Complete Canadian Curriculum

7

- Math
- Language
- History
- Geography
- Science

Printed in China

Contents

Mathematics

English

History

Geography

Science

Answers

MATHEMATICS

1

Exponents

- identify the base and exponent in a power
- write powers in exponent form, expanded form, and standard form
- compare powers
- identify a power as a perfect square or perfect cube

Write each power in expanded form.

1. 3^8 ____________ 2. 4^5 ____________

3. 8^7 ____________ 4. 12^4 ____________

5. 9^6 ____________ 6. 7^8 ____________

Fill in the missing numbers.

7. $\square^5 = 3 \times 3 \times 3 \times 3 \times 3$

8. $9^{\square} = 9 \times 9 \times 9 \times 9 \times 9 \times 9$

9. $2^3 = \square \times \square \times \square$

10. $\square^4 = 7 \times 7 \times 7 \times 7$

11. $4^{\square} = 4 \times 4 \times 4 \times 4$

12. $\square^7 = 8 \times 8 \times 8 \times 8 \times 8 \times 8 \times 8$

13. $11^4 = \square \times \square \times \square \times \square$

14. $3^{\square} = 3 \times 3 \times 3$

Find the base and exponent for each power.

15. 5^3 ______ base ______ exponent

16. 7^5 ______ base ______ exponent

17. 22^{10} ______ base ______ exponent

18. 13^6 ______ base ______ exponent

19. 39^2 ______ base ______ exponent

20. 1^{100} ______ base ______ exponent

Write each in exponent form and standard form.

	Expanded Form	Exponent Form	Standard Form
21.	8 x 8	8^2	______
22.	3 x 3 x 3 x 3	______	______
23.	7 x 7 x 7	______	______
24.	5 x 5 x 5 x 5 x 5	______	______
25.	9 x 9 x 9	______	______
26.	2 x 2 x 2 x 2 x 2 x 2	______	______
27.	1 x 1 x 1 x 1 x 1 x 1 x 1 x 1	______	______

Read what the children say. Write each power in exponent form, expanded form, and standard form.

28.

5 to the power of 4

______ ; ______________________________ ; ______

29.

the sixth power of 7

______ ; ______________________________ ; ______

30.

the base of the power is 2 and its exponent is 8

______ ; ______________________________ ; ______

A Product of Powers:

e.g. $3 \times 7 \times 7 \times 7 \times 3$

$= 3 \times 3 \times 7 \times 7 \times 7$ ← Rearrange the order to group the numbers.

$= 3^2 \times 7^3$

3 and 7 are the bases of the powers; and 2 and 3 are their exponents respectively.

Comparing Powers:

- If the powers have the same base, the one with the greater exponent is greater.

  e.g. $7^3 < 7^4$ ← same base (7) ; 7^4 is greater

- If the powers have the same exponent, the one with the greater base is greater.

  e.g. $5^3 < 6^3$ ← same exponent (3) ; 6^3 is greater

Write each as a product of powers.

31. $2 \times 2 \times 5 \times 5 \times 5 =$ ________
32. $6 \times 4 \times 6 \times 4 \times 4 =$ ________
33. $9 \times 9 \times 5 \times 9 \times 9 =$ ________
34. $8 \times 1 \times 8 \times 8 \times 1 \times 8 =$ ________
35. $7 \times 7 \times 2 \times 2 \times 7 \times 2 \times 7 \times 7 \times 2 =$ ________
36. $8 \times 3 \times 3 \times 8 \times 3 \times 3 \times 3 \times 8 \times 3 =$ ________

Evaluate each power. Compare the powers with the help of their standard form. Then put ">", "<", or "=" in the circles.

37. $3^3 =$ ______ $6^4 =$ ______

$5^3 =$ ______ $2^5 =$ ______

$4^5 =$ ______ $7^3 =$ ______

$9^3 =$ ______ $8^4 =$ ______

a. $7^3 \bigcirc 5^3$

b. $3^3 \bigcirc 7^3$

c. $4^5 \bigcirc 2^5$

d. $8^4 \bigcirc 6^4$

Put ">", "<", or "=" in the circles.

38. $7^3 \bigcirc 7^2$
39. $8^4 \bigcirc 9^4$
40. $5^4 \bigcirc 5^6$
41. $6^5 \bigcirc 4^5$
42. $x^5 \bigcirc x^8$
43. $6^m \bigcirc 4^m$

A Perfect Square – a number that is the square of an integer

e.g. $\frac{1}{1 \times 1}, \frac{4}{2 \times 2}, \frac{9}{3 \times 3}, \frac{16}{4 \times 4}, \frac{25}{5 \times 5}, \frac{36}{6 \times 6}, \ldots$ ← perfect squares

A Perfect Cube – a number that is the cube of an integer

e.g. $\frac{1}{1 \times 1 \times 1}, \frac{8}{2 \times 2 \times 2}, \frac{27}{3 \times 3 \times 3}, \frac{64}{4 \times 4 \times 4}, \frac{125}{5 \times 5 \times 5}, \ldots$ ← perfect cubes

Rewrite each power as another power with an exponent of 2 or 3. Then evaluate the power and tell whether the number is a perfect square or perfect cube.

44. $5^4 = 5 \times 5 \times 5 \times$ ____
    $= 25 \times$ ____
    $= 25^{\square}$
    $=$ ________
    So, ______ is a ________________.

45. $8^6 = 8 \times 8 \times 8 \times 8 \times$ ______
    $= 64 \times$ ____ $\times$ ____
    $= 64^{\square}$
    $=$ ________
    So, ______ is a ________________.

46. $7^4 = 49^{\square} =$ ________
    So, ______ is a ________________.

47. $3^9 = 27^{\square} =$ ________
    So, ______ is a ________________.

Simplify each group of powers. Then describe the pattern that you can see in the answers.

48.  A

$8^1 =$ ____ $15^1 =$ ____

$415^1 =$ ____ $67^1 =$ ____

B

$9^0 =$ ____ $42^0 =$ ____

$7^0 =$ ____ $125^0 =$ ____

A *If the exponent of a power is 1, then the answer will be the number ________ (itself / multiplied itself).*

B ______________________________

2

Squares and Square Roots

- find the square of a number
- find the square root of a number
- draw squares with the given area
- solve problems involving squares and square roots

Complete the list of square facts. Then find the square roots with the help of the square facts.

1. **Square Facts**

$1^2 =$ ____	$6^2 =$ ____
$2^2 =$ ____	$7^2 =$ ____
$3^2 =$ ____	$8^2 =$ ____
$4^2 =$ ____	$9^2 =$ ____
$5^2 =$ ____	$10^2 =$ ____

2. $\sqrt{49} =$ ____
3. $\sqrt{36} =$ ____
4. $\sqrt{81} =$ ____
5. $\sqrt{4} =$ ____
6. $\sqrt{100} =$ ____
7. $\sqrt{16} =$ ____

Find the missing digit in the ones column of each number.

8. $19^2 = 36$ ☐
9. $37^2 = 136$ ☐
10. $54^2 = 291$ ☐
11. $23^2 = 52$ ☐
12. $32^2 = 102$ ☐
13. $75^2 = 562$ ☐
14. $42^2 = 176$ ☐
15. $57^2 = 324$ ☐
16. $29^2 = 84$ ☐
17. $18^2 = 32$ ☐

Hint

When you square the digit in the ones column of any number that has two or more digits, the ones digit of the product must be the same as the ones digit of the square of the number that you started with.

e.g. 18^2 ← The square of 8 is 64; 4 is the digit in the ones column.
$= 324$ ← 4 in the ones column

Fill in the blanks to complete the sentences. Then translate each sentence into a mathematical expression.

A Mathematical Expression

18. 16 is the square of ______ . $16 = \square^2$

19. 49 is the square of ______ . ______________________

20. 8 squared is ______ . ______________________

21. 25 squared is ______ . ______________________

22. 7 to the power of 2 is ______ . ______________________

23. 9 to the power of 2 is ______ . ______________________

24. 10 is the square root of ______ . ______________________

25. 12 is the square root of ______ . ______________________

Find the answers. Then write a matching fact.

26. $\sqrt{225}$ = ______
    15^2 = ______

27. $\sqrt{400}$ = ______
    ____

28. $\sqrt{121}$ = ______
    ____

29. 16^2 = ______
    ____

30. 17^2 = ______
    ____

31. $\sqrt{441}$ = ______
    ____

32. The square root of 64 is ______ . ______________________

33. 20 to the power of 2 is ______ . ______________________

Find the area or side length of each square.

34.

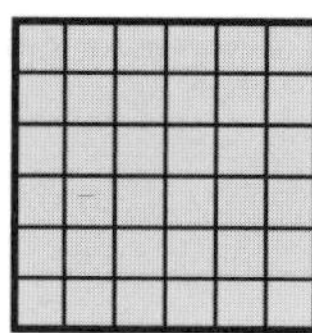

A = ▭^{2}

= ______ (square units)

35.

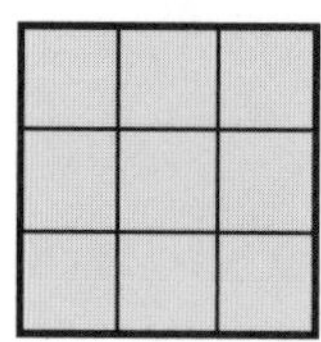

A = ______

= ______ (square units)

Hint

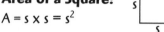

Area of a Square:
$A = s \times s = s^2$

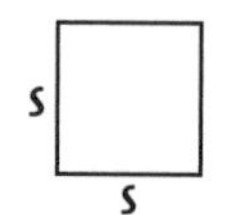

Side Length of a Square:
$s = \sqrt{A}$

36.

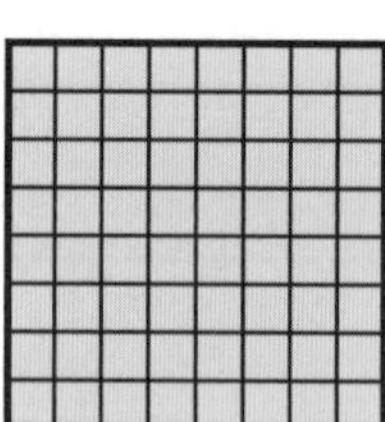

A = ______

= ______________

37.

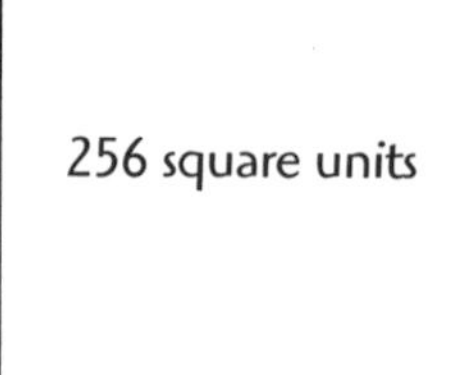

s = $\sqrt{}$

= ______ (units)

38.

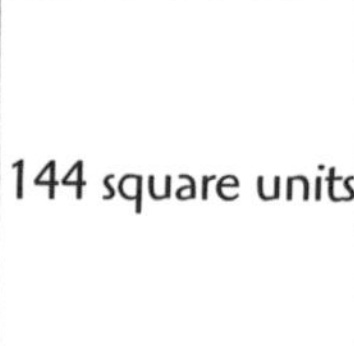

s = ______

= ______________

Find the areas and side lengths of the squares.

39. The big square is formed by a small square and 4 congruent isosceles right triangles.

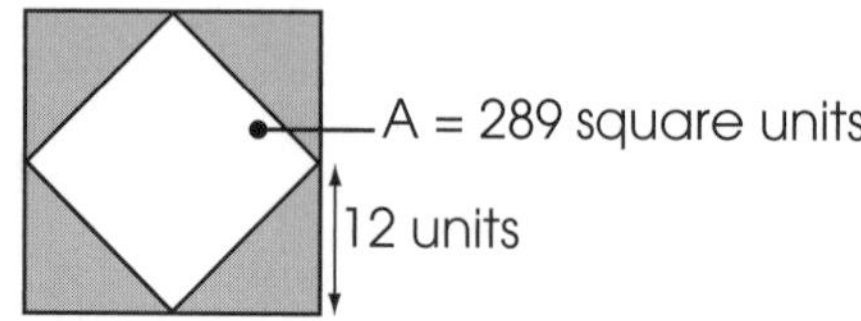

	Small Square	Big Square
Area (square units)		
Side Length (units)		

40. This figure is formed by 2 congruent rectangles and 2 squares of different sizes.

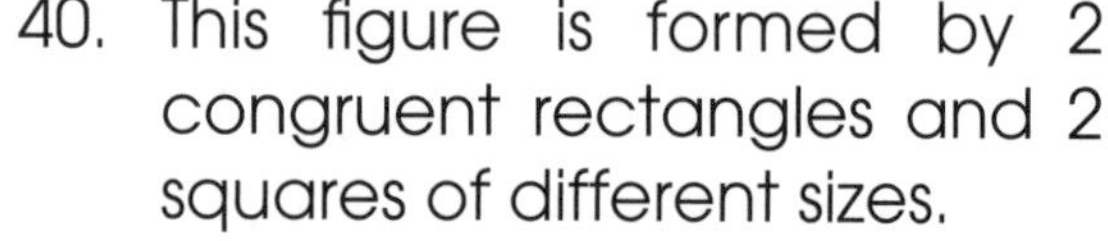

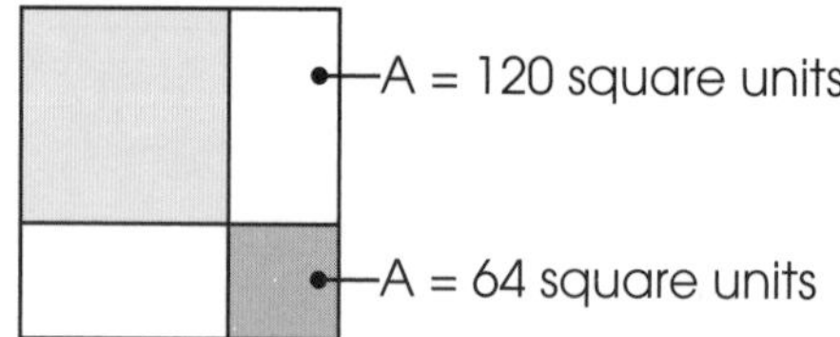

	Small Shaded Square	Big Shaded Square
Area (square units)		
Side Length (units)		

Draw and label the squares on the grid with the given areas.

41. **Area of Squares**

- (A) 36 cm^2
- (B) 16 cm^2
- (C) 4 cm^2
- (D) 9 cm^2
- (E) 25 cm^2

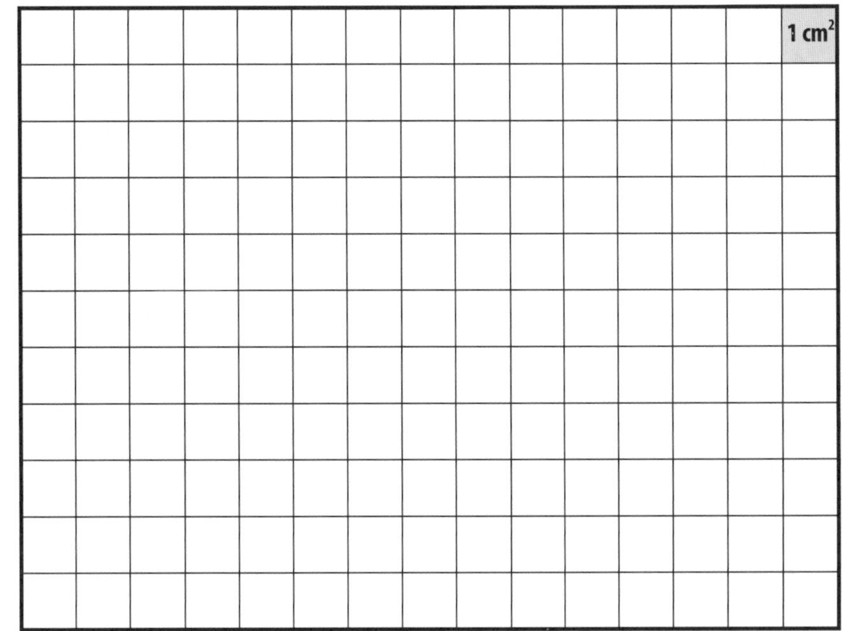

Solve the problems.

42. The area of the big and small squares are 169 cm^2 and 49 cm^2 respectively.

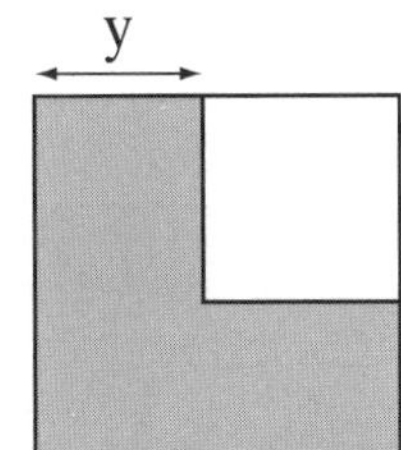

a. What are the side lengths of the two squares?

The side lengths are ________________ .

b. What is the value of y?

The value of y is ________ .

43. Jason cuts a square cardboard with an area of 576 cm^2 into 4 identical small squares. What is the side length of each small square?

The side length of each small square is _____ cm.

3

Factors and Multiples

- list out the factors of a number
- find the G.C.F. of a set of numbers
- list out multiples of a number
- find the L.C.M. of a set of numbers

List out all the factors of each number. Then circle the common factors of each group of numbers and find their greatest common factor (G.C.F.).

1. **6:** ______

   12: ______

   G.C.F.: ____

2. **15:** ______

   24: ______

   G.C.F.: ____

3. **14:** ______

   21: ______

   G.C.F.: ____

4. **12:** ______

   36: ______

   G.C.F.: ____

5. **8:** ______

   20: ______

   28: ______

   G.C.F.: ____

6. **48:** ______

   60: ______

   96: ______

   G.C.F.: ____

Look at the Venn diagram. Find the common factors of each group of numbers and their G.C.F.

7. 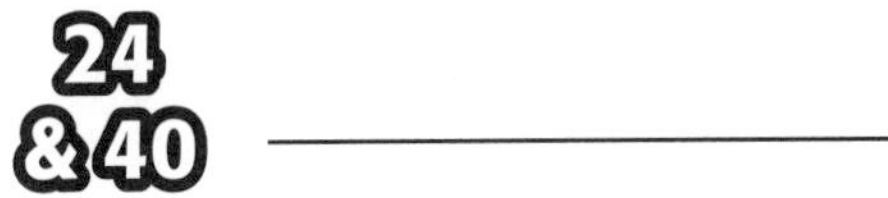

______________________ ; ______

8. 

______________________ ; ______

9. 24 & 60 ______________________ ; ______

10. 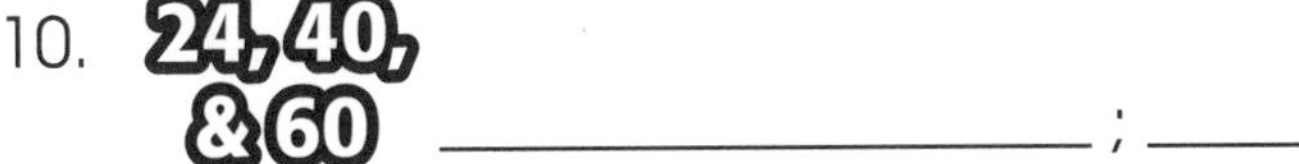

______________________ ; ______

Factors of 60
Factors of 40
Factors of 24

15
30
60
5
10 20
40
1 2
4
3
6 12
8
24

List out the factors of the numbers using Venn diagrams. Then find the G.C.F.

11. 30 and 42

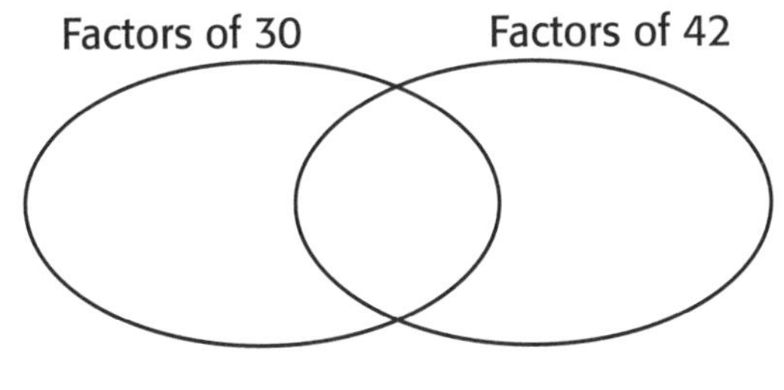

G.C.F. = ______

12. 28 and 35

G.C.F. = ______

13. 12, 20, and 36

G.C.F. = ______

14. 10, 45, and 60

G.C.F. = ______

Make a legend to mark the multiples of the numbers in the hundreds chart. Find the least common multiples (L.C.M.) of the numbers. Then answer the questions.

15.

1	2	3	4	5	6	7	8	9	10
11	12	13	14	15	16	17	18	19	20
21	22	23	24	25	26	27	28	29	30
31	32	33	34	35	36	37	38	39	40
41	42	43	44	45	46	47	48	49	50
51	52	53	54	55	56	57	58	59	60
61	62	63	64	65	66	67	68	69	70
71	72	73	74	75	76	77	78	79	80
81	82	83	84	85	86	87	88	89	90
91	92	93	94	95	96	97	98	99	100

☐ : multiples of 2 ☐ : multiples of 3

☐ : multiples of 4 ☐ : multiples of 10

a. common multiples of 3 and 10:

______

L.C.M.: ______

b. common multiples of 3 and 4:

______

L.C.M.: ______

c. common multiples of 4 and 10:

______

L.C.M.: ______

16. a. common multiples of 2 and 10:

______

b. Describe the pattern that you can see in the common multiples of 2 and 10.

______

c. Follow the pattern to find the next 5 common multiples of 2 and 10.

______

Write the first 12 multiples of each number. Circle the common multiples. Then fill in the blanks.

17. **4:** ______, 8, 12, ______

6: ______, 12, 18, ______

L.C.M. of 4 and 6: ______

The first 4 common multiples of 4 and 6: ______

List the first 12 multiples of each number. Then find the L.C.M. of each pair of numbers.

18.

Multiples	L.C.M.
3: ______	• **3 & 4:** ____
4: ______	• **5 & 6:** ____
5: ______	• **6 & 7:** ____
6: ______	• **5 & 7:** ____
7: ______	

Solve the problems. Show your work.

19. Tina has a sandwich for lunch every 4 days and Joe has it every 6 days. If they both have a sandwich for lunch today, how many days after will they both have sandwiches for lunch again?

Tina (multiples of 4): ______

Joe (multiples of 6): ______

They will both have sandwiches again after ____ days.

Hint

List the multiples. The L.C.M. is the least number of days that the two children will have sandwiches again.

20. Farmer Jack puts the eggs into the fewest cartons. Each carton holds the same kind and the same number of eggs. How many eggs does each carton hold? How many cartons are needed for each kind of egg?

factors of 18: ______

factors of 12: ______

Each carton holds ____ eggs.

We need ____ cartons for 18 brown eggs and ____ cartons for 12 white eggs.

This problem can be solved by finding the G.C.F.
18 brown eggs
12 white eggs

Integers

- locate integers on a number line
- relate integers to day-to-day activities
- compare and put integers in order
- add and subtract positive and negative integers

-2
-1
0
+1
+2
You haven't won this game yet. Don't you know that -2 is the opposite of +2? They have the same distance from 0.

Write the opposite of each integer and mark both integers on the number line.

1. **+3** ______

0

2. **-6** ______

0

3. **+7** ______

0

4. **+2** ______

0

5. **-5** ______

0

6. **+8** ______

0

Write an integer to represent each situation.

7. Today's temperature has risen by 5°C. ________
8. Louise's cat gained 2 kg. ________
9. Peter is 3 cm taller than last year. ________
10. The company lost $273. ________
11. Jason's wage has increased by $4/hour. ________
12. After the expansion, the park is 18 km² larger. ________

Locate the integers on the number line with arrows. Then compare them and put ">", "<", or "=" in the circle.

13.

-5 -4 -3 -2 -1 0 1 2 3 4 5

14.

-5 -4 -3 -2 -1 0 1 2 3 4 5

15.

-4 -3 -2 -1 0 1 2 3 4 5 6 7 8

16.

-7 -6 -5 -4 -3 -2 -1 0 1 2 3

Hint

Comparing Integers:

An integer is always greater than the integers on its left. Similarly, an integer is always smaller than the integers on its right.

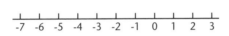

e.g. -5 -4 -3 -2 -1 0 1 2

- -5 is on the left of -1.
  -1 > -5
- 1 is on the right of -1.
  -1 < 1

Circle the greatest integer in each group.

17. +2 -3 +5

18. -3 -5 -8

19. -9 -2 -4

20. -1 -10 0

Put each group of integers in order from least to greatest.

21. +6 -2 +8 -4

____

22. +5 -3 -5 +2

____

23. -9 -1 0 -7

____

24. -11 +3 +12 -8

____

25. 0 -4 4 -2

____

26. -3 -15 -9 -6

____

Do each addition with the help of the number line.

27. (+3) + (+4) = ______

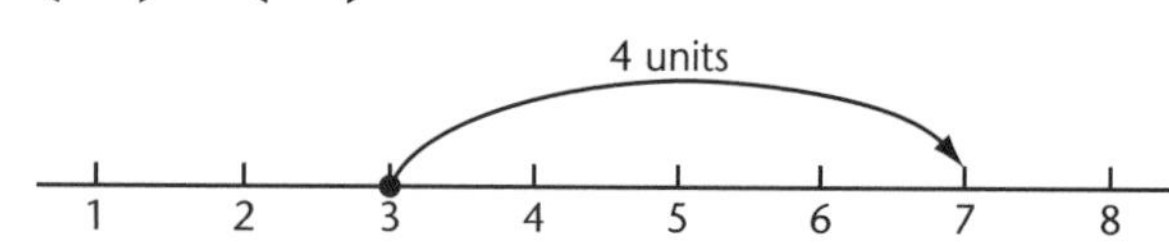

28. (+4) + (-5) = ______

29. (-2) + (+5) = ______

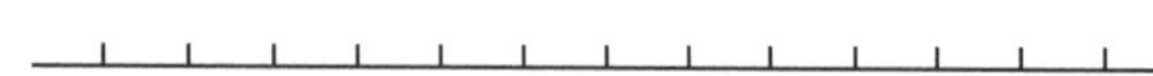

Hint

Adding Integers:

- Add a positive integer, move to the right.
- Add a negative integer, move to the left.

e.g. (+2) + (-3) = -1

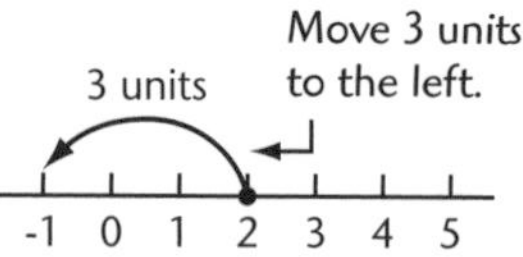

Do the addition.

30. (+8) + (-4) = ______

31. (-7) + (-5) = ______

32. (-12) + (+3) = ______

33. (+9) + (-3) = ______

34. (+5) + (-6) = ______

35. (-10) + (+4) = ______

36. (+2) + (-9) = ______

37. (+4) + (-7) = ______

Look at the table and answer the question.

38. Find the total scores of each child.

a. Jane ______ points

b. Leo ______

c. Bob ______

Scores			
Round	**Jane**	**Leo**	**Bob**
1	+13	+4	+6
2	-8	-2	-7

39. If Leo teams up with Bob to race against Jane, can the team beat Jane in these two rounds? If not, how many more points are needed?

______

Subtracting Integers:

- Subtract a positive integer, move to the left.
  e.g. (-4) – (+1) = -5

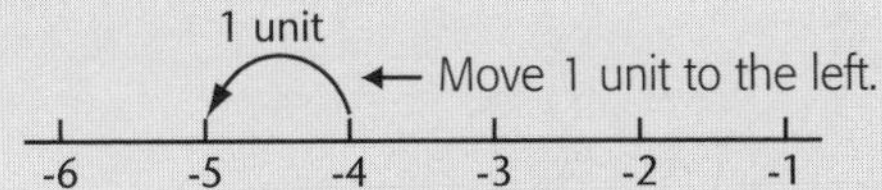

- Subtract a negative integer, move to the right.
  e.g. (-4) – (-1) = -3

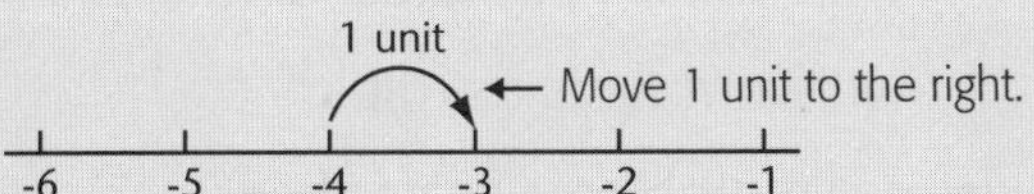

Do the subtraction with the help of the number line.

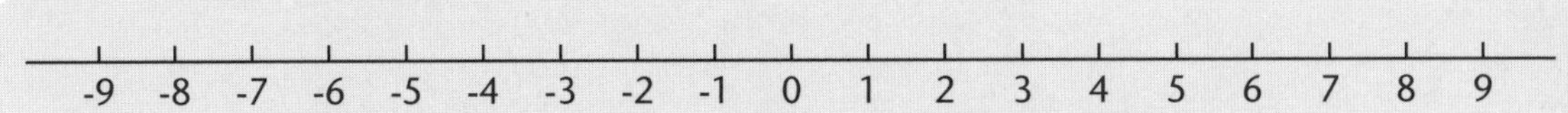

40. (-5) – (-1) = ______
41. (+8) – (+2) = ______
42. (+2) – (-9) = ______
43. (-7) – (-2) = ______
44. (+6) – (-3) = ______
45. (-10) – (-7) = ______
46. -6 – (+2) = ______
47. (-4) – (-4) = ______
48. -3 – (+3) = ______
49. 0 – (-5) = ______

Read what Susan says. Help her complete the table.

50. ***On Wednesday, the morning temperature was 4°C. It dropped 3°C in the afternoon and then another 4°C at night. On Thursday, the afternoon temperature was 5°C lower than the morning temperature. The temperature at night was -3°C and it was 8°C higher than the afternoon temperature.***

Temperature	morning	afternoon	night
Wednesday			
Thursday			

5

Ratios and Rates

- find ratios of a group of objects
- write equivalent ratios
- write ratios in simplest form
- write amounts as rates
- solve problems using ratios and rates

Ratio	1 Box		3 Boxes
:	2 : 3	=	6 : 9

x 3   x 3

Judy, don't you know that 2:3 and 6:9 are equivalent ratios?

Write the ratios for each group.

1. 

a. cups to mugs = ____ : ____

b. cups to bottles = ________

c. mugs to bottles = ________

d. bottles to all = ________

2.

a. hearts to stars = ________

b. flowers to hearts = ________

c. shaded shapes to unshaded shapes = ________

Colour the shapes to match the given ratios. Then find the ratios.

3. green circles to all shapes = 5:16
red rectangles to all shapes = 3:8

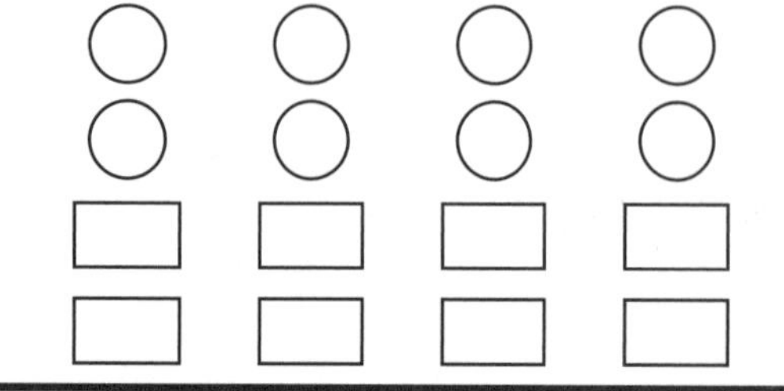

green ◯ : red ▭ = ______

4. red squares to blue stars = 3:3
red triangles to yellow stars = 3:2

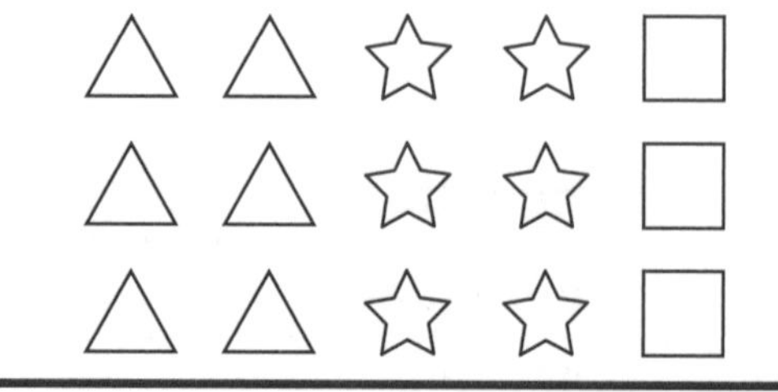

red □ : red △ = ______

Jane has a collection of marbles. Read what she says. Then help her complete the table.

5. *If my sister gives me 4 blue marbles and 1 red marble, what will be the new ratios?*

Marbles	Ratio	Ratio (New)
green : blue	3:2	
red : green		
blue : all		
red : all		

Find the equivalent ratios.

6. (× 2) 3 : 5 = ___ : ___ (× 2)

7. (× 4) 2 : 7 = ___ : ___ (× 4)

8. (÷ 2) $\frac{8}{6}$ = ___ (÷ 2)

9. (÷ 5) $\frac{15}{25}$ = ___ (÷ 5)

10. 4:12 = ______

11. 10:20 = ______

12. 30:8 = ______

13. 6:15 = ______

Hint

Finding Equivalent Ratios:

You may multiply or divide each term in a ratio to find an equivalent ratio.

e.g. (× 4) 2 : 3 = 8 : 12 (× 4) | (× 4) $\frac{2}{3} = \frac{8}{12}$ (× 4)

* Multiply both terms by 4.

Equivalent ratios: 2:3 and 8:12

Write two equivalent ratios for each.

14. 6:4 ______

15. 4:10 ______

16. 8:5 ______

17. 10:25 ______

18. 12:15 ______

19. 1:7 ______

Fill in the missing numbers.

20. 3:8 = ___ : 24

21. 6:4 = 3 : ___

22. ___ : 3 = 4:12

23. 7 : ___ = 21:6

24. 12:20 = ___ : 10

25. 24 : ___ = 8:6

Ratio in Simplest Form:

Divide both terms in the ratio by their G.C.F.

e.g. Write 6:9 in simplest form.

Think: The G.C.F. of 6 and 9 is 3.

÷ 3

6 : 9 = 2 : 3

÷ 3

The simplest form of 6:9 is 2:3.

There are 3 muffins and 4 doughnuts in a box. If there are 20 doughnuts, how many muffins are there?

Think: It is a ratio problem. Write as a ratio.

muffins : doughnuts = 3:4

x 5

3 : 4 = 15 : 20 ← Multiply both terms by 5 to figure out the answer.

x 5

There are 15 muffins.

Find the G.C.F. of the terms. Then write each ratio in simplest form.

26. 9:27 = ______
G.C.F. = ______

27. 18:45 = ______
G.C.F. = ______

28. 35:14 = ______
G.C.F. = ______

29. 30:18 = ______
G.C.F. = ______

30. 15:24 = ______
G.C.F. = ______

31. 42:18 = ______
G.C.F. = ______

Solve the problems.

32. The ratio of the height of a triangle to its base is 2:3. If the height of the triangle is 18 cm, what is the length of the base?

______

33. *The number of candies that Tom has to the number that I have is in the ratio of 4:5. If I have 35 candies, how many candies does Tom have?*

______

Rate:

a comparison, or a type of ratio, of two measurements with different units

e.g. It takes Sue 10 days to build 15 models.

Rate = 15 ÷ 10 = 1.5

Sue's rate is 1.5 models/day.

Unit Rate:

a rate with the second term being one unit

e.g. The cost of 8 pizzas is $63.92.

Unit rate = $63.92 ÷ 8 pizzas
= $7.99/pizza

The unit rate of a pizza is $7.99.

Write each as a rate.

34. travelling 82.4 km in 6 hours ____________

35. 8 chicken balls for $4.72 ____________

36. reading 36 pages in 4 days ____________

37. assembling 15 bicycles in 3 hours ____________

Find the unit rates. Then check the one with a higher unit rate in each group.

38. (A) type 378 words in 9 minutes
unit rate: ______ words/min

(B) type 990 words in 15 minutes
unit rate: ____________

39. (A) travel 382.6 km in 5 hours
unit rate: ____________

(B) travel 32.44 km in 0.5 hour
unit rate: ____________

40. *I can finish 326 g of food in 4 days and Sam can finish 39.25 g of food in half a day.*

	Unit Rate
(A) Judy the Cat	
(B) Sam the Cat	

6

Fractions

- write equivalent fractions
- add, subtract, and multiply fractions
- solve problems that involve the addition, subtraction, and multiplication of fractions

$6 \times \frac{3}{8} = \frac{18}{8} = 2\frac{1}{4}$
Don't worry, Jane. You still have $2\frac{1}{4}$ boxes of chocolates left.

Find an equivalent fraction for each fraction.

1. **By using multiplication:**
   multiply the numerator and denominator by the same number

   a. $\frac{3}{7} = \frac{3 \times 5}{7 \times 5}$ = ______

   b. $\frac{2}{5} = \frac{2 \times 3}{5 \times \square}$ = ______

   c. $\frac{5}{6} = \frac{5 \times \square}{6 \times 4}$ = ______

2. **By using division:**
   divide the numerator and denominator by the same number

   a. $\frac{12}{15} = \frac{12 \div 3}{15 \div 3}$ = ______

   b. $\frac{8}{10} = \frac{8 \div 2}{10 \div \square}$ = ______

   c. $\frac{5}{20} = \frac{5 \div \square}{20 \div 5}$ = ______

3. $\frac{5}{15}$ = ______

4. $\frac{1}{4}$ = ______

5. $\frac{16}{30}$ = ______

6. $\frac{10}{25}$ = ______

Find the equivalent fractions for each pair of fractions so that the equivalent fractions have the same denominator. Then colour the correct number of parts to find the sum.

7. $\frac{1}{2}$ and $\frac{2}{5}$

   $\frac{1}{2}$ = ______ $\frac{2}{5}$ = ______

   $\frac{1}{2}$ and $\frac{2}{5}$ = ______

8. $\frac{3}{4}$ and $\frac{1}{10}$

   $\frac{3}{4}$ = ______ $\frac{1}{10}$ = ______

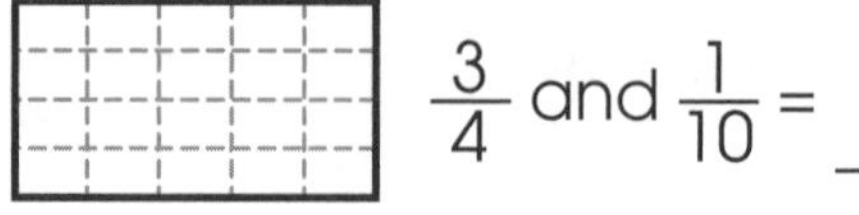

   $\frac{3}{4}$ and $\frac{1}{10}$ = ______

Adding fractions with different denominators:

1st Find the least common denominator (L.C.D.) and equivalent fractions.

2nd Add the numerators and keep the denominator the same.

3rd Write the answer in simplest form.

Add the numbers.

e.g. $\frac{1}{4} + \frac{7}{12} = \frac{3}{12} + \frac{7}{12} = \frac{10}{12} = \frac{5}{6}$

The L.C.M. of 4 and 12 is 12. So, 12 is the L.C.D.

Fractions in Simplest Form:

A fraction is in its simplest form if the greatest common factor of the numerator and denominator is 1.

e.g. $\frac{2}{7}$ ← in simplest form

Do the addition. Write the answers in simplest form.

9. $\frac{3}{5} + \frac{1}{10}$
   $= \_\_\_\_ + \frac{1}{10}$
   $= \_\_\_\_$

10. $\frac{3}{4} + \frac{1}{5}$
   $= \frac{}{20} + \_\_\_\_$
   $= \_\_\_\_$

11. $\frac{3}{10} + \frac{8}{15} = \frac{}{30} + \_\_\_\_$
   $= \_\_\_\_$
   $= \_\_\_\_$ ← in simplest form

12. $\frac{5}{9} + \frac{7}{36} = \_\_\_\_\_\_ = \_\_\_\_$

13. $\frac{2}{7} + \frac{5}{14} = \_\_\_\_\_\_ = \_\_\_\_$

14. $\frac{3}{4} + \frac{4}{5} = \_\_\_\_\_\_ = \_\_\_\_$

Write the answer as a mixed number.

15. $\frac{1}{2} + \frac{17}{18} = \_\_\_\_\_\_ = \_\_\_\_$

Solve the problems.

16. What is the total weight of one bag and one box of cookies?

______ = ____ ______

17. Sue has $\frac{5}{6}$ kg of cookies. If she buys a bag of cookies, how many kg of cookies will she have in all?

______ = ____ ______

Subtracting fractions with different denominators:

1st Find the least common denominator and equivalent fractions.

2nd Subtract the numerators and keep the denominator the same.

3rd Write the answer in simplest form.

e.g. $\frac{5}{6} - \frac{1}{3}$ ← L.C.D. = 6

$= \frac{5}{6} - \frac{2}{6}$

$= \frac{3}{6}$ ← Subtract the numerators; keep the denominator the same.

$= \frac{1}{2}$ ← in simplest form

Do the subtraction. Write the answers in simplest form.

18. $\frac{9}{10} - \frac{1}{2}$ ← L.C.D. = ____

$= \frac{9}{10} - \_\_\_\_$

$= \_\_\_\_$

19. $\frac{5}{6} - \frac{11}{15}$ ← L.C.D. = ____

$= \_\_\_\_ - \_\_\_\_$

$= \_\_\_\_$

20. $\frac{2}{3} - \frac{1}{6} =$ ____

21. $\frac{3}{10} - \frac{2}{15} =$ ____

22. $\frac{3}{4} - \frac{5}{12} =$ ____

23. $\frac{4}{5} - \frac{3}{10} =$ ____

24. $\frac{17}{20} - \frac{3}{5} =$ ____

25. $\frac{8}{15} - \frac{1}{3} =$ ____

Solve the problems. Write the answers in simplest form.

26. How much farther does Billy the Dog go than Ted in one minute?

________ = ____

____

I can run $\frac{9}{10}$ km in one minute.
Ted
Billy

27. If Billy slows down his speed by $\frac{1}{6}$ km/min, what will be his new speed?

________ = ____

____

Do the multiplication using addition. Write the answers in simplest form.

28. $3 \times \frac{5}{8} = \frac{5}{8} + \_\_\_\_ + \_\_\_\_$

$= \frac{\_\_}{8}$

$= \_\_\_\_$

29. $4 \times \frac{5}{6} = \frac{5}{6} + \_\_\_\_\_\_\_\_$

$= \frac{\_\_}{6}$

$= \_\_\_\_$

Do the multiplication. Write the answers in simplest form.

30. $6 \times \frac{4}{9} = \_\_\_\_$

31. $3 \times \frac{2}{7} = \_\_\_\_$

32. $8 \times \frac{3}{10} = \_\_\_\_$

33. $5 \times \frac{4}{15} = \_\_\_\_$

34. $\frac{3}{8} \times 6 = \_\_\_\_$

35. $\frac{5}{7} \times 4 = \_\_\_\_$

36. $\frac{7}{10} \times 5 = \_\_\_\_$

37. $3 \times \frac{7}{12} = \_\_\_\_$

Hint

A whole number x A fraction

1st Multiply the numerator by the whole number.

2nd Simplify the answer.

e.g. $5 \times \frac{8}{15}$

$= \frac{40}{15}$

$= 2\frac{2}{3}$ ← Write as a mixed number.

38. Joe drinks $\frac{3}{5}$ L of milk every day. How much milk does Joe drink in a week?

________ = ____ ______

39. A basket of apples weighs $\frac{11}{12}$ kg. What is the total weight of 3 baskets of red apples and 5 baskets of green apples?

________ = ____ ______

40. *If it takes us $\frac{5}{6}$ h to make 3 models, how many hours will it take to make 24 models?*

________ = ____

______

7

Decimals

- round decimals to thousandths
- estimate and find sums and differences
- follow the order of operations on decimals
- solve problems with decimals involving different operations

$$\begin{array}{r l} 8.95 & \leftarrow \text{2 decimal places} \\ \times \quad 0.2 & \leftarrow \text{1 decimal place} \\ \hline 1.790 & \leftarrow \text{3 (2 + 1) decimal places} \end{array}$$

Amount eaten: 0.2 kg

Invoice
$1.79

$8.95/kg

You have to pay me $1.79.

Round the decimal to the nearest ones, tenths, hundredths, and thousandths.

1. 2.8037 2. 11.5491 3. 4.0675 4. 25.8023

Estimate the sum and difference of each pair of decimals by rounding the decimals to the nearest ones. Then find the actual sums and differences.

5.

Estimate		Actual	
sum	difference	sum	difference
+			

6.

Estimate		Actual	
sum	difference	sum	difference

Estimate the product. Then put a decimal point in the correct place of the given product with the help of the estimated answer.

7. 2.6 x 5 = 130

   Estimate: 3 x ______ = ______

8. 4.38 x 2 = 876

   Estimate: ______________

9. 5.4 x 0.6 = 324

   Estimate: ______________

10. 7.9 x 2.3 = 1817

    Estimate: ______________

Do the multiplication.

11.
```
   22.4   ← 1 decimal place
 x  1.8   ← 1 decimal place
 ------
 [    ]   ← 8 x 224
 [    ]   ← 10 x 224
 ------
 [    ]   ← 2 decimal places
```

12.
```
   1.76   ← 2 decimal places
 x  3.7   ← 1 decimal place
 ------
 [    ]   ← 7 x 176
 [    ]   ← 30 x 176
 ------
 [    ]   ← 3 decimal places
```

13.
```
   8.7
 x 3.1
```

14.
```
   14.6
 x  0.5
```

15.
```
   1.06
 x  4.3
```

16.
```
   13.4
 x  0.8
```

Solve the problems.

17. Distance travelled

    a. in 1.6 h: ______________ = ______

    b. in 2.3 h: ______________ = ______

    c. in 3.5 h: ______________ = ______

    d. in 4.7 h: ______________ = ______

Our average speed is 82.46 km/h.

Decimals ÷ Decimals

1st Change the divisor into a whole number by moving the decimal point to the right end, and move the decimal point of the dividend the same number of places.

2nd Divide as "Decimals ÷ Whole numbers".

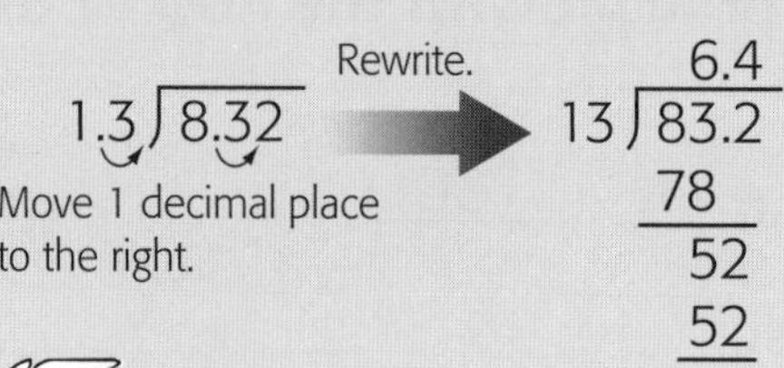

Estimate. Then do the division.

18. 41.76 ÷ 5.8 = ______

Estimate: 42 ÷ ______ = ______

5.8⟌41.76 ➡

19. 32.24 ÷ 2.08 = ______

Estimate: ______

2.08⟌32.24 ➡

20. 12 ÷ 6.25 = ______

Estimate: ______

6.25⟌12 ➡

21. 21.6 ÷ 1.5 = ______

Estimate: ______

1.5⟌21.6 ➡

Do the division.

22. 39.52 ÷ 1.6 = ______

23. 15.036 ÷ 2.8 = ______

24. 9.66 ÷ 2.3 = ______

25. 19.18 ÷ 3.5 = ______

26. 15.6 ÷ 2.4 = ______

27. 35.524 ÷ 4.15 = ______

Find the answers.

28. (1.6 + 2.3) x 4

29. 7.5 – 5 ÷ 2.5 x 1.25

30. 4.6 x 1.3 – 1.05 ÷ 0.5

31. 8.4 + 2.73 ÷ 1.3 = ______

32. 11.85 ÷ (3.21 + 6.27) x 5 = ______

33. 3.5 x 4.2 – 5.42 = ______

34. 10.32 ÷ 3.44 + 1.3 x 3.6 = ______

35. 29.61 ÷ (1.73 + 2.97) = ______

36. (8.96 + 1.8) x (10.54 – 6.09) = ______

Check the correct number sentence that describes each situation. Then solve it. Show your work.

37. Mrs. Kay bought 4 bags of 2.83-kg flour and used 3.07 kg of it to make bread. Then she put the rest of the flour equally into 5 jars. How much flour is there in each jar?

   (A) (2.83 x 4 – 3.07) ÷ 5

   (B) (3.07 – 2.83) x 4 ÷ 5

   There are ______ kg of flour in each jar.

38. Tommy the Mouse ran at a speed of 30.6 km/h in the first 0.35 h and 25.2 km/h in the next 0.25 h. What was his average speed?

   (A) (30.6 + 25.2) ÷ (0.35 + 0.25)

   (B) (30.6 x 0.35 + 25.2 x 0.25) ÷ (0.35 + 0.25)

____

8

Fractions, Decimals, and Percents

- describe parts of a whole in fractions, decimals, and percents
- shade diagrams to match the given percents
- do conversions between fractions, decimals, and percents
- solve word problems involving conversions

= 75% = 0.75 = $\frac{75}{100}$
75%
0.75
$\frac{75}{100}$
Actually, all three of us got the same score on the test. But how come he thinks that his is the highest among us?

Write the fraction, decimal, and percent for each shaded part.

1. 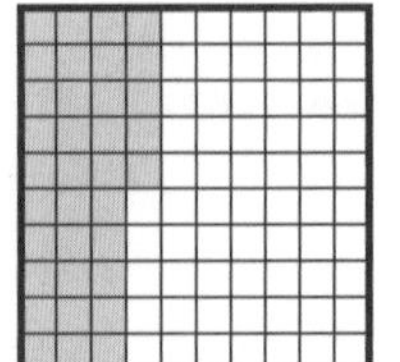

   ____ ____ ____

2. 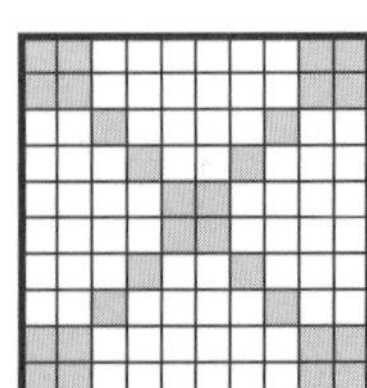

   ____ ____ ____

3. 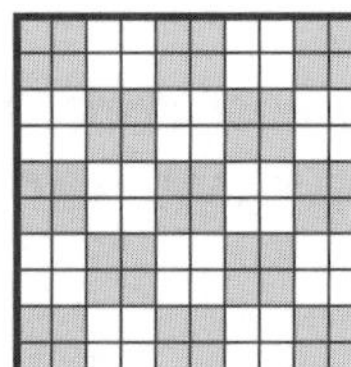

   ____ ____ ____

4. 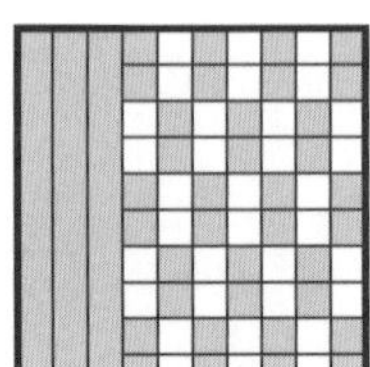

   ____ ____ ____

5. 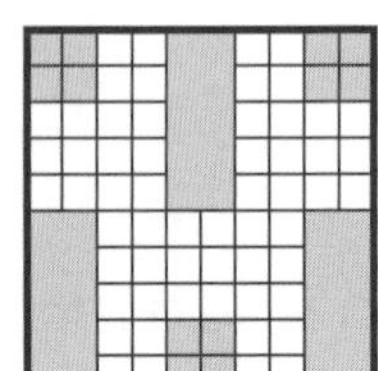

   ____ ____ ____

6. 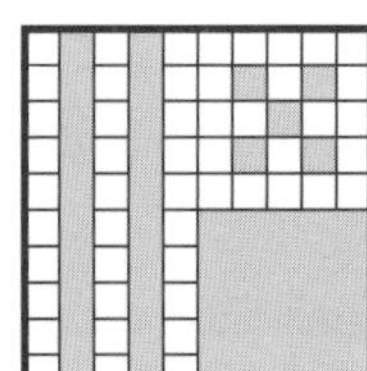

   ____ ____ ____

Shade the diagram to match each percent.

7. 

8. 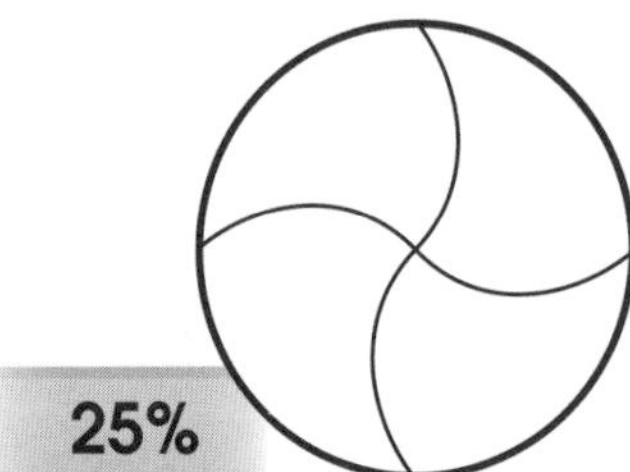

9. 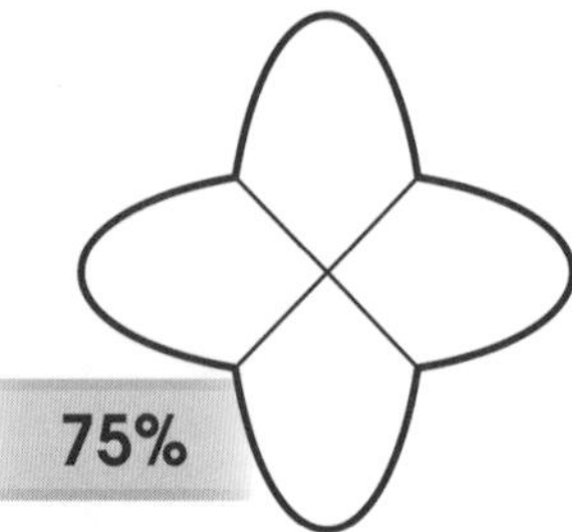

Converting a Decimal to a Percent:

1st Move the decimal point 2 places to the right.

2nd Add the "%" sign.

e.g. 0.328 = 32.8%

2 places to the right — Add "%".

Converting a Percent to a Decimal:

1st Move the decimal point 2 places to the left.

2nd Take out the "%" sign.

e.g. 32.8% = 0.328

2 places to the left — Take out.

Do the conversions.

10. **Decimal ⟶ Percent**

a. 0.48 = ________

b. 0.8 = ________

c. 2.15 = ________

d. 0.279 = ________

e. 0.082 = ________

f. 1.05 = ________

11. **Percent ⟶ Decimal**

a. 52% = ________

b. 15.4% = ________

c. 200% = ________

d. 0.5% = ________

e. 8.9% = ________

f. 7% = ________

Write a decimal and a percent to match the shaded part of each diagram, or shade the diagram to match the given decimal or percent.

12. 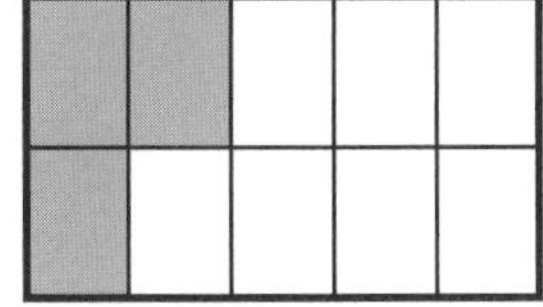

____ ____

13. 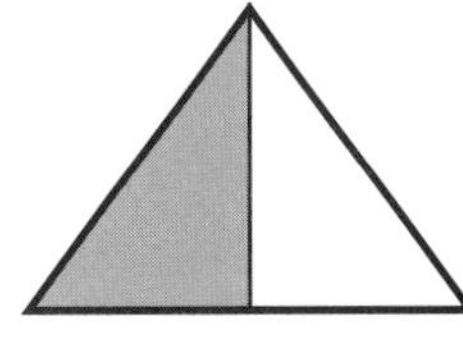

____ ____

14. 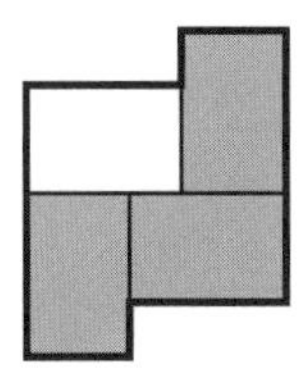

____ ____

15. 

0.9

____

16. 

____

120%

Converting a Fraction to a Percent:

Way 1 (using equivalent fractions)

1st Find the equivalent fraction with a denominator of 100.

2nd Write the numerator and add "%".

e.g. $\frac{18}{25} = \frac{72}{100} = 72\%$ (× 4)

↑ a fraction with a denominator of 100

Way 2 (using division)

1st Divide the numerator by the denominator.

2nd Write the quotient as a percent.

e.g. $\frac{18}{25} = 0.72$

$= 72\%$

$$\begin{array}{r} 0.72 \\ 25\overline{)18.0} \\ 175 \\ \hline 50 \\ 50 \\ \hline \end{array}$$

Find the equivalent fraction with a denominator of 100 for each fraction. Then write it as a percent.

17. $\frac{3}{10} = \frac{}{100} =$ ____ %

18. $\frac{9}{50} =$ ____ = ____

19. $\frac{16}{25} =$ ____ = ____

20. $\frac{3}{4} =$ ____ = ____

21. $\frac{19}{20} =$ ____ = ____

22. $\frac{3}{5} =$ ____ = ____

Write each fraction as a percent using division.

23. $\frac{8}{50}$ $50\overline{)8}$

= ____

= ____ %

24. $\frac{9}{25}$

=

25. $\frac{17}{20}$

=

Write each percent as a fraction in simplest form.

26. 24% = ____

27. 52% = ____

28. 78% = ____

29. 83% = ____

30. 36% = ____

31. 62% = ____

Hint

Percent ⟶ Fraction

e.g. 35%

$= \frac{35}{100}$ ← Drop the "%". Write as a fraction with a denominator of 100.

$= \frac{7}{20}$ ← Simplify.

Write a fraction, a decimal, and a percent to match the shaded part in each shape.

32.

	Fraction	Decimal	Percent
circle			
parallelogram			
triangle			
square			
rectangle			

Solve the problems. Show your work. You may draw diagrams to illustrate your answers.

33. Jason has $\frac{4}{5}$ cup of raisins, George has 0.7 cup, and 75% of Tim's cup is filled with raisins. Who has the most raisins?

_____ has the most.

34. 25% of the buttons a box are black, 0.1 are green, and the rest are red. What fraction of the buttons in the box are red?

_____

35. *Look at my record. Do you know which is my best subject?*

1st Term

English: $\frac{19}{20}$

Math: 89%

History: 0.92

Science: 23 out of 25

_____

9

Percents

- find the percent of an amount
- find the whole with the given amount of a percent
- solve problems relate to finding amount and the amount of one whole

Don't cry, Judy. There are 5 columns of chocolates in this box. I'll give you 40%.

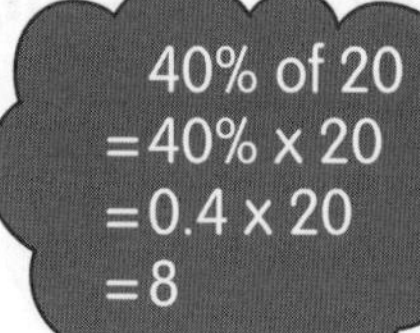

Each column contains 20% of a box of chocolates; 2 columns contain 40%, which means 8 chocolates.

Thank you. So, I'll have 8 chocolates.

Shade the diagram. Then find the amount.

1. 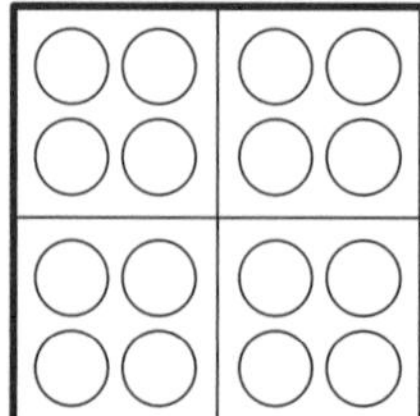

   25% of 16 = ______

2. 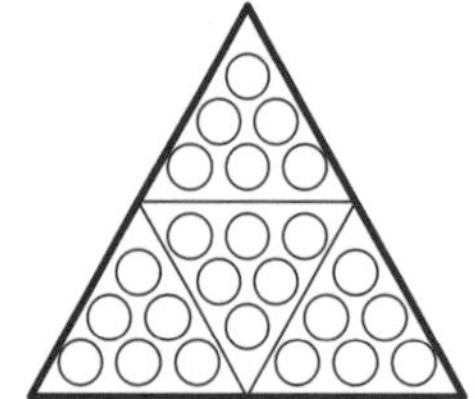

   75% of 24 = ______

3. 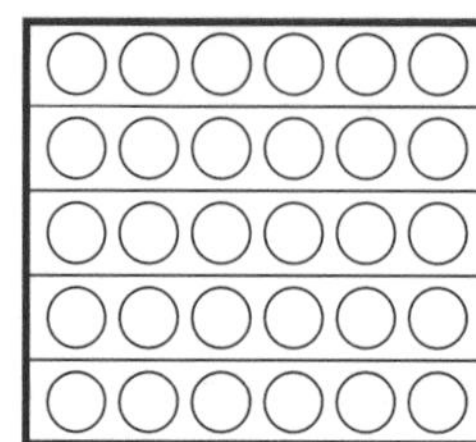

   60% of 30 = ______

4. 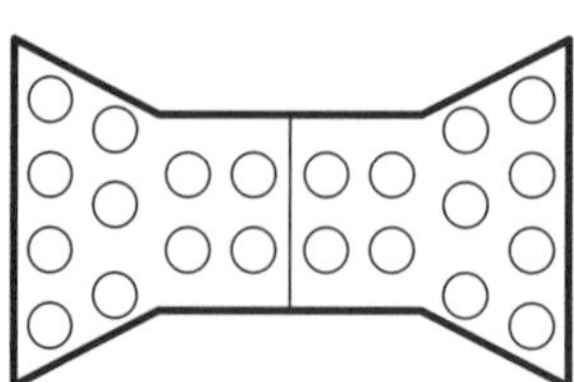

   50% of 22 = ______

5. 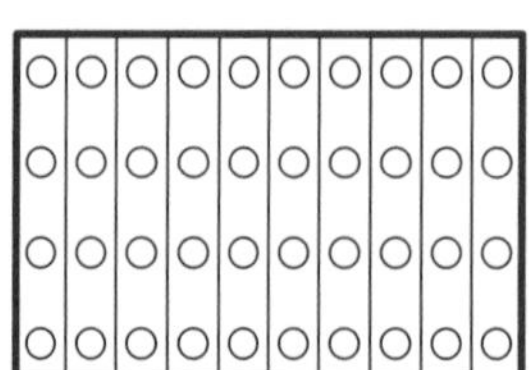

   80% of 40 = ______

6. 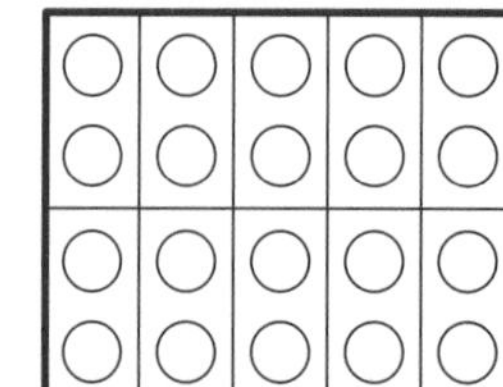

   70% of 20 = ______

Draw arrays in the diagrams to help you find the amounts.

7. 40% of 25 = ______

   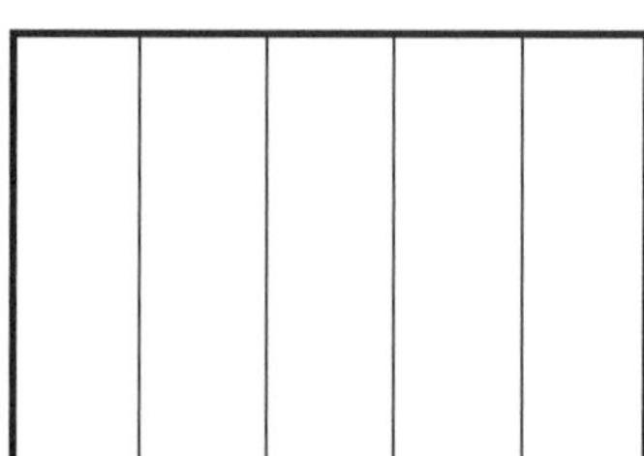

8. 25% of 12 = ______

   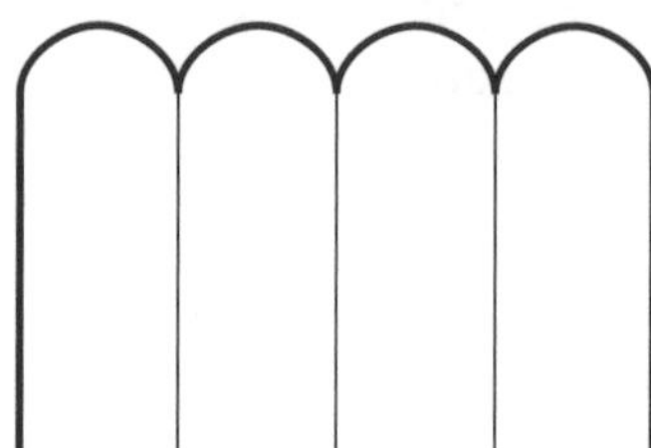

Using Multiplication to Find a Percent of an Amount:

1st Write the percent as a decimal.

2nd Multiply the decimal with the amount.

20% of 80
= 20% x 80
= 0.2 x 80
= 16

If I have $80, I'll give you 20%.

It means you'll give me $16.

Find the answers.

9. 15% of 20
   = ______% x 20
   = ______ x 20
   = ______

10. 30% of 90

11. 10% of 27

12. 7.5% of 360

13. 35% of 60

14. 3.2% of 50

Read what Emily says. Find how many children like each colour. Then answer the questions.

I've surveyed 80 children. 20% of the children like yellow, 25% like green, 30% like blue, 10% like red, and the rest of the children like orange.

15.

Colour	No. of Children
Yellow	20% x ______ = ______

16. If 70% of the children who like green are boys, how many boys like green?

______

When the percent and the value of the percent are known, use proportion to find the number.

Steps:

1st Set up a proportion.

2nd Find the value of 1% using division.

3rd Find the value of 100% using multiplication.

e.g. 5% of a number is 10.

Percent	Value
5%	10
1% ($\frac{5\%}{5}$)	2 ($\frac{10}{5}$)
100% (1% x 100)	200 (2 x 100)

So, the number is 200.

Find the numbers.

17. 3% of a number is 18.

3% → ______

1% → ______

100% → ______

So, the number is ______ .

18. 12% of a number is 24.

12% → ______

1% → ______

100% → ______

So, the number is ______ .

19. 4% of a number is 5, so the number is ______ .

20. 30% of a number is 21, so the number is ______ .

21. 15% of a number is 9.6, so the number is ______ .

Solve the problems.

22. 28% of the jar is filled with water. What is the capacity of the jar?

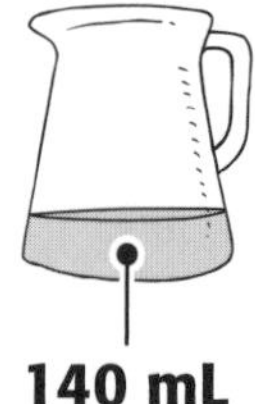

140 mL

____

23. Jane uses 25% of her savings to buy a doll for her sister. What were Jane's savings?

____

Solve the problems.

24. Find the number of marbles that each child has.

160 marbles
Judy – 20%
Sam – 45%
Tina – the rest

30 marbles
Ken – 40%
Judy – the rest

50 marbles
Sam – 48%
Ken – 20%
Tina – the rest

Judy

____

Ken

____

Sam

____

Tina

____

25. If Sam gives 25% of his marbles to his sister Pamela, how many marbles will Pamela get from Sam?

____

26. *70% of my marbles are red. Let me give you 80% of my red marbles.*

How many red marbles does Erica get from Judy?

____

10

Angles

- identify and measure angles formed by intersecting lines
- draw lines with the given measures of angles
- identify transversal and corresponding angles
- identify and draw parallel lines and perpendicular lines

Which pair of lines intersect at the given angles? Mark the angles in the diagrams and name the lines.

1. **Intersecting Lines**

   a. 80°: ____________

   b. 105°: ____________

   c. 35°: ____________

   d. 55°: ____________

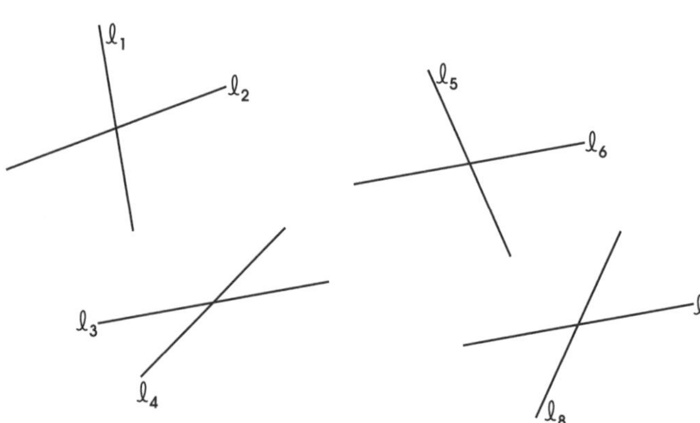

Draw lines that intersect at the given angles. Then mark the angles.

2. 65°

3. 110°

4. 97°

5. 83°

Transversal:
a line intersecting 2 or more lines

Parallel lines:
2 or more lines that never intersect

Corresponding angles:
angles in the matching corners that are formed when a transversal crosses 2 lines

e.g.

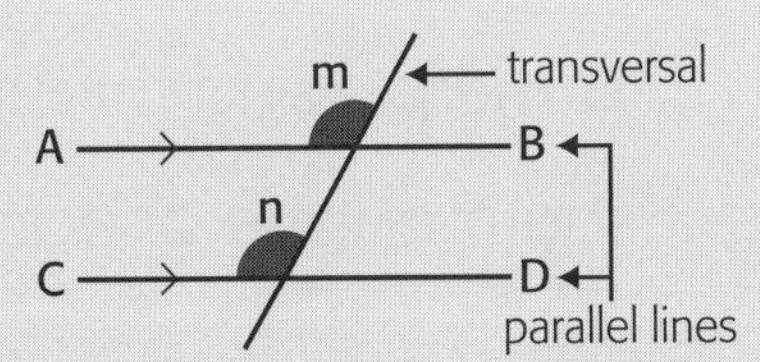

m and n are corresponding angles.
Since AB//CD, so ∠m = ∠n.

If a transversal crosses two lines that are parallel, then the measures of the corresponding angles are the same.

Name the transversal and find the corresponding angles for each set of lines.

6.

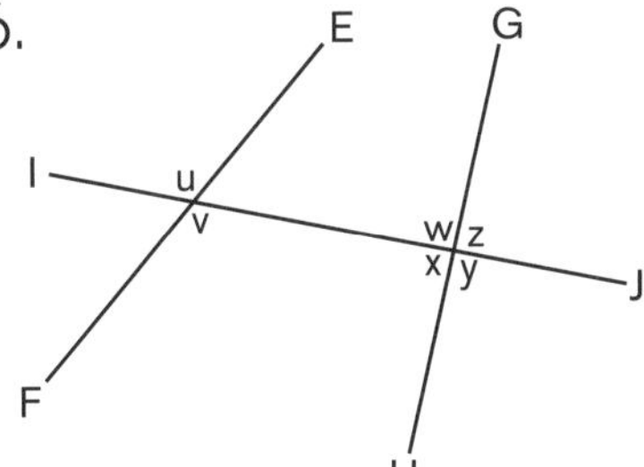

transversal: ______

corresponding angles:

- u and ______
- v and ______

7.

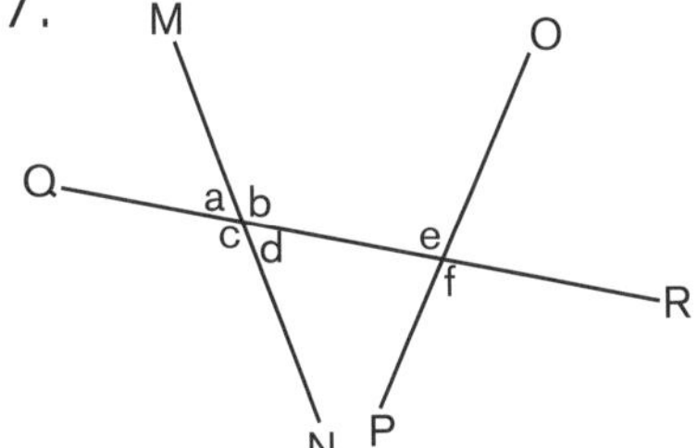

transversal: ______

corresponding angles:

- ______
- ______

8.

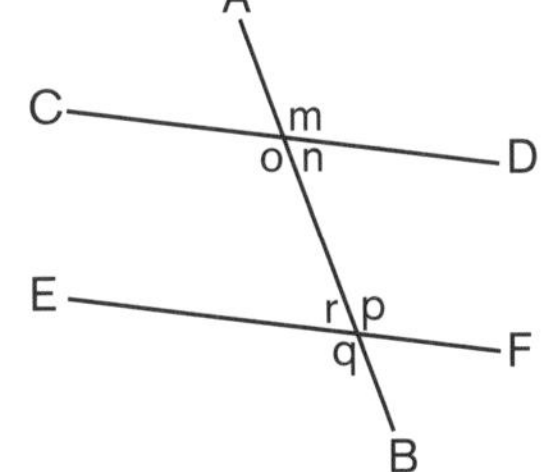

transversal: ______

corresponding angles:

- ______
- ______

Measure and record the marked angles. Then find the parallel lines.

9.

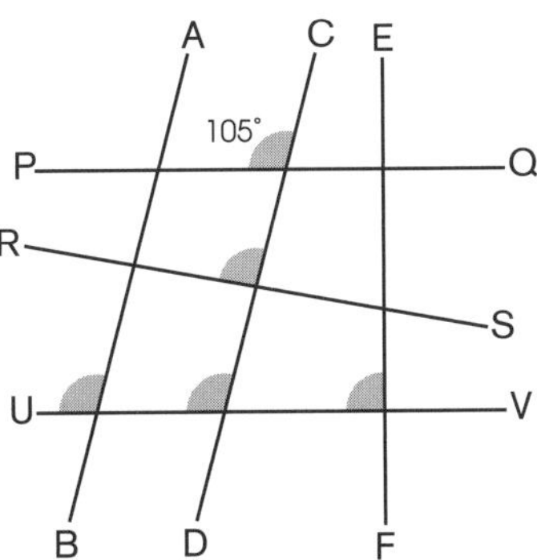

- ______ // ______
- ______ // ______

10.

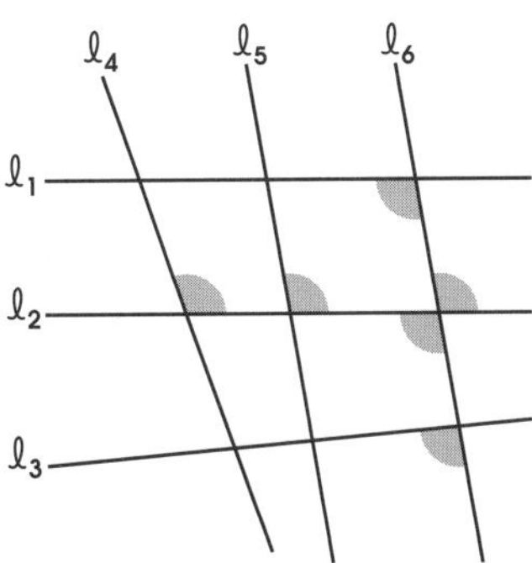

- ______
- ______

Draw lines as described. Then find and label one pair of corresponding angles.

11. a. a line passing through A and parallel to IJ

    b. the measure of each corresponding angle:

    ____

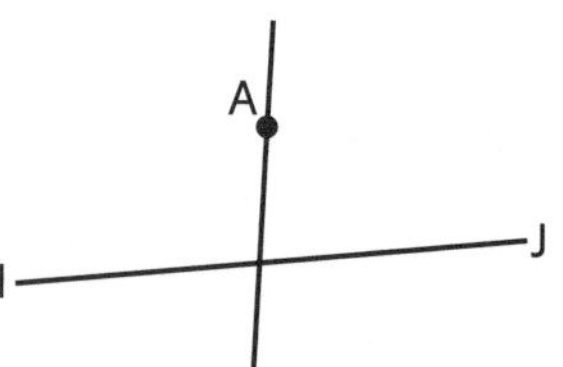

12. a. a line passing through points A and B

    b. the measure of each corresponding angle:

    ____

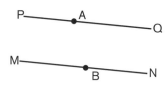

13. a. a line parallel to AB and intersecting XY

    b. the measure of each corresponding angle:

    ____

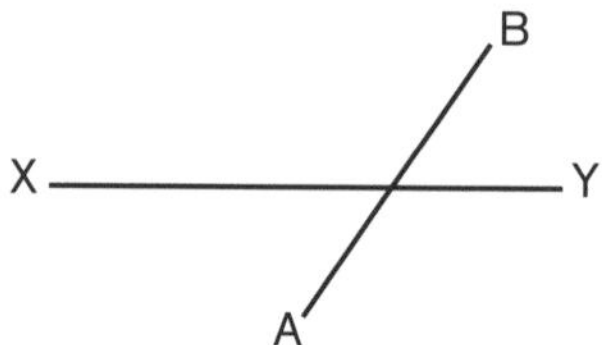

Fill in the blanks to complete what Jimmy says. Look at each highlighted angle. Then put a checkmark in the circle if the lines are perpendicular.

14. *Lines which meet at 90° angle are called* ____________ *.*

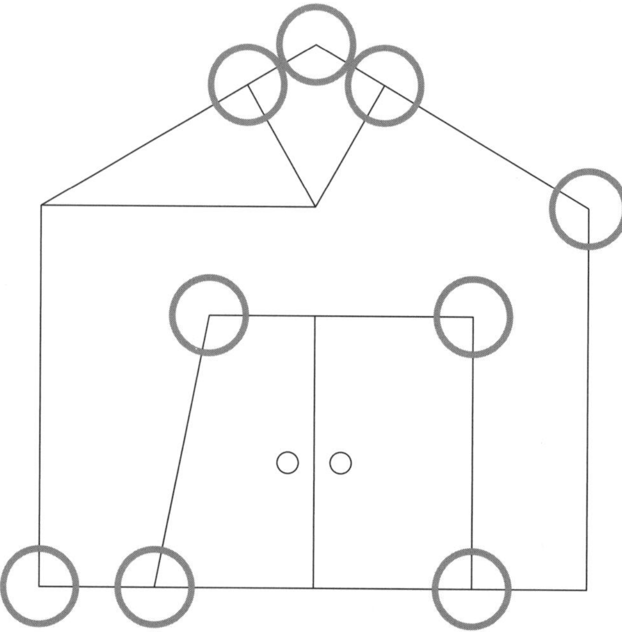

Steps to draw a perpendicular bisector to bisect a line segment with a compass and a ruler:

1st Draw a line AB.

2nd Take A and B as centres and a compass with radius longer than half the length of AB. Draw two arcs intersecting at the points C and D.

3rd Join C and D.

Bisect means "to cut in half". CD is perpendicular to and bisects AB.

Draw a perpendicular bisector to each given line with a compass and a ruler.

15.

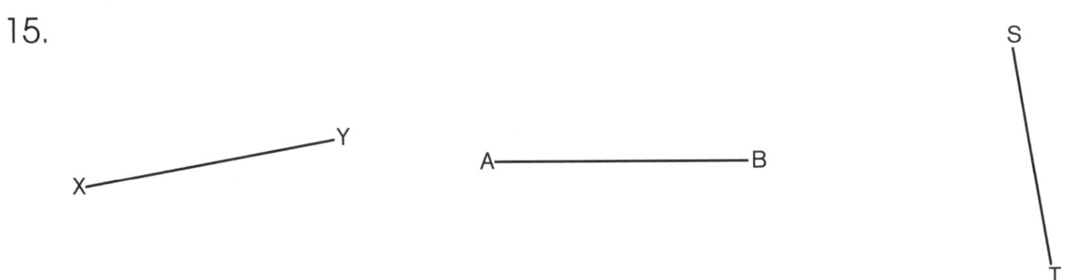

Draw the perpendicular bisector. Then find the measure of the angles and fill in the blanks.

16. Draw a perpendicular bisector to AB.

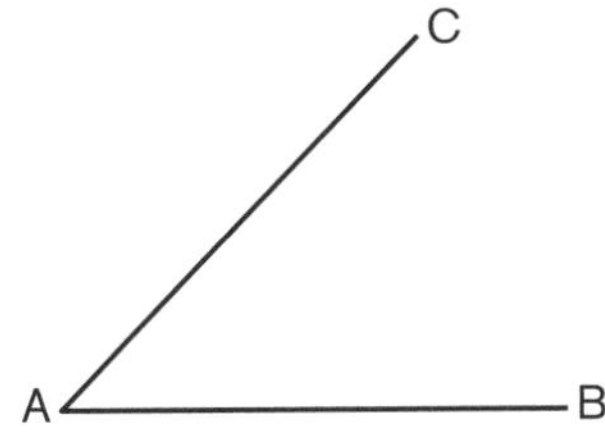

The measures of the adjacent angles formed by AC and the bisector are ______ and ______ .

17. ***Draw a perpendicular bisector to MN. Mark a point K on the bisector. Then draw two lines from K to M and N.***

M

N

The measures of the angles of the triangle NKM are ____________ .

It is a/an ____________ triangle.

Angles and Lines in Shapes

- identify properties of quadrilaterals
- identify and mark equal angles and sides
- identify convex and concave figures
- find the size of an angle using the sum of the angles in a triangle
- draw angle bisectors

Jason, why did you break the triangle?
a
b
c
a + b + c = 180°
Because I want to show you the sum of the angles of a triangle is always 180°.

Read each sentence. Write "T" for true and "F" for false.

1. A quadrilateral with 4 angles is a rectangle. ______
2. All triangles are symmetrical. ______
3. All the angles of a parallelogram can be equal in size. ______
4. A parallelogram always has two pairs of parallel sides. ______
5. A trapezoid has no obtuse angles. ______

Measure and mark the equal angles and sides in each figure if there are any. Then colour the regular polygons.

6.

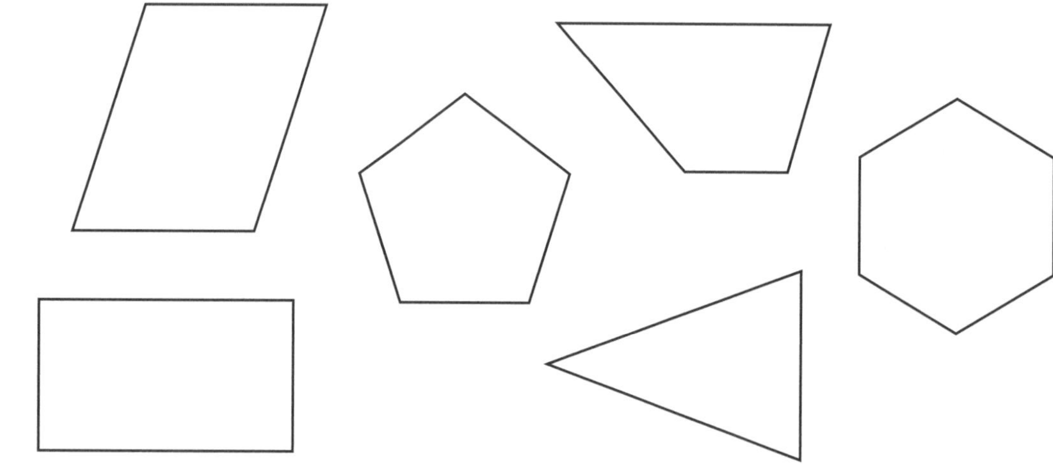

We can name a triangle 2 ways.

Naming Triangles:

by Angles:

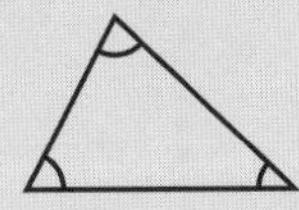

acute triangle
all angles are less than 90°

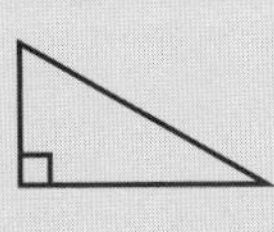

right triangle
with an angle of 90°

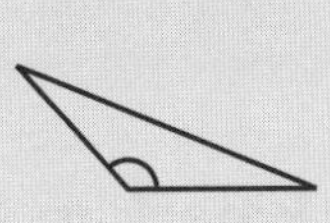

obtuse triangle
with an angle that is between 90° and 180°

by Sides:

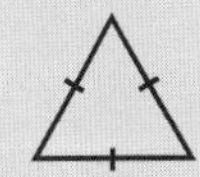

equilateral triangle
all sides are equal

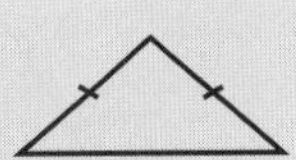

isosceles triangle
two sides are equal

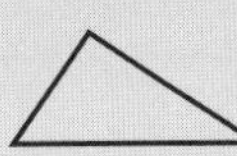

scalene triangle
no sides are equal

Mark the equal sides and angles in each triangle. Then name each triangle in two ways.

7.

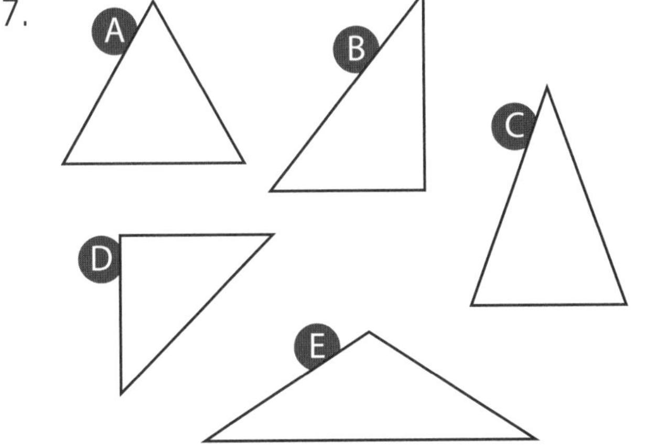

Name

A ____________________

B ____________________

C ____________________

D ____________________

E ____________________

Colour the convex shapes yellow and the concave shapes red.

8.

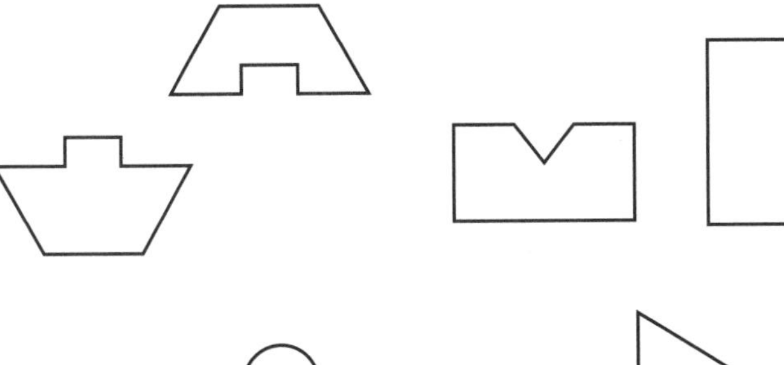

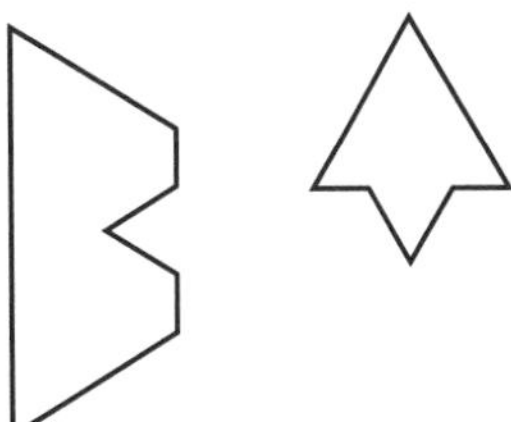

Hint

convex | concave

Convex is a line or surface that curves outward.

Concave is a line or surface that curves inward.

The sum of angles of a triangle is always 180°.

$a + b + c = 180°$

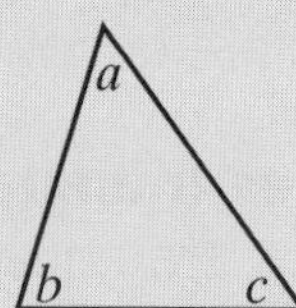

e.g. What is the measure of angle y?

66°
y
58°

$$66° + y + 58° = 180° \leftarrow \text{sum of the angles of a } \triangle$$
$$y + 124° = 180°$$
$$y + 124° - 124° = 180° - 124°$$
$$y = \underline{56°}$$

Are the angles in each set to be the angles of a triangle? Put a checkmark in the triangle if they are; otherwise, put a cross.

9. 60°, 36°, 94° △
10. 47°, 82°, 52° △
11. 36°, 98°, 46° △
12. 15°, 15°, 150° △
13. 85°, 80°, 20° △
14. 64°, 52°, 64° △

Find the measures of the marked angles in the triangles. Show your work.

15.

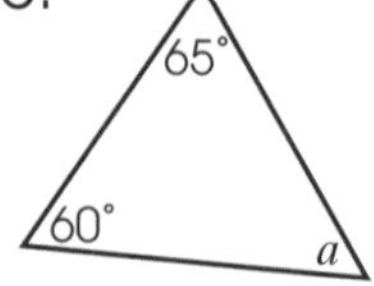

16.

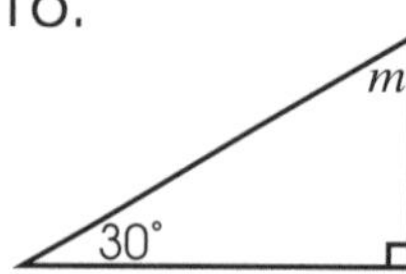

17.

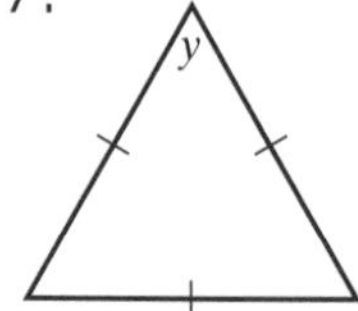

18.

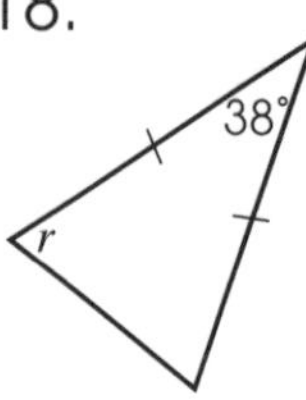

19.

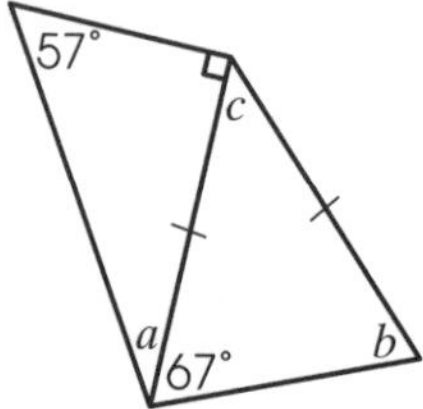

20.

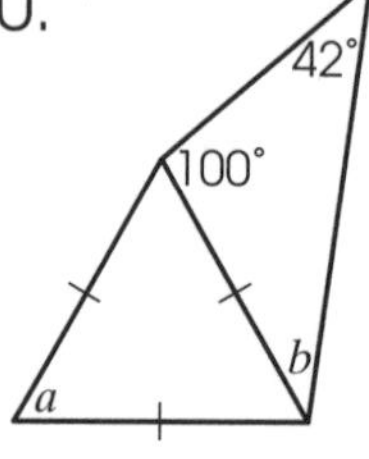

Steps to draw an angle bisector with a compass and a ruler:

1st Take A as centre and draw an arc that intersects the arms of the angle at B and C.

2nd Take B and C as centres and draw 2 arcs that intersect at D.

3rd Join A and D. Line AD is the angle bisector of $\angle A$.

AD is the angle bisector of $\angle A$.

Draw the angle bisector for each marked angle.

21.

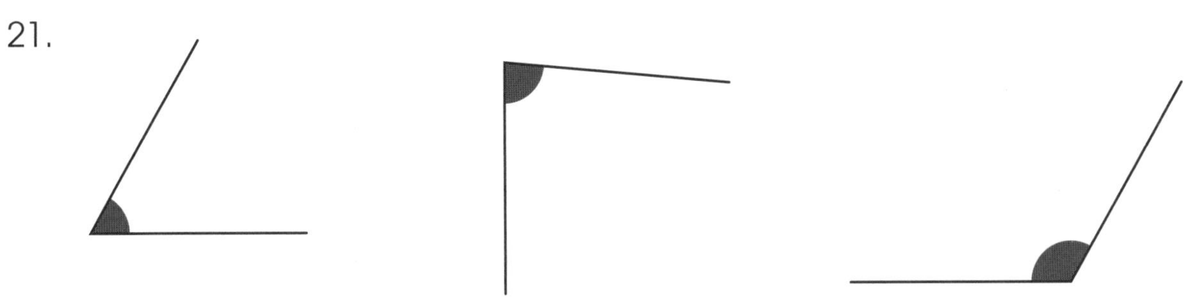

Look at Justin's straws. Draw the triangle that can be built with Justin's straws and name it in two ways. Then bisect one of the angles in the triangle and answer Justin's question.

22.

Name: ______________________

23. *If the long straws make an angle of 40°, what are the measures of the other two angles?*

____

12

Congruent and Similar Figures

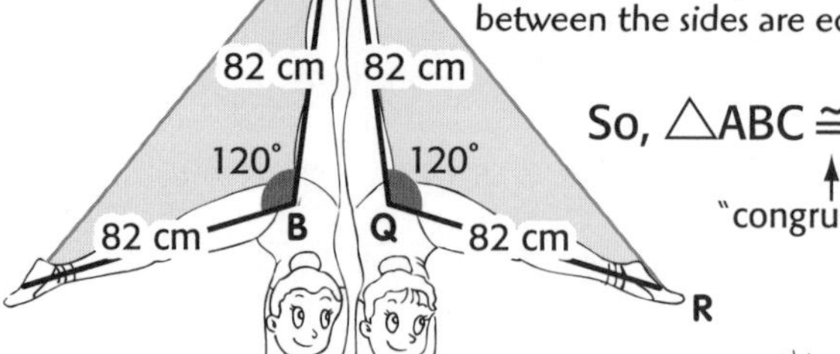

2 pairs of corresponding sides and 1 pair of corresponding angles between the sides are equal.

So, △ABC ≅ △PQR.

"congruent to"

- name equal sides and angles
- identify and name congruent triangles
- show how triangles are congruent by rules
- identify similar figures

Hold on, let me capture the congruent triangles that you've made.

List the corresponding sides and angles for each pair of congruent triangles. Then use "≅" to name the congruent triangles.

1.

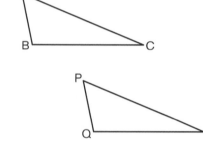

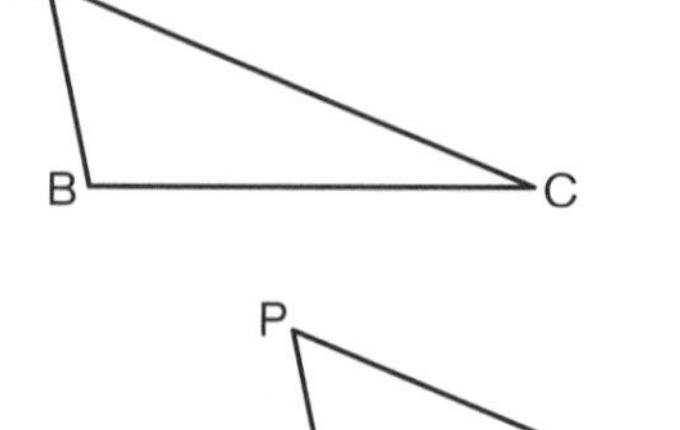

Sides: AB = ______ BC = ______ AC = ______

Angles: ∠A = ______ ∠B = ______ ∠C = ______

△ABC ______ △PQR

2.

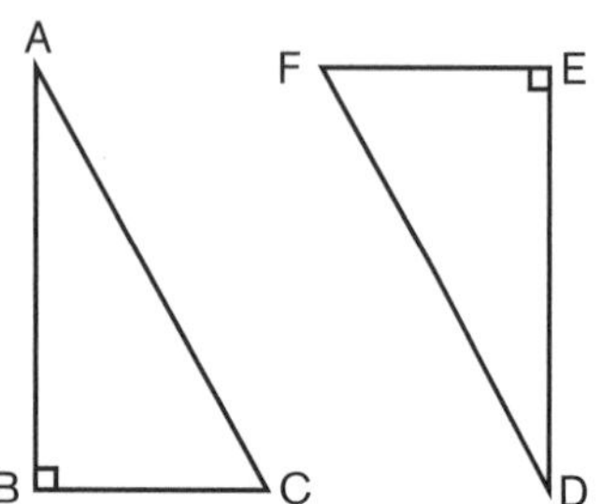

Sides	**Angles**
AB = ______	∠A = ______
______	______
______	______

△ABC ______

3.

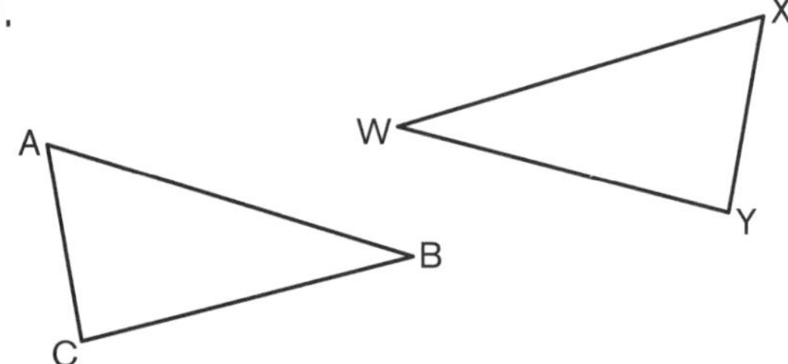

Sides	**Angles**
______	______
______	______
______	______

△ABC ______

Rules to prove that two triangles are **congruent**:

side-side-side

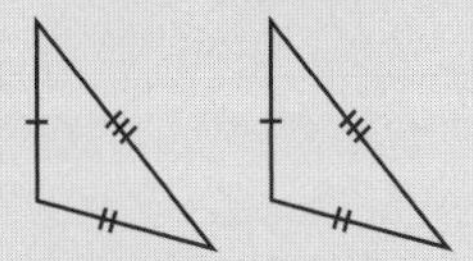

3 pairs of corresponding sides are equal

side-angle-side

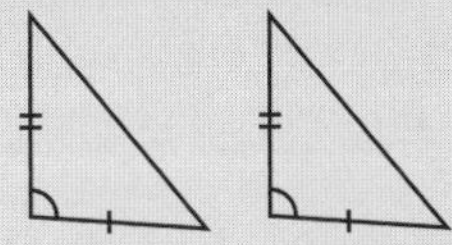

2 pairs of corresponding sides and 1 pair of angles between the sides are equal

angle-side-angle

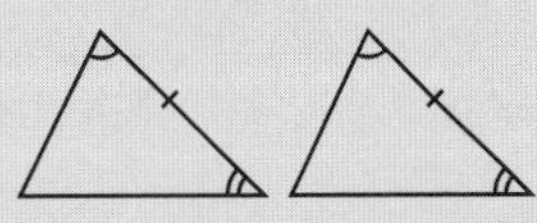

2 pairs of corresponding angles and 1 pair of sides between the angles are equal

angle-angle-side

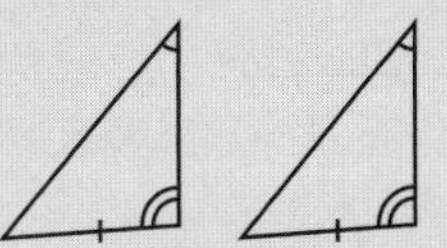

2 pairs of corresponding angles and 1 pair of corresponding sides are equal

Look at the markings on each pair of congruent triangles. Then write which rule can be used to prove that they are congruent.

4\.

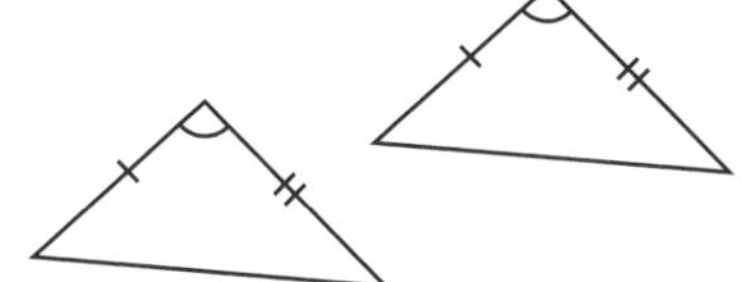

____

5\.

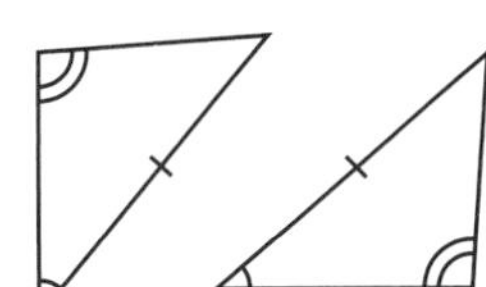

____

6\.

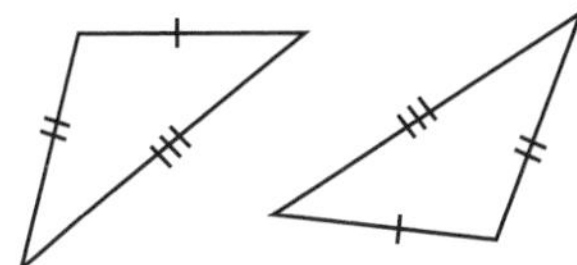

____

7\.

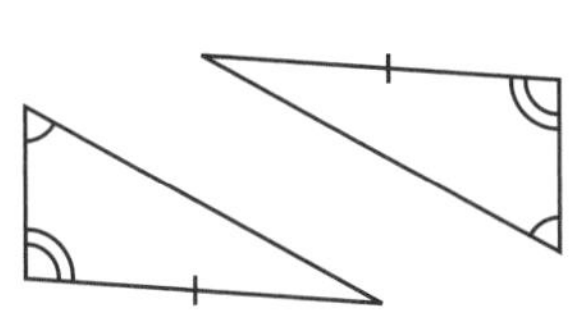

____

8\.

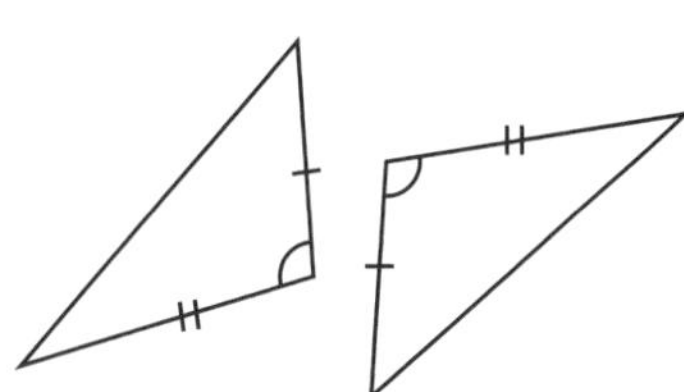

____

9\.

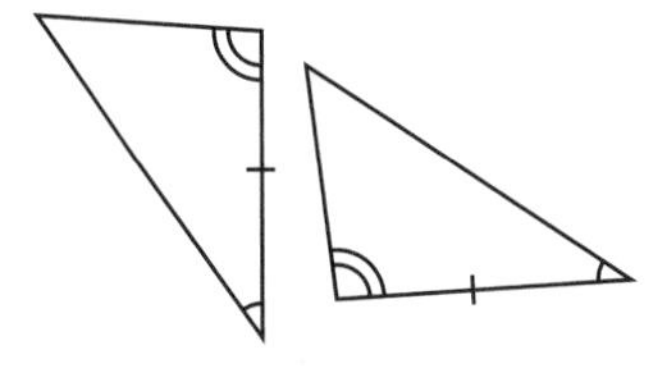

____

For each pair of congruent triangles, label the measurements on the shaded triangle the same as the other one. Then write the rule that proves they are congruent.

10\.

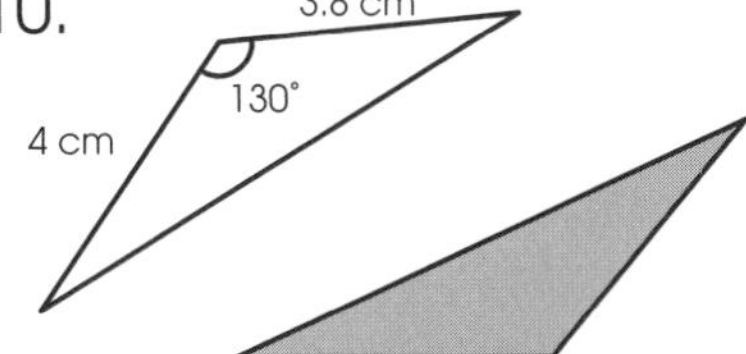

____

11\.

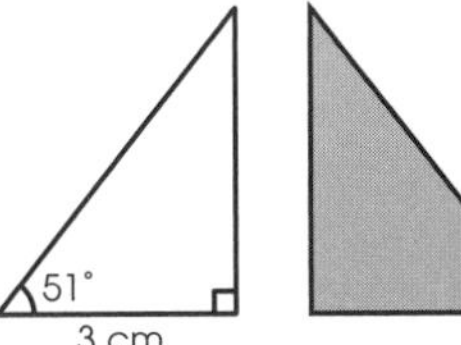

____

12\.

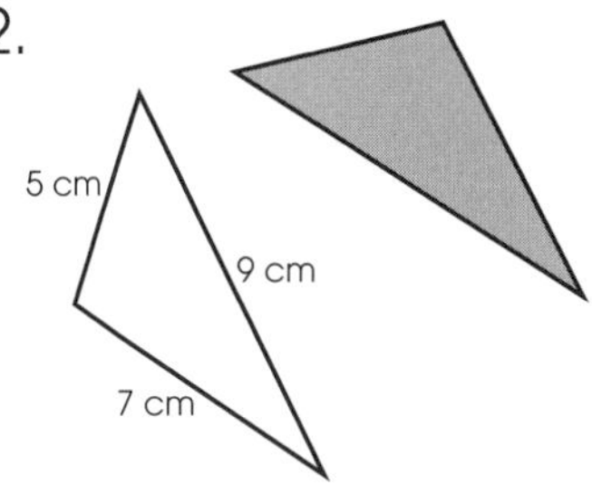

____

Complete each list to show how the two triangles are congruent.

13.

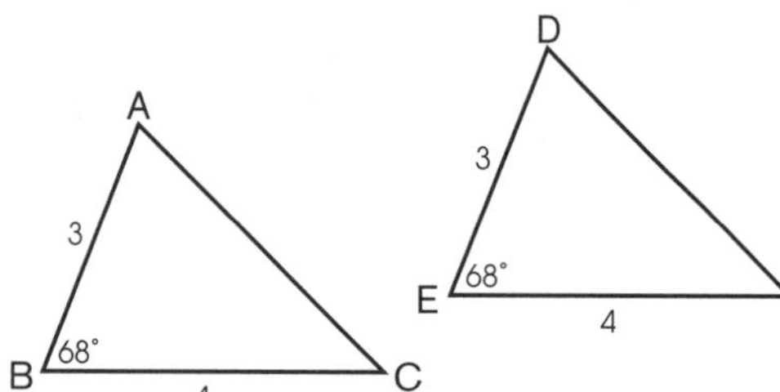

- AB = _____ = 3 units
- ∠B = _____ = _____
- BC = _____ = _____

So, △ABC ≅ _____ by side- _____ - _____

14.

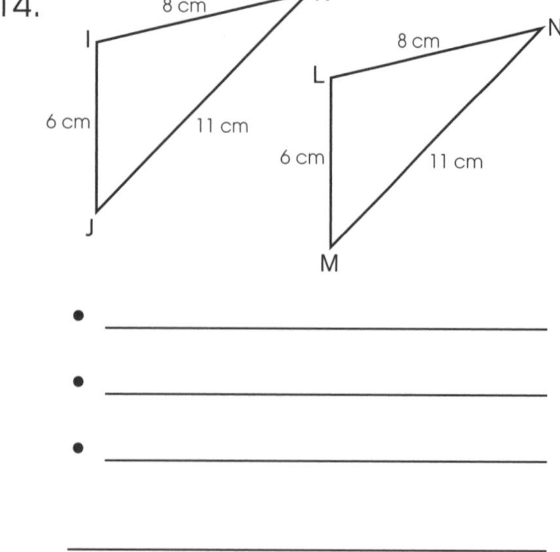

- _______________
- _______________
- _______________

____

____

15.

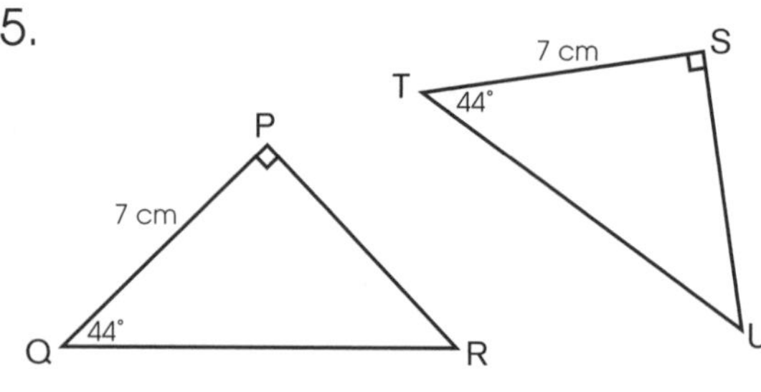

- _______________
- _______________
- _______________

____

____

Circle the two congruent triangles. Then show how they are congruent.

16.

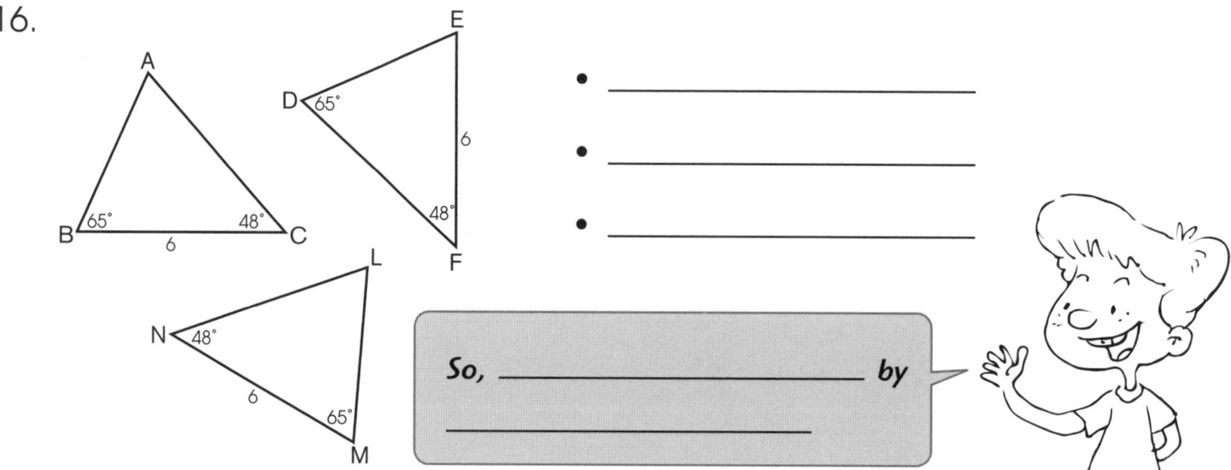

- _______________
- _______________
- _______________

So, _______________ *by*

____

Similar Figures – a similar figure can be made by shrinking or enlarging another figure

A, B, and C are similar figures.

You may use grid systems to draw similar figures.

A

B

C

This grid has a smaller scale. This figure is shrunk.

This grid has a larger scale. This figure is enlarged.

Draw a similar figure on each grid.

17.

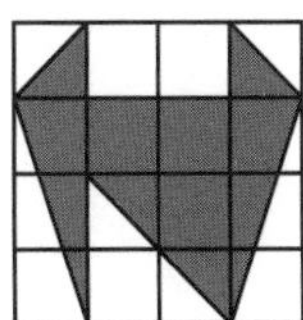

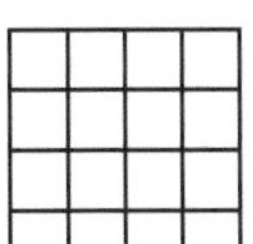

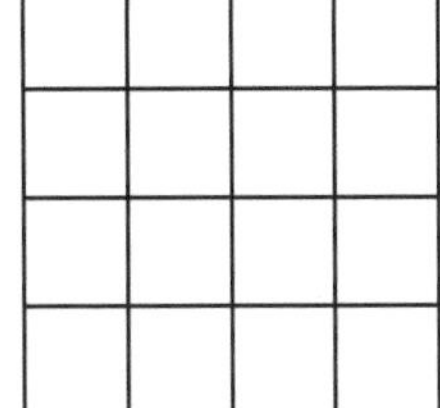

18.

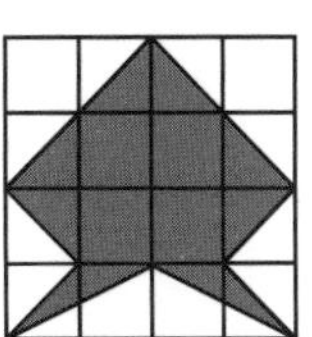

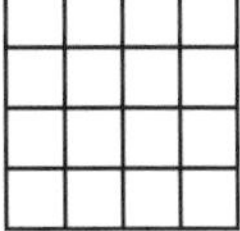

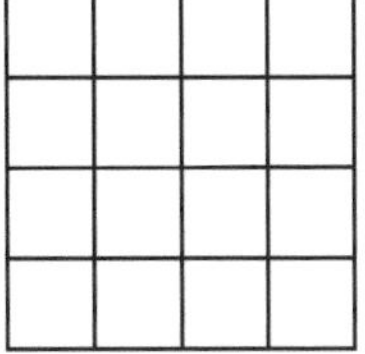

19.

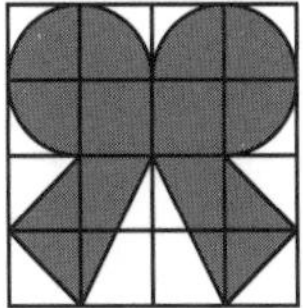

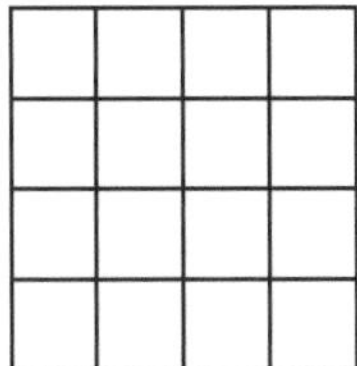

Give an example to support what Joanne says.

20.

All equilateral triangles are similar.

13

Solids

- draw 3-D solids on a grid
- identify and draw different views of a solid
- draw a 3-D solid with the given views
- identify solids from nets
- draw the nets of solids

Top
Back
Left side
Right side
Front

Excuse me, I want to look at the right side of the structure.

Front View

Back View

Top View

Left-side View

Right-side View

Draw the missing parts of each solid.

1.

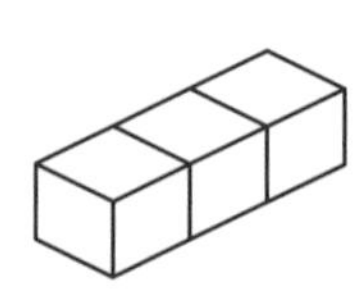

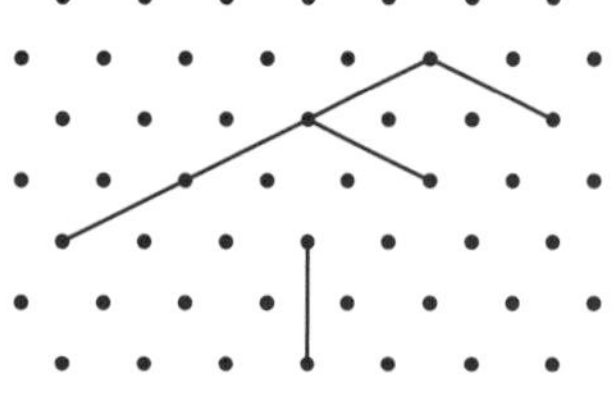

2.

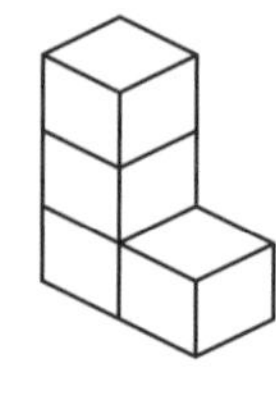

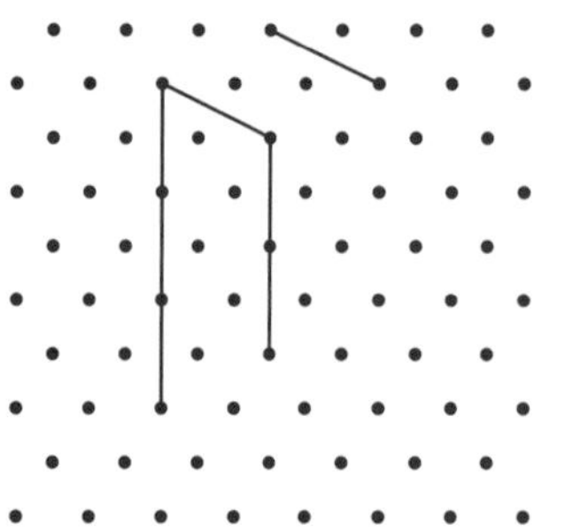

3.

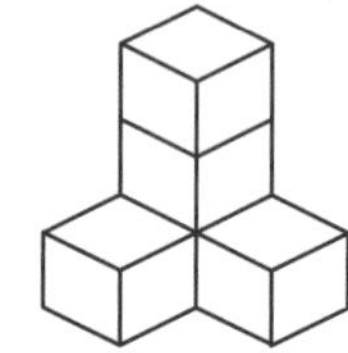

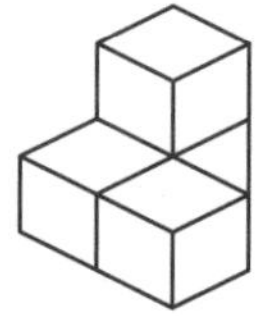

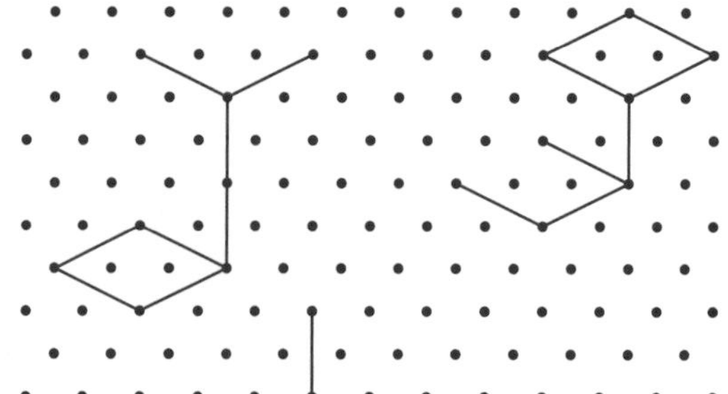

Look at different views of the solid. Write the letters in the circles.

4.

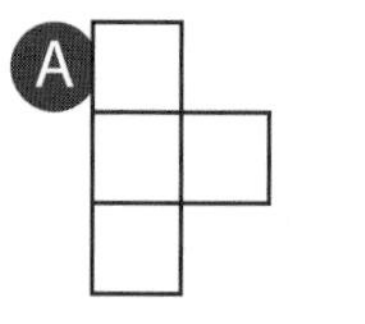

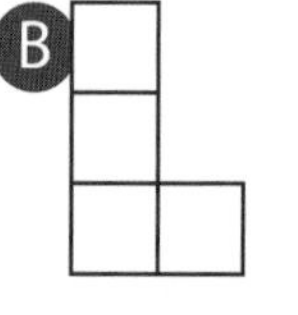

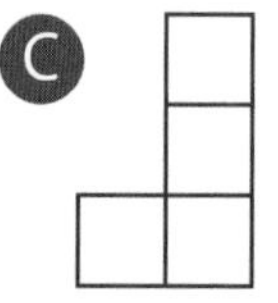

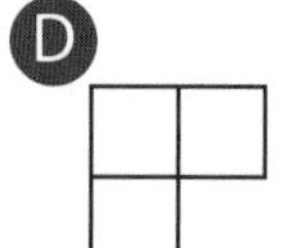

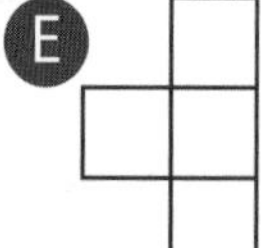

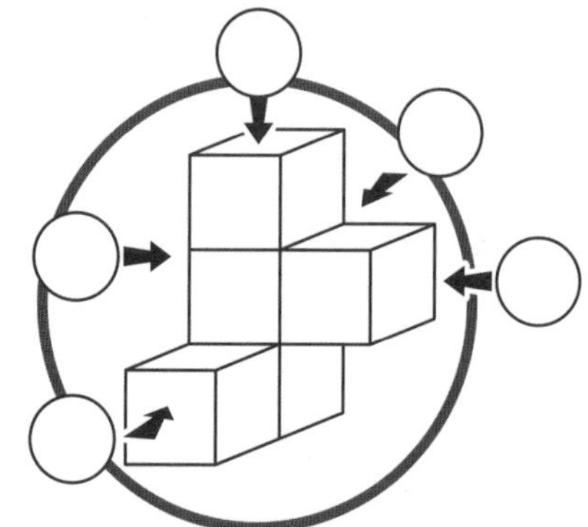

Check the solid that has the given views. Then draw the top view.

5.

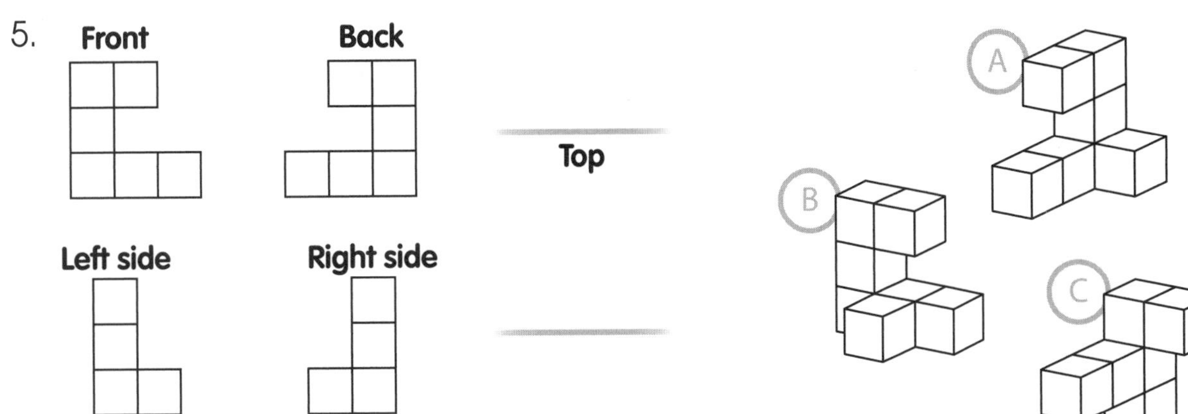

Draw the five views of each solid.

6.

Front

Back

Top

Left side

Right side

Draw the solids with the given views.

7\. Front Top Right side

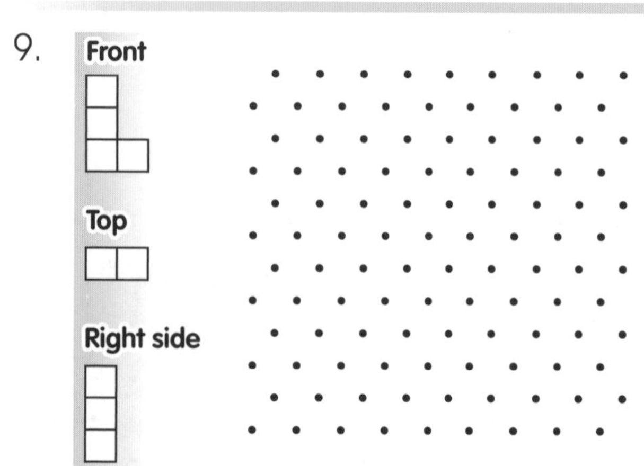

8\. Front Top Left side

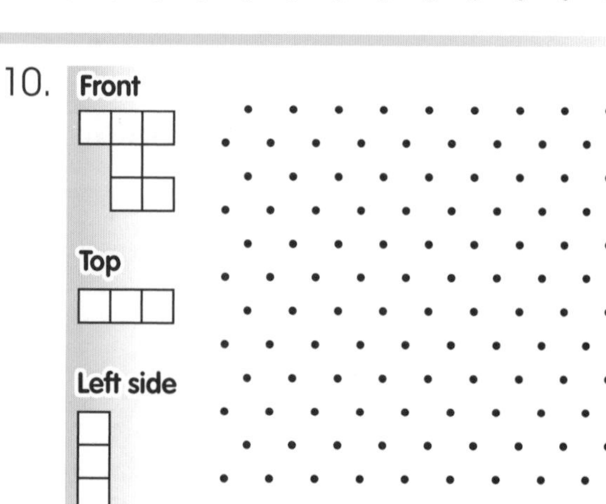

9\. Front

Top

Right side

10\. Front

Top

Left side

Identify the net of each solid. Name the solid.

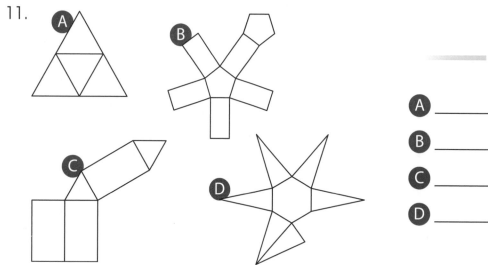

11\.

A

B

C

D

Name

A ____________________

B ____________________

C ____________________

D ____________________

Drawing a Prism:

1st Draw the end.

2nd Slide a congruent figure to the right and up a bit.

3rd Join the matching vertices.

Drawing a Pyramid:

1st Draw a base.

2nd Draw a point away from the base.

3rd Join each vertex of the base to the point.

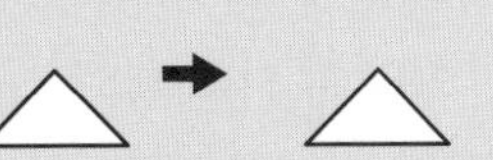

Count and write the numbers. Then sketch the polyhedron that is made by folding each net. Name the polyhedron.

12. _____ faces

_____ edges

_____ vertices

Congruent faces:

_____ hexagon(s) and

_____ rectangle(s)

Name: ____________________

13. _____ faces

_____ edges

_____ vertices

Congruent faces:

_____ octagon(s) and

_____ triangle(s)

Name: ____________________

Sketch the polyhedron as described. Then draw two different nets for that polyhedron.

14.

The polyhedron has 1 pentagonal face and 5 congruent triangular faces.

14

Area

I can change a parallelogram to a rectangle, but keep its area the same.

Area of a ▱
= Area of a ▭ (b, h)
= **b x h**

- find areas of parallelograms
- find missing measurements in parallelograms
- find areas of triangles
- find areas of trapezoids
- find areas of irregular shapes

This is a fact. Everyone can do this.

Trace the base and height of each parallelogram. Then find the area.

1.

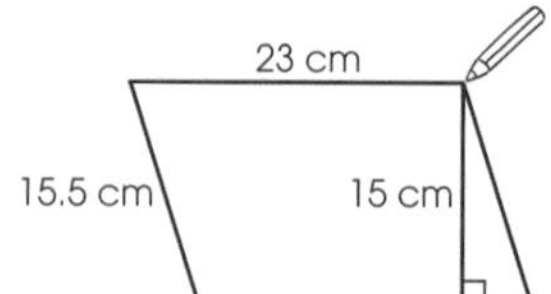

b = ______

h = ______

Area of parallelogram

= b x h

= ______ x ______

= ______ (cm^2)

2.

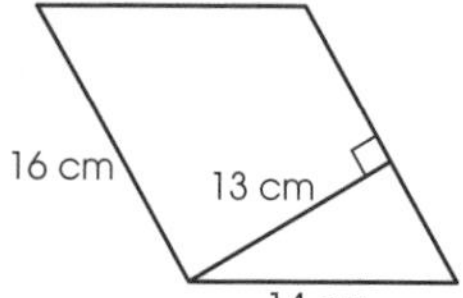

b = ______

h = ______

Area of parallelogram

= ______________

= ______

3.

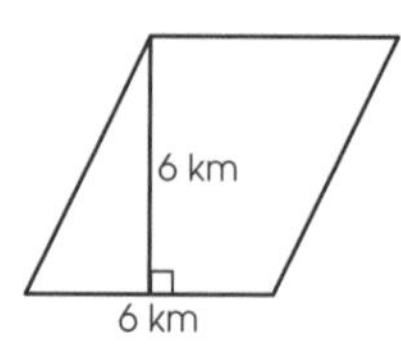
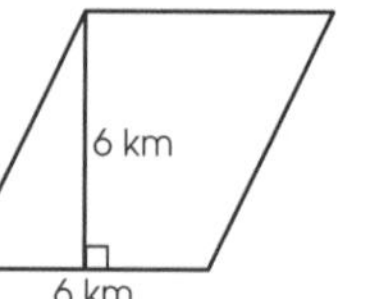

Area = ________

= ______

4.

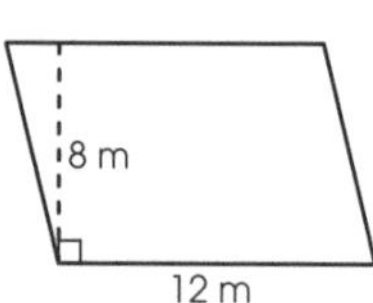

Area = ________

= ______

5.

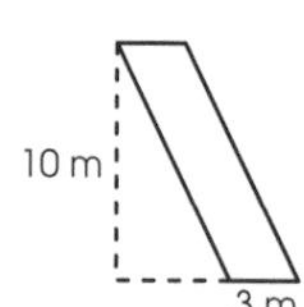

Area = ________

= ______

Find the missing measurement for each parallelogram.

6.

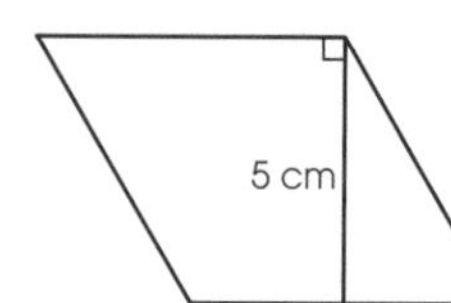

Area = 30 cm^2

Base = ______

7.

Area = 27 m^2

Height = ______

A parallelogram is formed by 2 identical triangles.

Area of a △ = Area of a ▱ ÷ 2

= **b** x **h** ÷ **2**

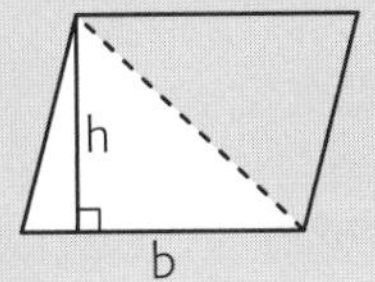

e.g. Area of △

= (b x h) ÷ 2

= (13 x 8) ÷ 2

= 52 (cm^2)

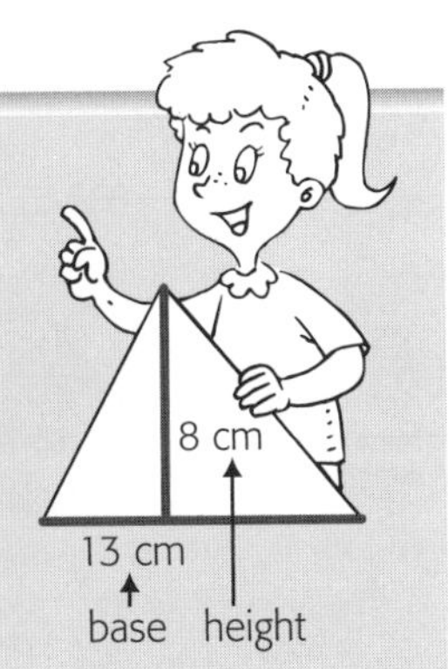

Trace the base and height of each triangle. Then find the area.

8.

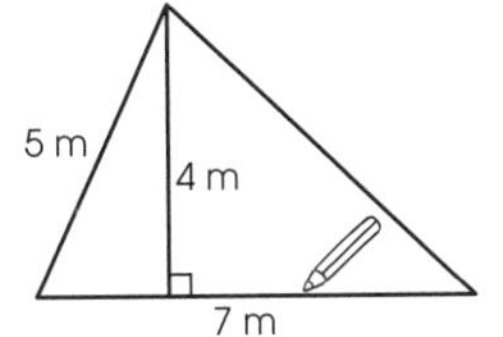

b = ______

h = ______

Area = (b x h) ÷ 2

= (______ x ______) ÷ 2

= ______ (cm^2)

9.

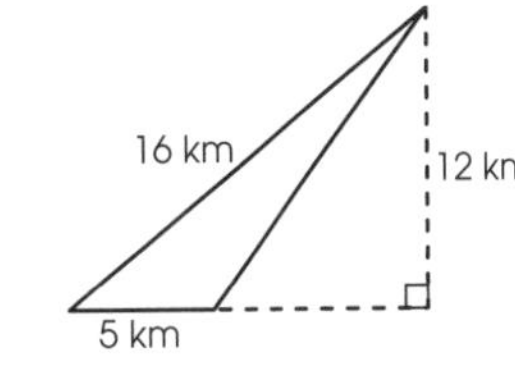

b = ______

h = ______

Area =

10.

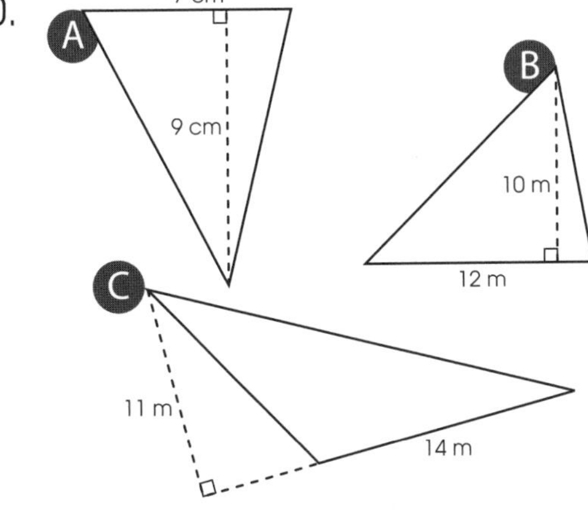

A Area =

B Area =

C Area =

Find the missing measurement for each triangle.

11.

Area	Base	Height
35 cm^2	7 cm	
42 cm^2	6 cm	
24 m^2	8 m	

12.

Area	Base	Height
20 cm^2		5 cm
19.5 m^2		10 m
42 m^2		3 m

Find the area of a trapezoid by cutting it into 2 triangles or 1 triangle and 1 parallelogram.

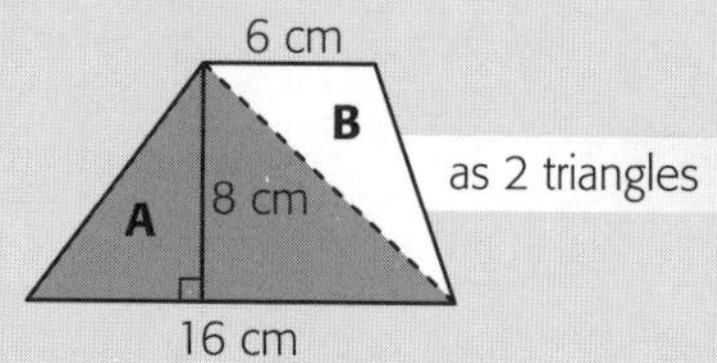

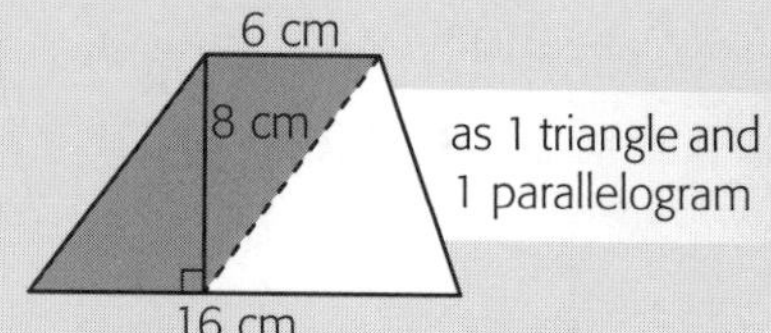

Area of A = (16 x 8) ÷ 2 = 64 (cm^2)
Area of B = (6 x 8) ÷ 2 = 24 (cm^2)
Area of trapezoid = 64 + 24 = 88 (cm^2)

Area of triangle = (10 x 8) ÷ 2 = 40 (cm^2)
Area of parallelogram = 6 x 8 = 48 (cm^2)
Area of trapezoid = 40 + 48 = 88 (cm^2)

Find the area of each trapezoid by cutting it into the specified shapes.

13.

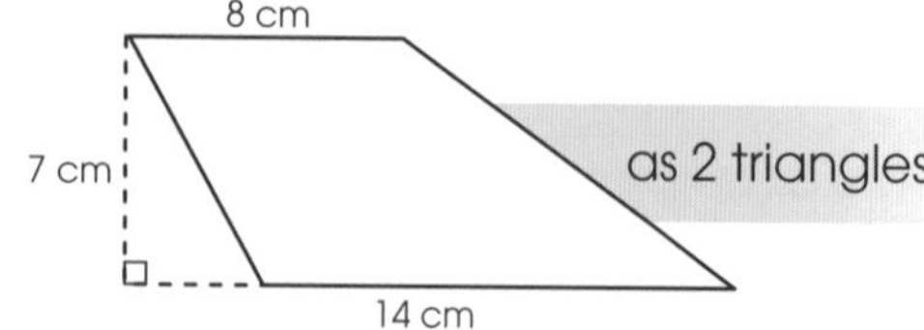

14.

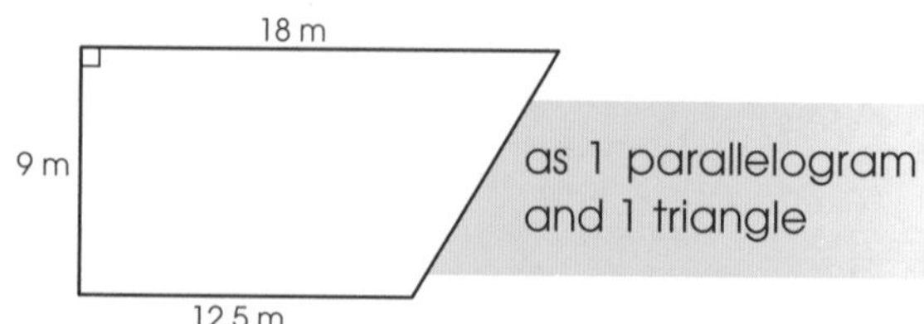

Find the area of each trapezoid.

15.

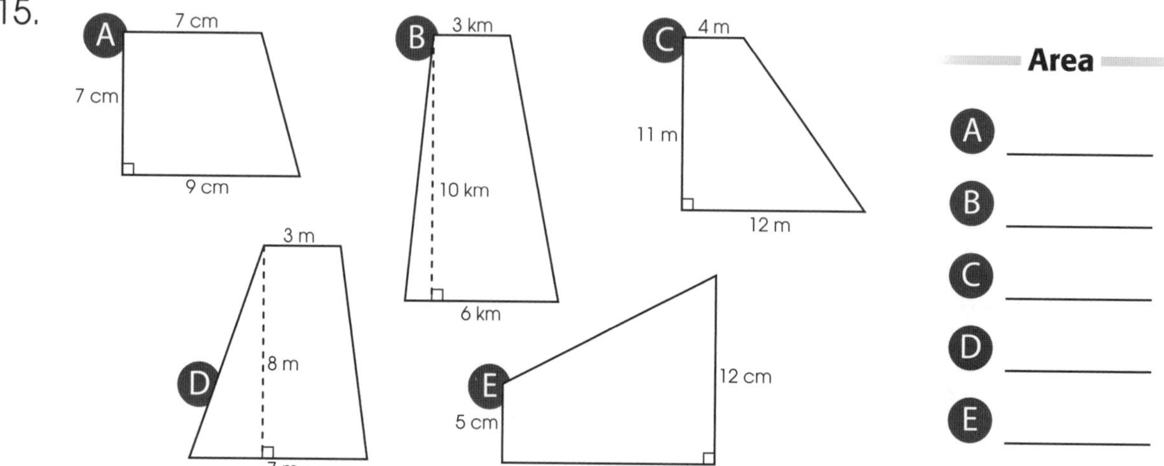

Area

A ____________

B ____________

C ____________

D ____________

E ____________

Trace the dotted lines to divide each irregular figure into several shapes. Find the area of each shape. Then add to find the area of the irregular figure.

16.

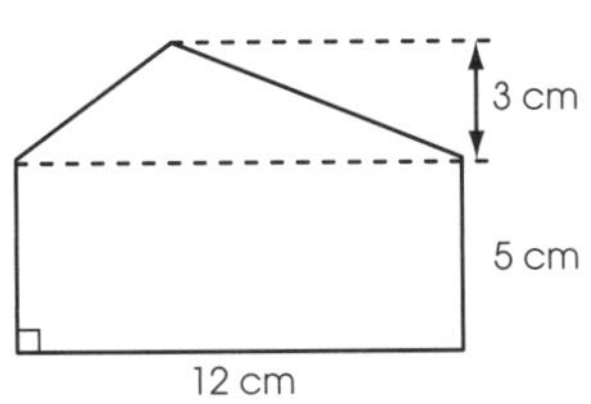

17.

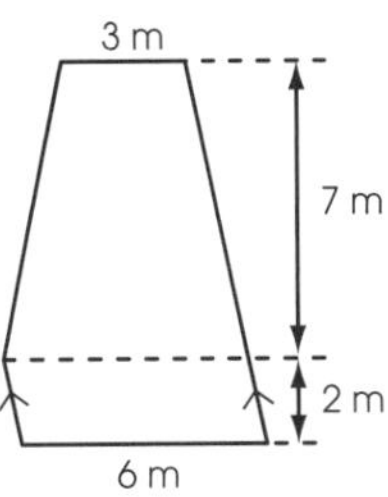

Find the area of each irregular figure.

18.

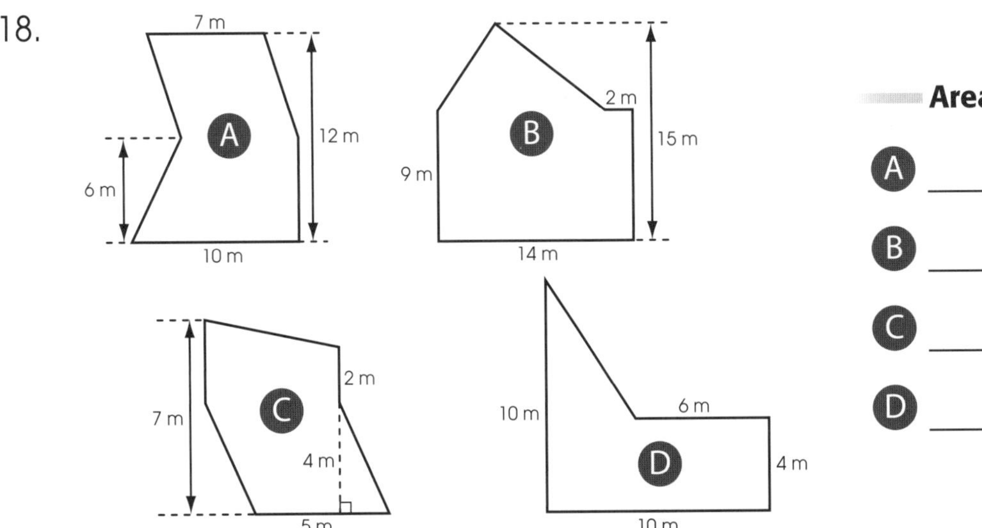

Area

A ________

B ________

C ________

D ________

Read what Harry says. Find the area of the trapezoid.

19.

You may use subtraction to find the area of this trapezoid.
1 cm
1 cm

Review 1

Fill in the missing numbers. Then evaluate.

1. $6^{\square} = 6 \times 6 \times 6 =$ ______

2. $\square^{5} = 3 \times 3 \times 3 \times 3 \times 3 =$ ______

3. $2 \times 3^2 = 2 \times 3 \times \square =$ ______

4. $4^2 \times 5^3 = 4 \times 5 \times 4 \times \square \times 5 =$ ______

5. $2^4 \times 5^3 \times 8^{\square} = 2 \times 2 \times 2 \times 2 \times 5 \times 5 \times 5 =$ ______

6. $2^3 \times 10^2 \times 11 = 2 \times 2 \times 10 \times 10 \times 2 \times \square =$ ______

Find the area of each polygon. Then solve the problems.

7.

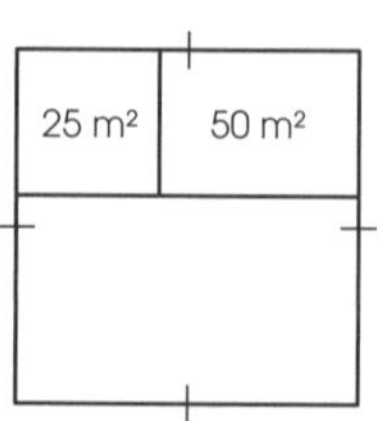

8.

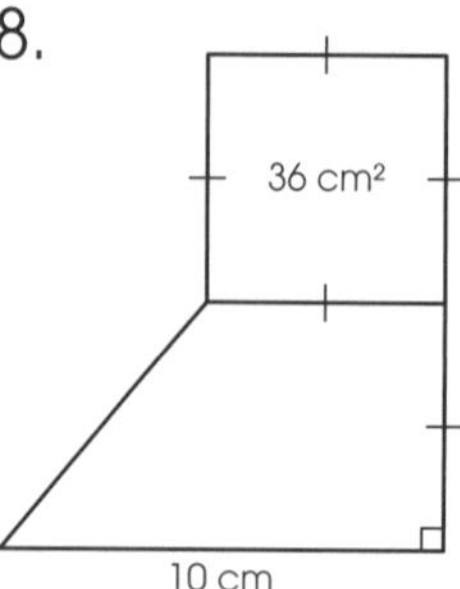

9.

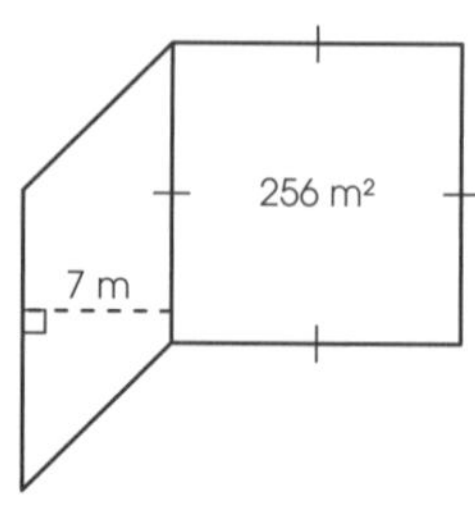

10.

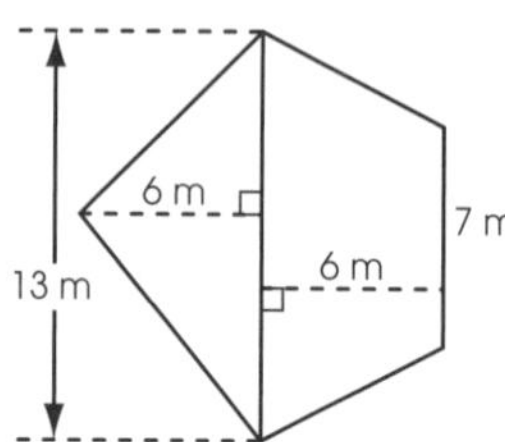

11. a. What is the side length of the big square?

______

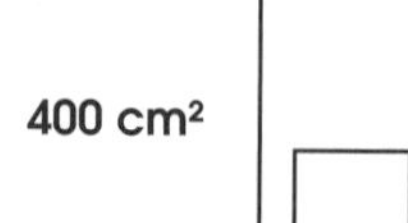

b. What is the ratio of the area of the small square to that of the big square?

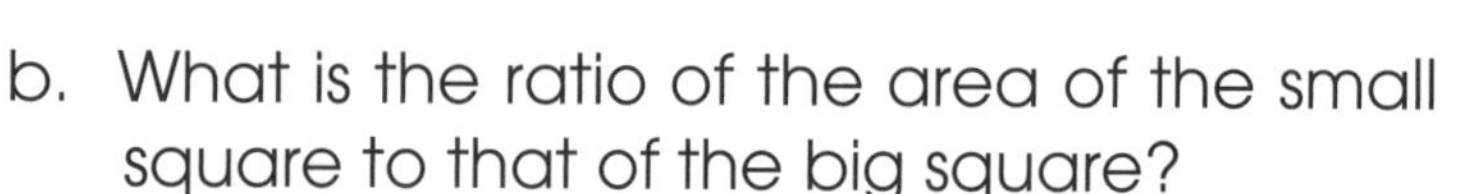

$\frac{\text{side length of small square}}{\text{side length of big square}} = \frac{2}{5}$

______

Find the G.C.F. of the terms. Then write each ratio in simplest form.

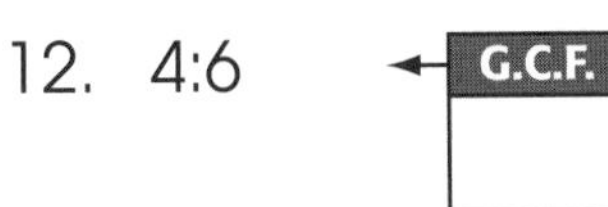

12. 4:6 ← G.C.F. ____ ______

13. 12:9 ← G.C.F. ____ ______

14. 16:2:8 ← G.C.F. ____ ______

15. 10:25 ← G.C.F. ____ ______

16. 14:30 ← G.C.F. ____ ______

17. 21:28:7 ← G.C.F. ____ ______

18. *I want to put 27 boys and 21 girls into teams. The number of players with the same gender on each team should be the same. Each team will have as many boys and girls as possible.*

a. How many teams will there be?

____

b. How many boys and girls will there be on each team?

____

We'll have more than 1 team.

List the first 10 multiples of the numbers. Find the L.C.M. of each group of numbers. Then answer the questions.

19. 3: ______________________________

4: ______________________________

5: ______________________________

6: ______________________________

7: ______________________________

8: ______________________________

L.C.M.

5 and 6 ______

7 and 8 ______

4 and 5 ______

3, 4, and 6 ______

3, 5, and 6 ______

20. A box of gumballs can be divided equally into groups of 2, 3, or 5. What is the least number of gumballs are there in a box?

____

Find the unit rate of each person and check the one with a higher rate. Then answer the question.

21. (A) Katie makes 9 lemon pies in 3 hours. rate: ____

(B) Jane makes 10 lemon pies in 4 hours. rate: ____

How many pies do the girls make in total in 12 hours?

____

22. (A) Jack builds 3 patios in 2 days. rate: ____

(B) Tom builds 6 patios in 3 days. rate: ____

How many more days does Jack take than Tom to build 15 patios?

____

Find the answers. Then solve the problems.

23. $\frac{2}{3} + \frac{5}{6} =$ ____

24. $\frac{9}{10} - \frac{2}{5} =$ ____

25. $14 \times \frac{6}{7} =$ ____

26. $(\frac{7}{9} - \frac{1}{18}) \times 18 =$ ____

27. $\frac{7}{15} - \frac{3}{10} =$ ____

28. $10 \times \frac{3}{5} =$ ____

29. $\frac{5}{8} + \frac{1}{6} =$ ____

30. $2 \times \frac{11}{30} + \frac{4}{15} =$ ____

31. $4 \times \frac{5}{28} + \frac{2}{7} =$ ____

32. Marco has a bottle of marbles. If he gives $\frac{2}{5}$ of his marbles to his brother, how many marbles will he have left?

____

Do the multiplication and division. Round the answers to 2 decimal places.

33. $17.6 \times 4.1 =$ ______

34. $9 \div 2.5 =$ ______

35. $18.25 \div 7.3 =$ ______

36. $13.53 \times 1.5 =$ ______

37. $18.41 \div 5.26 =$ ______

38. product of 6.75 and 10.2

The product is ______ .

Write each number as fractions, decimals, and percents. Then answer the questions.

39. 18% ______ ______

40. $\frac{10}{16}$ ______ ______

41. $\frac{2}{5}$ ______ ______

42. 2.5 ______ ______

43.

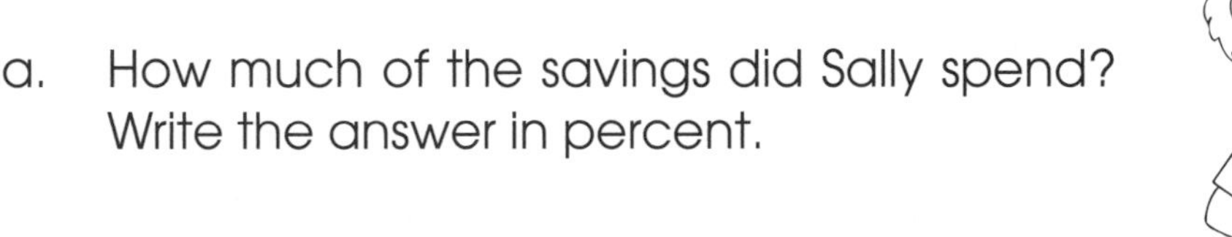

I spent 1/5 of my savings on food and 25% on clothes.

a. How much of the savings did Sally spend? Write the answer in percent.

____

b. If she spent $45 in all, what was her savings at the beginning?

____

Draw a line joining the two dots to form a transversal. Then label, measure, and record the size of two different sets of corresponding angles.

44.

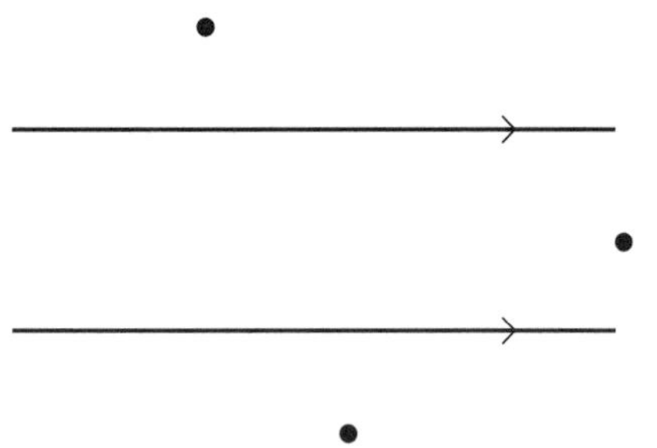

45.

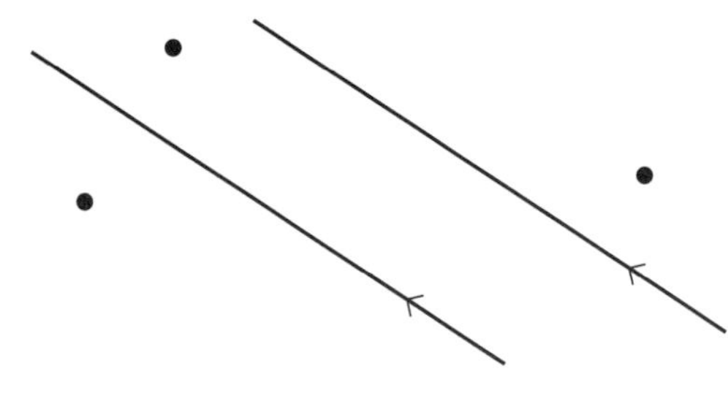

46.

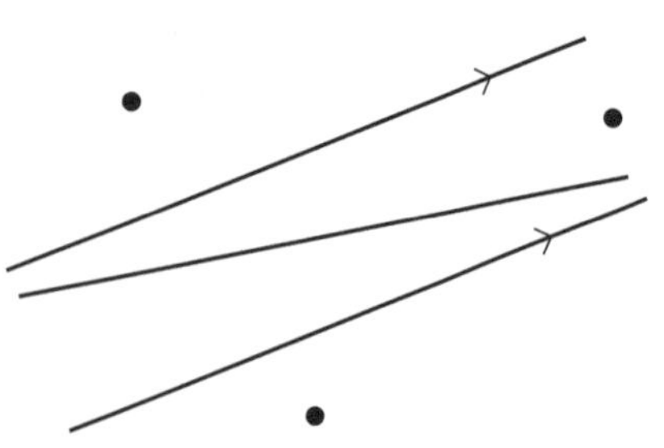

47.

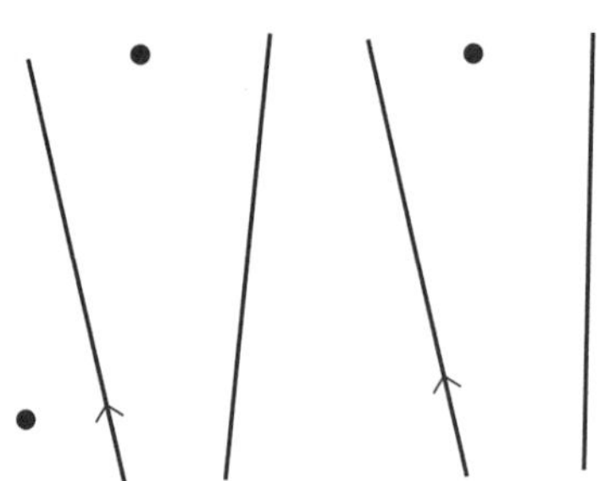

Draw the bisectors and answer the questions.

48. Bisect A. Then bisect one of the small angles.

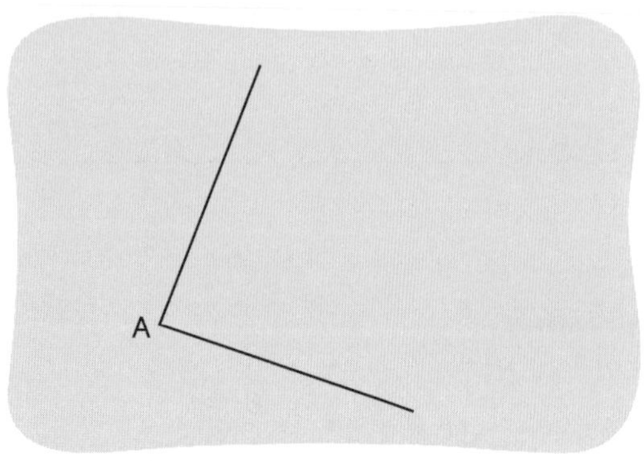

How does the measure of one of the smallest angles relate to A?

____

____

49. Bisect line AB.

C

A

B

If the perpendicular bisector of $\overline{AB}$ also bisects angle C, are the two small triangles congruent? Explain.

____

____

Tell which rule can be used to prove that the triangles in each pair are congruent. Then answer the questions.

50. 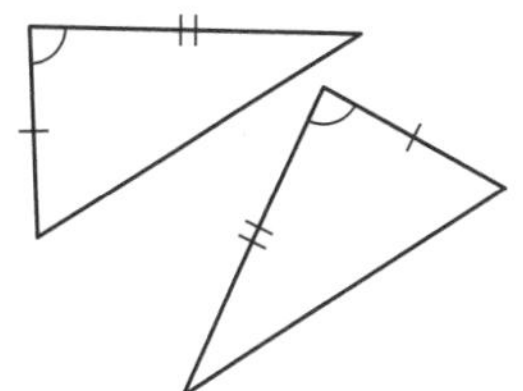

side - ______ - ______

51. 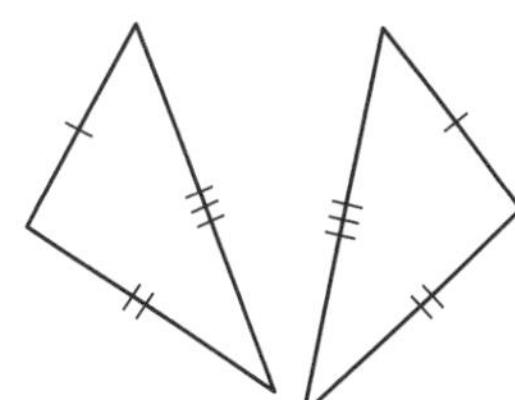

______

52. 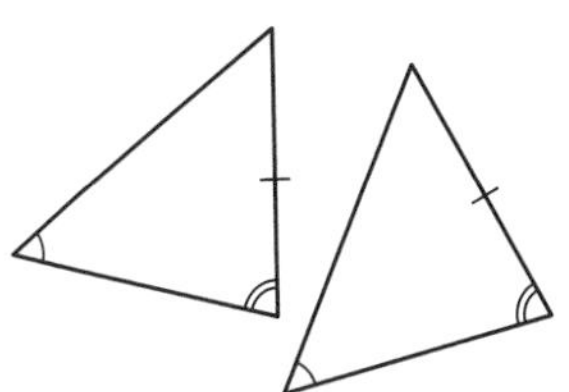

______

53. Circle the triangle that is congruent to $\triangle$ABC. Then prove your choice.

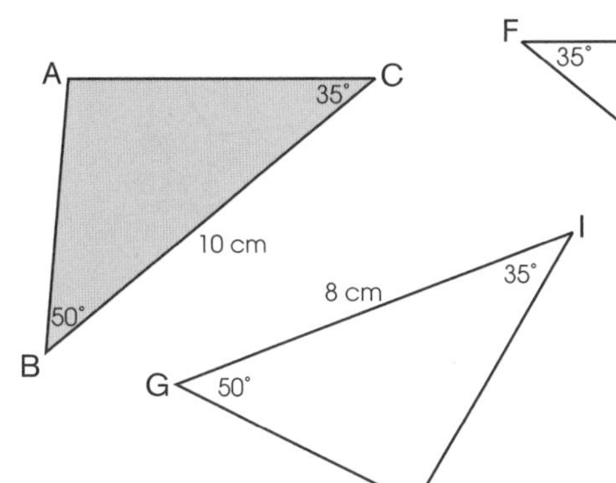

Reason

- $\angle$B = ______ = 50°
- ______
- ______

So, $\triangle$ABC ≅ ______ by

______

Draw the solids with the given views.

54. 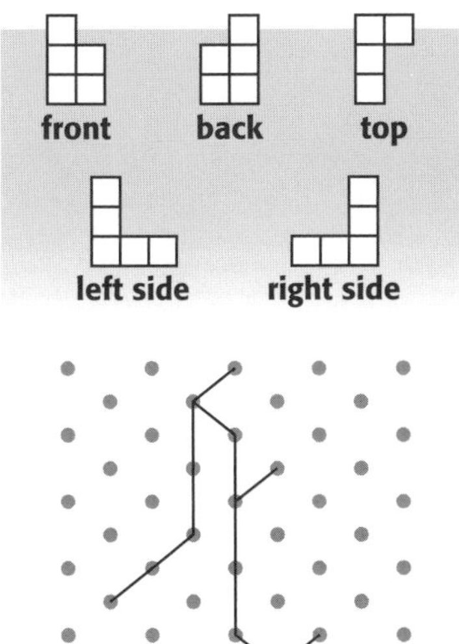

55. *The left-side, right-side, and back views of this solid are the same as its front view.*

front

top

Surface Area

- find surface areas of rectangular prisms
- find surface areas of triangular prisms
- find surface areas of different prisms
- find surface areas of combined prisms

There are 5 faces on a triangular prism with a total surface area of 420 cm². Let me hold this for you and you can start painting it.

Area

❶ 5 x 12 = 60
❷ 12 x 13 = 156
❸ 12 x 12 = 144
❹ & ❺
(12 x 5) ÷ 2 x 2 = 60

Total: 420 cm²

Find the surface area of each rectangular prism.

1.

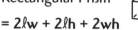

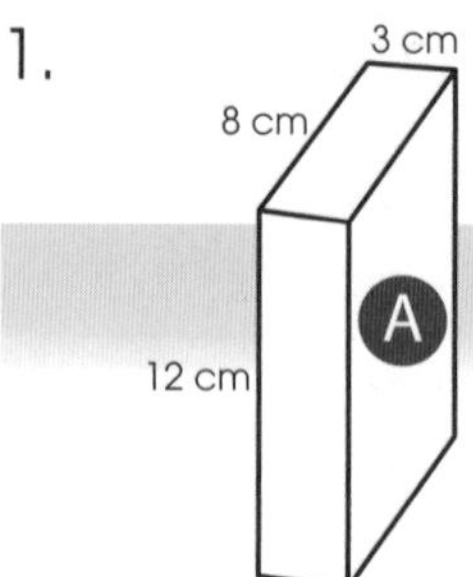

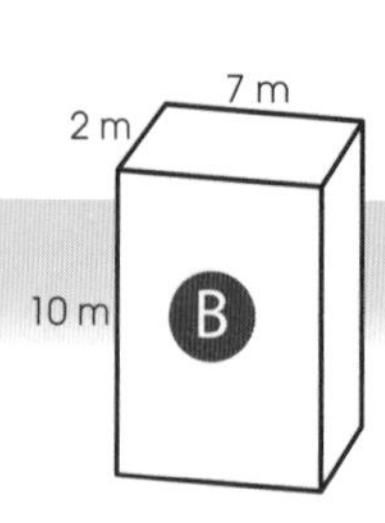

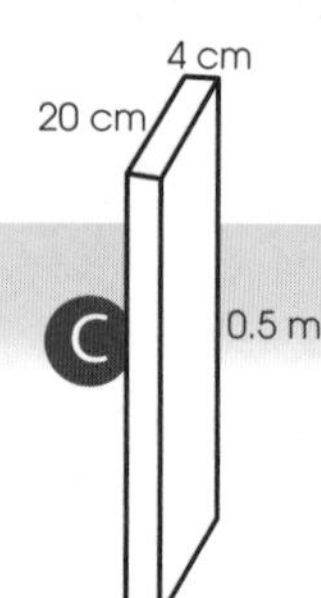

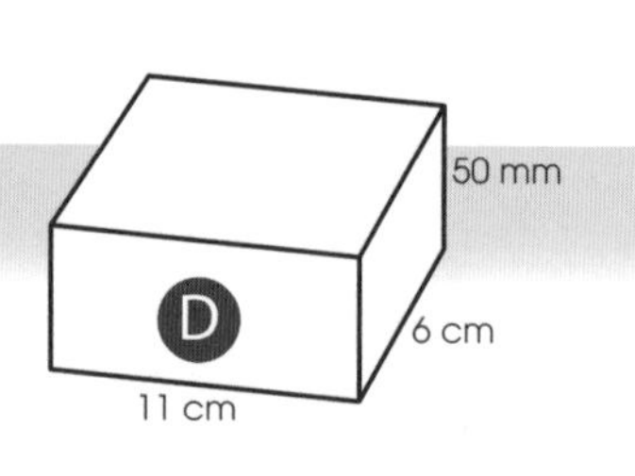

Surface Area

2 x ________ + 2 x ________ + 2 x ________

= ________ + ________ + ________

= ________ (cm²)

Surface Area of a Rectangular Prism

= 2ℓw + 2ℓh + 2wh

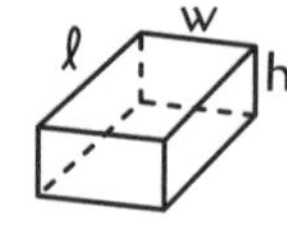

Remember to have all the dimensions with the same units before doing the calculation.

Label the measurements on the net. Find the area of each face. Then find the total surface area of each triangular prism.

2.

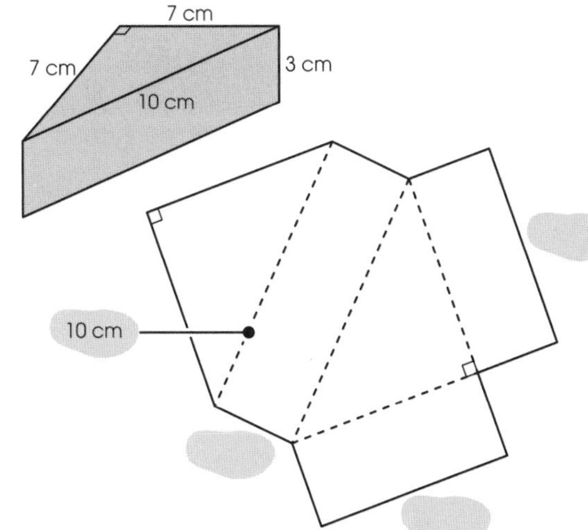

Area of each face:

Total surface area of the triangular prism:

3.

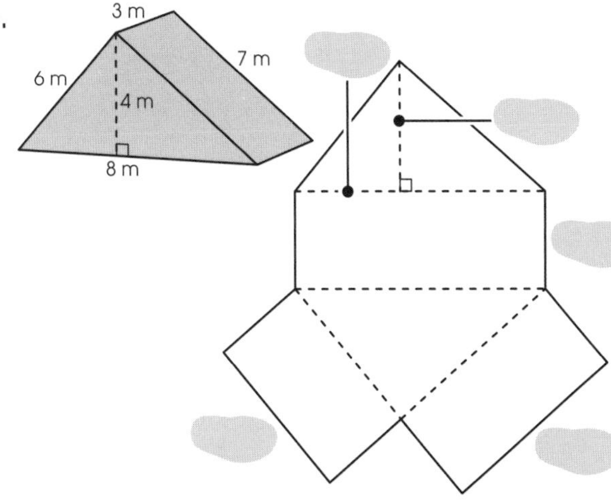

Area of each face:

Total surface area of the triangular prism:

4.

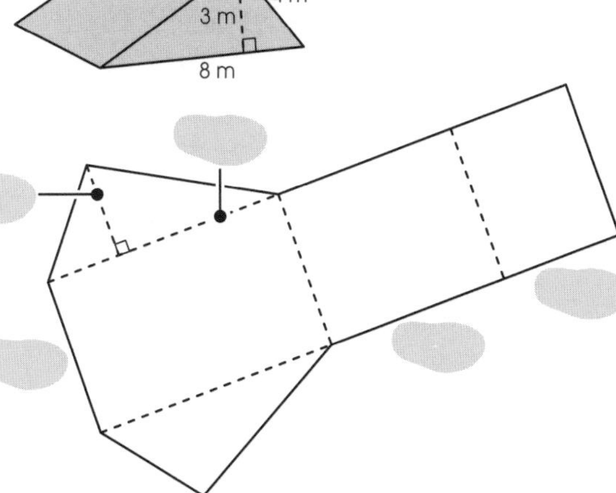

Area of each face:

Total surface area of the triangular prism:

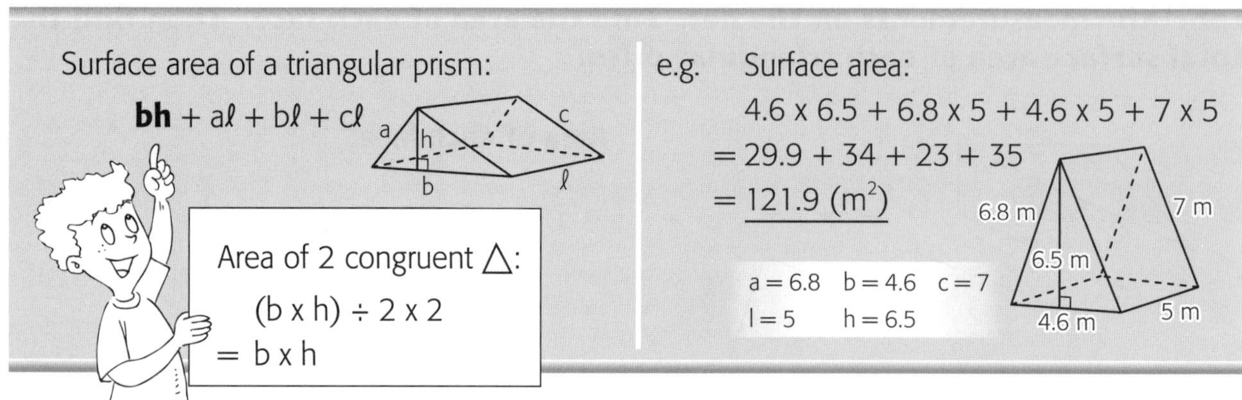

Surface area of a triangular prism:
bh + aℓ + bℓ + cℓ
a
h
b
c
ℓ
Area of 2 congruent △:
(b x h) ÷ 2 x 2
= b x h
e.g. Surface area:
4.6 x 6.5 + 6.8 x 5 + 4.6 x 5 + 7 x 5
= 29.9 + 34 + 23 + 35
= 121.9 (m²)
6.8 m
7 m
6.5 m
4.6 m
5 m
a = 6.8 b = 4.6 c = 7
l = 5 h = 6.5

Find the surface area of each triangular prism by using the formula above.

5.

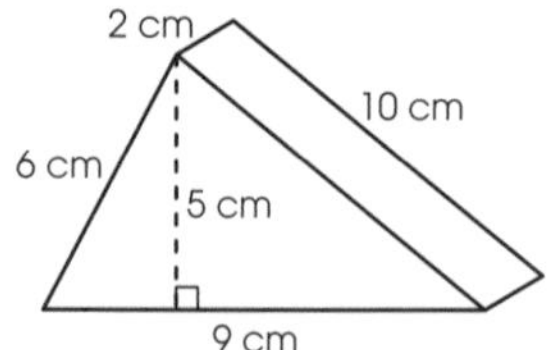

Surface area:

6.

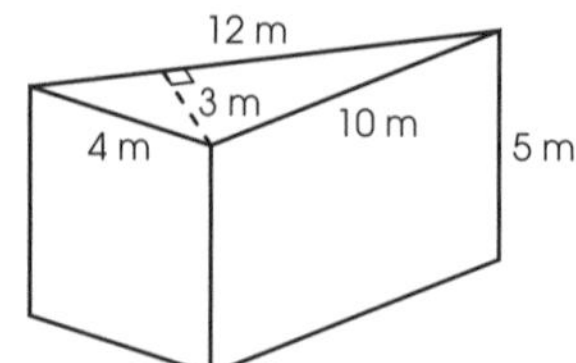

Surface area:

Find the surface area of each gift box. Then choose the most appropriate wrapping paper to wrap each box. Write the letter in the circle.

7.

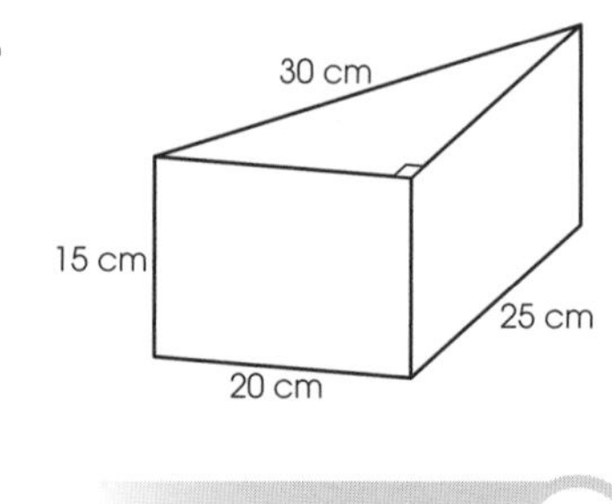

a.

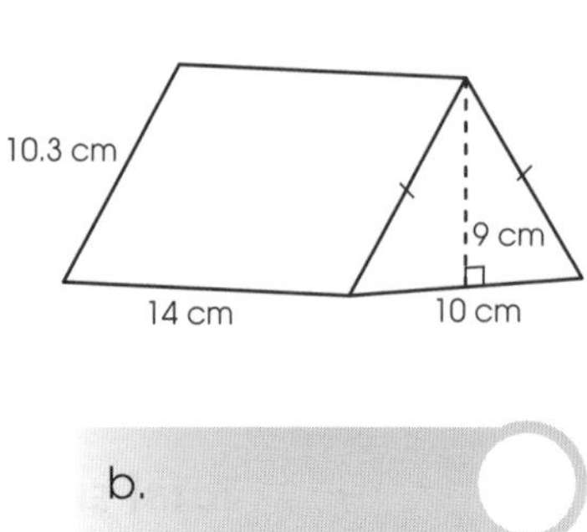

b.

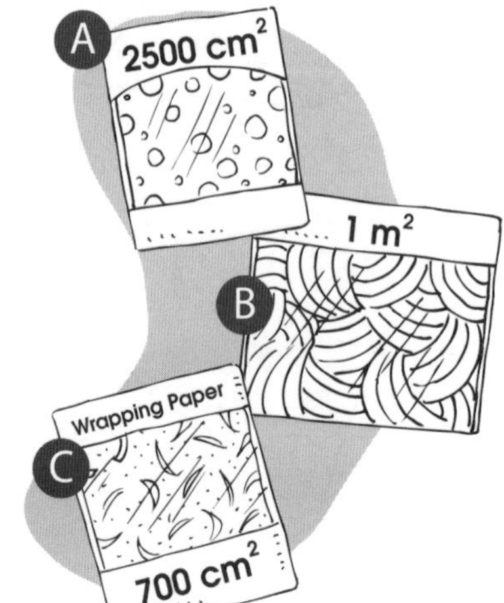

Complete the net of the solid and write the measurements. Then find the total surface area of the solid.

8.

Surface Area

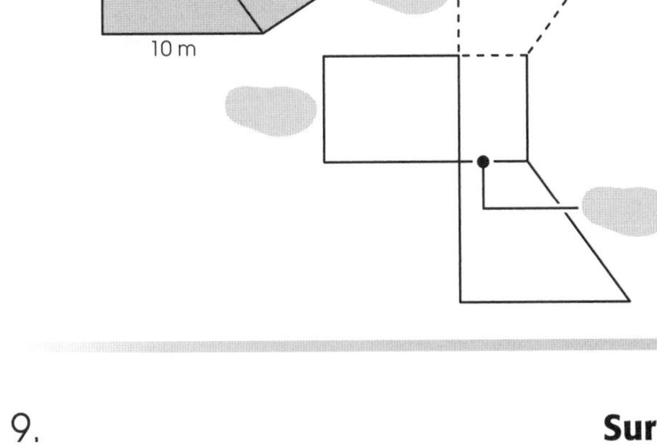

9.

Surface Area

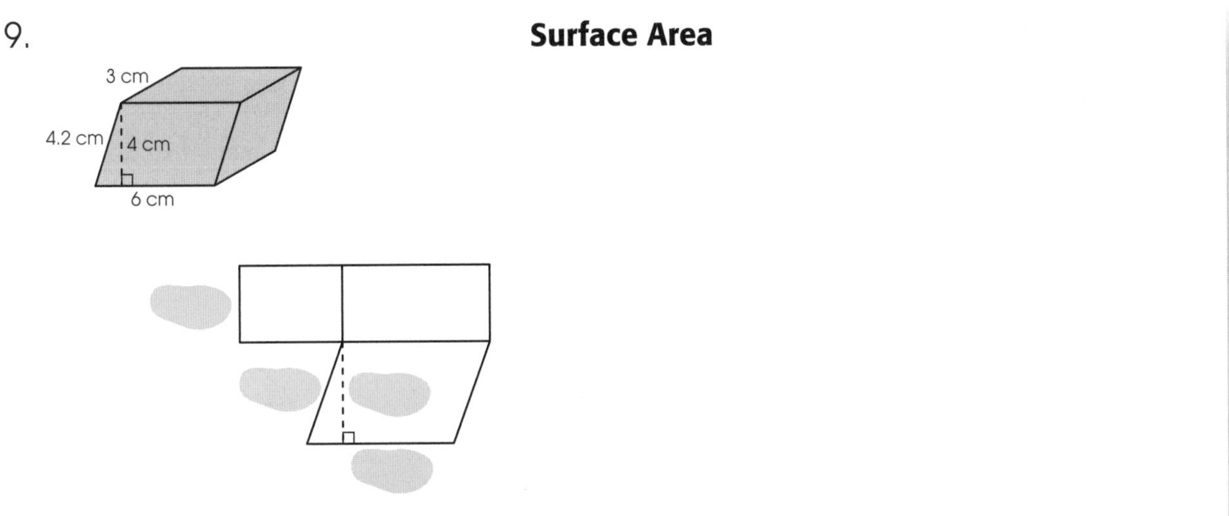

Joe has built two different towers with his two blocks. Find the surface area of each tower, and find out which tower has a smaller surface area.

10.

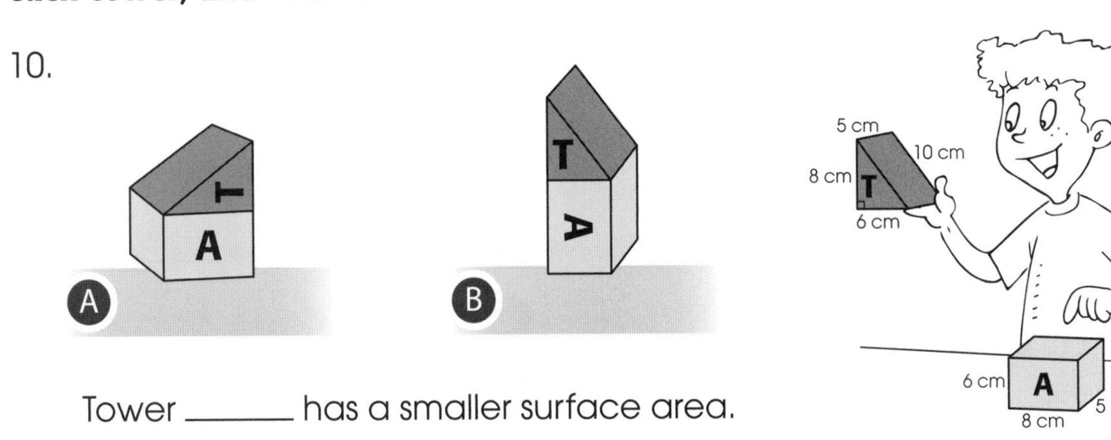

Tower ______ has a smaller surface area.

16

Volume

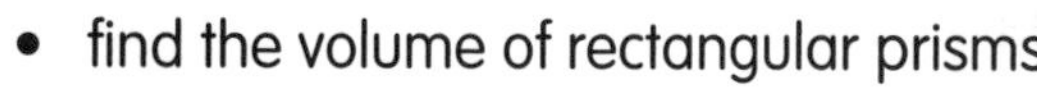

- find the volume of rectangular prisms
- find the volume of prisms that have different shapes in the base
- find the unknown measurements of prisms
- relate cm^3 to mL
- solve problems involving volume and capacity

Find the volume (V) of each prism.

1.

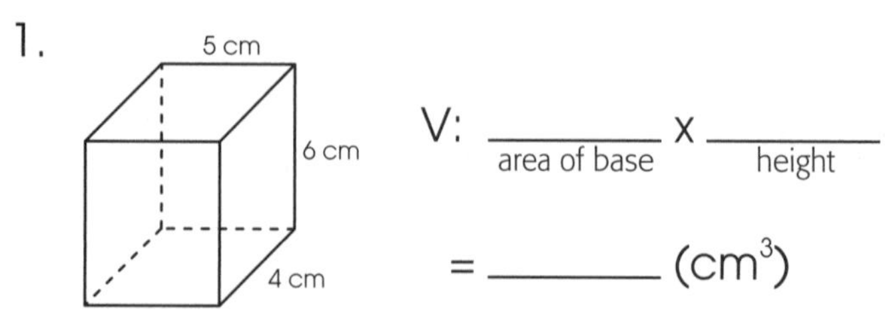

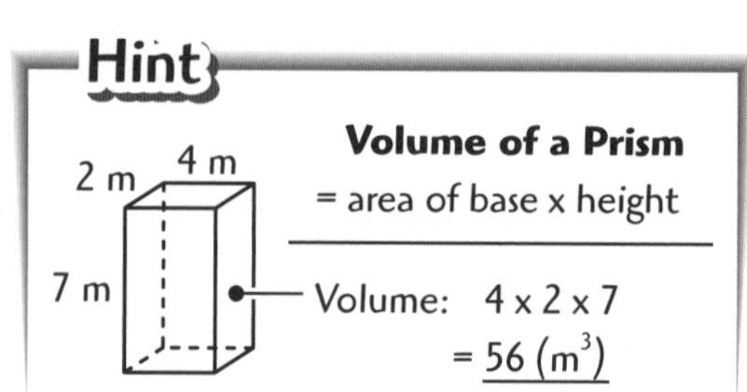

2.

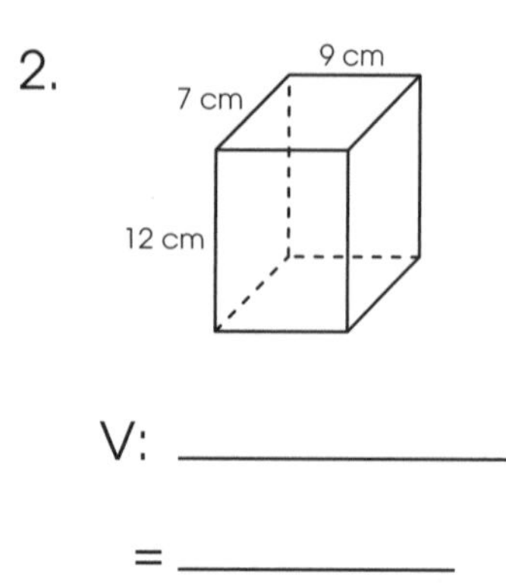

V: ______

= ______

3.

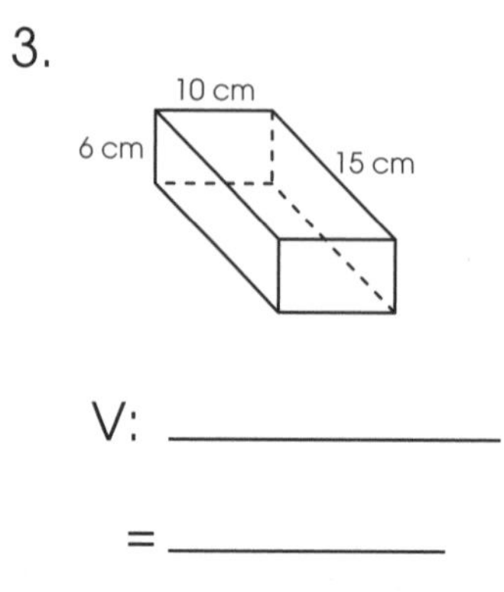

V: ______

= ______

4.

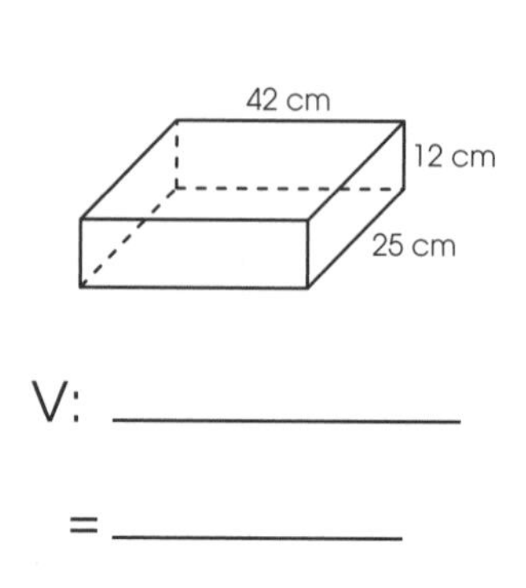

V: ______

= ______

5.

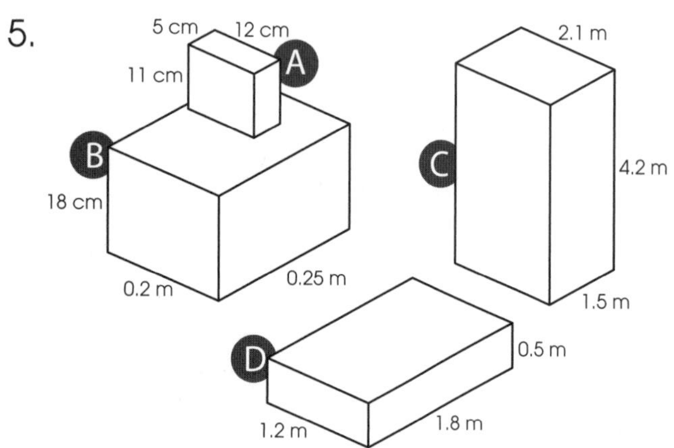

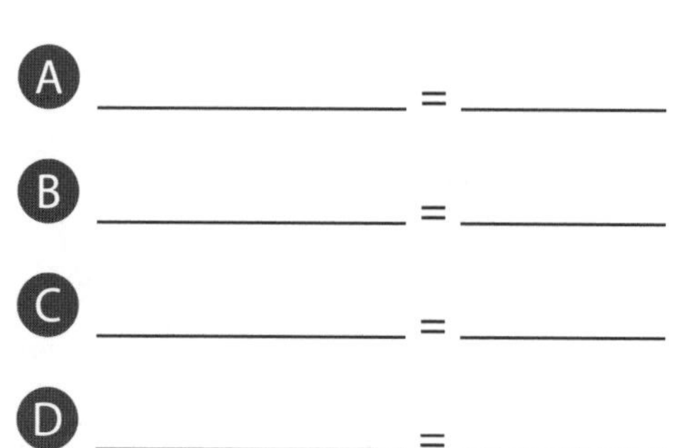

Finding the unknown side of a rectangular prism with the given volume:

1st Multiply to find the area of the base.

2nd Divide the volume by the area of the base.

e.g.

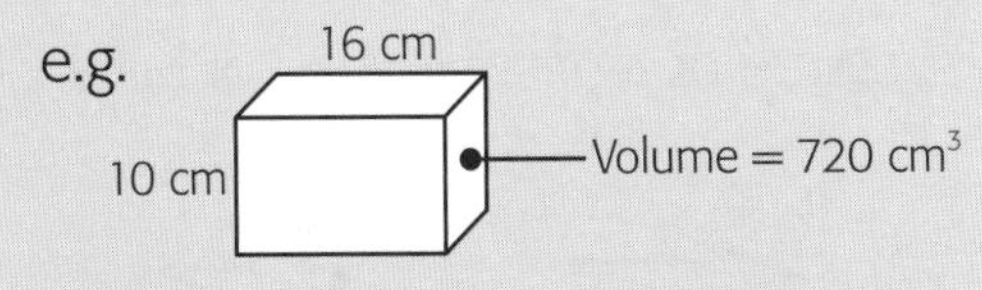

Area of base: 16 x 10 = 160

Width: 720 ÷ 160 = 4.5 (cm)

Find the unknown side of each rectangular prism.

6. volume: 13.2 m^3
   length: 2 m
   width: 1.8 m
   height: ______

7. volume: 118.69 cm^3
   length: ______
   width: 3 cm
   height: 11 cm

8. volume: 13.2 m^3
   length: 1.24 m
   width: ______
   height: 4.5 m

Find the length of the unknown side of each container. Then answer the question.

9.

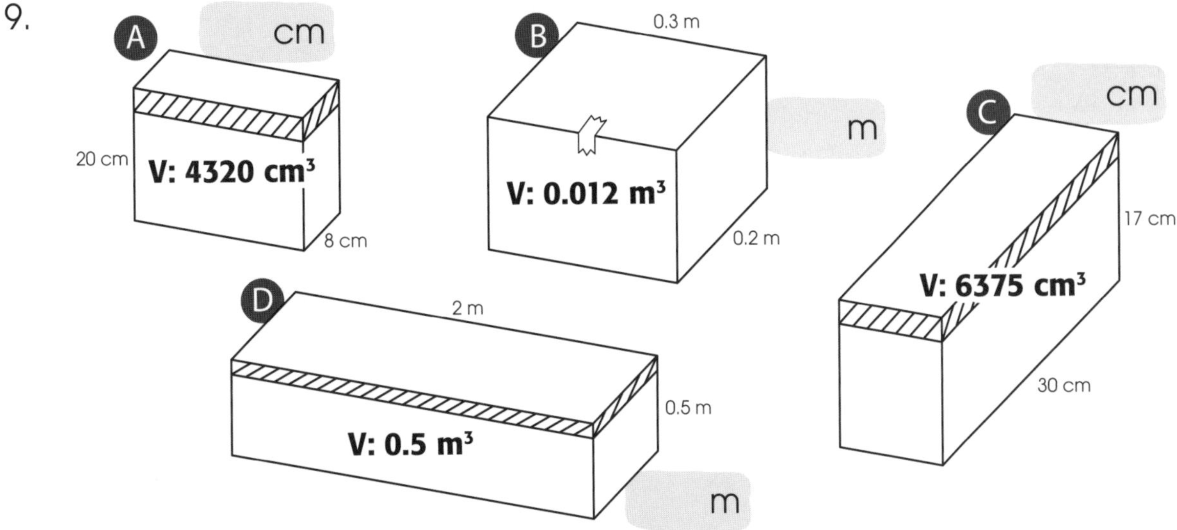

10. *How many cubes with sides of 3 cm are needed to fill up each container?*

______

______

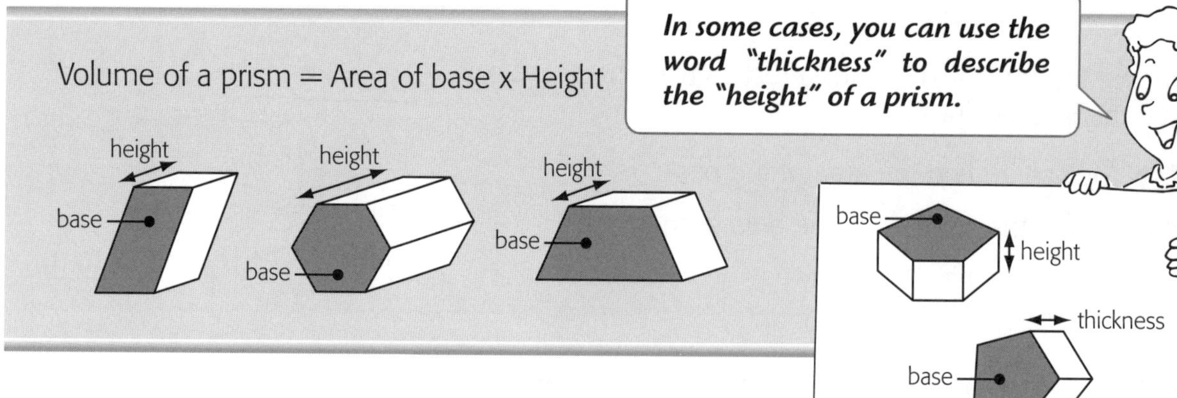

Find the volume of each prism.

11.

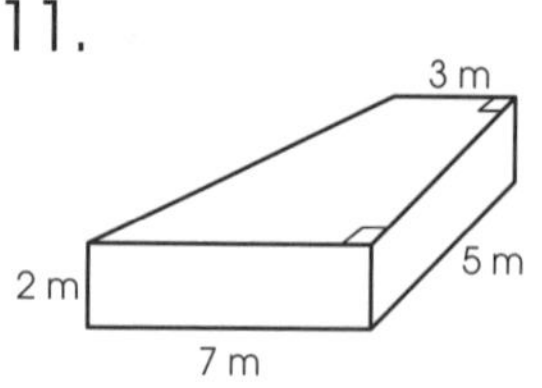

12.

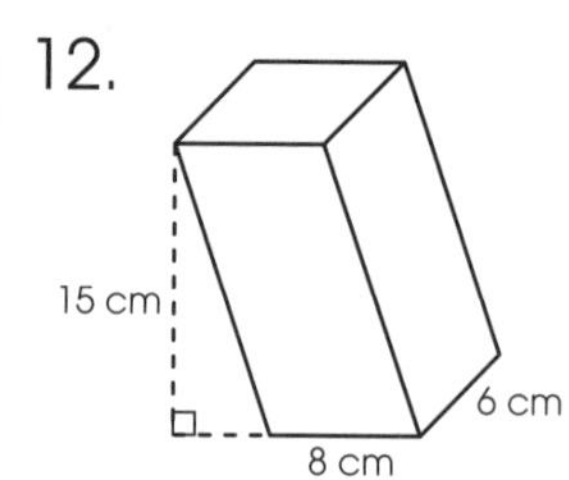

13.

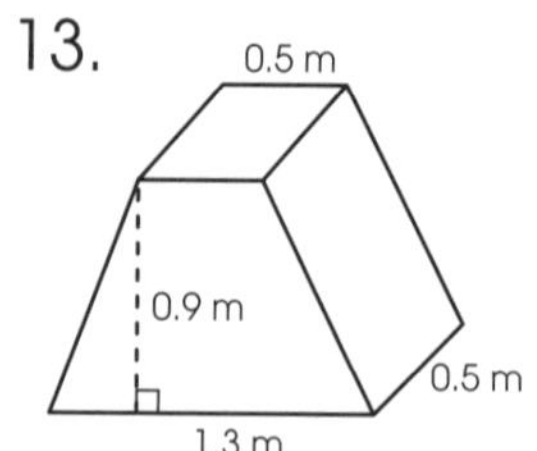

14.

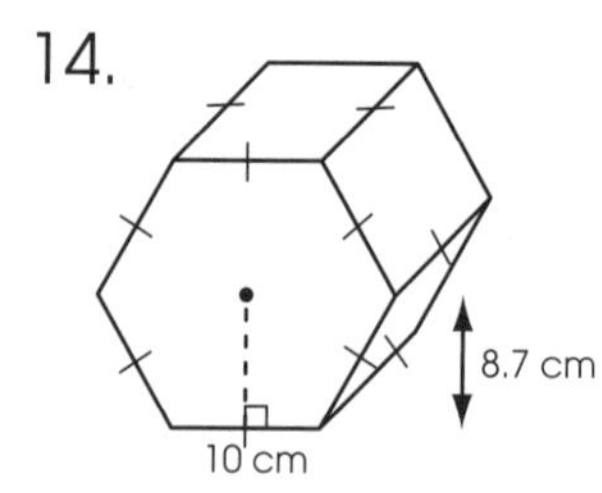

15.

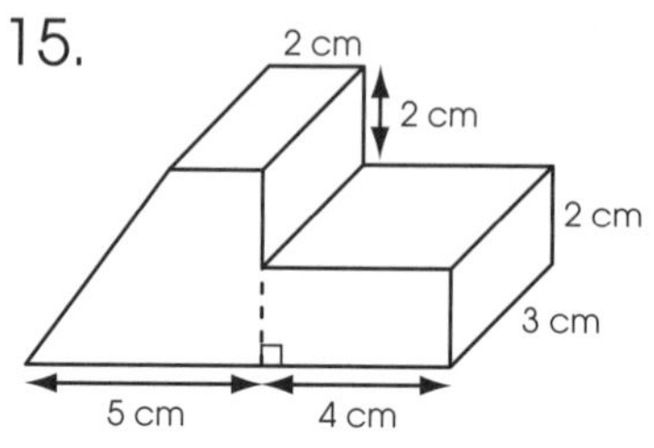

16.

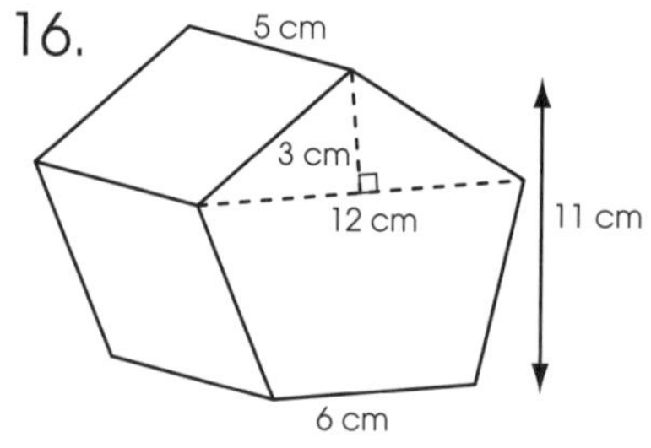

Cut the base into 2 friendly shapes. Find the area of each shape. Then add to find the base area.

Find the capacity of each vase. Then answer the questions.

17.

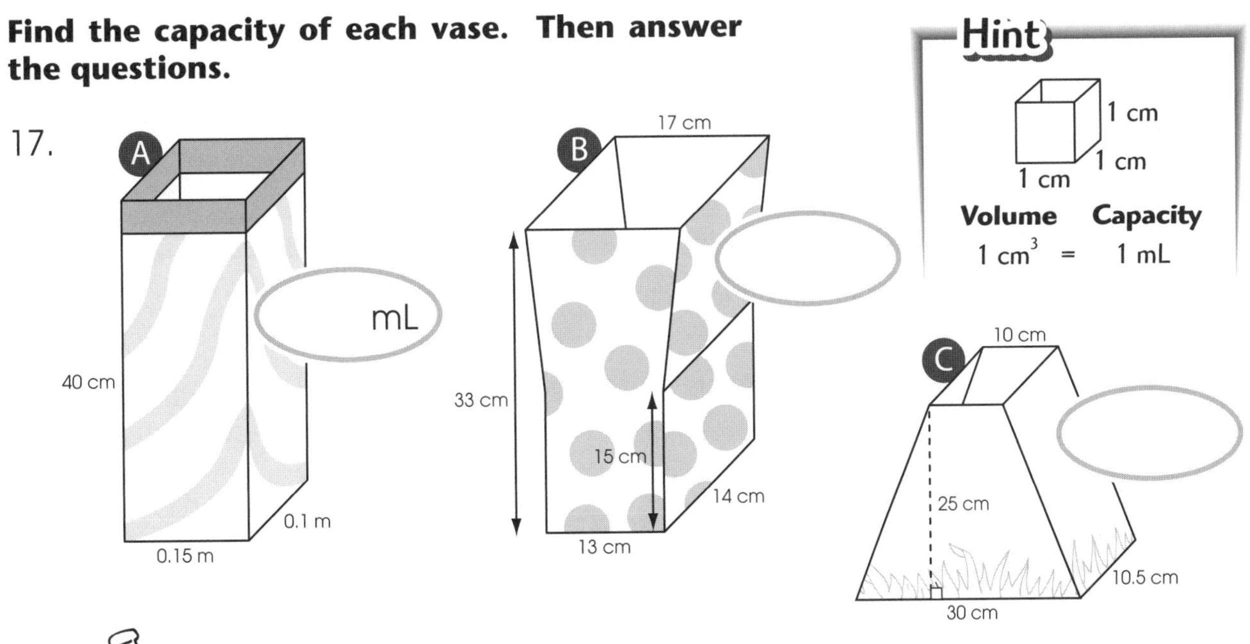

18. How many bottles of water are needed to fill up each vase?

Ⓐ _____ bottles Ⓑ __________ Ⓒ __________

19. The volume of each pebble is 3.6 cm^3. If Jack puts 40 pebbles into A, how much water can A hold now?

____

20.

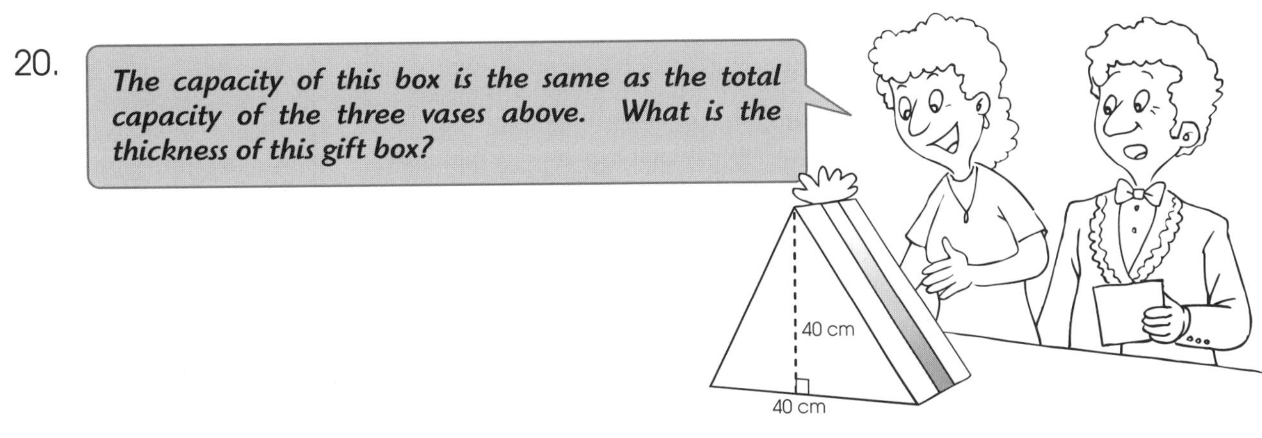

The capacity of this box is the same as the total capacity of the three vases above. What is the thickness of this gift box?
40 cm
40 cm

____

Coordinates

- identify the 4 quadrants
- identify which quadrants the points belong to
- plot and write the coordinates of the points
- make similar figures on the grid and write the vertices of the figures
- draw points with the given movements

...go 5 units left and 4 units down to find the treasure.

You are here.

Do you mean that the treasure is at (-3,-1)?

Label the xy-axis and the four quadrants. Then write whether the values are positive or negative in each quadrant.

1.

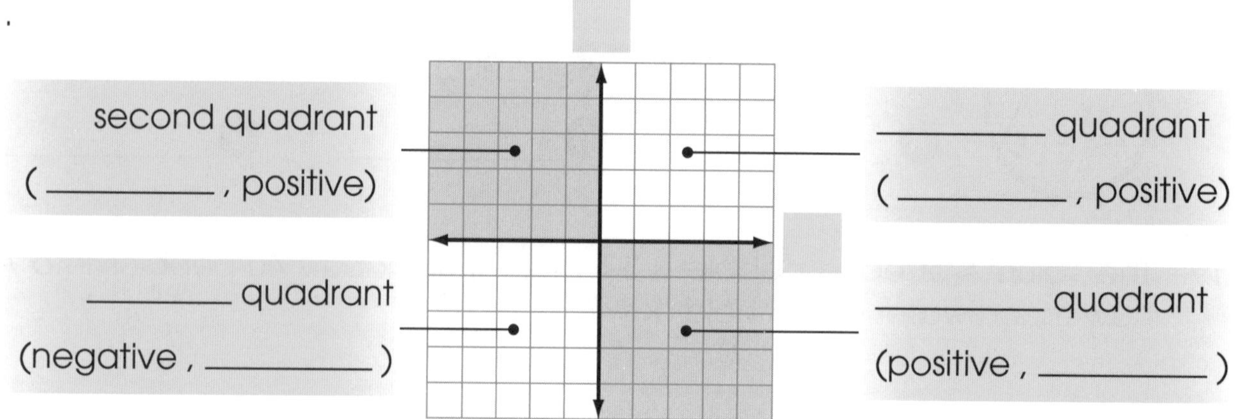

Look at the coordinates of each point. Write the point in the correct quadrant.

2. (8,-2) (6,4) (5,-3)
(10,-11) (-8,7) (19,2)
(14,5) (-2,13) (-7,-9)
(-20,28) (-15,-1) (16,4)
($\frac{1}{2}$,-1) (-6,-3.5) (-2.7,-4)
(-0.8,$\frac{1}{3}$)

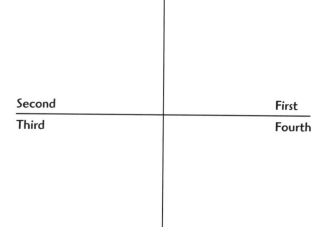

Second First
Third Fourth

Complete the grid. Then plot the points on the grid.

3. A(3,-7)
   B(-5,4)
   C(-1,2)
   D(0,-6)
   E(-2,-5)
   F(-6,3)
   G(7,0)
   H(2,-1)
   I(-3,4)
   J(1,8)

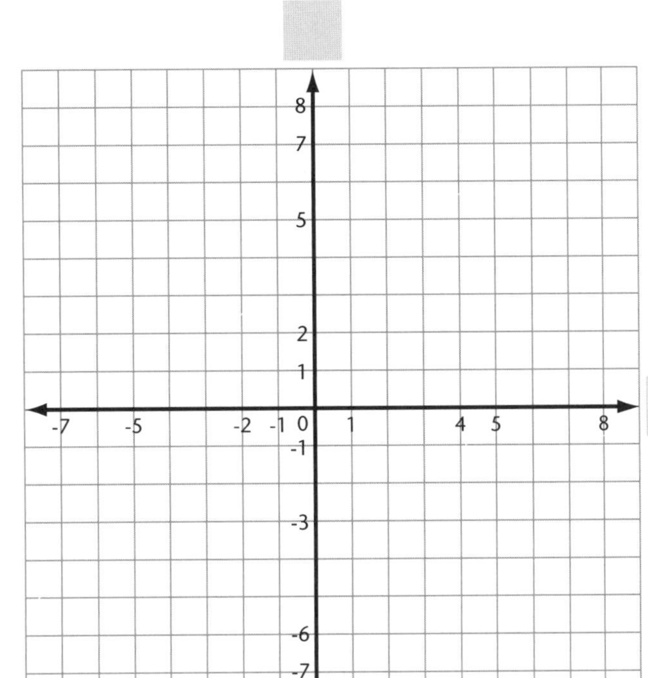

Write the coordinates of the points. Then answer the questions.

4.

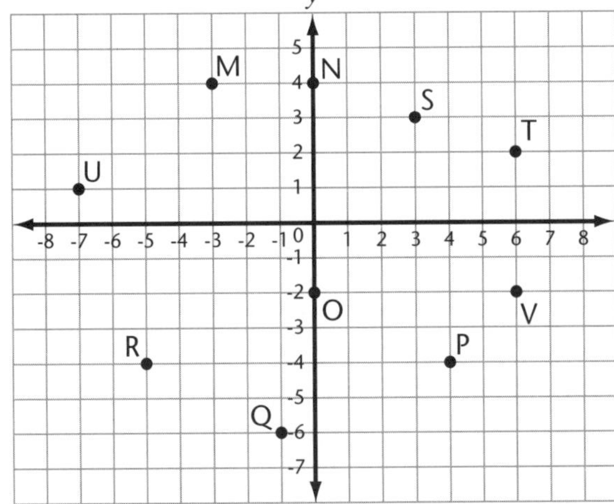

M ________ N ________

O ________ P ________

Q ________ R ________

S ________ T ________

U ________ V ________

5. *The points L, M, N, and O are the vertices of a rectangle. What are the coordinates of L?*

____

6. Name the polygon formed by OPQR: ____________________

Plot the points. Draw lines to complete each symmetrical polygon and write the coordinates of the missing vertices.

7.

Square	Pentagon	Rectangle
(-1,2) 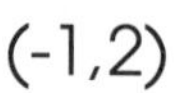	(-1,-1) 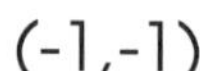	(-2,-6)
(-5,1)	(2,1)	(-2,1)
(-4,-3)	(5,-1)	(3,1)
	(4,-4)	

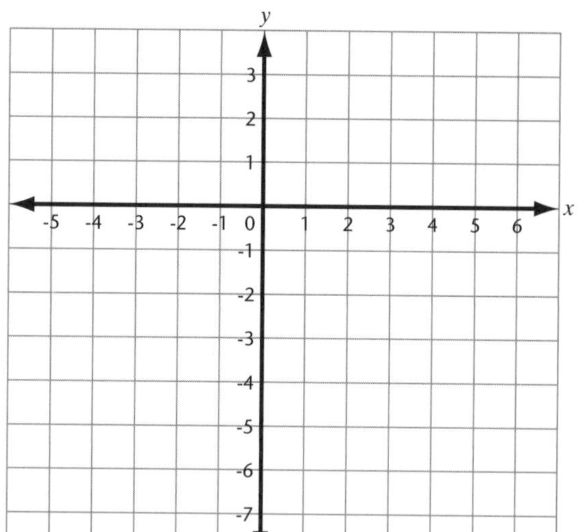

Complete and draw a similar figure of each shape with the help of the dotted lines. Then write "enlarge" or "shrink" in the shaded box and the coordinates of the vertices of the new figure.

8.

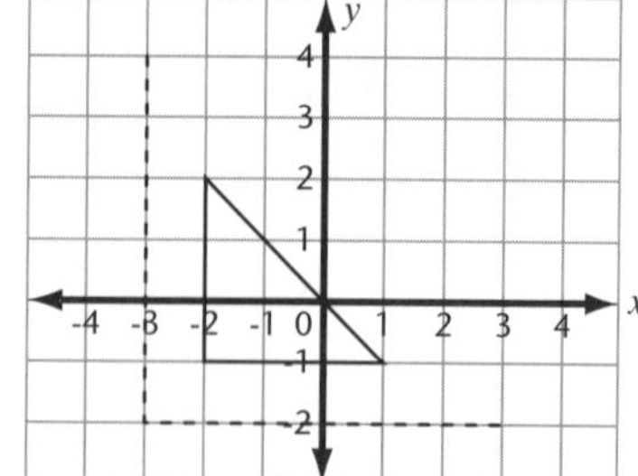

original figure ⟶ new figure

coordinates of the vertices of the new figure:

____

9.

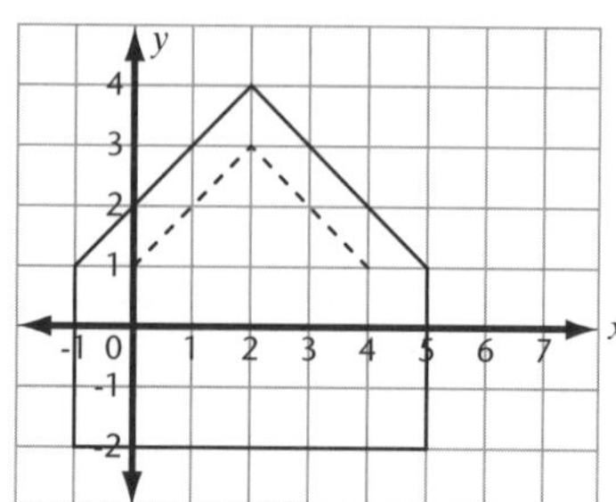

original figure ⟶ new figure

coordinates of the vertices of the new figure:

____

10.

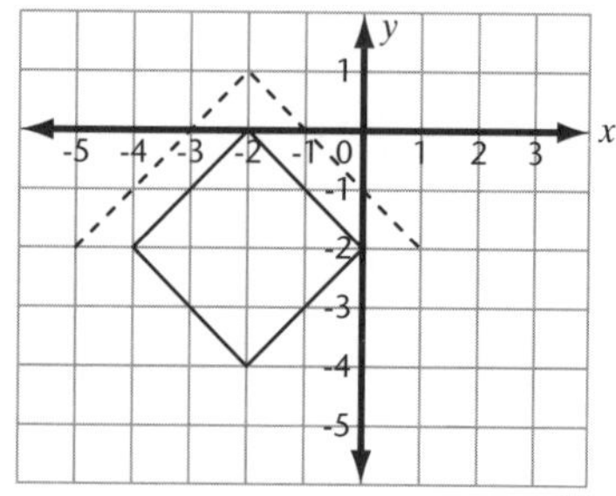

original figure ⟶ new figure

coordinates of the vertices of the new figure:

____

Plot the points on the grid and find the coordinates. Then answer the questions.

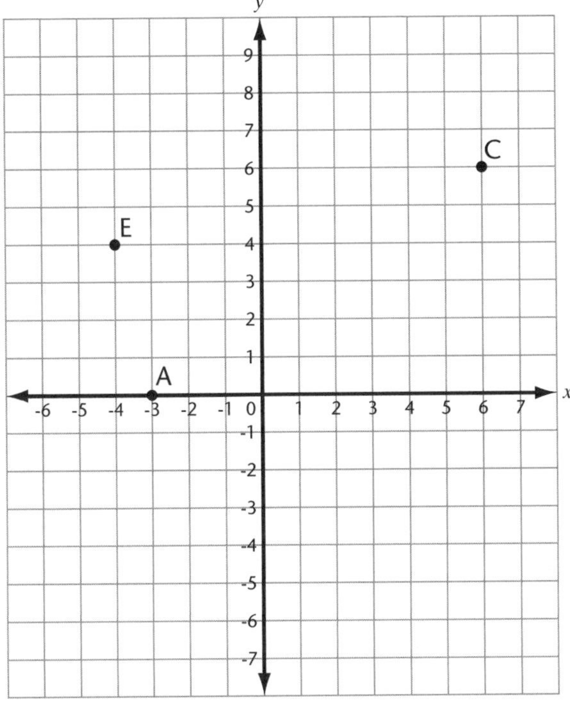

B__________

B is 3 units left and 2 units up from A.

D__________

D is 6 units left and 9 units down from C.

F__________

F is 8 units right and 8 units down from E.

12. Draw a line to join A and B, C and D, and E and F.

13. Is the point (-4,1) on line AB? __________

14. Is the point (3,-3) on line EF? 

15. Write the coordinates of any three points that are on line CD.

____

Write the coordinates of any three points that are on line EF. Then describe the pattern the points follow.

____

____

____

18

Transformations

- identify each of the three transformations
- transform figures and draw images
- describe simple transformations
- follow steps to draw images
- describe combined transformations
- complete and describe tiling design

This stop sign was damaged by the gusty wind yesterday. It's now showing a $\frac{1}{4}$ turn clockwise.

Identify each transformation. Write "translation", "reflection", or "rotation" on the line.

1.

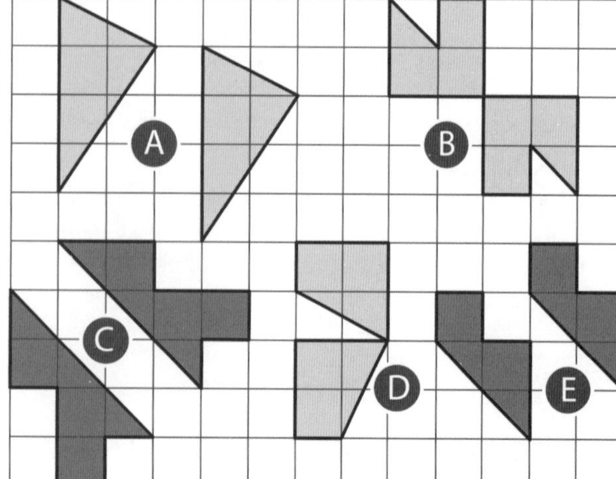

A ____________________

B ____________________

C ____________________

D ____________________

E ____________________

Each labelled figure is the image of the figure in the centre. Identify each transformed image. Write the letter.

2.

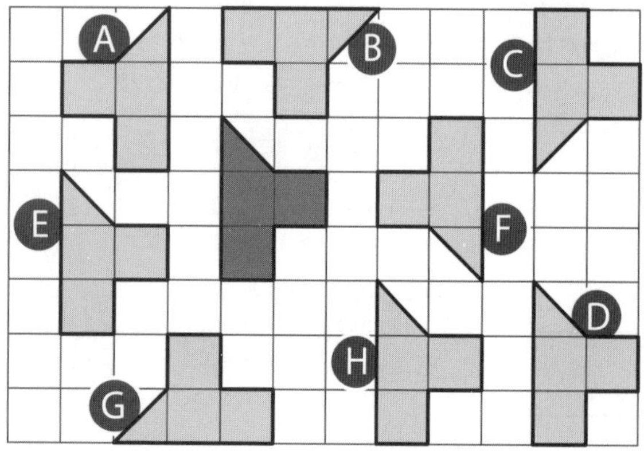

Translation Image	Reflection Image

Rotation Image

Draw the missing sides to complete the images. Then draw images for the other figures.

3. Translate each figure 2 units right and 3 units up.

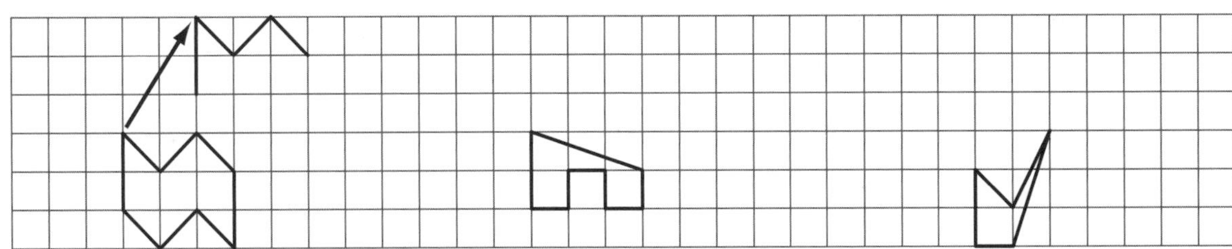

4. Rotate the first, second, and last figure a $\frac{1}{4}$ turn clockwise, $\frac{1}{2}$ turn, and $\frac{3}{4}$ turn clockwise at points P, Q, and R respectively.

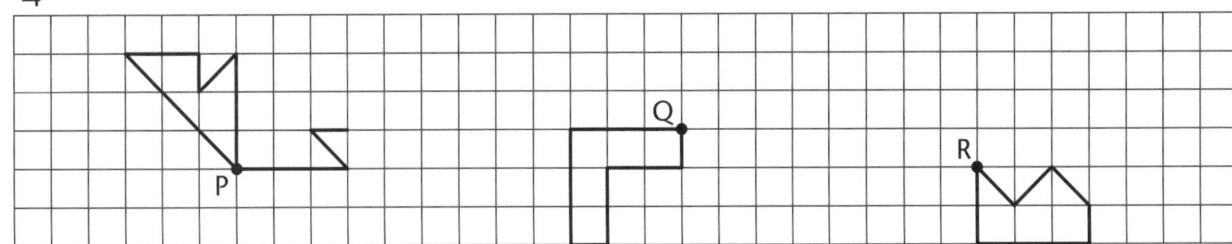

5. Flip the figures over the lines.

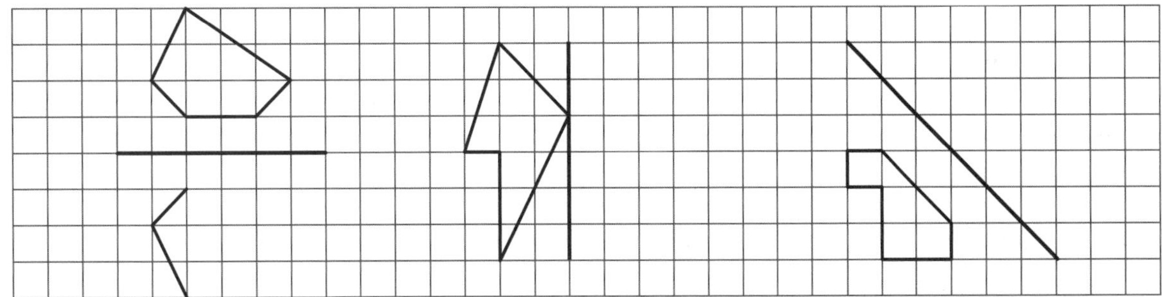

Identify and describe each transformation. Draw points, lines, or arrows in the diagram if needed.

6.

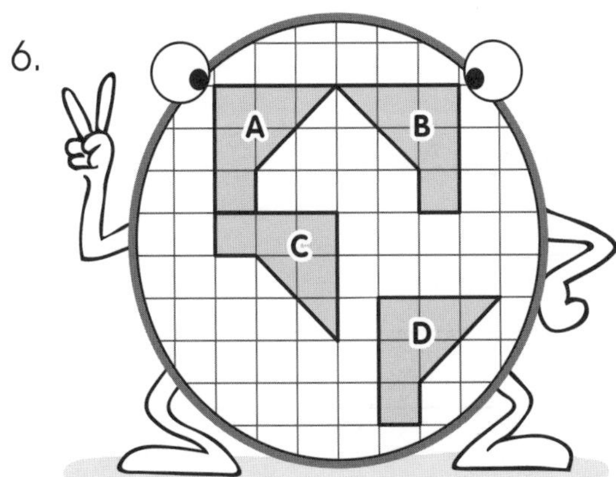

A → B: ______________________

____

A → C: ______________________

____

A → D: ______________________

____

Follow the steps to draw images.

7.
- Reflect A in line K. Label the image B.
- Translate B 3 units left and 6 units up. Label the image C.
- Rotate C a $\frac{1}{4}$ counterclockwise turn about point M. Label the image D.

8.
- Rotate P a $\frac{1}{4}$ clockwise turn about point O. Label the image W.
- Translate W 3 units up and 5 units right. Label the image X.
- Reflect image over line L. Label the image Y.

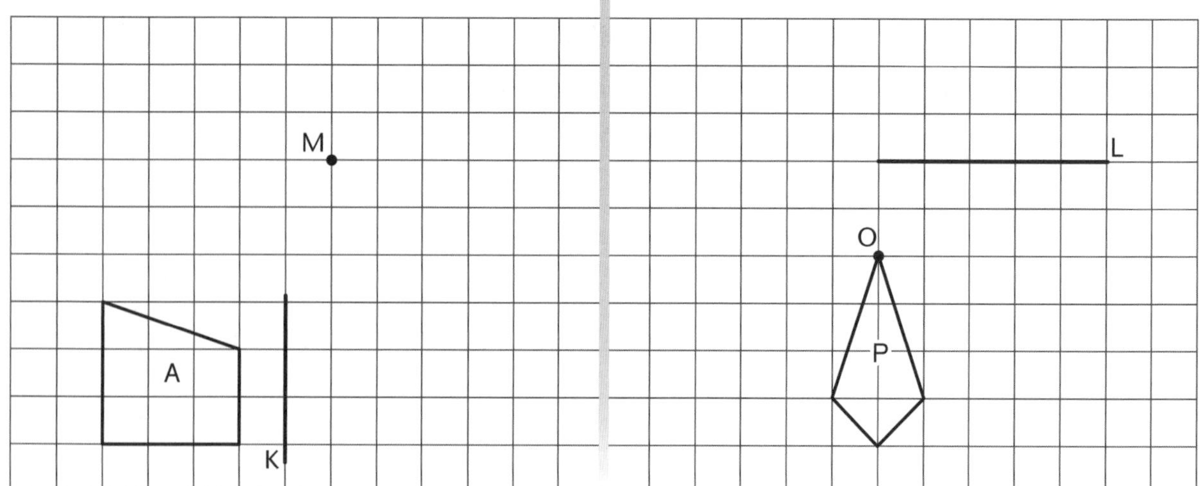

Describe two different combinations of transformations that could result in the images.

9.

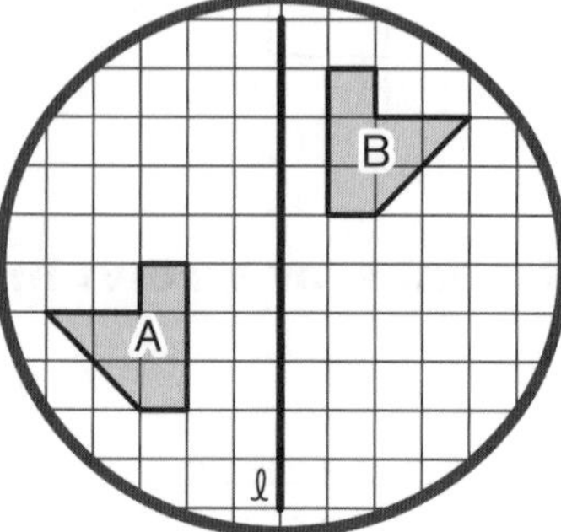

From figure A to its image B:

- ____
- ____

10.

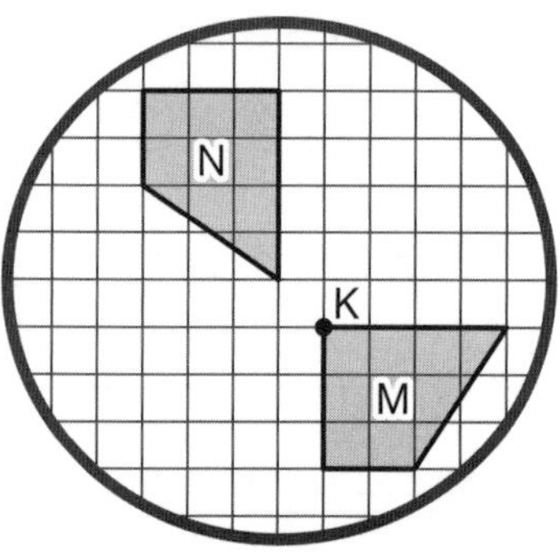

From figure M to its image N:

- ____
- ____

Can each shaded figure tile the plane by itself? If it can, put a checkmark in the circle; otherwise, put a cross. Then complete the tile pattern on the grid.

11. 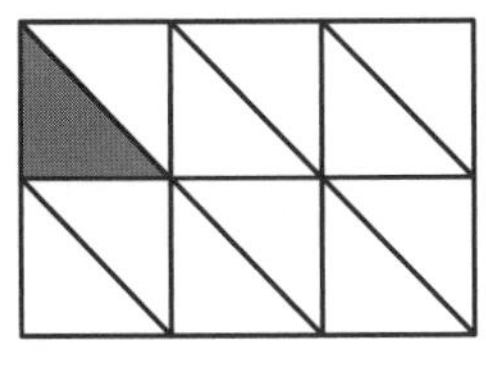

12. 

13. 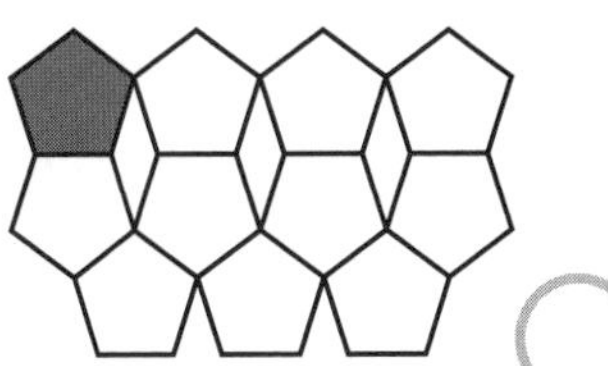

14. 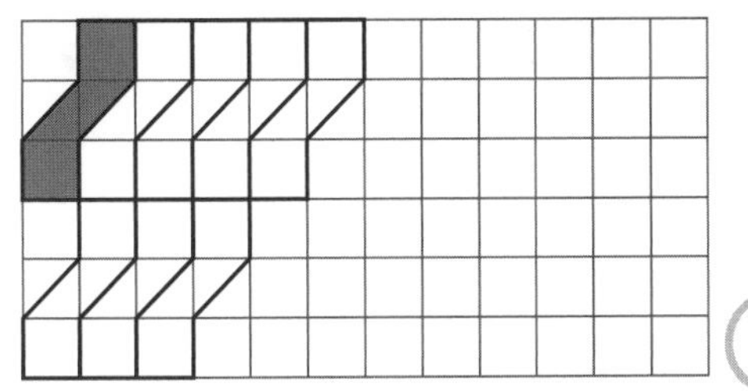

15. 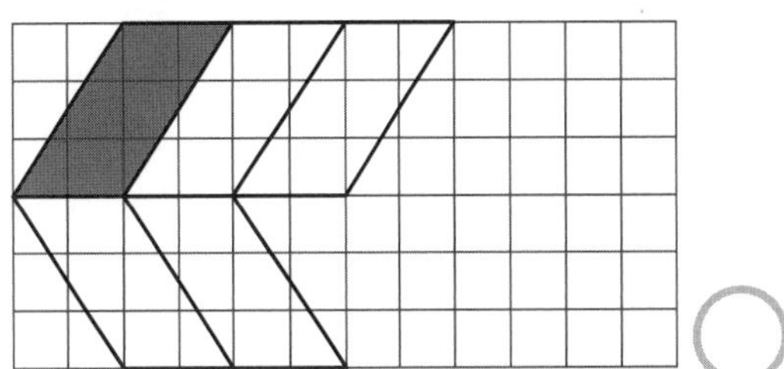

Complete the design and describe the transformations. Then complete the description of the design.

16. 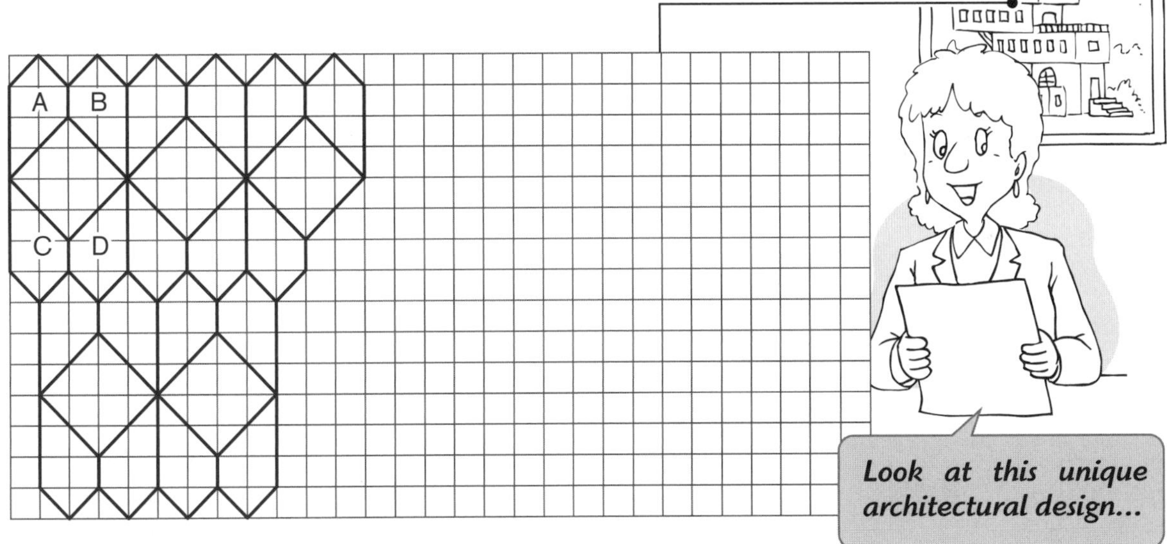
A
B
C
D
Look at this unique architectural design...

A → B: A is reflected in a vertical line along its ________ side to make B.

A & B → C & D: ____

Description of the design:

____

____

____

19

Patterning

- identify the core in a pattern
- find terms in a pattern
- find and write pattern rules
- relate term numbers to their terms
- make a graph to show the pattern

Wow! I found this structure in my first archaeological dig. Following the pattern, there must be 11 cubes in the 5th layer.

No. of Layers	No. of Cubes
1	**3** (2 x **1** + 1)
2	**5** (2 x **2** + 1)
3	**7** (2 x **3** + 1)
4	**9** (2 x **4** + 1)

Look at each pattern. Circle the core. Then answer the questions.

1.   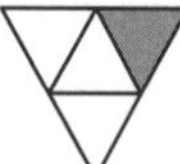 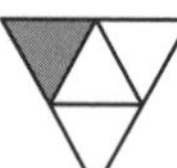  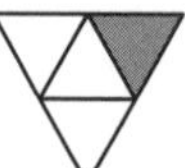 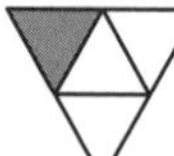  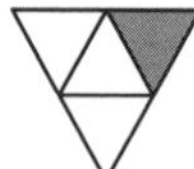

   a. Number of terms in the core: ______

   b. Number of times the core repeated: ______

   c. Draw:

   - **the next term**
   - **the 12th term**

Each picture or number in a pattern is called a term.

core

e.g. 1 2 4 1 2 4 1 2 4

This is the 4th term.

2. 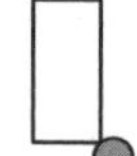 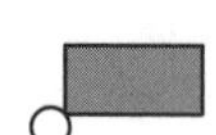 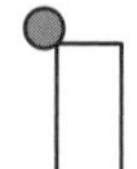 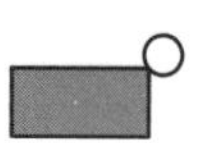 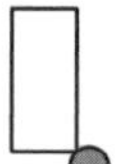  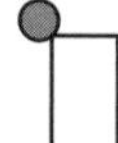  

   a. Number of terms in the core: ______

   b. Number of times the core repeated: ______

   c.

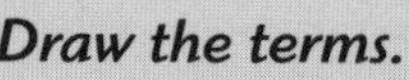

   - **the 12th term**
   - **the 15th term**

Finding terms in a pattern:

ADKADKADK...

There are 3 terms in the core.

What is the 19th term?

Steps:

1. The last term in each repeated core is K. (AD**K**AD**K**AD**K**...)
2. Compare the term number, 19, with the multiples of 3.

   Multiples of 3: 3, 6, 9, 12, 15, 18, 21...

   Since the 18th term is the last term in the core, the 19th term must be the first term in the core.

So, the 19th term is "A".

Look at each pattern. Describe the pattern and find the terms.

3. **4 A K M 4 A K M 4 A K M ...**

The core of the pattern: ____________

No. of terms in a core: ______

Multiples of 4: ____________

Pattern: Every ______ terms is M.

- the 20th term: ______
- the 31st term: ______
- the 40th term: ______
- the 53rd term: ______

4.  (house) (person) (house) (person) (house) (person) (house) (person) (house) (person) ...

The core of the pattern: ____________

No. of terms in a core: ______

Multiples of ______ : ____________

Pattern: Every ______ terms is (house).

- the 15th term: ______
- the 28th term: ______
- the 37th term: ______

5. 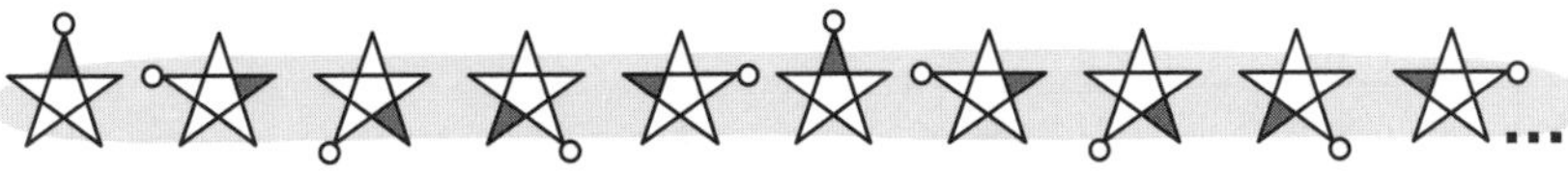 (stars) ...

The core of the pattern: ____________

No. of terms in a core: ______

Multiples of ______ : ____________

Pattern: Every ______ terms is (star).

- the 16th term: ______
- the 31st term: ______
- the 47th term: ______

Mr. Curtis has invented a cookie-making machine. Complete the descriptions and the table. Find the pattern rule, graph the data, and answer the questions.

6. Descriptions:

- The input number starts at ____ and increases by ____ each time.
- The output number starts at ____ and increases by ____ each time.
- Each output number is ____ less than ____ times the input number.

Cookie-Making Machine

Time (min) Input	No. of Cookies Output	Multiples of 8
1	3	8
2	11	
3	19	
4	27	
5	35	
6	43	

Compare the output number with multiples of 8.

So, the pattern rules for this pattern is "Multiply the input number by ____ , then minus ____ ."

Output number = Input number x ____ – ____

7.

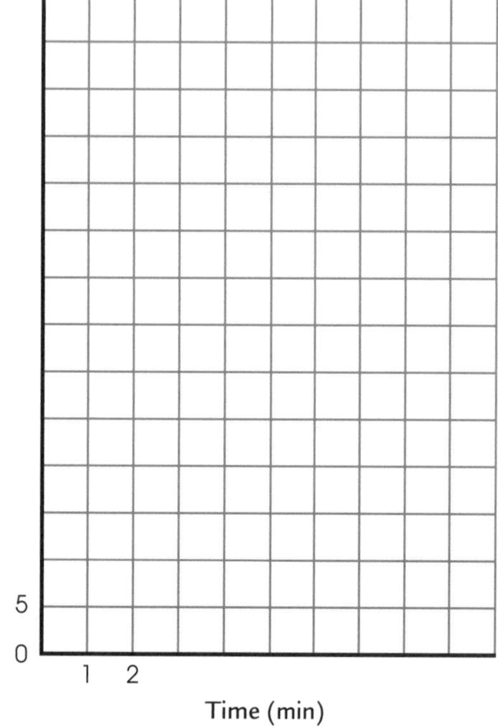

8. No. of cookies made in
- 8 minutes: ________
- 10 minutes: ________
- 15 minutes: ________

9. Time taken to make
- 67 cookies: ________
- 83 cookies: ________

Look at each pattern. Write descriptions and find the pattern rule. Then complete the table and find the terms.

10. a.

Input	Output
1	4
2	7
3	10
4	13
5	
6	

Descriptions:

- Each output number ________ (increases / decreases) by ____ each time.
- Compare the output number with multiples of ____ . Each output number is ____ more than ____ times the input number.

Pattern rule:

Output number = ____ x Input number + ____

b. Input: 15 Output: ______

Input: 19 Output: ______

Input: 24 Output: ______

Input: 35 Output: ______

11. a.

Input	Output
1	3
2	7
3	11
4	15
5	
6	

Descriptions:

Pattern rule:

b. *The input number is the number of digs, and the output number is the number of bones found. How many bones will be found in the 20th dig?*

____

20

Algebraic Expressions (1)

- match algebraic expressions with statements
- identify and write algebraic expressions for different situations
- evaluate expressions
- solve problems by evaluating expressions

Don't worry, Jane. I've only eaten 4 more than half of a box of chocolates.
No. of Chocolates Eaten:
(y ÷ 2) + 4
y chocolates
To: Jane

Match each algebraic expression with the correct statement.

1.	A number increased by 7 •	• $6x$
	6 times a number •	• $8 - z$
	A number subtracted from 8 •	• $y + 7$
	A number divided by 5 •	• $n - 9$
	A number multiplied by $\frac{1}{2}$ •	• $m \div 5$
	9 less than a number •	• $u \times \frac{1}{2}$

Write an algebraic expression for each statement. Use the variable n.

2. Triple a number __________
3. 4 less than a number __________
4. 50 divided by a number __________
5. A number increased by 9 __________
6. A number divided by 2 __________
7. 11 more than a number __________
8. The difference between 5 and a number

____

There are two possible answers to question 8.

Check Jenny's algebraic expressions. Put a check mark in the space provided if it is correct; otherwise, write the correct expression.

	's expressions	Check
9. 6 times a number, then add 7.	$7x + 6$	
10. Take away 2 from the sum of 5 and a number.	$2 + x - 5$	
11. 15 less than 3 times a number.	$3x - 15$	
12. Divide 10 by a number and double it.	$x \div 10 \times 2$	
13. Twice a number and decrease by 4.	$4 - 2x$	
14. Add 8 to half a number.	$\frac{x}{2} + 8$	
15. Divide a number by 3 and add 5.	$5 + \frac{x}{3}$	

Circle the correct algebraic expression for each situation.

16. m slices of pizzas cost: $\$3m$ $\$\frac{m}{3}$

17. Cost of a slice of pizza and a bowl of soup:

$\$(3n)$ $\$(3 + n)$

18. The cost of a plate of pasta is k times the cost of a slice of pizza. How much is a plate of pasta?

$\$(3 + k)$ $\$(3k)$

19. Jane and her sister buy a plate of pasta and share the cost. How much does each girl pay?

$\$(\frac{3k}{2})$ $\$(3k) \times 2$

Write an algebraic expression for each situation.

at noon

20. The temperature rises at a rate of y°C per hour. What will the temperature be

    a. at 2:00 p.m.? ________

    b. at 3:00 p.m.? ________

21. What was the temperature an hour ago?

____

Joe

108 mL

22. Joe has applied sunblock twice. Each time he uses p mL. How much sunblock does he have left?

____

23. Amy applies 5 mL more than twice the amount of sunblock that Joe applies each time. How much sunblock does Amy use each time?

____

Evaluate each expression by replacing the variable with the given value.

24. $7 + n$

$=$

$n = 8$

$n \div 2$

$=$

25. $4c - 5$

$=$

$c = 3$

$9 + \frac{c}{2}$

$=$

Hint

Evaluate the expression $3y + 2$ when y = 5.

$3y + 2$
$= 3(5) + 2$ ← Replace y with 5.
$= 15 + 2$
$= \underline{17}$

26. $k = 4$

    a. $5 + 3k =$ ______

    b. $\frac{2k}{8} =$ ______

    c. $\frac{12 + k}{2k} =$ ______

Evaluate each expression by substituting the numbers 0 to 4 for n.

27. **$8n + 2$**

Input n		Output $8n + 2$
0	$8(0) + 2$	

28. **$n - n \div 2$**

Input n		Output $n - n \div 2$

Each girl has written an algebraic expression for the money that she put into her piggy bank each week. Evaluate each expression by substituting the numbers 1 to 4 for n. Then answer the questions.

29. Jenny: $\$(4 + 7n)$ Erica: $\$(6n - 4)$ Stella: $\$(12 - 2n)$

n	$\$(4 + 7n)$
1	
2	
3	
4	

n	$\$(6n - 4)$

n	$\$(12 - 2n)$

30. Describe the savings pattern of each girl.

Jenny: __________

Erica: __________

Stella: __________

31. *This piggy bank has the money you saved in weeks 6 and 7. Do you know how much you have saved?*

____

Algebraic Expressions (2)

- evaluate algebraic expressions to complete charts
- make graphs with algebraic expressions
- model real-life problems with algebraic expressions
- solve problems with algebraic expressions

Grandma, I can run at a constant rate. My rate is 10 rounds per minute.

Complete the tables and graph the data. Then answer the questions.

1. 

$d = 50t$,
where d = distance travelled in km
t = time taken in h

Time t	Distance Travelled $d = 50t$
1	
2	
3	
4	

$d = 120t$,
where d = distance travelled in km
t = time taken in h

Time t	Distance Travelled $d = 120t$
1	
2	
3	
4	

2. 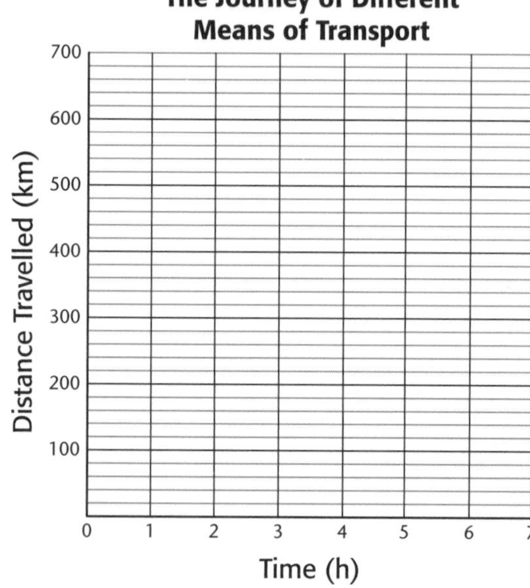

3. How far will the car travel in 6 h?

____

4. How long will it take the airplane to travel 660 km?

____

5. Describe the constant rate of the airplane.

____

____

The children participate in the regional newspaper distribution program. Find their earnings and graph the data. Then answer the questions.

6. *Let w be the number of weeks and s be the earnings.*

Karen's Earnings
$s = 4w + 10$

w	s
1	
2	
3	
4	
5	

Mike's Earnings
$s = 16 + 2w$

w	s
1	
2	
3	
4	
5	

7. **Children's Earnings**

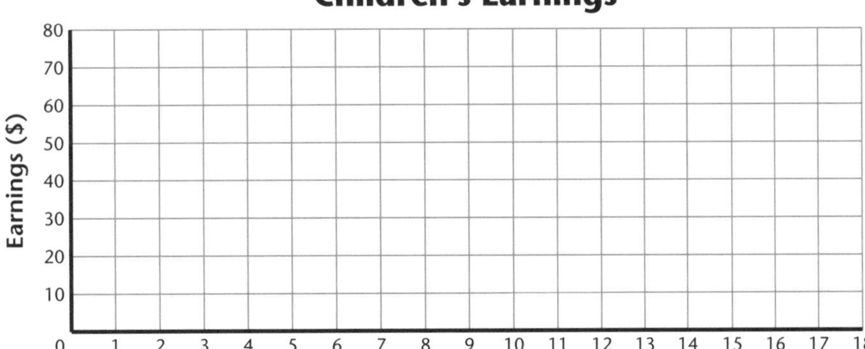

8. How much does each child earn in week 11?

Karen: ________ Mike: ________

9. Is there an intersection point in the graph? If so, what does it mean?

____

____

10. Whose pattern of earnings would you prefer if you could participate in the regional newspaper distribution program? Why?

____

____

Write an algebraic expression for each situation. Complete the tables and answer the questions.

11. Perimeter of Field A: (___ s) m

Perimeter of Field B: ______________

The fields are both in the shape of a square.

200 m longer than that of A

s m Field A

Field B

Perimeter (m)

s	A (s)	B ( )
400		
500		
600		
700		

12. Each metre of fencing costs \$$y$ and the labour fee per field is \$480.

a. If the side length of Field A is 600 m, how much is needed to fence each field?

Cost of Fencing (\$)

y	A (+)	B ( )
3		
4		
5		
6		

b. If the side length of Field B is 700 m, how much is needed to fence each field?

Cost of Fencing (\$)

y	A ( )	B ( )
3		
4		
5		
6		

Write expressions and complete the table. Then make a graph to show the total cost of admission and answer the question.

13. Write an expression for the total cost of m visits of each kind of membership.

    General: $ (______________)

    Silver: ______________

    Gold: ______________

Fun Waterpark

General Admission
$20 per person

Membership

Silver **$6 per year**
10% off each admission

Gold **$16 per year**
20% off each admission

14. Find the total costs of the first four visits for general admission and membership admission.

Total Cost

Number of Visits	General $ ( )	Silver	Gold
1			
2			
3			
4			

15.

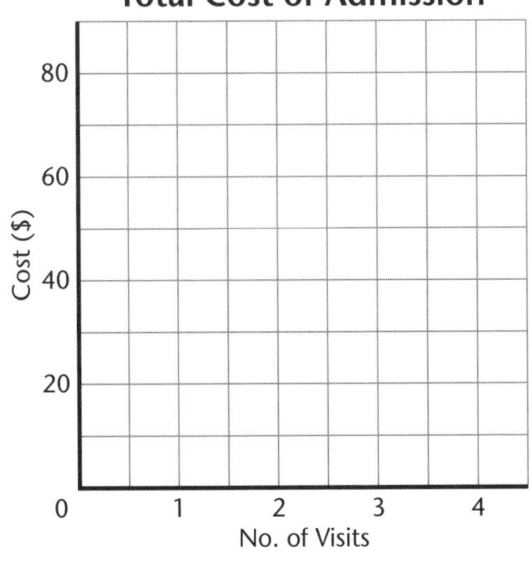

16. *Which type of admission should Jane choose if she plans to visit the waterpark 4 times this year? Explain.*

____

____

____

____

22

Equations

- match equations with statements
- write equations
- solve equations and check answers for different situations
- write appropriate situations to match equations

Match the equations with the correct statements.

1. $5x - 7 = 60$ •
   - • 7 less than a number multiplied by 5 is 60.
   - • 7 times a number decreased by 5 is 60.

2. $x \div 12 = 7$ •
   - • A number divided by 12 equals 7.
   - • 12 divided by a number equals 7.

3. $2 + 3x = 16$ •
   - • 3 more than double a number is 16.
   - • The sum of 2 and triple a number is 16.

Complete or write the equations for the sentences.

4. 18 divided by a number is 3. 18 ☐ ____ = ____

5. 21 less than a number is 20. y ☐ ____ = ____

6. A number increased by 5 is 34. ____ ☐ 5 = ____

7. Triple a number is 18. ________

8. One sixth of a number is 9. ________

Solve the equations by inspection.

9. $a + 8 = 12$ $a =$ ____

10. $s - 14 = 22$ $s =$ ____

11. $7x = 49$ $x =$ ____

12. $t \div 5 = 8$ $t =$ ____

13. $\frac{28}{k} = 14$ $k =$ ____

14. $\frac{n}{7} = 5$ $n =$ ____

Solve the equations. Show your work and check the answers.

15. $s + 7 = 21$

$s + 7 -$ ____ $= 21 -$ ____

$s =$ ____

Check

____ + 7 | 21

16. $t \div 2 = 15$

Check

____ ÷ 2 | 15

Hint

Steps to solve equations:

1st Undo the + or –.

2nd Undo the x or ÷.

e.g.

$2x + 1 = 9$

$2x + 1 - 1 = 9 - 1$ ← Undo the +.

$2x = 8$

$2x \div 2 = 8 \div 2$ ← Undo the x.

$x = 4$

Check $2(4) + 1 \mid 9$

$9 \mid 9$

17. $2n - 4 = 10$

$2n - 4 +$ ____ $= 10 +$ ____

$2n =$ ____

$2n \div 2 =$ ____ $\div 2$

$n =$ ____

Check

2(   ) – 4 | 10

18. $3m + 2 = 8$

Check

Check the correct equation to match each situation. Then solve it.

19. Build 7 identical towers with a box of 546 blocks. How many blocks are there in each tower?

(A) $546 + 7x = 0$

(B) $7x = 546$

(C) $x + 7 = 546$

There are ______ blocks in each tower.

20. The cost of renting a party room is $20 and $4 per guest. How many guests are there if the total cost is $68?

(A) $4x - 68 = 20$

(B) $4 + 20x = 68$

(C) $4x + 20 = 68$

There are ______ guests.

21. The number of marbles that Irene has is 2 times the number of Tony's plus 17. If Irene has 89 marbles, how many marbles does Tony have?

(A) $2x + 17 = 89$

(B) $17 - 2x = 89$

(C) $2x - 89 = 17$

Tony has ______ marbles.

22. *I have paid $54 for 6 boxes of cookies each with a $1 off coupon. What is the price of each box of cookies before the coupon?*

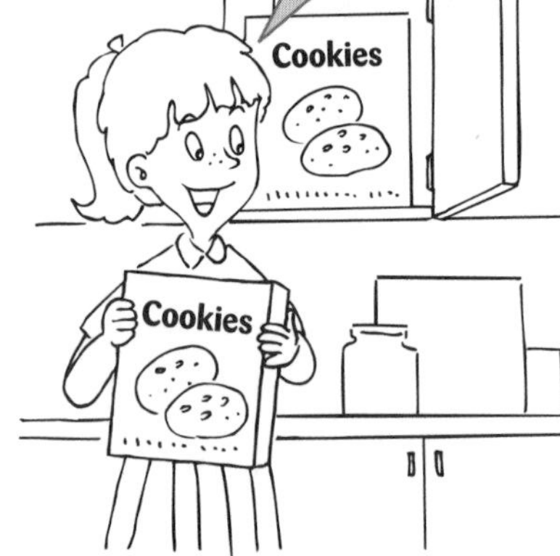

(A) $6(y - 1) = 54$

(B) $6(y + 1) = 54$

(C) $54 = (1 - y)6$

The price of each box of cookies is ______ .

Write an appropriate statement to match each equation and picture.

23.

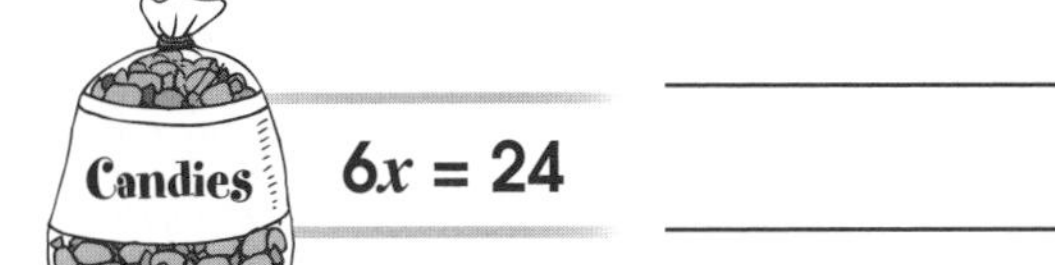

____

____

24.

$\frac{8 + n}{5} = 11$

____

____

Write an equation to describe each situation. Then solve it and check the answer.

25. The cost of a big tub of dog treats is 2 times that of a small one plus $3. If a big tub of treats costs $25, how much does a small tub of treats cost?

Let ____ be the cost of a small tub of treats.

2 ____ + ____ = ____

A small tub of treats costs ________ .

26. *If Joey and I share a small tub and a big tub of treats, each of us will get 92 treats. How many treats are there in a small tub?*

____

Data Management (1)

- identify discrete and continuous data
- classify primary and secondary data
- identify unbiased and biased questions
- determine whether sampling or census should be used
- record data in stem-and-leaf plot
- solve problems using given data

Tell whether the data collected in each situation is discrete or continuous.

1. the number of correct answers on a student's quiz __________
2. the height of a tree at a nursery __________
3. the weight of Josie's cat __________
4. the amount of air leaking from a balloon __________
5. the ages of a family's members __________

Describe what kind of data is collected by each child. Write "primary data" or "secondary data" on the lines.

I surveyed my classmates to find out the number of fruits they ate yesterday.
6. __________
I collected some data from the Internet and found that India has the fastest growing population.
7. __________
I found out that it takes an average of 8 years for the doctors that I interviewed to get a medical degree.
8. __________

Decide whether the survey questions are "biased" or "unbiased".

9. *I survey my friends on whether they prefer indoor or outdoor activities.*

- Do you enjoy indoor activities more than outdoor activities? ____________
- Are you interested in indoor or outdoor activities? ____________
- Do you think it is more fun to play outdoors? ____________

10. *Let me ask my friends to see what subjects they like the most.*

- What is your favourite subject? ____________
- Is Science your favourite subject? ____________
- Which subject do you like the most: Science, English, or Social Studies? ____________

Decide whether you would study each situation below by "sampling" or "census".

11. the top five best-selling novels

____

12. the average height of a female

____

13. the amount of calories in a lemon

____

Hint

Sampling

a part of the population that we collect data from

Census

the data obtained from the entire population

e.g. Length of battery life - sampling
No. of people in the world - census

14. the lifespan of butterflies ____________

15. the illness related to most employees' sick leave at a company ____________

16. the average running speed of the 10 fastest runners in Canada ____________

Jason recorded the daily highest temperatures in June. Help him complete the tally chart and the bar graph. Then answer the questions.

17.

Temperature (°C)	Tally	Frequency
11 – 15		
16 – 20		

Daily Highest Temperatures (°C) in June

22	34	20	11	17	30
21	29	31	30	27	33
28	30	29	16	21	24
31	32	14	19	24	28
31	30	18	25	24	35

18.

Daily Highest Temperatures (°C) in June

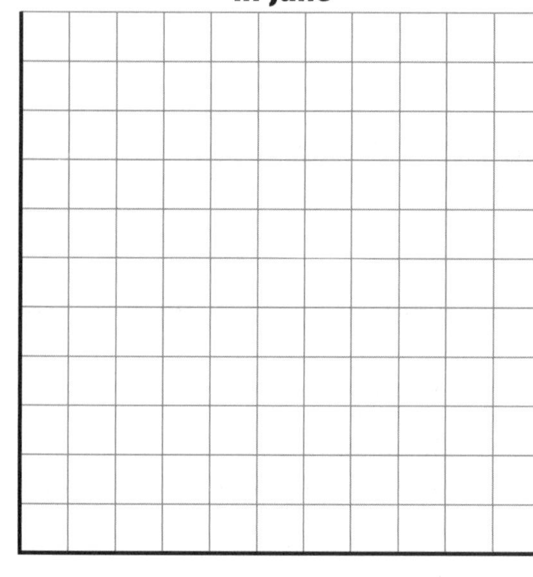

19. Describe the collected data with the help of the given terms.

____

20. What is the range of temperatures of most of the days in June?

____

21. If Jason puts the thermometer in a shed to collect data, do you think he will get the same result? Explain.

____

Read the stem-and-leaf plot. Answer the questions.

22. **Ages of the Drivers**

Stem	Leaf
1	8 8 9
2	0 1 4 7 7 8
3	1 2 4 6 6 6 9
4	2 2 5 5 5 8 8 8
5	0 1 3 3 7
6	2 3 3 5

a. ________ drivers were surveyed.

b. ________ drivers were between 16 and 25 years old.

c. The range of the drivers' ages is ________ years old.

Daven chose 35 data randomly from a record of the heights of 100 13-year-old children. Help him complete the stem-and-leaf plot and answer the questions.

23. **Heights (cm) of the Children**

Stem	Leaf
13	
14	
15	
16	
17	

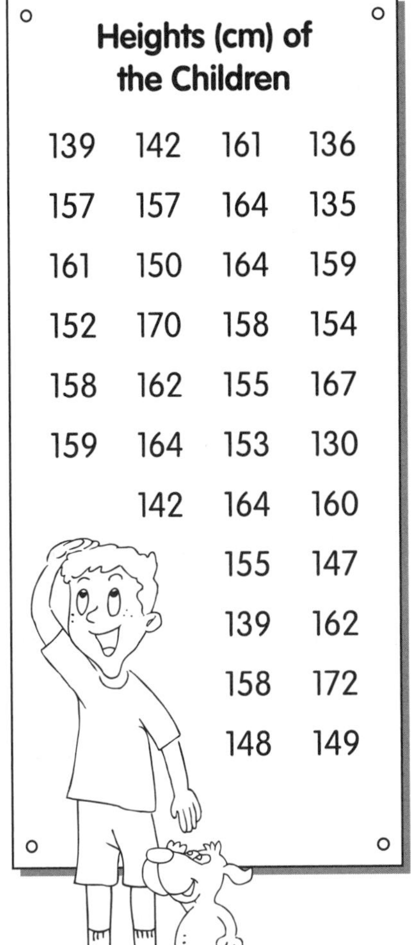

Heights (cm) of the Children

139	142	161	136
157	157	164	135
161	150	164	159
152	170	158	154
158	162	155	167
159	164	153	130
	142	164	160
		155	147
		139	162
		158	172
		148	149

24. What is the range of the children's heights?

____

25. How many children are taller than 1.6 m?

____

26. *Is this a set of primary or secondary data? Explain.*

____

____

Data Management (2)

- plot and make a line graph with given data
- make a circle graph
- determine the most appropriate kind of graph to show different sets of data
- answer questions using information presented in graphs

The value of your necklace is \$20 higher than mine. But why do you make a graph showing that the value of your necklace is about 2 times higher than mine?

Plot the points and draw lines to complete the line graph. Then answer the questions.

1. **Water Leaks from a Water Dispenser**

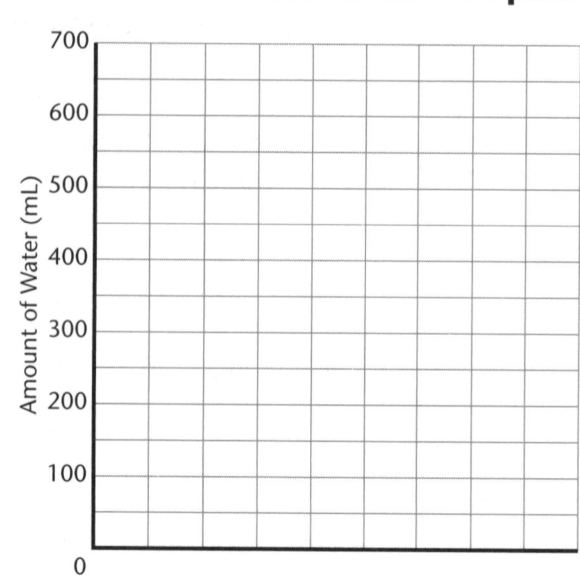

Time (a.m.)	Amount of Water Collected (mL)
7:01	0
7:02	105
7:03	205
7:04	300
7:05	390
7:06	475
7:07	555
7:08	630

2. In which period of time was the most water collected? ____________

3. Was the water leaking at a constant rate? If not, describe the changes of the rate.

____

____

4. Describe the trend. Predict the amount of water collected at 7:09 a.m.

____

Making Circle Graphs:

1st Find the size of angle for each group.

2nd Graph each group in a circle graph using a protractor.

e.g.

Fruit	No. of People	Size of Angle
apple	17	153°
orange	5	45°
banana	18	162°

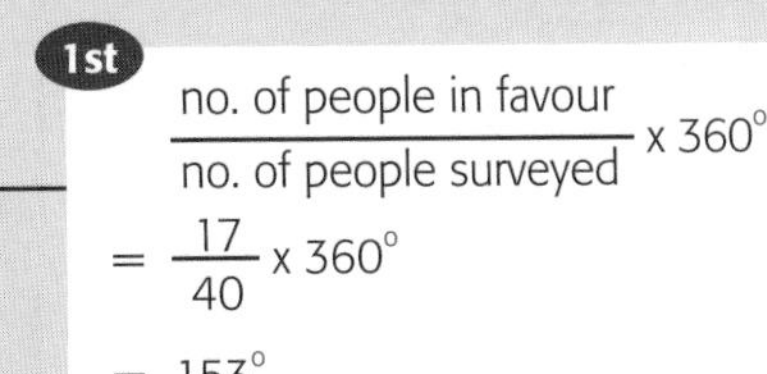

1st
no. of people in favour / no. of people surveyed x 360°
= 17/40 x 360°
= 153°

Joyce surveyed 30 students to see how they come to school. Help her complete the table and the circle graph. Then answer the questions.

5. **Ways to Come to School**

Means of Transport	No. of Students	Size of Angle
by bus	11	$\frac{11}{30}$ x 360° = ____
by car	5	
by subway	1	
by bike	2	
on foot	9	
others	2	

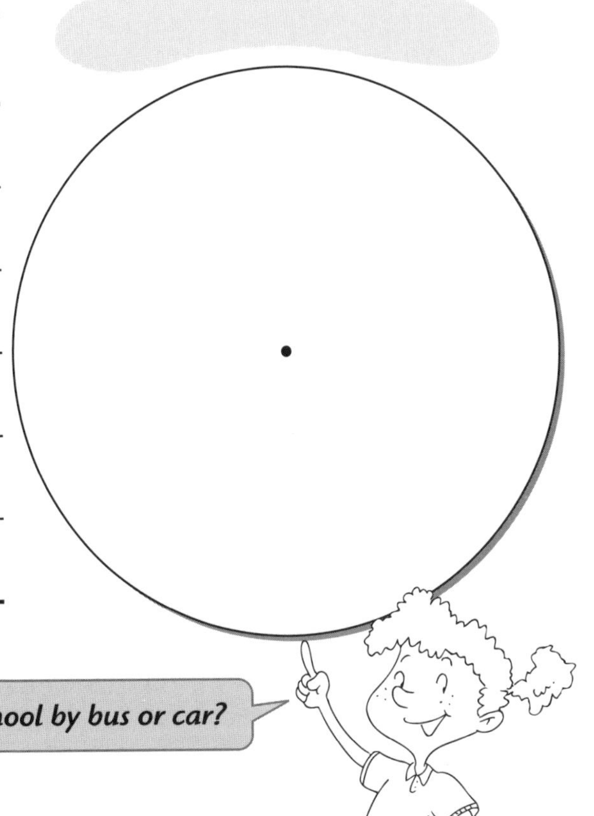

6. *About what percent of the students go to school by bus or car?*

____

7. Write two sentences to describe the circle graph.

____

____

Different Types of Graphs:

Bar graph – shows the relationship between 2 or more groups
e.g. the number of each kind of fruit in a basket

Line graph – shows continuous data over time
e.g. the height of a tree measured yearly in the past 5 years

Circle graph – shows how a part relates to the whole
e.g. the population of different nationalities in a city

Determine whether you would use a bar graph, a line graph, or a circle graph to show the data in each situation. Then give an example to go with each type of graph.

8. ____________
- the temperatures at different times in a day
- ____________

9. ____________
- the price of popsicles at different stores
- ____________

10. ____________
- the percent of different kinds of plant in a forest
- ____________

Look at the graphs showing the height of a fertilized plant. Check the biased one and answer the questions.

11. (A) Height of a Plant — Height (cm): 10, 15, 20; Week: 1, 2, 3, 4

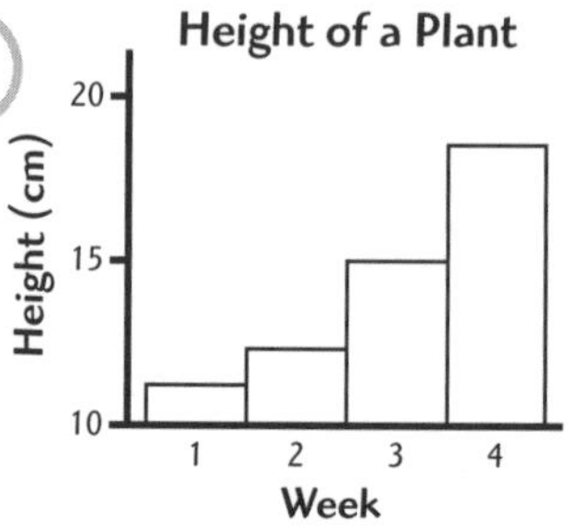

(B) Height of a Plant — Height (cm): 0, 10, 20; Week: 1, 2, 3, 4

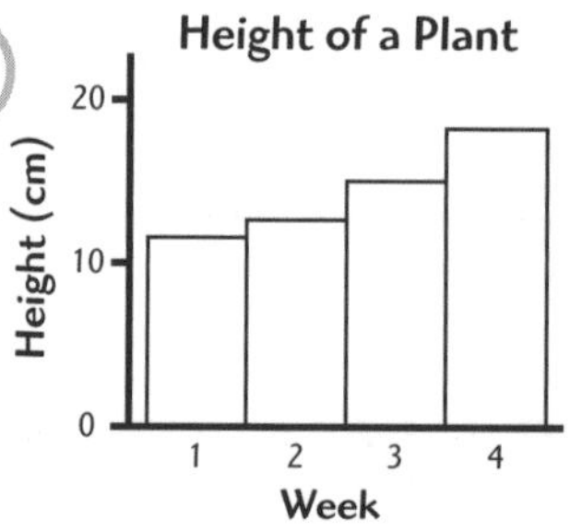

Hint

Biased graphs are misleading and usually do not start at 0 on the vertical axis.

12. *I'm the sales manager of fertilizers. Which graph do you think I should present to my customers? Why?*

____

____

Fertilizer

Jackson is inflating a balloon. Follow the pattern to complete the table that shows the amount of air in the balloon at different times. Then answer the questions.

13.

Time Elapsed (s)	**1**	**2**	**3**	**4**	**5**	**6**	**7**
Amount of Air in the Balloon (cm^3)	70	220	370	520			

14. How long does Jackson take to blow up the balloon?

____

I can hold 4570 cm^3 of air when I am fully inflated.

15. Which type of graph is the most appropriate to show the data? Explain your choice and make the graph to show the data.

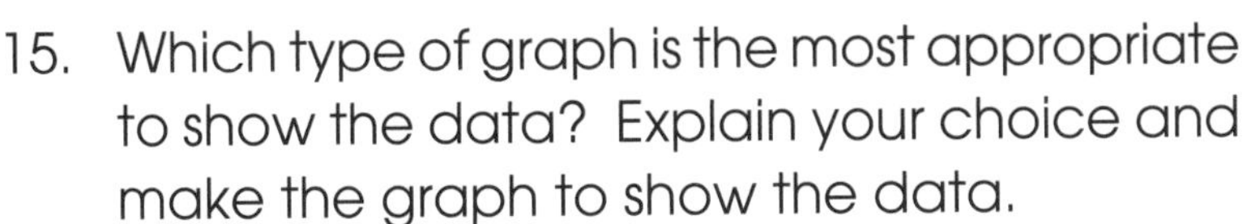

____

____

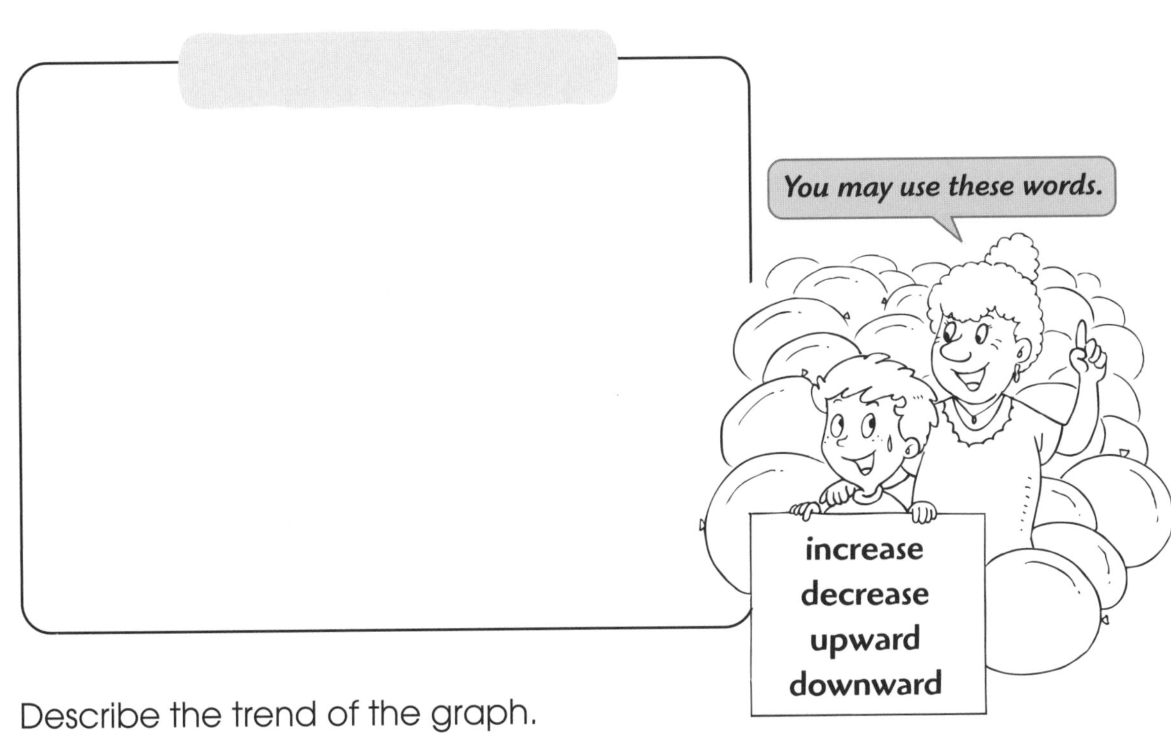

16. Describe the trend of the graph.

____

____

Mean, Median, Mode

- define each central tendency
- identify the central tendency used
- determine which central tendency should be used in different situations
- find the mean, median, and mode
- record data in stem-and-leaf plots
- solve problems involving mean, median, and mode

You did a good job, Tim. Each of the mean, median, and mode times taken is around 12 s.

Lap	Time Taken
1	12.5 s
2	11.8 s
3	12.6 s
4	11.8 s
5	12.3 s

Sum of the data

Mean: 61 ÷ 5 = 12.2 (s)

In order:

11.8 s, 11.8 s, 12.3 s, 12.5 s, 12.6 s

Median: 12.3 s

Mode: 11.8 s

Write the meaning of each central tendency.

1. Central Tendency

   Mean: ______________________

   Median: ______________________

   Mode: ______________________

Name which central tendency the children are talking about. Then find the value.

2.

Scores	
74	83
62	57

I added all the scores and divided the sum by 4.

__________ ; ____

3.

I told my mom the score that I got most of the time.

__________ ; ____

Scores	
81	64
53	80
72	64

My middle score is the same as that of the whole class.

__________ ; ____

Hint

If there are 2 middle values, find the average of these 2 values to get the median.

Write and explain which central tendency should be used in each situation.

4. **Amount of Funds Raised in 5 Events**

mean: $567
median: $623
mode: $300

I want to let the community know that I am a successful fundraiser.

____

____

5. **Members' Ages**

mean: 22 years old
median: 18 years old
mode: 20 years old

My club wants to attract new members who are around 20 years old.

____

____

Find the mean, median, and mode for the number of computers sold at different stores. Solve the problems.

6. **Number of Computers Sold at 10 Stores**

11	20	4	6	12
6	9	11	13	18

mean: ____________

median: ____________

mode: ____________

7. *I've collected the data from 3 more stores. The new mean, median, and mode are shown. I've put all the data in order. What is the missing data?*

NEW

mean: 11 computers
median: 10 computers
mode: 6 computers

Number of Computers Sold at 13 Stores

4 6 6 ____ 9 10 ____ 11 11 13 18 ____ 20

The children had a skipping contest. The tables below show the number of times the children skip in one minute. Find the mean, median, and mode for each set of data. Then answer the questions.

8.

The Skipping Record of the Children in Mrs. Jerkin's Class

Stem	Leaf
11	0 1 3 3 4 5 7
12	2 3 4 4 4 8
13	1 1 5 9

_______ mean _______ median _______ mode

9.

The Skipping Record of the Children in Mrs. Winter's Class

Stem	Leaf
10	1 2 5 5
11	2 4 5 5 6 7
12	0 3 9
13	7 7 7 8

_______ mean _______ median _______ mode

10. The class with a higher mean wins. Which class won the contest?

____

11. *If I want to reset the rule for winning this game, which central tendency should I refer to?*

____

Record the data in the stem-and-leaf plot. Find the mean, median, and mode of the data.

12.

Children's Heights (cm)

Stem	Leaf

Children's Heights (cm)

154	162	140	147
152	170	154	163
159	154	162	145
143	163	169	152
158	146	175	150

13. Mean: __________ Median: __________ Mode: __________

See how many bags of marbles the children have. Help them find the mean, median, and mode. Then answer the questions.

14. *1 bag – 15 marbles each*
2 bags – 16 marbles each
4 bags – 18 marbles each

mean: ______ marbles

median: ____________

mode: ____________

15. *1 bag – 25 marbles each*
2 bags – 10 marbles each
3 bags – 15 marbles each
4 bags – 20 marbles each

mean: ____________

median: ____________

mode: ____________

16. Jay has 8 bags of marbles with a mean of 18 marbles in each bag after Ann gave a bag of her marbles to him. How many marbles does Jay have now?

Hint

Multiply the mean by the total number of groups to find the total.

mean x total no. of groups = the total

Jay now has ______ marbles.

Solve the problems.

17. How many seconds did Tom take to run 5 laps if the mean time taken for each lap is 15.1 s?

Tom ran ______ seconds.

18. How many seconds did Tom run in the 5th lap if the mean time taken for the first 4 laps is 14.7 s?

Tom ran ______ seconds in the 5th lap.

Tom's Record

Lap	Time Taken (s)
1	12.9
2	13.1
3	15.8

26

Experimental Probability

- find relative frequency
- write relative frequency as fractions, decimals, and percents
- solve problems that involve relative frequency
- make circle graphs using relative frequency

They spin the spinner 100 times. It lands on "Bone" 15 times and "Fish" 85 times.

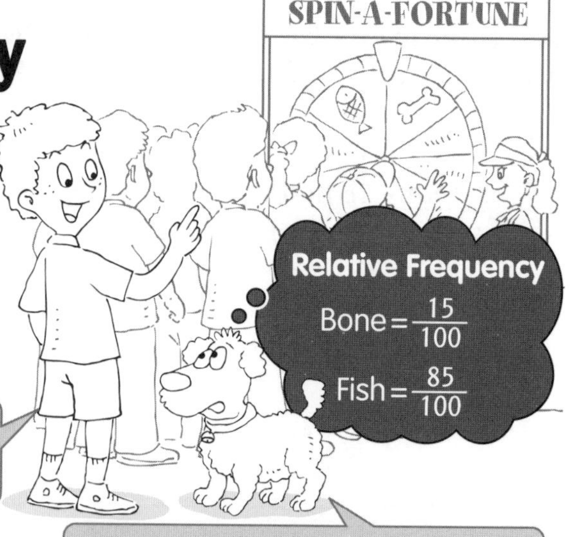

Well, the relative frequency of landing on "bone" is so low.

Joe tosses a coin. Find the relative frequency for each case.

> **Hint**
>
> Relative frequency is a ratio as described below:
>
> $\frac{\text{no. of successful outcomes}}{\text{total no. of trials}}$

1. **Toss 10 times** – heads: 7 and tails: 3

   Relative frequency of heads: ______

   Relative frequency of tails: ______

2. **Toss 50 times** – heads: 22 and tails: 28

   Relative frequency of heads: ______

   Relative frequency of tails: ______

Look at the records. See how many times the children picked a ball from each box. Fill in the blanks and find the relative frequency for each kind of ball.

3. Mary's Record

Ball	No. of Times	Relative Frequency
	5	
	9	
	6	

Total: ______

4. Kevin's Record

Ball	No. of Times	Relative Frequency
red	6	
blue	9	
green		

Total: 30

Find the relative frequency for each case. Write the answers as fractions, decimals, and percents.

5. In a fair, some children are asked if they like French fries, cotton candy, or corn on the cob.

	No. of Children
French fries	135
cotton candy	64
corn on the cob	81

Relative Frequency

a. French fries = ____________

b. cotton candy = ____________

c. French fries and cotton candy = ____________

6. Lucy draws a ball from a bag and records the result.

	No. of Times
red	15
green	4
blue	1
yellow	45
white	20

Relative Frequency

a. red = ____________

b. blue or yellow = ____________

c. white or green = ____________

d. not yellow = ____________

Help Katie complete the table that shows the relative frequency for each number tossed. Then answer the question.

7. *The relative frequency for tossing odd numbers is $\frac{12}{25}$.*

a dice labelled from 1 to 6

a.

Number Tossed	Relative Frequency
1	$\frac{3}{25}$
2	$\frac{5}{25}$
3	$\frac{4}{25}$
4	$\frac{2}{25}$
5	
6	

b. How many times did the dice land on each number?

1: ____ 2: ____ 3: ____

4: ____ 5: ____ 6: ____

c. What is the relative frequency for tossing even numbers?

____

Find the passing rate for each subject. Write the answers in percents. Then answer the questions.

8.

	Number of Children taking a test	Number of Children passing the test	Passing Rate
Mathematics	31	27	
English	29	23	
Science	15	10	
History	28	23	
Geography	34	32	

Hint

You may use division to find the passing rate.

Passing rate $= \frac{\text{No. of children passing the test}}{\text{No. of children taking the test}}$

9. Which subject has the highest passing rate? ____________

10. If Mr. Winston, the school principal, wants to offer an after school enrichment program to help the children, which subject should the program focus on? ____________

Look at the record. Find the relative frequency in decimals. Then answer the questions.

11.

Result \ Team	Maple No. of Times	Maple Relative Frequency	St. Jacob No. of Times	St. Jacob Relative Frequency
Win	18		15	
Loss	20		10	
Tie	5		9	

12. Which team has a better result? ____________

13. *If the Maple plays 5 more games, how many games does it need to win to have a better result than St. Jacob? Show me your work.*

Identify and label the circle graphs that show the sales records of the salespersons. Then fill in the boxes with the relative frequencies in decimals.

14.

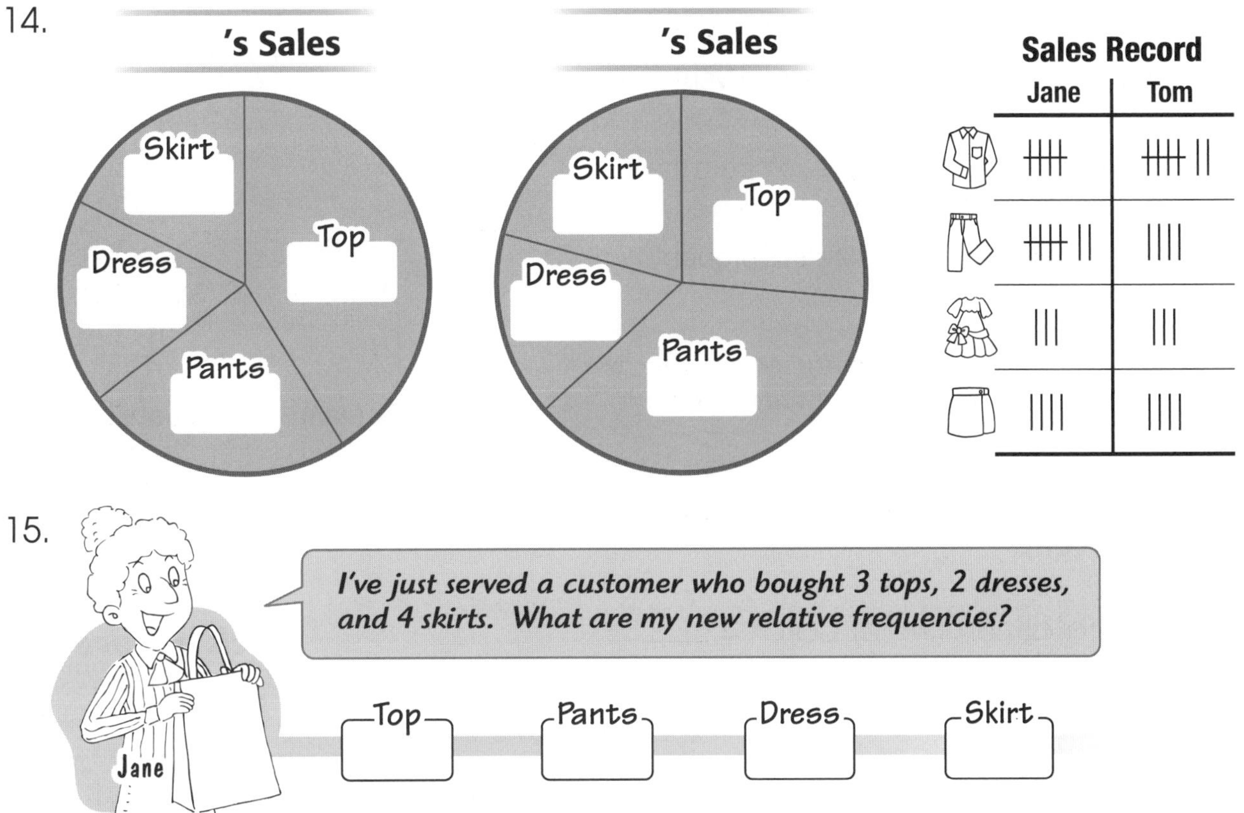
's Sales
Skirt
Top
Dress
Pants
's Sales
Skirt
Top
Dress
Pants

Sales Record

	Jane	Tom
(top)	卌	卌 II
(pants)	卌 II	IIII
(dress)	III	III
(skirt)	IIII	IIII

15.

I've just served a customer who bought 3 tops, 2 dresses, and 4 skirts. What are my new relative frequencies?
Jane
Top
Pants
Dress
Skirt

The table below records the results of spinning Kevin's spinner. Help Kevin complete the table and make a spinner that matches the result. Then answer the question.

16.

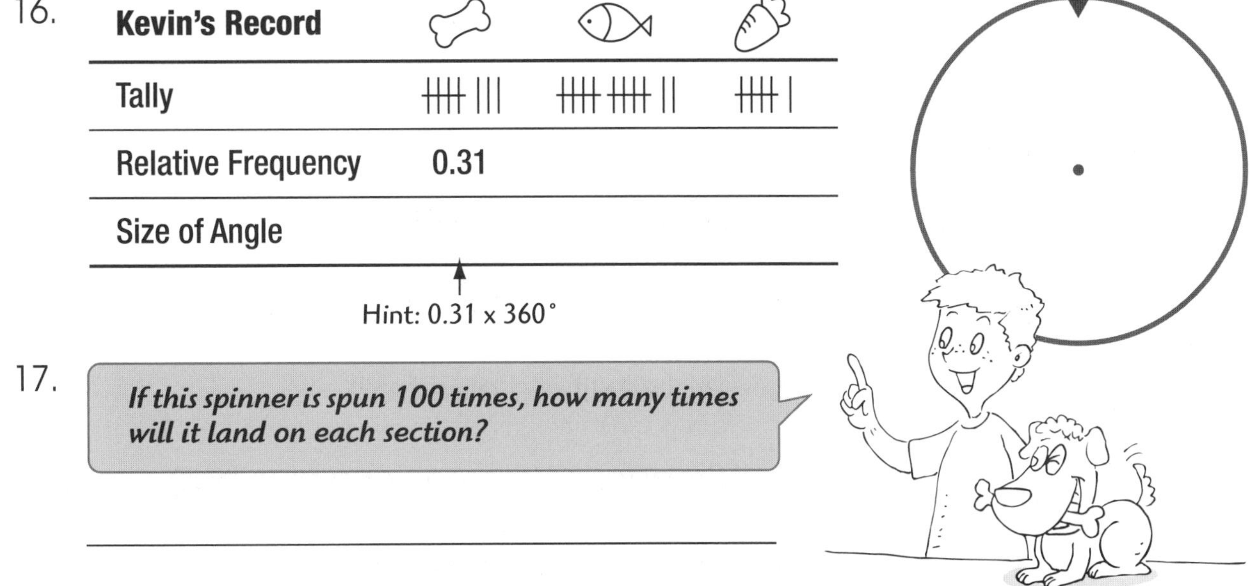

Kevin's Record	(bone)	(fish)	(carrot)
Tally	卌 III	卌 卌 II	卌 I
Relative Frequency	0.31		
Size of Angle			

Hint: 0.31 x 360°

17.

If this spinner is spun 100 times, how many times will it land on each section?

27

Theoretical Probability

- find the probabilities of different events
- predict the number of times an event will occur
- find relative frequencies and compare them to theoretical probabilities
- solve problems using theoretical probability and prediction

Her probability of winning the prize is much greater than ours.

Fill in the blanks and find the probability for each event.

1. a. Total number of cards = ______

Pick a Card

18	5	3	●
☆	4	10	9
A	15	C	♡

b. Probability (a shape) = $\frac{\square}{\square}$ ← No. of cards with a shape / ← Total no. of cards

c. Probability (a letter) = $\frac{\square}{\square}$ ← No. of cards with a letter / ← Total no. of cards

d. Probability (a number or a letter) = $\frac{\square}{\square}$ ← No. of cards with a number or a letter / ← Total no. of cards

2. **Draw a Ball**

a. Total number of balls = ______

b. Probability (a red ball) = ______

c. Probability (a blue ball) = ______

d. Probability (a green or a blue ball) = ______

e. Probability (not a green ball) = ______

Read what the children say. Find each probability.

I like milk chocolates and almond chocolates the most.

Milk chocolates:	9 pieces
Dark chocolates:	8 pieces
Mint chocolates:	11 pieces
Almond chocolates:	2 pieces

3. Find the probability of picking out

   a. a milk chocolate: ______

   b. a dark chocolate: ______

   c. a mint chocolate: ______

   d. an almond chocolate: ______

   e. a chocolate that Elaine likes the most: ______

   f. a chocolate without nuts: ______

   g. a milk or a mint chocolate: ______

4. Pick a dice and toss it.

Each dice is labelled from 1 to 6.

Find the probability of

a. picking a red dice: ______

b. not picking a yellow dice: ______

c. tossing a "2": ______

d. tossing an odd number: ______

e. tossing a prime number: ______

5. Spin the spinner labelled with 26 letters.

I've got W, L, and L already. Let me spin it one more time.

Find the probability that he will form the word

a. WILL: ______

b. WALK: ______

c. WALL or WILL: ______

d. WALK or WELL: ______

Predicting an Outcome:

1st Find the probability of getting the outcome.

2nd Multiply the probability by the number of repeated actions.

e.g. Predict how many times the pointer lands on "lollipop" if it is spun 40 times.

Probability (lollipop) = $\frac{3}{8}$

Number of times getting "lollipop" = $\frac{3}{8}$ x 40 = 15

If I spin it 40 times, it will land on "lollipop" 15 times.

Find the probabilities and answer the questions.

6. Lily shuffles a deck of cards and picks one without looking.

There are 3 kinds of cards in the deck. I'll pick out a card and put the card back. I'll repeat this 100 times.

Hint

The sum of the probabilities of all outcomes of an experiment is 1.

	Probability	Prediction (No. of Times)
draw a	0.1	0.1 x 100 = ______
draw a	0.54	
draw a		

7. Ken draws a red ball from either one of the boxes to win a prize.

a. If Ken wants to win a prize, from which box should he draw a ball?

____

b. How many red balls should there be in box B so that it has the same winning probability as box A?

____

Follow the instructions to do the activity 50 times. Record each outcome and complete the table. Then answer the questions.

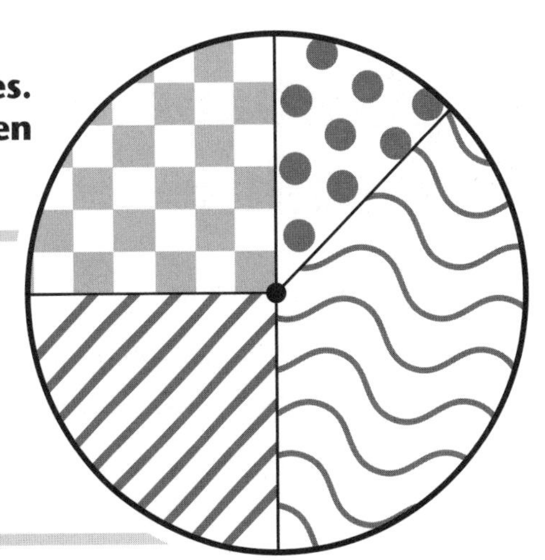

8. **Instructions**
   1. Secure a paper clip in the centre of the spinner with a pencil.
   2. Spin the paper clip and record the pattern that it lands on.

	Tally	Relative Frequency	Theoretical Probability
"dots"			
"wavy lines"			
"stripes"			
"checkers"			

9. 

Compare the relative frequency with the theoretical probability.

10. *If I swing the paperclip 800 times, how many times will the paperclip land on each sector?*

11. *About how many times do I need to swing the paperclip to get 150 times of "wavy lines"?*

28

Applications of Probability

- draw tree diagrams
- find the number of outcomes
- find probabilities from tree diagrams
- solve problems using tree diagrams

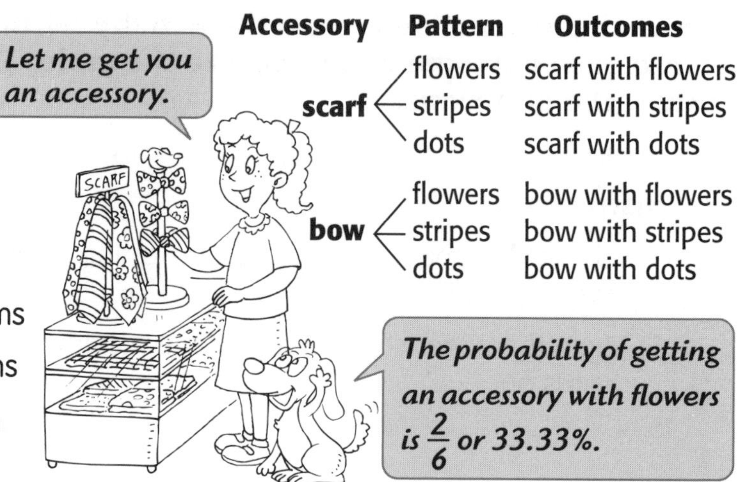

Complete the tree diagram. Then answer the questions.

1.

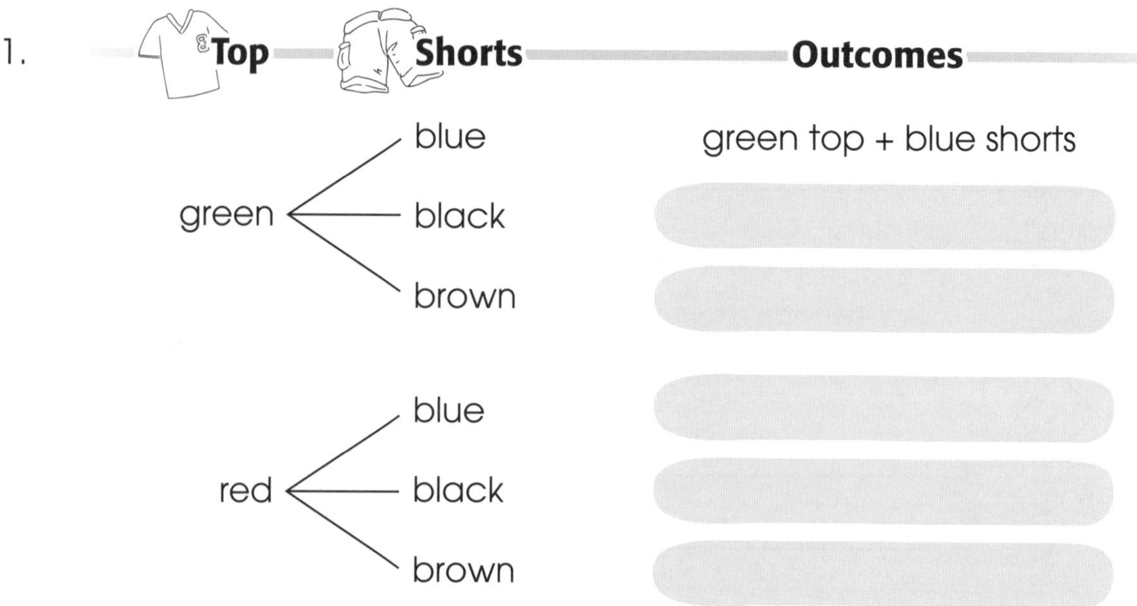

2. How many possible outcomes are there? ________

3. How many outcomes are there with blue shorts? ________

4. How many outcomes are there with a red top? ________

5. A customer is going to buy a top and a pair of shorts. What is the probability of choosing

   a. a green top and a pair of black shorts? ________

   b. a red top and a pair of brown shorts? ________

James is drawing a letter ball from each of the three boxes. Complete the tree diagram. Then answer the questions.

6. **Box 1 Box 2 Box 3 Formed Words**

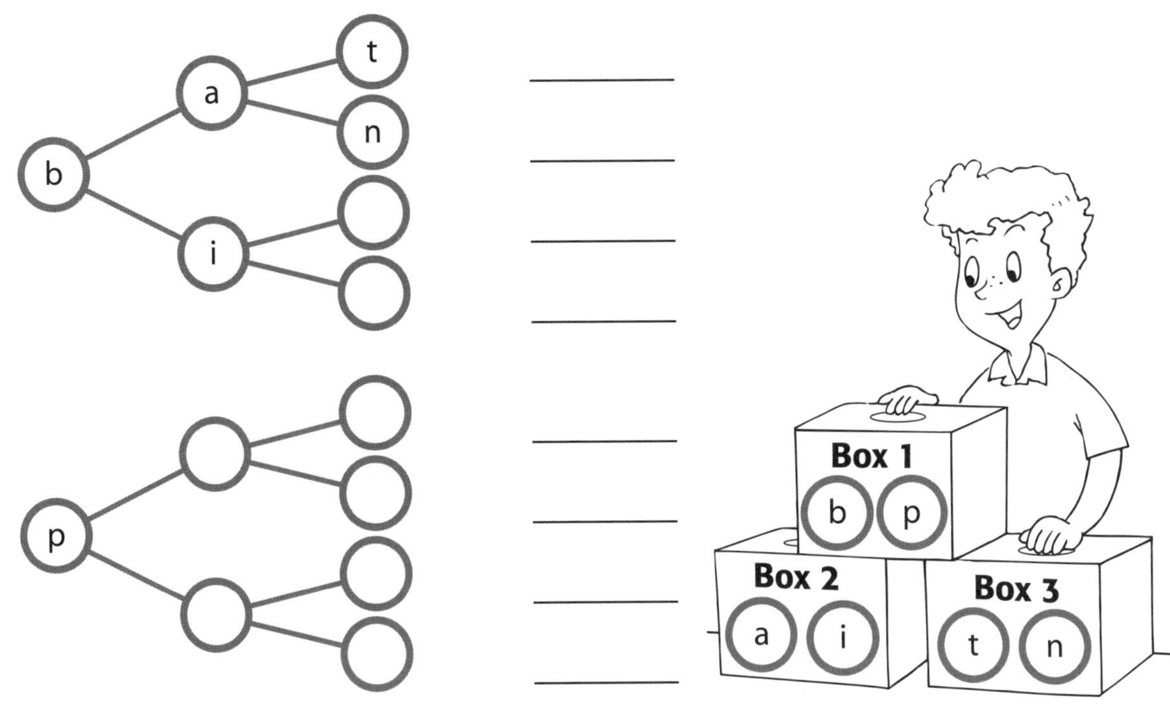

7. How many possible words are there? ________

8. What is the probability of getting "bin"? ________

9. What is the probability of getting "pan"? ________

10. What is the probability of getting a word with a letter "a"? ________

11. If James puts a ball with a letter "g" into box 3 and draws a ball from each of the three boxes again,

    a. how many possible words are there? ________

    b. what is the probability of getting "bag"? ________

    c. what is the probability of getting a word with a letter "g"? ________

Draw a tree diagram to show the possible outcomes for ice cream cones with different toppings. Then answer the questions.

12. **Flavour** — **Topping** — **Outcomes**

Make Your Own Cone
Flavour
• vanilla
• chocolate
Topping
• nuts
• sprinkles
• fruits

13. ***What is the probability that each kind of ice cream cone is chosen?***

a. vanilla flavoured ______

b. chocolate flavoured with nuts ______

c. vanilla flavoured without fruits ______

14. If the "fruit" topping is sold out, what will be the probability that each kind of ice cream that remains is chosen? Will the probability of choosing vanilla with sprinkles be greater than before? Show your work.

Jason is designing a treasure hunt game. Help him draw a tree diagram to show the ways to the treasure. Then answer the questions.

15. 

Character

- *a scientist*
- *an explorer*

Path

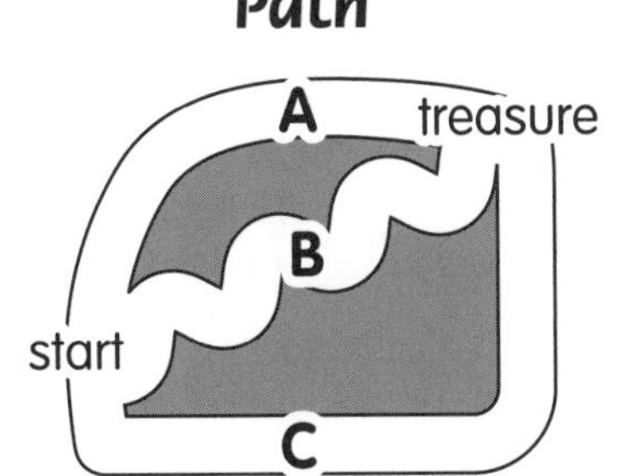

Treasure Chest

- *jewellery*
- *snakes*

16. What is the probability that a player gets jewellery? ________

17. What is the probability that a player is a scientist and gets snakes? ________

18. ***Paths B and C are very muddy. Find the probability that a player is***

a. an explorer and gets jewellery without getting muddy?

____

b. a muddy scientist and gets snakes?

____

Review 2

Find the volume and surface area of the building blocks.

1.

Volume

Surface Area

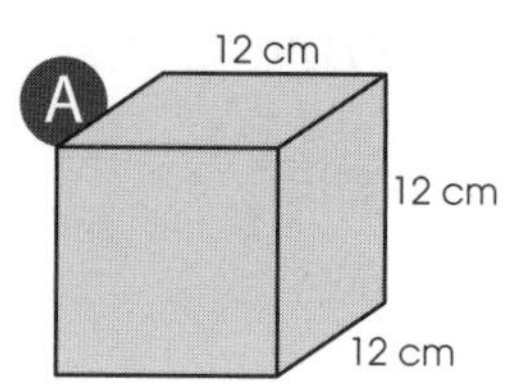

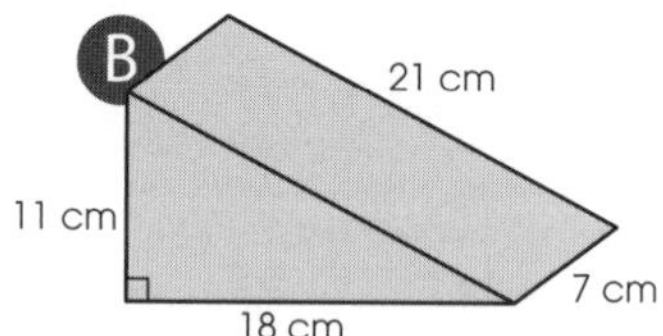

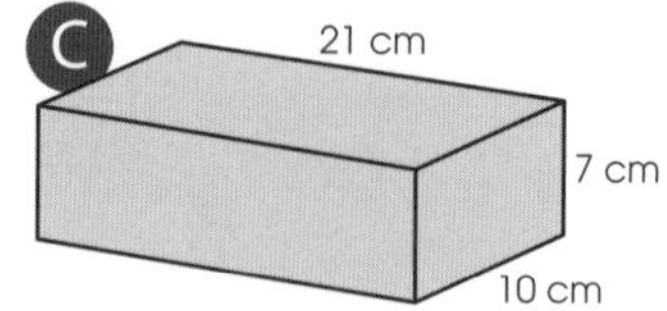

Check the correct answers.

2.

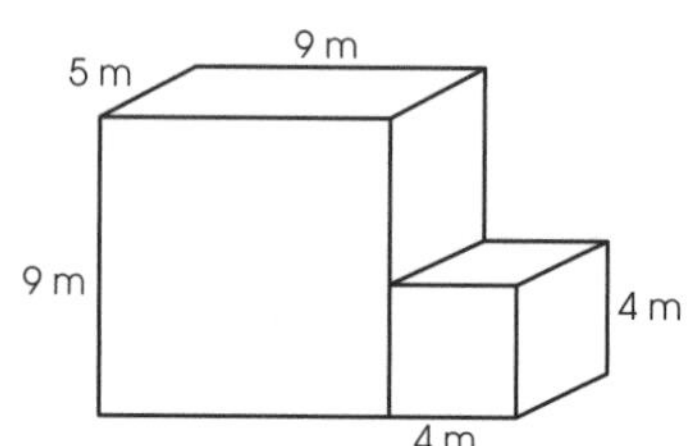

Volume:

Surface Area:

Volume:	Surface Area:
(A) 469 m^3	(A) 414 m^2
(B) 485 m^3	(B) 438 m^2
(C) 793 m^3	(C) 470 m^2

3.

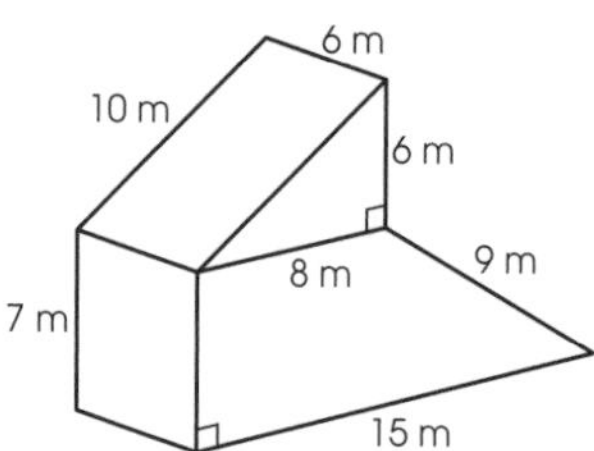

Volume:	Surface Area:
(A) 627 m^3	(A) 406 m^2
(B) 771 m^3	(B) 491 m^2
(C) 1110 m^3	(C) 587 m^2

Draw the images and record the coordinates of the vertices of the images. Then plot another image of each shape and describe the transformation.

4.

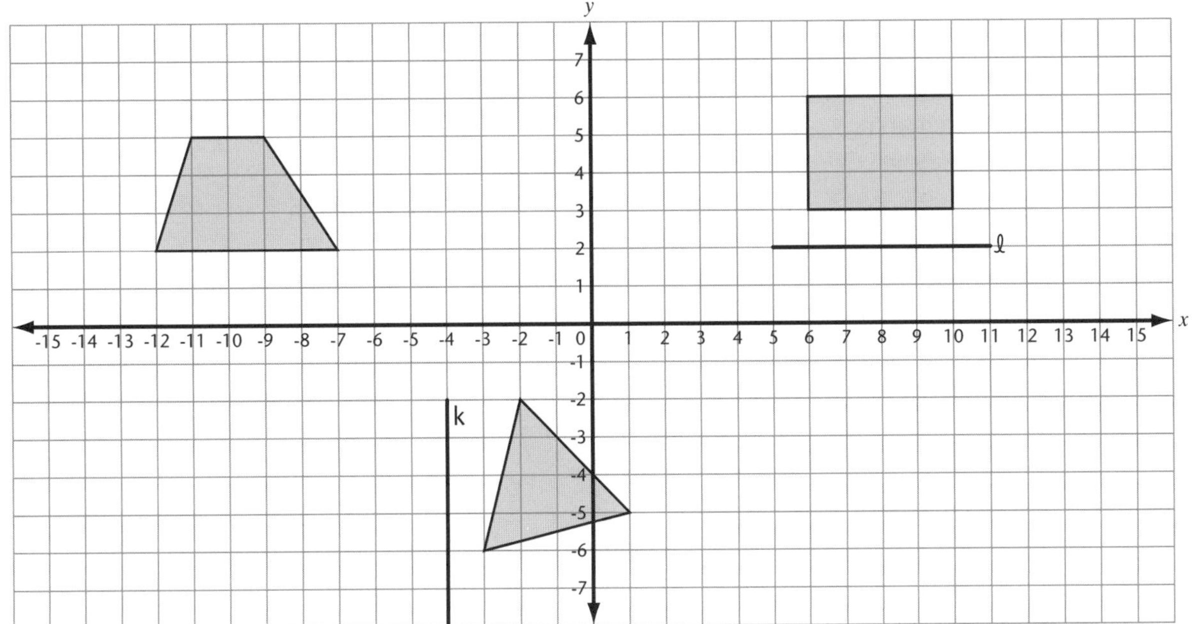

Coordinates

a. Translate the trapezoid 2 units left and 3 units up. ________________

b. Rotate the rectangle a $\frac{1}{4}$ counterclockwise turn at (6,3). ________________

c. Reflect the triangle at line k and translate it 1 unit right and 2 units down. ________________

5. Draw another image of each shape.

a.

Image of trapezoid	Image of triangle	Image of rectangle
(-7,2) (-7,-3) (-10,-2) (-10,0)	(6,-3) (9,-6) (5,-7)	(6,1) (10,1) (10,-2) (6,-2)

b. Describe each transformation.

trapezoid : ____________________________

triangle : ____________________________

rectangle : ____________________________

Review 2

Look at the core of each pattern. Find the terms. Then help Jason find the core of a pattern.

6. **Y B 5 K**

- the 13th term: ________
- the 36th term: ________

7. 

- the 10th term: ________
- the 29th term: ________

8.
- the 6th term: **A**
- the 9th term: **M**
- the 20th term: **H**
- the 27th term: **T**

There are 4 terms in the core of this pattern.

core: ____________

Uncle Sam has recorded the number of rabbits seen on his farm. Complete the descriptions and the pattern rule. Then answer the question.

9. **Descriptions**

a. The number of weeks starts at ________ and ________________ (increases / decreases) by ________ each time.

b. The number of rabbits seen starts at ______________________________.

c. The number of rabbits is ________ more than ________ times the number of weeks.

No. of Rabbits Seen

No. of Weeks	No. of Rabbits
1	7
2	13
3	19
4	25
5	31

10. **Pattern Rule**

No. of Rabbits = No. of Weeks x ________ + ________

11. How many rabbits will there be in 9 weeks? ________ rabbits

Write an algebraic expression with variable m for each statement. Then evaluate.

12. Subtract 8 from 4 times a number.

    Expression: ____________

    If $m = 5$, ____________ = ______

13. Take away 3 from half a number.

    Expression: ____________

    If $m = 8$, ____________ = ______

14. Add 3 to one third of a number.

    Expression: ____________

    If $m = 24$, ____________ = ______

15. Triple a number and add 6.

    Expression: ____________

    If $m = 12$, ____________ = ______

Aunt Annie wants to buy a cookies store in either store A or store B. Write the algebraic expressions and answer the questions.

16. *My monthly profit is the amount I earn minus the expense. Each cookie is sold at $0.60 in store A and $0.70 in store B.*

    Let c be the number of cookies Aunt Annie sells each month. Find her monthly profit in

    a. store A: $(____________)

    b. store B: $(____________)

Monthly Expense	
Store A	$300
Store B	$550

17. Which store should Aunt Annie buy if she expects to sell

    a. 2400 cookies?

    b. 3500 cookies?

    c. 5000 cookies?

Solve the unknowns and check the answers. Then solve the problems.

18. $8k + 4 = 44$

Check

19. $\frac{m + 7}{2} = 13$

Check

20. $5(p - 6) = 15$

Check

21. Josh ran 2 fewer than 5 times the number of laps that Kay ran. How many laps did Kay run?

____

22. Kay ran 1 more minute than half of Josh's time. How long did Josh run if Kay ran 9 minutes?

____

I ran a total of 18 laps.
Josh

Read the data Jenny found from the Internet on the number of babies born between January and June. Then answer the questions.

23. Circle the terms that describe the data.

   a. discrete / continuous

   b. primary data / secondary data

24. The mean number of babies born each month is 1216. How many babies were born in April?

____

Number of Babies Born in Springview

Month	No. of Babies Born
Jan	1050
Feb	1154
Mar	1212
Apr	
May	1390
Jun	1245

Katie rolled a dice that she made from a net 1000 times. Find each relative frequency in percent and answer the question.

25.

Number Tossed	No. of Times Tossed	Relative Frequency
1	165	
2	340	
3	170	
4	159	
5	166	
6	0	

26. Check the net that Katie used to make the dice.

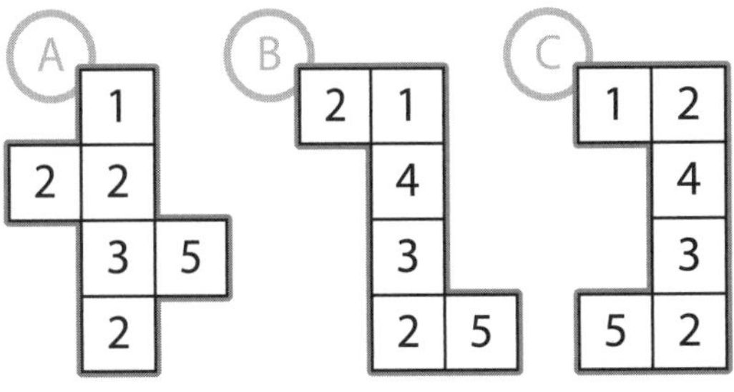

A player spins the spinner 2 times in one game. Draw a tree diagram to show all the possible outcomes in one game. Then answer the questions.

27. **Tree Diagram**

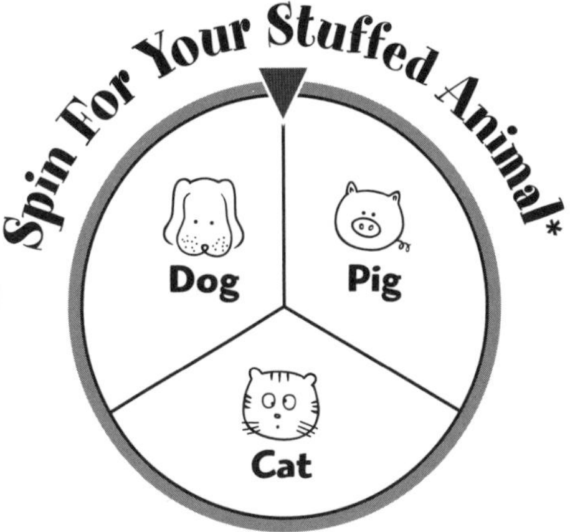

*A player who gets the same animal in one game wins.

28. What is the probability that a player gets 1 cat and 1 dog? __________

29. What is the probability that a player wins a game? __________

30. If you play the game 18 times, how many times will you expect yourself to win? __________

ENGLISH

Everyone, including you and me, has made New Year's resolutions, but how well did you follow through with them? It seems that very few people can let the new year roll in without giving a thought to how they can improve their lives, and make the coming year better than the last. Actually, the making of New Year's resolutions is a tradition dating back to the early Babylonians. One of their most popular resolutions was a promise to return borrowed farm equipment!

A New Year's resolution is a promise one makes to do something to better oneself. Resolutions usually involve a commitment to a lifestyle change or to ending a bad habit. Of course, resolutions need not be made with the New Year, but the fact that everyone is doing away with the old and welcoming the new often provides the motivation needed to even consider such ideas. Some resolutions are very personal, such as getting fit, quitting smoking, and becoming more assertive. Others are more community-minded, such as giving to charity more often and becoming more environmentally responsible.

Although the making of New Year's resolutions is a very secular activity, there are some parallels in religion. For example, many Christians give up things such as favourite sweets and cigarettes during the Christian fasting period of Lent, though the motive is more one of making sacrifices than trying to consciously improve oneself. Yom Kippur, Judaism's holiest holiday, is a time to reflect upon one's wrongdoings in the previous year and to seek and offer forgiveness.

Losing weight, as well as getting a better job, is among the most popular New Year's resolutions for adults. But resolutions are not just for adults! The American Academy of Pediatrics has lists of resolutions for children ranging from pre-school age to the teen years. Their list for youth aged 13 years old and up includes:

New Year's Resolutions

1. I will eat at least one fruit and one vegetable every day, and I will limit the amount of soda I drink.
2. I will take care of my body through physical activity and nutrition.
3. I will choose non-violent television shows and video games, and I will spend only one to two hours each day on these activities.

4. I will help out in my community by volunteering, working with community groups, or joining a group that helps people in need.

5. I will wipe negative "self talk" (e.g. "I can't do it" or "I'm so dumb") out of my vocabulary.

6. When I feel angry or stressed out, I will take a break and find constructive ways to deal with the stress, such as exercising, reading, writing in a journal, and discussing my problem with a parent or friend.

7. When faced with a difficult decision, I will talk with an adult about my choices.

8. I will resist peer pressure to try drugs and alcohol.

A. Fill in the blanks with words from the passage.

1. Many people make resolutions to ________________ their lives in the coming year.

2. Very often, a resolution involves a ________________ to give up a bad habit.

3. Making New Year's resolutions is a ________________ activity for many. However, some people make resolutions for religious reasons.

4. We make resolutions to improve ourselves ________________ .

5. Some teenagers resolve to find ________________ ways to deal with stress.

B. Suppose it is the beginning of a new year. Write two New Year's resolutions for yourself.

1. ____

____

2. ____

____

Subject-Verb Agreement

The verb in a sentence must **agree** with its subject in both person and number. A singular subject takes a singular verb and a plural subject takes a plural verb.

Example: One of their most popular resolutions was a promise to return borrowed farm equipment.

Note that the noun or pronoun right before the verb may not be the "real" subject of the sentence. Make sure to identify the subject and use the correct form of the verb.

With indefinite pronouns like "everybody", "someone", and "nothing", singular verbs are used.

Example: Everyone is doing away with the old and welcoming the new.

C. Circle the correct form of the verb for each sentence.

1. Everybody in class has / have to make a list of New Year's resolutions.
2. Each of the lists represents / represent the commitments made by each student.
3. The list of resolutions was / were handed in to the teacher by the end of the lesson.
4. Someone has / have left the list on the teacher's desk.
5. Nothing is / are impossible if you is / are set on it.
6. Some of the students' resolutions includes / include going to bed earlier, eating less chocolate, and saving more money.
7. All of us wants / want to get better grades in the coming year.
8. Has / Have anybody thought of eating less fast food?
9. Whoever makes / make a resolution will have to follow it through.

Other Vexing Agreement

When "either" and "neither" are used as subjects, singular verbs are required. When they are used as correlative conjunctions, the subject closer to the verb determines whether the singular or plural form of the verb should be used.

Examples: Neither of the two boys has thought about any resolutions.

Neither Issac nor his friends need to lose weight.

Words and phrases like "including" and "as well as" do not join the nouns or pronouns they introduce to the subjects, so they do not affect the forms of verbs used.

Examples: Everyone, including you and me, has made New Year's resolutions before.

Losing weight, as well as getting a better job, is among the most popular New Year's resolutions for adults.

D. The subject-verb agreements in the following sentences are incorrect. Rewrite the sentences to make them correct.

1. Either of the two resolutions are made by me.

____

2. Neither the girls nor Bosco think that making resolutions are useless.

____

3. Working out, as well as reading, are some ways to release stress.

____

4. Mrs. Bauer, together with her students, volunteer to help out after school.

____

5. Either Angie or Carl are going to be the first to tell us the resolutions.

____

6. Everybody, including all teachers, are going to the New Year Camp.

____

2

The Three Roses: *a Czech Folktale*

Once upon a time, there was a mother who had three daughters. As she was preparing to go to the market, she asked her daughters what she should bring back for them. Two of them began to list many things, and demanded that she buy them all. When the mother had heard enough, she asked her third daughter, "And you, don't you want anything?"

"No, but, if you like, you can bring me three roses, please," she replied. Once the mother knew what the girls wanted, she set off to the market. She bought everything she could afford, piled it high on her back, and started for home. But soon nightfall overtook her. The poor woman was lost and could go no further. She wandered aimlessly through the woods until she grew tired. Then, she came upon a palace, which was quite strange since she had never before heard of any palace in the woods. A large rose garden surrounded the palace, and it seemed to the woman that all the roses were smiling at her. Then she remembered her youngest daughter, who had asked sweetly for just such beautiful roses. She thought, "There are so many lovely roses here. No one will mind if I take just three."

She tiptoed into the garden and picked the roses. At once, an old wizard came down and demanded the woman's daughter in exchange for the roses. The woman was petrified and attempted to throw the flowers away, but the wizard laughed and threatened to send her into the dark woods forever. The woman promised him her daughter, and then sadly made her way home, roses in hand. She gave the three roses to her daughter and said, "Here are the roses you asked for, but I had to pay dearly for them. You must now go to the palace in the woods in return for them. I don't know if you will ever come back."

But the youngest daughter seemed not to mind at all, and the woman led her back to the palace. The wizard reappeared and told the girl that she had to feed him three fine meals a day.

For a long time, the girl worked hard to prepare fine meals for the old wizard. Then one day, the wizard asked her to cut his head off! She protested, but the wizard raged, and so she did it. The wizard's head rolled onto the ground, and from out of his body came a terrible hissing snake! Again, the snake asked her to cut his head off. This time, the girl did not hesitate, and cut his head off at once. The evil serpent changed immediately into a handsome young man, and said to the girl in a pleasant and grateful voice, "This castle is mine and, now, because you have saved me, I wish to marry you."

There was a great wedding, and the young man and the girl lived happily ever after.

A. Answer these questions.

1. Why was it strange for the woman to have found a palace in the woods?

____

2. If you were the woman, would you promise the old wizard your daughter?

____

3. Why did the wizard ask the girl to cut off his head?

____

4. Think of a different ending to the story.

____

____

____

5. Can you think of a fairy tale similar to this? Explain how they are similar.

____

____

____

Past Perfect Tense

The **past perfect tense** is formed with "had + past participle" and is used:

- to indicate that something had happened before another past action
- to show that an action had been completed before a specific past time
- for an action that began before, and was still continuing at, a past time
- in indirect speech introduced by a past verb of saying or thinking to talk about something that had happened before the speech took place

Examples: Then she remembered her youngest daughter, who <u>had asked</u> sweetly for just such beautiful roses.

The young man said he wished to marry the girl because she <u>had saved</u> him.

B. Check if the sentences contain the past perfect tense. If not, put a cross.

1. The old woman had three daughters. ☐
2. She had bought all the things her daughters needed before she headed home. ☐
3. The woman had not heard of a palace in the woods before. ☐
4. She has not seen such beautiful roses before. ☐
5. She picked three roses for her youngest daughter. ☐
6. The woman had never before been so scared. ☐
7. The young girl had to stay in the palace because her mother had picked roses from the garden. ☐
8. The girl had to feed the wizard three meals a day. ☐
9. The wizard asked the girl if she had prepared lunch. ☐

C. Fill in the blanks with the correct form of the verbs.

1. After she (hear) ______________ enough from her first two daughters, the old woman (ask) ______________ her youngest daughter what she (want) ______________ .

2. The woman (not be) ______________ able to get out of the woods before night (fall) ______________ .

3. An old wizard (appear) ______________ after the woman (pick) ______________ the roses.

4. The woman (give) ______________ the roses to her daughter before she (take) ______________ her to the palace.

5. After the girl (cut) ______________ the head off the serpent, it (change) ______________ into a handsome young man.

D. Complete the following.

1. Write about something you had done before you went home from school yesterday.

____

____

____

2. Write about a special event that had happened before you were in Grade 7.

____

____

____

Mythical Creatures from the *World of Fantasy*

Do you remember the old fairy tales you were told as a child? Your favourite stories no doubt included some of the more well-known fantasy creatures, such as mermaids, dragons, and unicorns. If you have read ancient Greek myths, then you may also be familiar with creatures like the *Centaur* (half human, half horse), the *Satyr* (human with goat-like features), and perhaps the *Griffin* which is often depicted as an eagle with the body of a lion. In addition to reading about them in books and seeing them in movies, we can find these mythical creatures on vases and in old paintings and ancient mosaics. They also appear as gargoyles in historical and modern architecture, such as in the churches and cathedrals of Paris, and the skyscrapers of New York and Chicago.

In fact, there are hundreds of such mythical creatures from the world of fantasy, myth, and legend. Not only have these mythical creatures been with us through the ages, but they appear throughout the cultures of the world. For example, the South Pacific nation of the Solomon Islands has mermaid-like creatures in their mythology. These "merpeople" (*mer* is the French word for "ocean") are called *Adaro*. They are part man and part fish, but this is probably where similarities with the better-known merpeople end; an Adaro has a swordfish spear growing out of his head, lives in the sun, comes to earth by sliding along rainbows, and is not very nice to humans!

Dragon-like sea creatures appear in many different cultures as well. For example, the *Tarasque*, the French version of a dragon, has a lion's head, a turtle's shell, a scorpion's sting, and legs like a bear's! This particular dragon not only spews fire, but likes to swim, and is said to inhabit the waters of Ha Long Bay, off the coast of northern Vietnam, which used to be a French colony. It joins the pantheon of other mysterious sea creatures throughout the world, which includes *Amemasu*, the lake monster of Ainu mythology in Japan; *Jormungandr*, the sea spirit of

Norse mythology; and the fearsome water demons of Slavic lore, the *Bagiennik*. There are more recent examples of mysterious sea creatures, which people claim to see today. There are the Canadian sea monsters, such as *Ogopogo*, which inhabits Lake Okanagan in British Columbia, and *Manipogo*, which has been sighted in Manitoba's Lake Winnipeg. And, of course, there is the world-famous *Loch Ness Monster* in Scotland. But it seems these more modern sea monsters are friendly sorts and good for tourism!

In many cases, it is not difficult to understand the folklore roots of these mythical creatures. There often seems to be a grounding in the nature of the area. For example, in Inuit lore, the *Akhlut* is part wolf and part whale. And in Irish lore, there is the *Dobhar-chu*, half dog and half fish, and the *Kelpie*, a water-horse. It is not surprising to discover that the folklore of many of the world's desert-dwelling people focuses more on ants and bats and birds, rather than fish and whales.

There will never be a list that includes all the mythical creatures of the world, since our collective imaginations will forever be creating more!

A. Give a brief description of the physical features of each creature below.

1. Centaur

____

2. Satyr

____

3. Griffin

____

4. Adaro

____

5. Tarasque

____

6. Akhlut

____

Active and Passive Voices

A sentence in the **active voice** focuses on the doer of the action while one in the **passive voice** puts the emphasis on the thing or person being acted upon.

Examples: Painters depict the griffin as an eagle with the body of a lion. (active)

The griffin is depicted as an eagle with the body of a lion. (passive)

Note that in using the passive voice, we sometimes leave out the doer so that the reader's attention is further directed to the person or thing being acted upon.

If it is necessary to mention the doer of the action in a passive voice sentence, the word "by" is used.

Example: The griffin is depicted as an eagle with the body of a lion by the famous painter Tobias Malone.

B. Write "active" if the sentences are in the active voice and "passive" if they are in the passive voice.

1. Grandma told me lots of fairy tales when I was young. ________________

2. The mythological "merpeople" of the South Pacific nation of the Solomon Islands are called Adaro. ________________

3. The Tarasque is said to inhabit the waters of Ha Long Bay. ________________

4. Some mythical creatures appear as gargoyles in modern architecture. ________________

5. The Manipogo has been sighted in Lake Winnipeg in Manitoba. ________________

6. Nessie, the Loch Ness Monster, has attracted many tourists to Scotland. ________________

7. Mythical creatures have appeared in different cultures' myths around the world for ages. ________________

C. Rewrite each sentence below using the active voice.

1. A lecture on mythical creatures was delivered by Professor Rayner.

2. *Exploring the World of Fantasy* was written by Nina Kirwan.

3. That picture of a unicorn flying in the sky was drawn by me.

4. The Inuit legend was staged by Mr. Reid's class.

5. All the costumes and props for the play were made by the students themselves.

D. Rewrite each sentence below using the passive voice. Leave out the doer if it does not affect the clarity of the sentence.

1. Our teacher told us to do a project on Greek mythology.

2. A thief stole the famous painting *The Rebirth of the Phoenix*.

3. They built a statue of the Ogopogo in a park in Kelowna.

4. Elves and fairies inhabit the island nation of Iceland.

5. Someone has sent a picture of Nessie to the press.

Facebook – Are You Revealing Too Much?

Most young people know what Facebook is: a free-access Internet social networking website popular among teenagers, and adults, too. It was founded by a Harvard University student named Mark Zuckerberg and launched on February 4, 2004. Initially, it was intended only as a networking site for Harvard's campus community, providing a handy tool to help everyone on campus – students, faculty, and other staff – get to know one another. Almost immediately, it expanded to include Stanford, Columbia, and Yale Universities, and then several more Ivy League schools, including MIT and Northeastern. Now, Facebook has evolved into a vast social network for anyone over the age of 13, with more than 65 million active users.

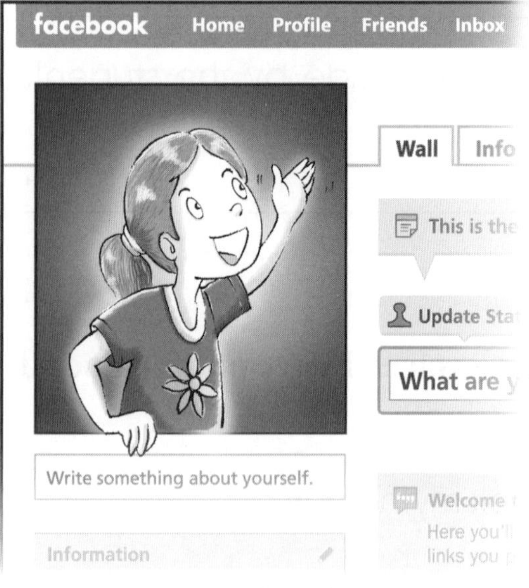

As the name suggests, faces are an integral part of the website – and of social networking, too, one could say. Facebook.com is the top Internet site for uploading photos, with 14 million photos uploaded every day! People continue to expand their personal profiles with photos, though a feature that allows blogging was soon added to the site. Some of the other features now include a Marketplace site, allowing users to post free classified ads. Similarly, under other network headings, people can let others know about events and post videos. There is even a way to send friends virtual "gifts" – such as happy face balloons, heart-shaped boxes of virtual chocolates, and dog bones – from Facebook's virtual gift shop! In this way, Facebook has increased in popularity and broadened the demographic of its usership, and it has increased its value for the owner. So far, Zuckerberg has declined to sell his site (rival networking site MySpace.com was sold to News Corp) even though he has received offers of up to a billion dollars!

But sometimes success can lead to a downfall of sorts; Facebook is not without controversy. Ironically, at least one university has blocked access to the site saying that logging onto Facebook violates its acceptable use policy. The government of Ontario blocked access to the site for its public employees in 2007. Privacy is also a major concern. In some cases, the identities of people, such as those involved in crimes as victims or perpetrators, are released to the general public through posts on such sites, even before permission is granted by the families or by the police. When this happens, it seems that website administrators cannot keep up with users who are determined to keep the information posted, no matter how many times it is taken down. There are instances of unflattering, embarrassing, or even unlawful material being posted about third parties, resulting in real damage to people's reputations, sometimes with tragic results.

Moreover, as some people have become more and more interested in chatting with their new online friends, their real-life relationships have suffered. Psychologists are seeing an increase in problems among people who are addicted to such sites. Backlash against the use of these social networking sites is now occurring, and once-devoted fans of sites like Facebook are committing "Facebook Suicide" – saying a virtual goodbye to their virtual friends and returning to their "real" lives, developing friendships with people in real life, and enjoying the real warmth and rewards that only face-to-face friendship can offer.

A. Write "T" for the true sentences and "F" for the false ones.

1. Facebook is a free social networking website for any students. ______
2. Facebook was intended to be a website to help those at Harvard University get to know one another. ______
3. There is a total of 14 million photos on Facebook now. ______
4. Classified ads for virtual gifts can be posted on Facebook's Marketplace. ______
5. The founder of Facebook sold his site for a billion dollars. ______
6. Ontario government employees cannot access Facebook at work. ______

B. In your own words, state the pros and cons of Facebook.

Pros

____

____

Cons

____

____

Verbals

A **verbal** is a form of a verb that does not act as a verb in a sentence. There are three types of verbals.

A **gerund** is the "ing" form of a verb, which acts as a noun.

Example: Some people have become more and more interested in <u>chatting</u> with their new online friends.

A **participle** is the present or past participle form of a verb which acts as an adjective.

Examples: There are instances of <u>embarrassing</u> materials being posted about third parties. (present participle)

Some of the other features now include a Marketplace site, allowing users to post free <u>classified</u> ads. (past participle)

An **infinitive** is the "to" form of a verb which can be a noun, an adjective, or an adverb in a sentence.

Example: There is even a way <u>to send</u> friends virtual gifts. (adjective)

C. Identify the types of verbals underlined in the sentences below. Write "G" for gerunds, "PSP" for present participles, "PTP" for past participles, and "I" for infinitives.

1. My friend sent me a <u>dancing</u> happy face on Facebook. ______
2. <u>Chatting</u> with friends online can be time-consuming. ______
3. You need to be 13 years old or above <u>to join</u> Facebook. ______
4. The Lintons like <u>putting</u> their family photos on Facebook. ______
5. They can share the <u>posted</u> albums with their friends. ______
6. This website has a large group of <u>devoted</u> fans. ______
7. <u>Visiting</u> the site has become his daily routine. ______
8. It's easy <u>to post</u> videos on Facebook. ______
9. The many <u>interesting</u> features and functions of Facebook have attracted many people to use this website. ______

D. Underline the infinitive in each sentence. State whether it functions as a noun, an adjective, or an adverb.

1. Kate promised her parents not to spend more than an hour on Facebook every day. ____________

2. Benny has chosen some photos to be put on Facebook. ____________

3. Remember to read the site's privacy agreement before signing up. ____________

4. You may be able to find your old friends on Facebook. ____________

5. The site continues to develop as more and more people join it. ____________

6. To have real-life interactions with others is essential. ____________

E. Change the verbs below to verbals and use them in sentences of your own.

1. visit (gerund)

____

2. participate (present participle)

____

3. write (past participle)

____

4. create (infinitive as noun)

____

5. help (infinitive as adverb)

____

"My Olympic Hero" Speech Competition

Good morning Principal Smith, teachers, and fellow students. Even though Sang Lan has never competed in the Olympic games, I think of her as my Olympic hero. You might think my choice is strange, or perhaps not a proper topic for this speech, which should be about "My Olympic Hero". Allow me to explain.

More than ten years ago, Sang Lan was one of China's top gymnasts. While competing at the Goodwill Games in New York in 1998, she lost control during a practice vault and broke her neck. She thought that her dream of becoming an Olympic athlete was lost forever.

But soon Sang Lan realized she didn't want to live a life of despair, sorrow, and bitterness. After months of difficult rehabilitation in the United States, Sang Lan returned to China and created a life for herself as a friendly personality and an inspiration to other disabled people in China. She continued with daily physical therapy, gaining back the use of her arms and shoulders to a significant degree. She wanted to get on with her life and live it the best way she could. She went back to school to work on a journalism degree, impressing her classmates with her "courage and exceptional spirit".

Sang Lan also began to realize that she could achieve her Olympic dream in other ways. For example, she was part of the Beijing Olympic Games Bid Committee. In 2004, she carried the Olympic torch during the Athens Olympic Games torch relay. She also carried the torch through Beijing during the torch relay leading up to the 2008 games. In addition, she hosted a TV talk show in China about the games, called "Sang Lan Olympics 2008". Sang Lan dreamed of representing China in the 2008 Paralympic Games as a ping-pong player, but this dream was not realized as her hands cannot grasp. Though Sang Lan cannot participate in any Olympic Games as an athlete, she plans to continue to be involved in future Olympics.

The story of Sang Lan shows me that even tragedy does not have to remain forever, and even a catastrophic injury does not have to define you. We must remember that when things don't always go the way we want them to, we can find other ways to achieve our dreams, and help other people achieve their dreams, too. Sometimes it may require us to tweak our dreams, but the end result is that we simply achieve new goals, and feel just as good for it.

So, next time I am watching the Olympic events on television, I will also be thinking about Sang Lan, wondering if she is in the stadium, watching – and dreaming – along with me.

A. Read the clues and complete the crossword puzzle with words from the passage.

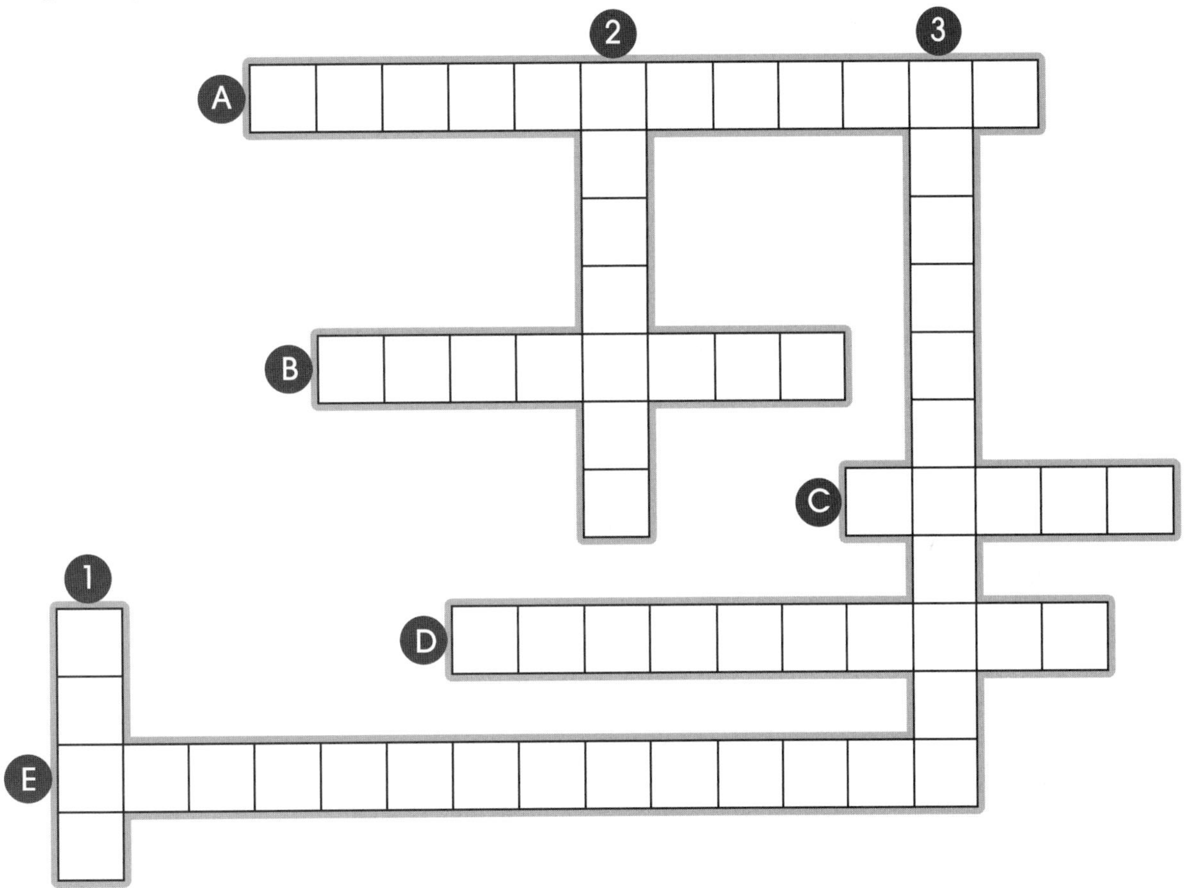

Across

A. Sang Lan's ____ injury did not cause her to live a life of despair and sorrow.

B. Sang Lan was among China's top ____ before the accident.

C. Sang Lan broke her neck during a practice ____ .

D. She wanted to get a degree in ____ .

E. Sang Lan's ____ in the United States was a hard experience.

Down

1. Sang Lan is the writer's Olympic ____ .
2. With daily physical ____ , Sang Lan regained the ability to use her arms.
3. Sang Lan is an ____ to other disabled people.

Noun Phrases

A **noun phrase** is a group of words that includes a noun as head and all its modifiers. It functions like a single noun in a sentence, and may be the subject, object, or complement of the sentence.

Examples: The story of Sang Lan shows me that even tragedy does not have to remain forever. (subject)

Sang Lan lost control in a practice vault and broke her neck. (object)

Ten years ago, Sang Lan was one of China's top gymnasts. (complement)

B. Identify the underlined noun phrases as the subject (SUB), object (OBJ), or complement (COM) of the sentences.

1. Sang Lan is the writer's Olympic hero. ________
2. Her tragic accident took place in 1998 at the Goodwill Games in New York. ________
3. Daily physical therapy helped Sang Lan gain back the use of her arms and shoulders to a significant degree. ________
4. Sang Lan has become an advocate for disabled people in China. ________
5. She is now taking journalism degree courses at Peking University. ________
6. "Sang Lan Olympics 2008" is a TV talk show hosted by Sang Lan. ________
7. Sang Lan's tough training to be a gymnast played an important role shaping her strong character. ________
8. Competing in the 2008 Paralympic Games as a ping-pong player was a dream that Sang Lan could not realize. ________

C. Read the following paragraph from the passage. Underline all the noun phrases.

Sang Lan also began to realize that she could achieve her Olympic dream in other ways. For example, she was part of the Beijing Olympic Games Bid Committee. In 2004, she carried the Olympic torch during the Athens Olympic Games torch relay. She also carried the torch through Beijing during the torch relay leading up to the 2008 games. In addition, she hosted a TV talk show in China about the games, called "Sang Lan Olympics 2008". Sang Lan dreamed of representing China in the 2008 Paralympic Games as a ping-pong player, but this dream was not realized as her hands cannot grasp. Though Sang Lan cannot participate in any Olympic Games as an athlete, she plans to continue to be involved in future Olympics.

D. Rewrite the following sentences by changing the underlined nouns to noun phrases.

1. All the people here are <u>athletes</u>.

   ____

2. <u>Rehabilitation</u> was a hard experience for Sang Lan.

   ____

3. What we all need is <u>practice</u>.

   ____

4. Every Olympic athlete has <u>dreams</u>.

   ____

Family "Memoirs" – the Gift of a Lifetime

Scrapbooking has become a booming industry in recent years. Walk into a scrapbooking shop or browse online, and the selection of colours, papers, patterns, stickers, borders, covers, and albums – not to mention entire scrapbooking furniture sets – will make your head spin. Why do so many people put such effort into this pastime? For many of us, it is important to remember life's lessons, good or bad, because these are the memories you want to share. It's about keeping your past alive in the present and future. The finished product is a keepsake, and the process itself also generates memories.

There are many ways to make memory books. Scrapbooking items can be bought online or in local shops. Pages can also be laminated and coil-bound, or slipped into the plastic pages of a clear book bought at any stationery store. If photography has been your preferred way to tell your family history, various websites specialize in making photo books. Doing an online search with the words "photo album making" will quickly put you onto a long list of online businesses that can create any family memento you can dream up. But this kind of family bookmaking needn't be only for photos. People are starting to write their own family history books. If you give it a try, you will be amazed at how grateful your cousins and aunts and uncles will be. The project will also inspire some of them to do a similar project relating to the other side of their family. Think of the fun you can have putting your favourite family photos on the book cover. You can hire printers to make any number of copies, large or small, and even hire book packagers and print-on-demand publishers to help see your project through to a more professional-looking finished product.

But family memories need not be on paper only – clothes can also be used and turned into precious family heirlooms. Old furs, woollen coats, chenille bedspreads, and ancient tweeds are being turned into gorgeous old-fashioned teddy bears, sold in the most up-market gift shops. The old baby clothes you are reluctant to part with can be given a new and practical lease on life by being sewn into quilts that can be kept for years and passed down – and used during the coldest weeks of Canadian winters. Making use of the clothes you feel you can't give away is a way of bringing memories back to life, not only for yourself but for others as well. And don't forget, there are other options as well: having your old baby shoes bronzed; having plaster casts of hands and feet (and not just a baby's!) made; turning favourite photos into canvas tote bags or coffee cups – all of these make treasured mementoes that have the benefit of utility as well.

So the next time you are wondering about what special gift you can give to family or friends – or yourself – think about creating family "memoirs" in any form. There is no better gift than the wisdom of a lifetime, or the chronicle of a life whose memories might otherwise fade way.

A. Use your dictionary to find the definitions of these words.

1. scrapbook ____________________
2. album ____________________
3. memoir ____________________
4. keepsake ____________________
5. memento ____________________
6. heirloom ____________________

Look at the definition of the word "memoir" you have found above. Do you know why the word is put in quotation marks in the title and the passage?

____

____

____

____

B. Among the different ways of creating family "memoirs" in the passage, which one will you choose? Why?

____

____

____

____

Verb Phrases

A **verb phrase** is a group of words that functions as a single verb in the sentence. It has a verb as its head.

Examples: Scrapbooking items <u>can be bought</u> online or in local shops. (head of verb phrase – "bought")

People <u>are starting</u> to write their own family history books. (head of verb phrase – "starting")

C. Underline the verb phrases and circle the head of each one in the following sentences.

1. Jenny is making a memory book.
2. She has taken a lot of photos to be put in the book.
3. She will bind the pages with a pretty ribbon.
4. Drawings of family members and friends can also be added.
5. What would be the best family "memoirs"?
6. You can buy any materials you can think of in this shop.
7. He would not have been able to think of what to make if I had not brainstormed ideas with him.
8. This quilt was made by Grandma and is treasured by everyone in the family.
9. My brother and I made a family photo DVD for our mother's birthday. She was so happy and surprised that she could not say a word.
10. This would be regarded as the best present Mom has ever received.

Verbal Phrases

A **verbal phrase** is a phrase that contains a gerund, a participle (present or past), or an infinitive. It functions as a noun, an adjective, or an adverb in the sentence.

Examples: It's about keeping your past alive with the present and future. (gerund phrase – noun)

Scrapbooking has become a booming industry in recent years. (present participle phrase – noun)

The finished product is a keepsake. (past participle phrase – noun)

For many, it is important to go through life and remember its lessons. (infinitive phrase – adverb)

D. Identify the types of verbal phrases below and make sentences of your own with them.

1. to organize the photos (phrase)

____

2. constructing a memory book ( )

____

3. the written family history ( )

____

4. getting the whole family involved ( )

____

5. to win the hearts of others ( )

____

6. the fading memories ( )

____

7

Superstitions around the World

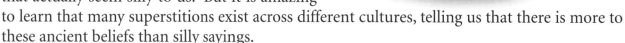

Have you ever walked around a ladder that was blocking your path, or turned down a side street to avoid walking where a black cat had just crossed? Have you ever worried about something bad happening if you saw a crack in a mirror or spilled some salt? We are all aware of superstitions, and have heard stories about how to avoid bad luck or gain good luck that actually seem silly to us. But it is amazing to learn that many superstitions exist across different cultures, telling us that there is more to these ancient beliefs than silly sayings.

A lot of superstitions are related to the naming of children. Based on the sheer amount of "dos and don'ts" regarding this topic, it is clear that the naming of children is an important undertaking in any culture and, it could be said, an indication of just how much we value our children. In the Dominican Republic, children are given nicknames ("apodo"), which are commonly used instead of given names. A given name is regarded as an important part of a person and must be kept secret to prevent the name from being used in a spell or a curse from a witch ("brujo"). Among Ashkenazi Jews, it is considered bad luck to name a child after a living relative. It is believed that this superstition originated from a common belief of the Middle Ages: that the Angel of Death could mistakenly take an infant instead of the aged relative it was named after. In the Jewish faith, it is popular practice to name a child after a deceased relative because doing so creates a deep bond between the soul of the child on earth and the soul of the person already in heaven, which will benefit the child.

In many places, such as India and Sri Lanka, parents are very concerned about their children being gazed upon by the "Evil Eye" (a malign spirit similar to the "brujo" of the Dominican Republic). To prevent this, parents used to give their children insulting names in the belief that it would save the child's life – after all, what spirit would want to take a child with the name of "Cowdung", "Rag", or "Rubbish"? Assigning infant children with such strange names was also practised in countries such as China and Korea for the same reason.

But perhaps we can think of superstitions – at least some of them – as common sense. For example, placing a hand over your mouth when sneezing may not have anything to do with preventing your soul from escaping – but it will cut down on the spread of germs! And why not make a wish next time you see a falling star or find a four-leaf clover? It is fun to be a hopeful and optimistic person. It certainly is bad luck to open an umbrella in the house – because in doing so you may easily knock something over and break it. And, as for bad luck happening when you walk under a ladder – face it, walking under a ladder is a tight fit for most of us, running the risk of knocking over the ladder and causing injury to yourself, if not others.

Perhaps there is more wisdom in those silly, old superstitions than we thought. Even so, it is undoubtedly a good thing that superstitions are no longer adhered to by so many people. After all, would you like to be given the nickname "Old Shoe"?

A. Read the clues and complete the crossword puzzle with words from the passage.

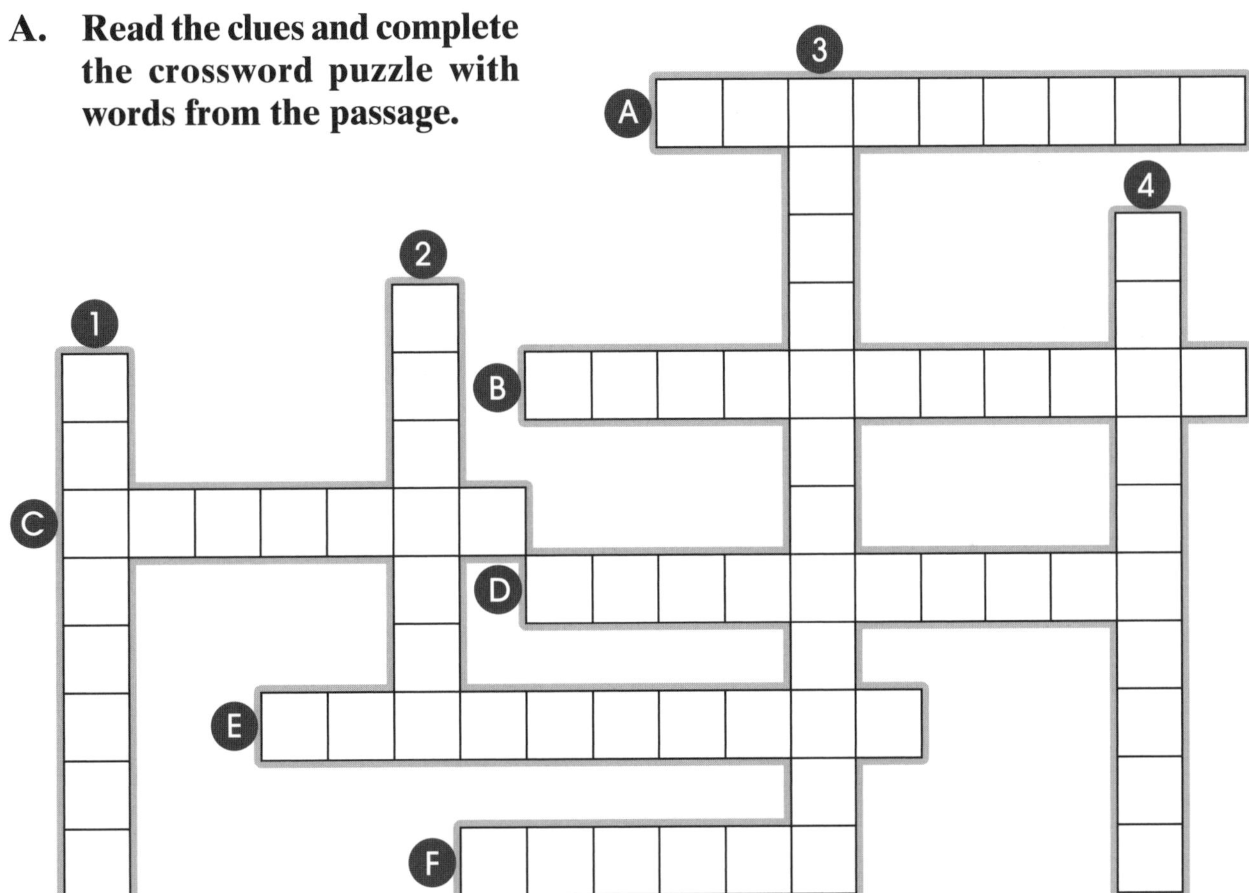

Across

A. giving
B. task or job
C. remained faithful
D. began to exist
E. hopeful about the future
F. harmful

Down

1. something that people do regularly
2. do good to
3. belief in things that cannot be explained
4. regarded as

Adjective Phrases

An **adjective phrase** is a group of words with one or more adjectives as head. It functions like a single adjective in a sentence.

Examples: In many places, parents are <u>very concerned</u> about their children being gazed upon by the "Evil Eye".
(head of adjective phrase - "concerned")

It is more fun to be a <u>hopeful and optimistic</u> person.
(heads of adjective phrase - "hopeful"; "optimistic")

B. Underline the adjective phrases and circle the head of each in the following sentences.

1. Making a wish upon seeing a shooting star is very common practice.
2. Some people give their children strange and insulting names out of superstition.
3. To convince others not to be so superstitious is somewhat difficult.
4. It is awfully silly of you to believe in the magical power of that product.
5. Mom is quite upset because, on her way home, a big black cat crossed her path.
6. Objective and scientific evidence does not affect some people's beliefs.

C. Write two sentences, each containing at least one adjective phrase.

1. ______________________________

____

2. ______________________________

____

Adjectival Phrases

An **adjectival phrase** can be any phrase that functions like an adjective. Adjectival phrases are usually hyphenated when they precede the nouns they are modifying.

Example: Make a wish next time you find a four-leaf clover.

D. Check if the underlined words form an adjectival phrase in the sentence.

1. The three-hour documentary unveils the strangest superstitions of different cultures. ☐

2. The professor is doing an in-depth study on the ancient beliefs of his country. ☐

3. The baby girl is named after her great-great-grandmother. ☐

4. She talked about the weird practice with a matter-of-fact look on her face. ☐

5. The play is a re-creation of the ancient practice on stage. ☐

6. Some people say that superstitions are by-products of people's ignorance. ☐

7. Janice is an easy-going person, so she doesn't care much about any superstitions. ☐

E. Write two sentences of your own using adjectival phrases.

1. ______________________________

____

2. ______________________________

____

Muhammad Yunus
and the Grameen Bank

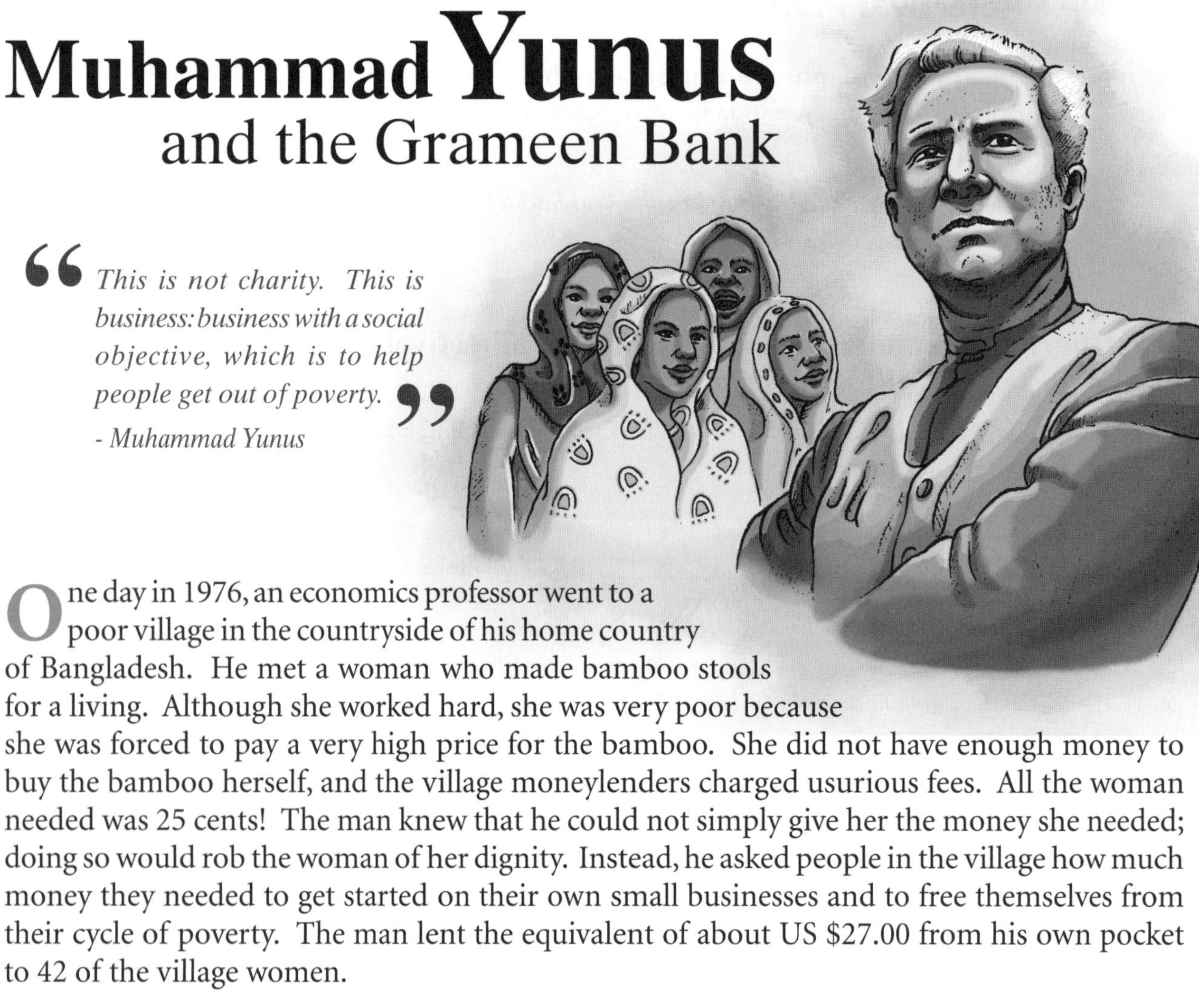

> *This is not charity. This is business: business with a social objective, which is to help people get out of poverty.*
>
> *- Muhammad Yunus*

One day in 1976, an economics professor went to a poor village in the countryside of his home country of Bangladesh. He met a woman who made bamboo stools for a living. Although she worked hard, she was very poor because she was forced to pay a very high price for the bamboo. She did not have enough money to buy the bamboo herself, and the village moneylenders charged usurious fees. All the woman needed was 25 cents! The man knew that he could not simply give her the money she needed; doing so would rob the woman of her dignity. Instead, he asked people in the village how much money they needed to get started on their own small businesses and to free themselves from their cycle of poverty. The man lent the equivalent of about US $27.00 from his own pocket to 42 of the village women.

That man was Muhammad Yunus, and that day in the village was the start of something big! Those women then started their own small businesses, earning money to support their families (their net profit on that first loan amounted to about two cents each). Muhammad Yunus went on to found the Grameen Bank, which has helped over two million Bangladeshi women escape the chains of poverty. The world now knows about the concept of "microcredit" – the granting of "micro-loans" to the very poor, to those without collateral and who would otherwise be rejected by conventional banks as loan recipients.

In 2006, the Nobel Peace Prize was awarded jointly to Muhammad Yunus and the Grameen Bank "for their efforts to create economic and social development from below". The Nobel Prize committee made a wise choice, reminding us that the road to peace must include concerted efforts to reduce the number of people living in poverty. The idea that microcredit can be a guiding principle for successful businesses is catching on throughout the developing world and also in developed nations like Canada and the United States. Like the Grameen Bank, the new microcredit lending institutions lend mostly to women.

Muhammad Yunus is a hero around the world. At one point, he was thinking about becoming involved in politics in Bangladesh, and formed a political party called "Citizens' Power" in 2007. So far, he has not embarked on a political career, but is a member of an international think tank of leaders called the Global Elders, of which Nelson Mandela is a founding member. He now speaks out about his theory of the "social business enterprise", which places value on enterprises that "generate social improvements and serve a broader human development purpose" in addition to focusing on economic gains. Yunus stresses that capitalism is too narrowly defined in that it focuses solely on profit maximization. Given what industrialization has done to this planet in the name of profit maximization, it is clear that the time has come for the world to get on board with Muhammad Yunus.

A. Write "T" for the true sentences and "F" for the false ones.

1. The woman Muhammad Yunus met in Bangladesh did not have money to buy stools, so she had to make her own bamboo stools. ______
2. Muhammad Yunus did not want to rob the woman of her dignity. ______
3. Muhammad Yunus lent money to the village women so that they could free themselves from poverty. ______
4. The village women started their own businesses and earned a net profit of two cents in all on the first loan. ______
5. "Microcredit" is the granting of "micro-loans" to very poor women in Bangladesh. ______
6. According to the writer, Muhammad Yunus's act of reducing the number of people in poverty will eventually lead to peace. ______
7. Microcredit lending institutions are set up in both developed and developing countries. ______
8. The Global Elders is a political party formed by Muhammad Yunus in Bangladesh. ______
9. Muhammad Yunus's theory of the "social business enterprise" does not simply emphasize economic gains. ______

Adverb Phrases

An **adverb phrase** is a group of words that describes a verb, an adjective, or an adverb. It functions like an adverb in a sentence.

Example: Yunus stresses that capitalism is too narrowly defined.

A **prepositional phrase** is an adverb phrase when it functions as an adverb.

Example: Yunus asked people how much money they needed to free themselves from their cycle of poverty.

An **infinitive phrase** can also be an adverb phrase.

Example: Those women then started their own small business to earn money.

B. Identify the underlined adverb phrases in the following sentences. Write "P" for prepositional phrases and "I" for infinitive phrases.

1. Muhammad Yunus is famous for introducing the concept of "microcredit" to Bangladesh. ______
2. Yunus founded the Grameen Bank to give loans to the poor in Bangladesh. ______
3. Conventional banks were not interested in giving loans to those without collateral. ______
4. Muhammad Yunus and the Grameen Bank were jointly awarded the Nobel Peace Prize in 2006. ______
5. Yunus would use part of his award money to set up a company to produce low-cost and high-nutrition food for poor people. ______
6. Yunus wrote *Banker to the Poor* to explain how he employed the idea of "microcredit" in the Grameen Bank to help the world's poor. ______
7. Many micro-lending programs have been established around the world. ______

C. Rewrite the following sentences by changing the underlined adverbs to adverb phrases.

1. The Global Elders consist of a group of <u>widely</u> respected world leaders.

2. The Global Elders contribute <u>greatly</u> to solving some very tough global problems.

3. The Elders are <u>generously</u> sponsored by a group of founders.

4. Nelson Mandela works <u>actively</u> in fighting for freedom and equality in African countries.

5. The Elders respond <u>quickly</u> to conflict situations around the world.

D. Write two sentences containing the following phrases as adverbs.

1. prepositional phrase

2. infinitive phrase

The New 7 Wonders of the World

You've heard of the Seven Wonders of the Ancient World: the Great Pyramid of Giza, the Hanging Gardens of Babylon, the Temple of Artemis at Ephesus, the Statue of Zeus at Olympia, the Mausoleum at Halicarnassus, the Colossus of Rhodes, and the Pharos of Alexandria. You've heard of the Seven Natural Wonders of the World: Mount Everest, the Great Barrier Reef, the Grand Canyon, Victoria Falls, the Harbour of Rio de Janeiro, Paricutin Volcano, and the Northern Lights. But that's not all; it seems that we love to make lists of wonders!

There are also the Seven Wonders of the Medieval Mind (including Stonehenge, the Leaning Tower of Pisa, and the Great Wall of China), the Seven Underwater Wonders of the World (including Lake Baikal, Palau, and the Galapagos Islands), and the Seven Wonders of the Modern World (including the Empire State Building, the Panama Canal, and the CN Tower). To add to the never-ending lists of seven wonders, there are the Seven Forgotten Natural Wonders (including the Bay of Fundy, Niagara Falls, and Mount Kilimanjaro), the Seven Forgotten Modern Wonders (including Mount Rushmore, the Eiffel Tower, and the Aswan High Dam), and the Seven Forgotten Wonders of the Medieval Mind (including Angkor Wat, the Parthenon, and Mont Saint-Michel).

On July 7, 2007, a New 7 Wonders of the World list was announced. With the help of Internet technology, people around the world were allowed to vote, and over 100 million online votes were cast. The website of the New 7 Wonders Foundation, which was administering the competition (www.new7wonders.com), was inundated with so many "hits" that its server crashed! From a whittled-down list of 21 sites, the final tally produced the definitive list of the world's top new man-made wonders: the Great Wall of China, Petra in Jordan, Brazil's statue of Christ the Redeemer, Peru's Machu Picchu, Mexico's Chichen Itza pyramid, the Colosseum in Italy, and India's Taj Mahal. The 14 runners-up included the Eiffel Tower, Timbuktu, the Statue of Liberty, Angkor Wat, Hagia Sophia, the Kremlin/St. Basil's, Stonehenge, and the Sydney Opera House.

The "New 7 Wonders" list is the idea of a Swiss businessman Bernard Weber, who felt that the people of the world should be able to decide – "not some government, not some individuals, not some institutions" – and that modern technology had finally made that prospect possible. UNESCO, the United Nations' cultural organization, is not affiliated with this "new wonders" project and has a much longer list of wonders in its World Heritage List – almost 900 sites at the moment – and it is still expanding (check it out at http://whc.unesco.org).

Whichever list you wish to peruse, there are plenty of places to imagine, to learn about, and even to visit – enough to fill many lifetimes. What a wonderful world we live in!

A. Complete the chart with the different lists of seven wonders in the passage and give an example for each.

List of Seven Wonders	Example

Prepositional Phrases

A **prepositional phrase** is a group of words with a preposition as head. It modifies a noun like an adjective, or a verb, an adjective, or an adverb like an adverb in a sentence.

Example: With the help of Internet technology, people around the world were allowed to vote.

"With the help of Internet technology" and "to vote" function like adverbs and modify the verbs "vote" and "allowed" respectively. "Of Internet technology" and "around the world" function like adjectives and modify the nouns "help" and "people" respectively.

B. Write "ADJ" if the underlined prepositional phrases function like adjectives and "ADV" if they function like adverbs.

1. There are various lists of wonders of the world. ________

2. Did you vote for the New 7 Wonders of the World online? ________

3. The new list was announced in Lisbon, Portugal in 2007. ________

4. You can visit the website of the New 7 Wonders Foundation to learn more about the new list. ________

5. The New 7 Wonders of Nature will be officially declared in the autumn of 2010. ________

6. The New 7 Wonders list is the idea of a Swiss businessman Bernard Weber. ________

7. "If we want to save anything, we first need to truly appreciate it," said Bernard Weber. ________

8. UNESCO has a World Heritage List of almost 900 sites. ________

C. Fill in the blanks with the appropriate prepositional phrases.

with 91 steps   at the centre   at the site

of the Mayan culture   in the Mayan language

for astronomical purposes   in 2007   of its four sides

Chichen Itza in Mexico is a UNESCO World Heritage Site and is rated as the most important archaeological site 1. ____________ . The name means "at the mouth of the well of the Itza" 2. ____________ . There are many outstanding ruins 3. ____________ , among which is the Temple of Kukulkan, also known as El Castillo (the castle), situated 4. ____________ of the city. The temple was voted one of the New 7 Wonders of the World 5. ____________ . It is a square-based pyramid 6. ____________ on each 7. ____________ . It is the largest and most important ceremonial structure at Chichen Itza and was built 8. ____________ .

D. Write two sentences, one using a prepositional phrase as an adjective and the other using one as an adverb.

1. ____________

____

2. ____________

____

10

Harmful Microorganisms

Some microorganisms are beneficial to us, while others can cause infectious diseases. Disease-producing microorganisms, such as viruses, bacteria, protists, and fungi, are called pathogens. They attach to the host tissue at the time of exposure, penetrate it, and then multiply. The host tissue becomes damaged, resulting in infectious disease. Most pathogens invade our body through skin wounds or through the layers of cells that line the cavities and surfaces of our digestive, respiratory, urinary, or reproductive systems.

At first, the number of pathogens that enter the host is too small to cause any damage; however, under favourable environmental conditions, such as an adequate nutrient supply, suitable temperatures, and suitable pH levels, the pathogens multiply rapidly in the host tissue, causing damage and illness. For example, viruses can take over the host cells' replication mechanisms and start multiplying in the host cells. Bacterial cells can block blood vessels or heart valves, or clog the lungs' air passages. A large number of pathogens may trigger an excessive inflammatory response in the host, as in the case of pneumonia. Many pathogenic bacteria, protists, and fungi damage the host by producing toxins or enzymes. Toxins diffuse into the host cells, disturbing their normal functions; enzymes break down the host's defence barriers, causing the spread of pathogens deeper into the tissues and further throughout the body.

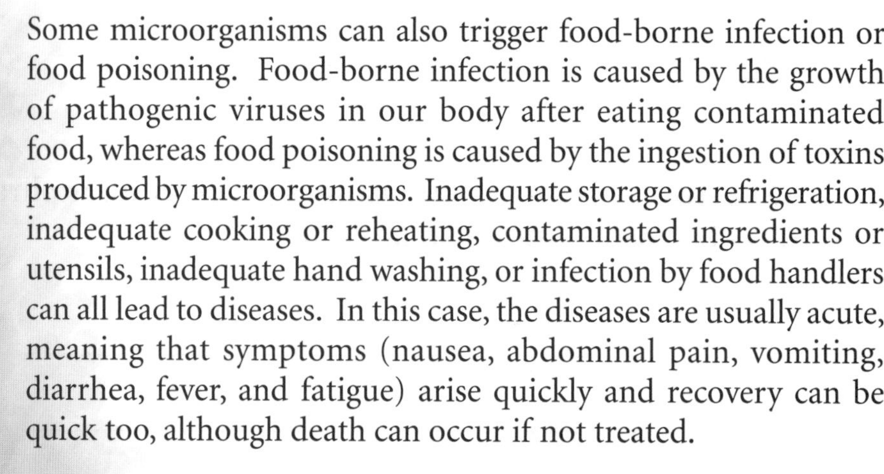

Some microorganisms can also trigger food-borne infection or food poisoning. Food-borne infection is caused by the growth of pathogenic viruses in our body after eating contaminated food, whereas food poisoning is caused by the ingestion of toxins produced by microorganisms. Inadequate storage or refrigeration, inadequate cooking or reheating, contaminated ingredients or utensils, inadequate hand washing, or infection by food handlers can all lead to diseases. In this case, the diseases are usually acute, meaning that symptoms (nausea, abdominal pain, vomiting, diarrhea, fever, and fatigue) arise quickly and recovery can be quick too, although death can occur if not treated.

The Salmonella bacterium is one of the most common causes of food-borne infection. Poultry, eggs, food made from raw eggs, and pre-cooked meat such as sausages, are commonly contaminated by Salmonella. Other causes include E. coli (found in the intestines of warm-blooded animals), which commonly contaminate undercooked beef, and noroviruses, found in faecal-contaminated water, which contaminate shellfish and vegetables washed in the water. The most common type of food poisoning is caused by the toxins produced by the Staphylococcus aureus bacterium. These bacteria exist in air, sewage, water, dust, milk, and on food equipment, humans, and animals. They are easily transferred to the skin, wounds, or nasal cavities of food handlers. When the contaminated food is left in a warm place (between 4°C and 60°C), the bacteria grow quickly and secrete a heat-stable toxin that disturbs the intestines of humans.

Since the SARS (Severe Acute Respiratory Syndrome – a serious and highly infectious form of viral-borne pneumonia) outbreak of 2003, we have become more concerned about the harmful effects of microorganisms and the occurrence of infectious diseases. It is good to know that most outbreaks can be mitigated or avoided by developing good hygiene habits and adhering to safe food preparation and handling methods.

A. Briefly describe the terms below.

1. pathogens

____

____

2. Salmonella

____

____

3. Noroviruses

____

____

4. Staphylococcus aureus

____

____

5. SARS

____

____

Clauses

A **clause** is a group of words that consists of a subject and a predicate. Every sentence consists of one or more clauses. A simple sentence is the most basic kind of sentence structure that is formed with one clause. A sentence with more than one clause has one or more conjunctions that link the clauses together.

Examples: Disease-producing microorganisms are called pathogens.
(a simple sentence with one clause)

Some microorganisms are beneficial to us, while others can cause infectious diseases.
(a sentence consisting of two clauses linked by "while")

B. Underline the clauses in the following sentences.

1. Pathogenic microorganisms are harmful because the diseases they cause may be fatal.

2. When meat is left at room temperature for many hours, the bacteria in it may multiply and contaminate the meat.

3. Illness caused by noroviruses is characterized by nausea, vomiting, and diarrhea.

4. Pathogens can evolve rapidly to avoid being detected by our immune system.

5. Most bacteria are harmless and a few are even beneficial, but some can cause infectious diseases.

6. Although influenza is often confused with the common cold, it is a more severe disease caused by a different kind of virus.

7. At human body temperature, flu viruses can remain infectious for a week but at 0°C, they can last for more than 30 days.

8. When we cough, we have to cover our mouth to avoid the spread of flu viruses.

Coordinate Clauses and Subordinate Clauses

Coordinate clauses are clauses linked by coordinating conjunctions such as "and", "or", and "but".

Example: <u>The symptoms arise quickly</u> and <u>recovery can be quick too</u>.

A **subordinate clause** is a clause that depends on another clause to complete its meaning. It is linked to the clause it depends on, known as the **main clause**, by a subordinating conjunction like "when", "if", or "since".

Example: <u>When the contaminated food is left in a warm place,</u>
(subordinate clause)
<u>the bacteria grow quickly</u>.
(main clause)

C. Find an example for each type of clause from the paragraph below.

We have to be very careful with what we eat, for food poisoning can be fatal. Even eating at home does not mean that we are safe from this infection. If we do not treat food properly, food poisoning can still occur. In fact, what we need to do is simple. Just remember the following: always wash your hands before and after preparing food. Never put raw meat together with cooked food and fresh fruit, and cook food thoroughly to destroy harmful germs. If you suspect that you have food poisoning, seek medical assistance immediately.

1. Coordinate Clause

____

____

2. Subordinate Clause

____

____

3. Main Clause

____

____

The Science of Dreams

It used to be that if someone called you a dreamer, it was an insult. But these days, people are beginning to appreciate the importance of being a dreamer – both during the day and at night! During the day, a form of "dreaming" is welcomed by innovative, creative businesses. For example, the company 3M (makers of Scotch Tape) allows employees to spend as much as 15% of their work time on their own "pet projects" and interests. This freedom to dream did provide a very good payoff to the company. Because of this policy, 3M employees Arthur Fry and Spencer Silver invented the Post-it note.

As for nighttime dreaming, it is now clear to us that we dream when we sleep, whether we remember it or not. We dream during the REM (rapid eye movement) stage of sleep, as well as at non-REM times. Some believe that dreams are a sort of re-creation of certain psychologically important events, and others ascribe meanings of dreams to long lists of all the things you see in your dreams, but the truth is that there are still many unanswered questions regarding the science of dreams.

Did you know?

- The word "dream" comes from the Middle English word "dreme" meaning *joy* and *music.*
- A third of your life is spent sleeping, and over a lifetime you will have spent six years dreaming.
- We dream about two hours per night.
- We can have, on average, four to seven dreams per night.
- Dreams not only are visual images, but also include sounds, smell, and tactility.
- Most dreams are forgotten within ten minutes of waking.
- Most people around the world dream about similar things, characters, social interactions, and emotions.
- Anxiety is the most common emotion associated with dreams.
- While people usually dream something once, many people experience recurring dreams. More females than males experience recurring dreams.
- People who cannot dream, due to sleep disorders, can suffer from personality disorders

due to lack of dreaming, in addition to sleep-related illnesses.

- Blind people dream, but only those that were once sighted say they dream with visual images.
- Scientific tests have shown us that our brains are more active when we are dreaming than when we are awake!
- You cannot dream when you are snoring.
- If you are awakened right after REM sleep, you may recall your dream better than if you were allowed to sleep until morning.
- Many people have reported experiencing déjà vu in their dreams. This is more common in females than in males.
- Not everyone dreams in colour. Some people's dreams are exclusively in black and white.

Who would have thought there is so much to know about the hours we sleep?

A. Choose and underline the correct answers.

1. "Pet projects" are ____ .

   A. projects related to the behaviours of different pets

   B. projects or goals pursued as personal favourites, rather than because they are regarded as necessary or important

2. Employees of 3M can spend ____ .

   A. no less than 15% of their work time on their own interests

   B. 15% of their work time at most on their own interests

3. We dream ____ .

   A. about two hours every night during both REM sleep and non-REM sleep

   B. about one third of our sleeping time during REM sleep

4. We can recall our dreams better if ____ .

   A. we sleep until morning

   B. we are awakened after REM sleep

Noun Clauses

A **noun clause** is a clause that functions as a noun in a sentence.

Example: Some people believe that dreams are a sort of re-creation of certain psychologically important events.

In this sentence, "that dreams are a sort of re-creation of certain psychologically important events" functions as the object of the verb "believe".

B. Check if the underlined words are noun clauses. Cross if they are not.

1. Whatever we dream of will be forgotten soon after we wake up. ______
2. A huge cockroach chased after me in my dream. ______
3. Do you remember the name of that famous dream interpreter? ______
4. I know that even animals have dreams. ______
5. Whether or not we understand the meaning of our dreams is not important. ______
6. Maggie writes down whomever she saw in her dreams. ______
7. I can tell that my baby brother is having a nightmare. ______
8. Sometimes my dreams are in black and white, but more often, they are in colour. ______
9. I am not surprised at what she dreamed of. ______
10. That he has never dreamed before is impossible. ______
11. I was so happy in the dream that I was still laughing the moment I woke up. ______

Adverb Clauses

An **adverb clause** is a clause that functions as an adverb in a sentence. It gives additional information about when, where, why, or how something happens.

Example: You cannot dream <u>when you are snoring</u>.

In this sentence, "when you are snoring" tells when you cannot dream.

C. Underline the adverb clauses in the text below.

Whenever you mention déjà vu to your friends, there will surely be one or two among them that tell you they have had this experience before.

Déjà vu means "already seen" in French. It refers to an uncanny feeling that you have experienced a new situation before.

When I was very young, I had this dream. I came to a temple on a beach. There was an open area built with concrete in front of it. I saw many old people sitting at big round tables. Although they were having a feast, I couldn't hear any sound. Then I saw a Chow-chow tied to a pole. I went over and played with it for a while. After I played with the dog, I turned round and found all the old people gone. I was all alone!

Many years later, I went on a trip with my family to an island in Southeast Asia. The tour guide took us to a beach. There I saw a temple with a concrete open area in front. It gave me the creeps the moment I saw it because it was the first time I had been to that island, but everything was exactly the same as in my dream, even the colours of the temple! The only difference was that there were no old people around. Do you know what the weirdest thing was? There was a Chow-chow tied to a pole near the temple!

It is said that "necessity is the mother of invention". This saying helps us understand why humans invented the wheel, learned to use fire for useful purposes such as cooking raw meat, and domesticated horses and dogs. Surely in this day and age there is nothing more we need, but maybe you disagree. Perhaps the need to create, or to invent, is part of our human DNA, or perhaps it is an irresistible urge, similar to the urge we have to express ourselves through the arts. There is still no shortage of weird inventions and crazy new contraptions, but it must be said that some of them may have been created to put a smile on our faces more than to serve a practical purpose.

In Japan, there seems to be quite a lot of these kinds of weird inventions. In fact, a word has been coined to describe such creations: *chindogu*. According to Kenji Kawakami, the amateur inventor and writer who coined the term in the late 80s, chindogu is "the art of invention based on an 'unuseless' idea". In other words, chindogu inventions may seem silly, but actually serve a real need. One example is a pillow with sensors that are meant to measure when the user has fallen into a deep sleep, at which time an alarm in the pillow will go off. This pillow is meant for the busy "salaryman" (a Japanese term for a busy office worker) who may be having a nap at his desk during lunchtime. Other chindogu inventions include: a hay-fever hat consisting of a roll of toilet paper strapped to one's head making it convenient for the person to blow his or her nose, a noodle-eater's hair guard consisting of a 15-centimetre-wide rubber ring fitted snugly around one's face to prevent liquids from splashing onto hair or clothes as he or she slurps up ramen or udon, a portable office tie fitted with tiny pockets on the underside – perfect for stashing necessities such as scissors, a calculator, paper clips, a pen, credit cards, etc.

Chindogu: Weird Inventions We Can Actually Use

According to Kawakami's "Ten Tenets of Chindogu", a chindogu contraption must exist, that is, a prototype must have been made. Also, these inventions cannot be for real use, and yet, paradoxically, they are tools for everyday life. Humour must not be the only reason for creating such items. Another tenet is that chindogu inventions should have the inherent spirit of anarchy. Kawakami adds that chindogu items are not for sale, are not propaganda, are never taboo, cannot be patented, and are without prejudice.

However, since chindogu inventions are a lot of fun and actually do serve a practical purpose, many things in Japan and elsewhere that seem chindogu at first have made it into the mainstream. In Canada, for example, one can buy a certain dental hygiene product that looks like quilted-cotton finger puppets, but are in fact bristle-less "toothbrushes" for people who feel they need to brush on the go. Such an item, albeit with bristles, is already in the chindogu catalogue. Also, at the 2006 Hong Kong Footwear Design Contest, a pair of running shoes made from computer keyboards, called "IT", won top prize in the sports category. Does this mean "IT" is something from which we can no longer run away? How chindogu!

A. Write in point form Kawakami's "Ten Tenets of Chindogu".

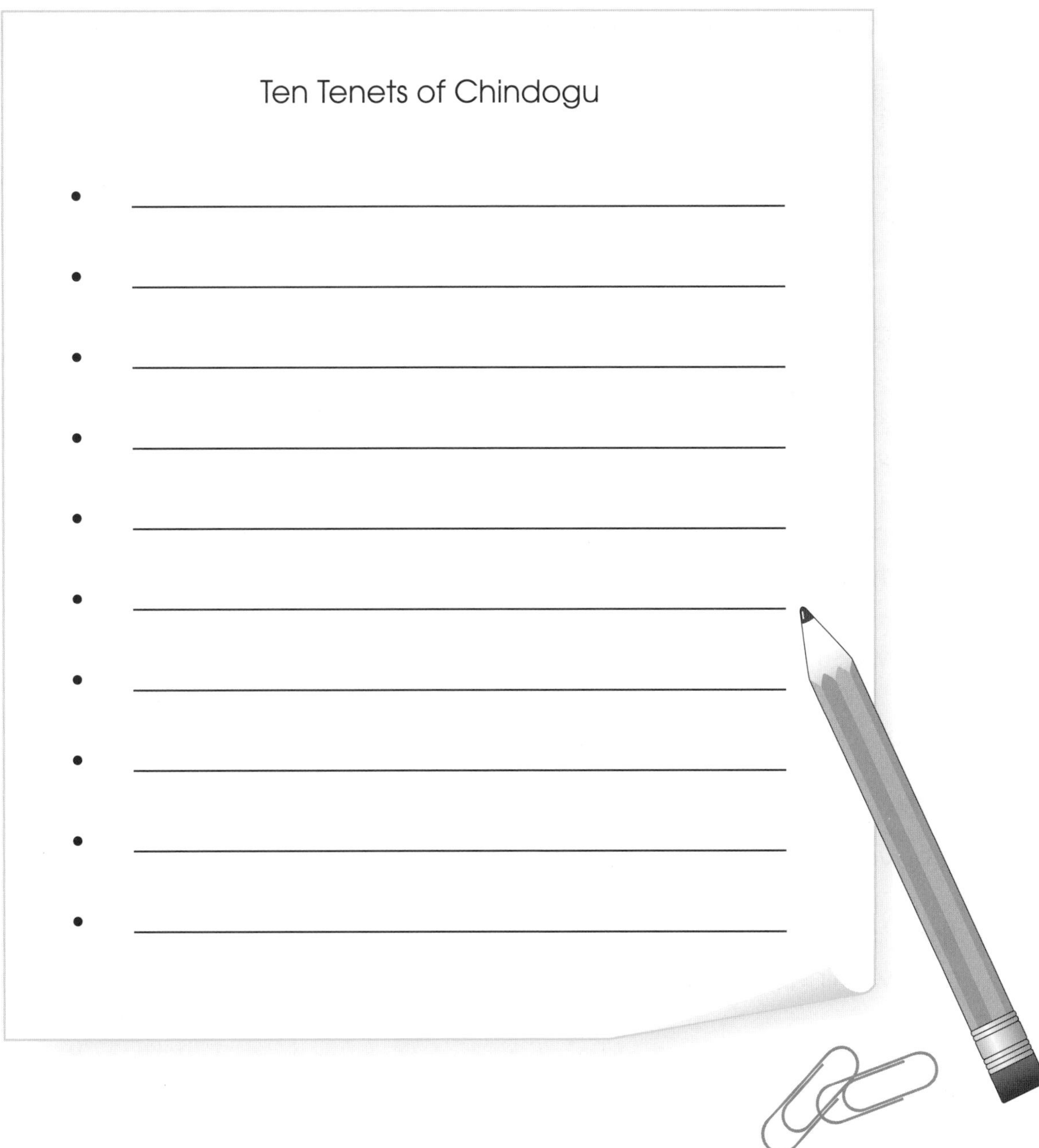

Relative Clauses

A **relative clause** is a subordinate clause that helps identify someone or something, or provides information about them. It is also called an adjective clause or adjectival clause since it describes a noun. It goes immediately after the noun it relates to. A **relative pronoun** (who, whom, whose, which, that) or a **relative adverb** (when, where, why) is used to link a relative clause to the part of the sentence it describes.

Example: The bristle-less "toothbrushes" are for people <u>who feel they need to brush on the go</u>.

B. Underline the relative clause in each of the following sentences.

1. Necessity is the reason why there are so many inventions.
2. The pillow has sensors that measure when the user has fallen into a deep sleep.
3. This invention is meant for the busy "salaryman" who may be having a nap during lunchtime.
4. Kenji Kawakami, whose books have been translated into many different languages, is the founder of the International Chindogu Society.
5. The inventor to whom the prize was awarded has become famous worldwide.
6. That was the time when these two great inventors first met in history.
7. Have you been to the country in which the design contest is held?
8. The convention centre where the exhibition was held will be closed for renovation.
9. The little problems that we encounter in our daily lives are inspirations for many chindogu inventions.
10. This is the invention that has been voted The Weirdest Invention of the Year.

Defining and Non-defining Relative Clauses

Relative clauses can be defining or non-defining.

A **defining relative clause** identifies or describes a particular person or thing.

A **non-defining relative clause** simply provides additional information about the person or thing. It is separated from the main sentence by commas.

Examples: The amateur inventor who coined the term "chindogu" is also a writer. (defining)

Kenji Kawakami, who coined the term "chindogu", is an amateur inventor and writer. (non-defining)

The relative clause in the first example is defining because without it, one cannot tell which amateur inventor the sentence is about.

C. Add a defining or non-defining relative clause to each of the following sentences.

1. The inventor ______________________________ ______________________________ has come up with a fun invention.

2. A chindogu invention should be one ______________________________ ______________________________.

3. Will you join the design competition ______________________________ ______________________________?

4. There are a lot of chindogu inventions in Japan, ______________________________ ______________________________.

5. The running shoes "IT", ______________________________ ______________________________, won top prize in the sports category.

6. The "Ten Tenets of Chindogu", ______________________________ ______________________________, was written by Kenji Kawakami.

Totem Poles

Have you ever seen a totem pole? Even if you have not had the good fortune of seeing them in person along the Pacific Northwest, you have probably seen them on television. They are monuments carved in wood, usually from large red cedar trees, and are an important tradition in many of the aboriginal cultures along the Pacific Northwest coast of North America. It is believed that the English word "totem" comes from an Anishinaabe word *doodem*, meaning "clan".

Totem poles are a type of heraldry recording a variety of information, depending on the group involved. Some totem poles record clan lineage, while others are in fact historical records of the community. There are also some that depict the group's legends. This art form is ancient, but due to the humid climate of the region (which encourages decay of organic matter), there are very few totem poles built prior to the 1800s still around today. The Royal British Columbia Museum in Victoria, BC, has one dated pre-1400s! Totem pole construction declined in the early 1900s as European settlers discouraged aboriginal groups from continuing with their traditional ways.

Ainu, the aboriginal people of the northern island of Hokkaido, Japan, are also makers of totem poles. Their totem poles are smaller because the sources of wood are much smaller trees than those found along the Pacific Northwest, and they are not painted. You can find Ainu totem poles in the Vancouver area at Burnaby Mountain Park, near Simon Fraser University. Staring up at these awesome carvings, you may wonder how it came to pass that the aboriginal culture of Japan – the Ainu – would have something similar to the First Nations' totem poles in Vancouver in their tradition. Perhaps it is more proof of the "land bridge" that is said to have existed across today's Bering Sea, and that the aboriginal cultures of Canada and Asia are indeed related.

Totem poles can also be found in other parts of the world, although they are a little different. The Maori people of New Zealand have smaller "totem poles", as do cultures in Tahiti, India, and parts of Africa. Anthropologists tend to make a distinction between the totem poles of Canada and the wooden figures of these other places. They refer to the latter carvings as "ancestor figures", "greet figures", "talismans", or "tikis". This is because, in the latter cultures, these wooden figures were made for the purposes of ancestor worship or identifying taboos, or as depictions of their gods.

Totem poles are sacred objects and cannot be made by just anyone. In Canada, authentic totem poles can only be made by trained members of West Coast Aboriginal groups. Only in very rare cases can a non-aboriginal be sanctioned to do this work. The totem pole must also be sanctioned or "blessed" in a special ceremony undertaken by qualified aboriginal elders.

The majestic and awe-inspiring totem poles we see in aboriginal villages, and in parks lucky enough to have been gifted one or several, are not only testaments to the beauty of aboriginal art, but also to the beauty of aboriginal heritage.

A. Based on the information in the passage, explain the cause or effect of the following.

1. Cause: Humid climate encourages decay of organic matter.

   Effect: ______________________________

   ____

2. Cause: ______________________________

   ____

   Effect: Totem pole construction declined in the early 1900s.

3. Cause: ______________________________

   ____

   Effect: Ainu totem poles are smaller.

4. Cause: Wooden figures found in places like Tahiti and India were made for ancestor worship or identifying taboos, or as depictions of their gods, unlike the totem poles found in Canada.

   Effect: ______________________________

   ____

5. Cause: ______________________________

   ____

   Effect: Authentic totem poles can only be made by trained members of West Coast Aboriginal groups.

Types of Sentences

Simple sentence: consists of one single clause

Compound sentence: made up of two or more coordinate clauses linked by "and", "or", or "but"

Complex sentence: made up of one main clause joined to one or more subordinate clauses with subordinate conjunctions like "because" and "although"

Compound-complex sentence: made up of two or more coordinate main clauses along with one or more subordinate clauses

B. Identify the types of sentences below. Write "S" for simple sentences, "CP" for compound sentences, "CX" for complex sentences, and "CPX" for compound-complex sentences.

1. My parents had a week's holiday last month, and they took my sister Angie and me on a trip to Vancouver. ________

2. We flew there so that we could have more time in Vancouver. ________

3. Since Angie has a great fear of heights, she didn't enjoy the flight. ________

4. We visited some tourist attractions, including Grouse Mountain, the Vancouver Aquarium, and the Burnaby Village Museum. ________

5. As my cousin Lucas studies at the University of British Columbia, and he resides on the campus, we went there to visit him. ________

6. He had planned to take us to the Museum of Anthropology to see the totem poles, but the museum was closed for innovations. ________

7. He took us to see the famous totem poles at Stanley Park instead. ________

C. Find an example of each below from the passage.

1. a simple sentence

2. a compound sentence

3. a complex sentence with the conjunction "while"

4. a complex sentence with the conjunction "although"

5. a complex sentence with the conjunction "even if"

6. a complex sentence with the conjunction "as"

7. a compound-complex sentence

One More Reason to Save the **Rainforest**

As we all know by now, the large rainforests scattered around the world, and the Amazon Rainforest in particular, are the "lungs" of our planet. They soak up much of the carbon dioxide we produce and give us life-sustaining oxygen in return.

The world's rainforests are also home to the majority of the planet's plant and wildlife species; we can thank rainforests for the *biodiversity* of our world, which has benefited the human species in many ways. For example, rainforest ecosystems have provided us with not only a variety of herbs and medicines, but also many very healthy things to eat! In fact, some of our favourite snacks contain ingredients originally sourced from the rainforest, such as the cocoa in chocolate and the kola nut from which cola drinks are derived, not to mention coconuts, cashews, macadamia nuts, ginger, vanilla, bananas, corn, and cinnamon. And what could we dip our nacho chips in if we didn't have the tomatoes and avocadoes needed for salsa?

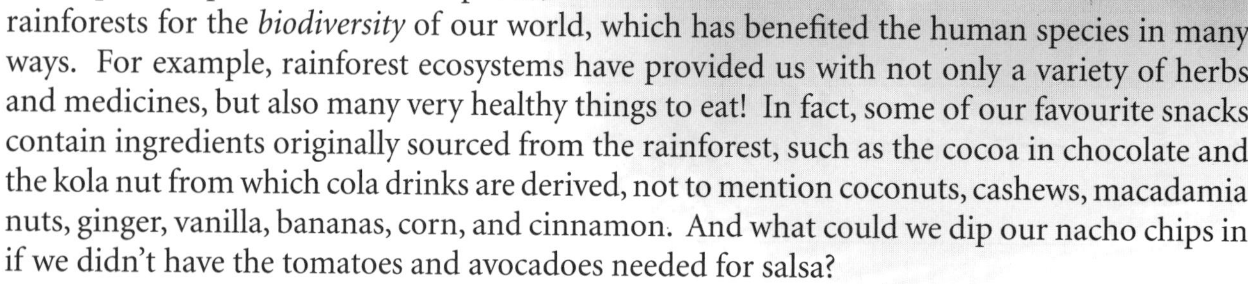

The foods listed above are all commercially grown now and are known to people around the world. We are also becoming familiar with a variety of rainforest foods that provide real health benefits. These are called "superfoods", and the indigenous peoples inhabiting the world's rainforests have long known about their healthy benefits. These days, urban dwellers and people in far-away places can also benefit from these "magical" plant items. Below are three "superfoods" that may be unknown to you.

The acai berry (pronounced as-sigh-ee) is a small purple fruit grown in bunches (like grapes) on tall palm trees. It tastes like a blend of field berries and chocolate, and is full of antioxidants, amino acids, and essential fatty acids. Antioxidants help lower the risk of heart disease, and these little berries have 30 times more antioxidants than red grapes. Fatty acids help brain function, and acai also provides loads of energy. It can be mixed into smoothies or sorbet, or drunk as a juice.

The yerba mate is a type of holly found in subtropical South American countries. A special tea can be made by steeping dried leaves and small twigs from this plant. It tastes like herbal tea – slightly grassy – but does not become bitter when steeped for a long time. It gives us minerals we need, such as potassium, magnesium, and manganese. It has a kind of caffeine-like stimulant, but is gentler on the stomach than coffee or tea.

The cupuassu is a tree found in the rainforests of Brazil. The fruit of this tree is encased in brown, fuzzy, oblong pods, up to two kilograms in weight and covered in a thick skin. The cream-coloured, pulpy fruit inside is wonderfully fragrant and contains theacrine, an alkaloid believed to boost our immune systems, lower cholesterol levels, and ward off cancer. It is often mixed into ice cream and jams or made into juice blends.

These three rainforest products – all from South America – are becoming increasingly popular among society's more health-conscious people. More and more special food items like these are being discovered every week. We need to protect our rainforests to make sure that such plants are not lost to us, before they are even "discovered".

A. Write in your own words the main idea of each paragraph.

Paragraph 1 ____

____

Paragraph 2 ____

____

Paragraph 3 ____

____

Paragraph 4 ____

____

Paragraph 5 ____

____

Paragraph 6 ____

____

Paragraph 7 ____

____

Word Roots

Many English words are derived from Greek and Latin **word roots**. Understanding these roots helps us get the meanings and spellings of the derivatives right more easily.

Example: word root – extra
meaning – outside; beyond
derivatives – extracurricular ; extraterrestrial; extraordinary

B. Find derivatives that contain the word roots below from the passage.

	Root	Meaning	Derivative
1.	maj	greater; larger	______________
2.	kilo	thousand	______________
3.	de	from	______________
4.	anti	against	______________
5.	di	two	______________
6.	bene	good	______________
7.	medic	heal; cure	______________
8.	bio	life	______________
9.	eco	home	______________
10.	pop	people	______________
11.	vari	different	______________
12.	super	beyond; more than	______________
13.	sub	below	______________
14.	con	with; together	______________

Prefixes and Suffixes

Groups of letters can be added to some base words to modify their meanings.

A **prefix** refers to a group of letters added to the beginning of a base word.

Example: perfect → <u>im</u>perfect (not perfect)

A **suffix** refers to a group of letters added to the end of a base word.

Example: perfect → perfect<u>ly</u> (in a perfect manner)

C. Find words from the passage that are derived from the base words below and have the meanings in the parentheses. Make sentences of your own with the derivatives.

1. dwell (people who dwell in a place) ______

____

2. know (not known) ______

____

3. herb (consisting of herbs) ______

____

4. gentle (with a higher degree of gentleness) ______

____

5. origin (with respect to origin) ______

____

6. cover (found something previously not known) ______

____

A. **Check if the subject-verb agreement in the following sentences is correct. If not, rewrite the sentences.**

1. All students gathers together every morning to sing the National anthem. ☐

   ____

2. Playing basketball, as well as doing yoga, are among my favourite hobbies. ☐

   ____

3. Whoever make the most beautiful cake wins the prize. ☐

   ____

4. Someone has tried to call you many times. ☐

   ____

5. Neither of your friends need a bus ticket to go home. ☐

   ____

B. **Fill in each blank with the simple past tense or past perfect tense of the given verbs.**

1. The boys (buy) ____________ some beautiful carnations for their mother before they (celebrate) ____________ Mother's Day.
2. Our boat (not be) ____________ able to reach the shore before the night (fall) ____________ .
3. Mom (make) ____________ sure she (turn) ____________ off the oven before we (go) ____________ out.
4. The snowstorm (hit) ____________ the city the day after we (leave) ____________ .

C. Using the words provided, write a sentence in the active voice and one in the passive voice.

1. **Daniel cooked delicious bowl of spaghetti**

   Active: ______________________________

   ____

   Passive: ______________________________

   ____

2. **Susan donate old toys charity**

   Active: ______________________________

   ____

   Passive: ______________________________

   ____

D. Change the verbs below to verbals and make your own sentences with the verbals.

1. limit (gerund)

   ____

2. post (infinitive)

   ____

3. fascinate (present participle)

   ____

4. devote (past participle)

   ____

E. Change the underlined nouns and verbs in the paragraph below to noun phrases and verb phrases.

Christmas (1) remains one of Canada's favourite holidays. The local malls are filled with (2) shoppers who (3) scramble for that very last gift on their shopping list. This (4) holiday is all about family gatherings. My family would gather around my grandmother's dining table to eat a hearty meal and share our interesting holiday stories. My favourite part of the holiday is the mystical and joyous Christmas spirit that fills every corner of downtown Toronto. The dazzling light bulbs and (5) ornaments hanging on every Christmas tree would surely bring a (6) smile to everyone.

1. ____________________ 2. ____________________

3. ____________________ 4. ____________________

5. ____________________ 6. ____________________

F. Write the type of verbal phrase in the parentheses. Then make a sentence with the given phrase.

infinitive **gerund** **present participle** **past participle**

1. the cascading waterfall (phrase)

____

2. building a doll house (phrase)

____

3. the completed ghost story (phrase)

____

4. to participate in athletic activities (phrase)

____

G. Underline the adjective phrases and adjectival phrases in the following sentences. Write "ADJ" for adjective phrases and "ADL" for adjectival phrases.

1. We will not go to that loud and rowdy theatre again. ________
2. I made a last-minute decision to join the team. ________
3. Tony is the fastest swimmer on his team. ________
4. My one-year-old nephew has recently begun talking. ________
5. For my birthday, my mother bought me a brown and white puppy. ________
6. Billy believes wholeheartedly in the magic of a four-leaf clover. ________
7. Rufus became completely hysterical when he saw the dog. ________

H. Complete the following paragraph with the specified phrases.

I have a 1.________________ (adjective phrase) pet dog. I call him Rocky. I take Rocky out for a walk 2.________________ (adverb phrase). We often play fetch 3.________________ (prepositional phrase – adverb). Rocky's favourite spot at home is the armchair 4.________________ (prepositional phrase – adjective). He enjoys sleeping in it whenever my family sits together to chat or watch television.

Review 1

I. Find an example of each type of clause from the passage below.

We have to be more aware of what we do to the environment since our planet is in peril. The mere act of taking the bus to school does not mean we are doing enough to help. Changing our daily activities, such as recycling plastic bottles instead of throwing them away and setting the air conditioning system to a lower temperature at home, can help a great deal. We should not let the tap run when we are brushing our teeth, and we should always remember to turn off the tap when we are finished. If we see our friends waste paper, we should tell them about the harmful effects of cutting down trees to produce paper.

Protecting our environment is not a job for one individual but rather a responsibility for all who inhabit this planet. Let's not be selfish and inconsiderate, but try our very best to save energy whenever possible.

1. Coordinate clause: ____________________

2. Subordinate clause: ____________________

3. Noun clause: ____________________

4. Adverb clause: ____________________

5. Relative clause: ____________________

J. Identify the types of sentences. Write "S" for simple sentences, "CP" for compound sentences, "CX" for complex sentences, and "CPX" for compound-complex sentences.

1. Many of us visited other places in Canada for our Christmas vacation, but Bob had fallen ill with chicken pox, and he was unable to participate in our Canadian adventure. ________
2. When all our guests have arrived, we will start our dinner. ________
3. We are planning to watch the ballet "The Nutcracker" this Christmas. ________
4. Should we start by mixing all the ingredients together or should we begin with preheating the oven? ________
5. As the temperature falls to below zero degrees in Northern Ontario, we should take advantage of the cold weather and go skiing, and maybe we can build a snowman, too. ________

K. Write the meaning of each word root in the parentheses. Think of a derivative and make a sentence with it.

1. hydro ( )

   ____

2. geo ( )

   ____

3. dis ( )

   ____

4. micro ( )

   ____

5. inter ( )

   ____

The Endangered Tibetan Antelope

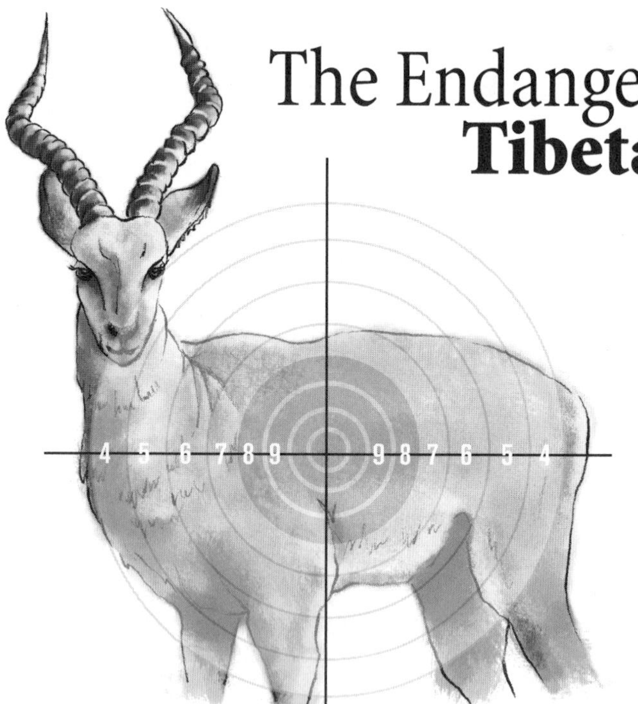

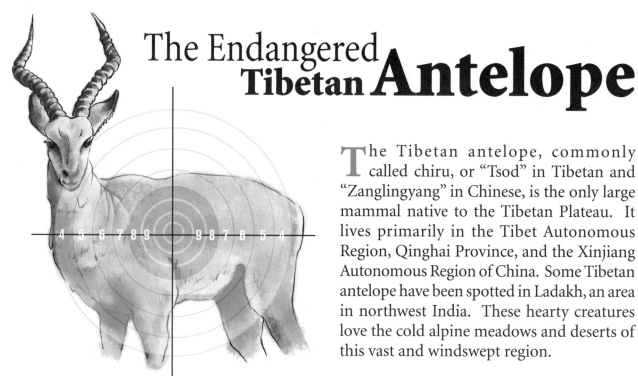

The Tibetan antelope, commonly called chiru, or "Tsod" in Tibetan and "Zanglingyang" in Chinese, is the only large mammal native to the Tibetan Plateau. It lives primarily in the Tibet Autonomous Region, Qinghai Province, and the Xinjiang Autonomous Region of China. Some Tibetan antelope have been spotted in Ladakh, an area in northwest India. These hearty creatures love the cold alpine meadows and deserts of this vast and windswept region.

The Tibetan antelope is related to wild goats and sheep. Males are 80 to 85 centimetres high at the shoulder and weigh about 35 to 40 kilograms. They have slender, curving black horns that can grow to as long as 50 to 60 cm! Females are slightly smaller and do not have horns. Their coat colouring ranges from grey to reddish-brown with a white underside. In the winter, the male Tibetan antelope develops black markings on its face and legs. The Tibetan antelope can survive in temperatures as cold as 40 degrees Celsius below zero, grazing on the sturdy plants and grasses of the region. It seems like an inhospitable place for such a gorgeous animal.

A hundred years ago, it is believed that herds of a million chiru roamed the Tibetan Plateau. Today the estimated number is less than 75 000. This is because these animals have been hunted down for the fine hair beneath their thick coat of wool (the secret to how they stay so warm), called shahtoosh. Each animal must be killed in order to harvest the ultra-fine hairs at the skin; the hair cannot be shorn as in the case of sheep's wool. This shahtoosh is desired by people all over the world. It is very warm, and can be woven into shawls so fine they can pass through a wedding ring! One shahtoosh shawl is worth thousands of dollars, and is one of the most sought-after items among wealthy people.

Because of this, people illegally hunt the Tibetan antelope, despite the fact that it is protected by Chinese law. Each year, between three and five thousand Tibetan antelope are killed by poachers to supply the illegal trade in shahtoosh fibre. Some estimate that the figure could be as high as 15 or even 20 thousand! Wildlife officials in the region are outnumbered by the armed hunters who shoot the animals and then sell the shahtoosh to international smugglers.

Why is it that so many people are willing to kill endangered animals when they know it is wrong? Just as in the trade of ivory, poverty causes some people to resort to criminal activity in order to feed their families and get their daily necessities. Many think we cannot blame the impoverished poachers. Instead, to solve the problem of illegal poaching, we must target not just the suppliers, but also those who demand the luxury product. Efforts are being made to ban the sale of shahtoosh around the world as a way to protect this endangered species, but this will not be enough. Fewer people are now wearing fur, compared to a couple of decades ago, due to the efforts of those against the slaughter of animals for fur. These same people must now turn their attention to the Tibetan antelope, and tell the world that it is not fashionable or glamorous to kill such a beautiful animal simply to wear a fabric that can fit through a wedding ring.

A. Complete the chart about the Tibetan antelope below.

The Tibetan Antelope

Other Names:	1. ______
Species:	related to 2. ______
Habitat:	3. ______ ______
Population:	4. ______
Size (Male):	5. ______ ______
(Female):	6. ______
Coat Colour:	7. ______
Special Features:	8. ______ ______ ______ ______
Main Diet:	9. ______

Easily Confused Words

We often confuse words that have similar sounds or spellings, or are related in meanings. We should look up words in a dictionary when in doubt, to make sure we are using the right words.

B. Fill in the blanks with the correct words to complete the paragraphs.

The Tibetan antelope 1. ______ (lives / leaves) in the Tibetan Plateau region, which is covered with widespread 2. ______ (deserts / desserts) and cold alpine meadows. They 3. ______ (grace / graze) on the sturdy plants and grasses in the region. Male Tibetan antelope have 4. ______ (slander / slender), black horns, while females are hornless. Tibetan antelope have ultra-fine hair called shahtoosh under 5. ______ (there / their) thick coat of wool. This is the 6. ______ (secret / secrete) to how they stay warm in their cold habitat, where temperatures can reach as low as 40 7. ______ (decrees / degrees) Celsius below zero.

Since shahtoosh can be woven into very warm shawls and sold at very high 8. ______ (prices / prizes), 9. ______ (porches / poachers) kill Tibetan antelope for these ultra-fine hairs and 10. ______ (sale / sell) them to smugglers, 11. ______ (despise / despite) the fact that it is against Chinese law to hunt these endangered animals.

C. Write sentences with the words below to show the difference in their meanings.

1. grace ______________________________

   graze ______________________________

2. slander ______________________________

   slender ______________________________

3. secret ______________________________

   secrete ______________________________

4. decree ______________________________

   degree ______________________________

5. sale ______________________________

   sell ______________________________

6. despise ______________________________

   despite ______________________________

As a Canadian student, you have access to a computer. Perhaps you even have one all to yourself. These days, especially for students, a computer is considered a necessity, not a luxury. You may even have spent time wondering how on earth people managed without computers, which is what we did in the years before you were born.

Canadian students are lucky; there is a high standard of living in this country, and most people can afford the cost of computers. But in developing countries, this cost is way beyond the reach of most people. How do students in those countries manage without computers? Imagine how much more those students could learn if they had their own computer! And not only that, imagine how students around the world could communicate with one another if each one had a computer. It could help to make the world a better place.

This was the dream of Nicholas Negroponte, the founding chairman of the Massachusetts Institute of Technology's Media Lab. To make it happen, he set about developing a computer that would cost only one hundred U.S. dollars. This price tag would motivate governments of poor countries to purchase computers for all their students. Negroponte met with government leaders and got assurances from several (including the leaders in Nigeria, Brazil, and Thailand) that they would buy millions. The more computers that could be produced for purchase, the cheaper the cost. And so began Nicholas Negroponte's One Laptop Per Child (OLPC) project.

One Laptop Per Child

In November 2005, at the World Summit on the Information Society in Tunisia, Negroponte and UN Secretary General Kofi Annan unveiled a working prototype of the computer, called XO. In addition to word processing capability, this green and white laptop had a built-in wireless network interface and a colour camera. It had no hard disk, but came with 1 GB of flash memory. To help save power (a major concern in developing countries), the computer had a dual-mode screen; it could switch from black-and-white to colour. By the end of 2006, the first prototypes had been shipped, and the first large-scale production line began in November 2007. The final cost of this computer turned out to be about US $188 per unit, but for many, it was close enough, and people around the world were looking forward to the notion of students in developing countries being given their own personal laptop computer, a better education, and a brighter future.

But the story of the $100 laptop has not been smooth sailing. Negroponte's plan was to supply computers to children as a not-for-profit endeavour. Companies who were in the business of making and selling computers knew that this would have an adverse effect on their profits. So the larger computer manufacturers began developing their own low-cost computers, with software to go with it, not to mention brand recognition. As a result, some of the governments of countries who, at first, pledged to buy the XO, backed out of the deal and bought the laptops developed by OLPC's new competitors. Whatever the future of the OLPC organization, Nicholas Negroponte and his team at MIT must be recognized as the leaders of the global movement to provide affordable computers to the children of the world.

A. Answer these questions.

1. In what ways can computers enrich our learning experience?

____

____

____

____

2. What problem did the OLPC project encounter?

____

____

____

____

3. If you were the government leader of a developing country, would you purchase computers for all students in your country? Why or why not?

____

____

____

____

Capitalization

Follow these basic rules of capitalization:

1. at the beginning of a sentence, except for one that is put in parentheses within another sentence
2. names of particular people, things, projects, and organizations
3. titles when used before names but not after names
4. names of places and countries, and adjectives derived from names of countries
5. days of the week, months, holidays, and special events
6. main words in titles – do not capitalize articles, prepositions, and coordinating conjunctions
7. abbreviations

B. Refer to the rules above. Decide which rules of capitalization the underlined words in the sentences below follow. Write the numbers on the lines.

1. Many Canadian students have access to a computer. ______
2. Nicholas Negroponte is the founding chairman of the Massachusetts Institute of Technology's Media Lab. ______
3. He began the One Laptop Per Child project. ______
4. Negroponte and UN Secretary General Kofi Annan unveiled a working prototype of the computer in 2005. ______
5. The computer was named XO. ______
6. It came with 1 GB of flash memory. ______
7. The computer could switch from black-and-white to colour. ______
8. The mass production of the computer started in November 2007. ______
9. I first got to know about OLPC from the article "OLPC Gives Poor Children Hope". ______

C. Rewrite the following sentences using proper capitalization.

1. xo was unveiled at the world summit on the information society held in tunisia in November 2005.

2. inspired by the olpc project, the brazilian government started to investigate the use of laptops in education.

3. i came across an article about the features of xo in the computer magazine today's technology.

4. mr. negroponte aims to eliminate poverty in developing countries through the one laptop per child project.

5. daisy told me her family has got a new computer, so she can do research on the internet for our english project.

6. this laptop has a maximum memory capacity of 5 gb.

Yummy International Desserts

Who doesn't love desserts? We all have our favourite desserts for different reasons, whether it's a fondness for certain flavours, or because they bring back memories of another time, place, event – or even person. Many desserts are made for special occasions, but every once in a while, we know that a specific food – especially a sweet one – will give us a lift when we feel we need it (we call such foods "comfort foods").

It's always fun to try new things, but even if we tried a new dessert every day for the rest of our lives, we'd never sample all the desserts the world has to offer! One thing we could do, however, is to try the desserts that are favourites in many parts of the world. These desserts show up more often than others on the menus of fine restaurants around the world.

Pies are the favourite desserts of many people. They are often fruity. The most popular fruit pies are peach, blueberry, raisin, rhubarb, strawberry, and of course, apple. Fruit pies can even include citrus fruits, like key lime and lemon meringue pies. There are also cream pies, such as banana cream, coconut cream, and chocolate cream pies. Some pies are made from non-fruit items, such as pumpkin pie and pecan pie.

Cakes come in many forms: high and spongy angel food cakes; flat, dense, and chewy brownies; cakes in layers covered in fruit or jam or icing; cheesecakes; spicy coffee cakes... The list is endless, and it's hard to know which are the most popular. But an old Italian dessert called tiramisu, made with coffee and mascarpone cheese, has become very popular in recent years.

Puddings are also very popular desserts. Some, like bread pudding or rice pudding, are made with cheap and abundant ingredients but loved by rich and poor alike. A list of some of the most popular puddings today includes chocolate mousse and its vanilla-flavoured equivalent, panna cotta. Custards (a kind of dessert similar to puddings) are also popular, especially in the form of almond-flavoured blancmange and egg-flavoured crème caramel, or a warm version called crème brûlée with its hard crunchy layer of burnt sugar on top.

With the rise of international travel and immigration, everyone can now know the favourite desserts of cultures in far-away places. Some of the best-loved "international" desserts would have to include the following: Baklava originating from the Middle-East and Mediterranean countries – a sweet, sticky dessert made of layers of phyllo pastry, honey, and pistachio nuts; English trifle – custard, fruit, jam, and bits of sponge cake or biscuits thrown in a bowl in layers and topped with whipped cream; Gulab Jamon from South Asian countries – delicious balls of cake soaked in a sweet rose water syrup; and Crêpes Suzette from France – thin pancakes rolled in a sauce of orange juice, sugar, and liqueur. There are too many international favourites to name! How fun life would be if we became our own experts on yummy desserts of the world!

A. Complete the chart below.

Dessert	Origin	Description
Baklava		
Trifle		
Gulab Jamon		
Crêpes Suzette		

B. If you were to recommend a dessert from your culture to your friends, what would your choose? Briefly describe this dessert and explain why you would recommend it.

____

____

____

____

____

____

Colons and Semicolons

We use a **colon** to set off a list, a quotation, or an explanation. It shows that what follows is closely related to the introducing clause.

We use **semicolons** to separate items in a list, especially when the items are long and contain commas within, or to separate closely related independent clauses.

Example: Cakes come in many forms**:** high and spongy angel food cakes**;** flat, dense, and chewy brownies**;** cakes in layers covered in fruit or jam or icing**;** cheesecakes**;** spicy coffee cakes...

C. Add colons and semicolons in appropriate places.

1. Rachel has a sweet tooth she likes all kinds of desserts.

2. We ordered three desserts cheesecake topped with blueberries, raspberries, and strawberries yogurt parfait with layers of yogurt, fruit, and granola crepe filled with bananas, fresh cream, and chocolate sauce.

3. The world-famous restaurant expects one thing from the new pastry chef creativity.

4. Have you heard of this saying "A world without ice cream is a world in darkness"?

5. The four-judge panel for the dessert competition includes Mrs. Emily Miller, Principal of the French Culinary Academy Mr. Ryan Cann, Executive Chef of North Windsor Hotel Ms. Hannah Evans, Chief Editor of *Fine Cuisine Magazine* Mr. Logan Ramos, former winner of the competition.

6. We need these ingredients to make waffles flour, sugar, eggs, milk, and baking powder.

7. This is the first cake I made a chocolate shortcake topped with sweetened strawberries and whipped cream.

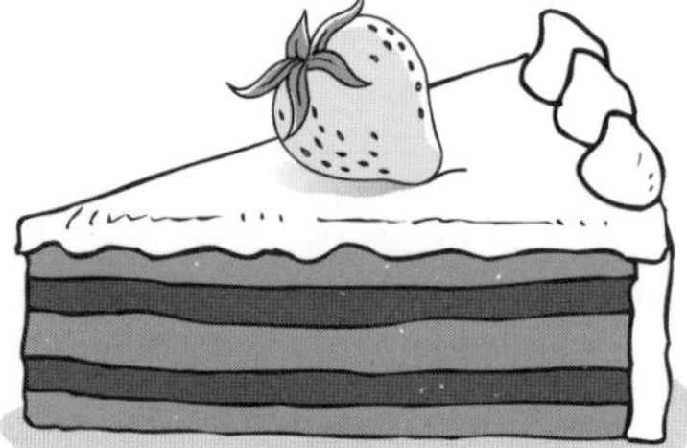

Dashes, Parentheses, and Quotation Marks

We use **dashes** to insert or set off appositions and explanations to further the reader's understanding of the sentence.

We use **parentheses** to enclose phrases or statements as additional information that is not an essential part of the main statement and that does not normally fit into the flow of the text.

We use **quotation marks** to enclose direct quotations or fragments of quotations, words or phrases used with special meanings, and titles of short stories, articles, and poems.

Example: Once in a while, we know that a specific food – especially a sweet one – will give us a lift when we feel we need it (we call such foods "comfort foods").

D. Add dashes, parentheses, and quotation marks in appropriate places.

1. The soufflé at this restaurant I don't remember its name is excellent. You must give it a try.

2. The article How to Make Award-Winning Desserts has given us useful information.

3. Simply Delight a cozy café in downtown Toronto offers a fantastic assortment of desserts and special drinks.

4. Wow, this is the most scrumptious lemon meringue pie I've ever had! exclaimed Josh.

5. Valeria is learning to make chocolate éclair a favourite dessert of everyone in her family.

6. This Japanese chef uses *nori* dried seaweed in many of his dessert dishes.

7. Tiramisu an Italian dessert made with coffee and masarpone cheese is loved by many.

8. Elmo gave the brownie a big bite he would have put the whole piece into his mouth if he could and was already reaching for the last piece on the plate.

"After the Boom"

Canada has its share of "boom" towns: places that began or grew rapidly in response to a certain commodity being found and developed nearby. Probably the best-known boom town is Dawson City, Yukon. When gold was discovered in 1896 in a nearby river, the Klondike Gold Rush began, and Dawson City went from being a fishing camp to a bustling town of 40 000. The gold rush ended only a few years later, and people began to leave in large numbers. Although there were "mini-booms" over the decades related to the fortunes of the mining industry, the search for gold was all but over by the 1960s. Today, Dawson City is a town of 2000 year-round, growing to 5000 during the summer. There have been many towns like Dawson City all over Canada over the decades. Some of these towns have been able to "reinvent" themselves, primarily as "eco-tourism" destinations, but most of them are simply sad reminders of what once was.

At present, Canada's biggest and most "booming" boom town is Fort McMurray, located about 450 kilometres northeast of Edmonton. The reason it exists has mostly to do with the "oil sands" (a mixture of sand, clay, water, and heavy crude oil) located in this area in vast quantities. The First Nations peoples of the area have long known about these oil sand deposits. For example, they used the tar-like substance to waterproof their canoes. The oil sands were first described by the explorer Alexander MacKenzie in his 1790 chronicles.

Fort McMurray was established as a Hudson's Bay Company trading post in 1870 at the confluence of the Athabaska and Clearwater Rivers, but it grew because of the oil sands. The first company to exploit the resource was Abasands Oil, back in the 1930s. However, the process by which the oil could be extracted from the sand was not cost effective. As the price of oil increased, greater efforts were made to tap into the vast reserves. In 1966, the population of Fort McMurray was only 2000, but with the opening of the Suncor plant in 1967 and then the Syncrude consortium mine in 1978 (still the biggest mining operation of any kind in the world), the population grew to over 30 000 by 1980. During these years, the price of oil was relatively high due to tensions in the Middle East, the world's main oil-producing region. The growth of Fort McMurray levelled off during the late 1980s and 1990s when the price of oil fell sharply.

Now, however, the price of oil has surged again. Companies like Syncrude are no longer worried about the cost of extracting the oil from sticky oil sands. All the companies involved are stepping up production. The population of Fort McMurray is now reaching 70 000. As is the case with such towns, there is a significant social and environmental impact stemming from the oil-extraction and processing industry. Pollution from the tailing ponds is said to be contaminating the land, rivers, and also the local wildlife population. Among the inhabitants of the area, there is a high rate of depression, drug abuse, illness, and social dysfunction.

What will become of Fort McMurray after the boom?

A. Write the events that took place in the following years.

1790 ____________________

1870 ____________________

1896 ____________________

1930s ____________________

1960s ____________________

1967 ____________________

1978 ____________________

B. Do you think Fort McMurray will face the same fate as other boom towns like Dawson City one day? Why or why not?

Spelling Rules

1. Drop the silent "e" when the suffix begins with a vowel.
   Examples: bustling, mining, trading

2. Retain the silent "e" when the suffix begins with a consonant.
   Examples: relatively, movement, useful

3. Change the ending "y" to "i" before a suffix, except when the "y" follows a vowel or when the suffix is "ing".
   Examples: companies, played, studying

4. Double the ending consonant of a word when the suffix begins with a vowel, except when the ending consonant is preceded by two vowels.
   Examples: logging, booming, tailing

5. Do not double the ending consonant of a word with more than one syllable when the word is accented on the first syllable.
   Examples: murmuring, tutored, comforting

6. Put "i" before "e", except after "c" and for words that rhyme with the letter "a".
   Examples: yield, deceive, weight

C. Circle the correctly spelled word in each pair.

1. heating / heatting
2. steming / stemming
3. worryed / worried
4. purposeful / purposful
5. heirarchy / hierarchy
6. employed / emploied
7. referred / refered
8. visuallized / visualized
9. speculative / speculateive
10. terrifiing / terrifying
11. reciever / receiver
12. reindeer / riendeer
13. hurries / hurrys
14. development / developement

D. Read the clues and complete the following crossword puzzle.

Across

A. that can be proven right or reasonable
B. sound made by a horse
C. produce
D. attractive
E. someone who examines accounts officially
F. dishonest

Down

1. filled with deep regret
2. working something out in detail
3. moved from one place to another
4. providing food and services for a banquet
5. making something free of dirt or harmful substances
6. gave something to someone for approval

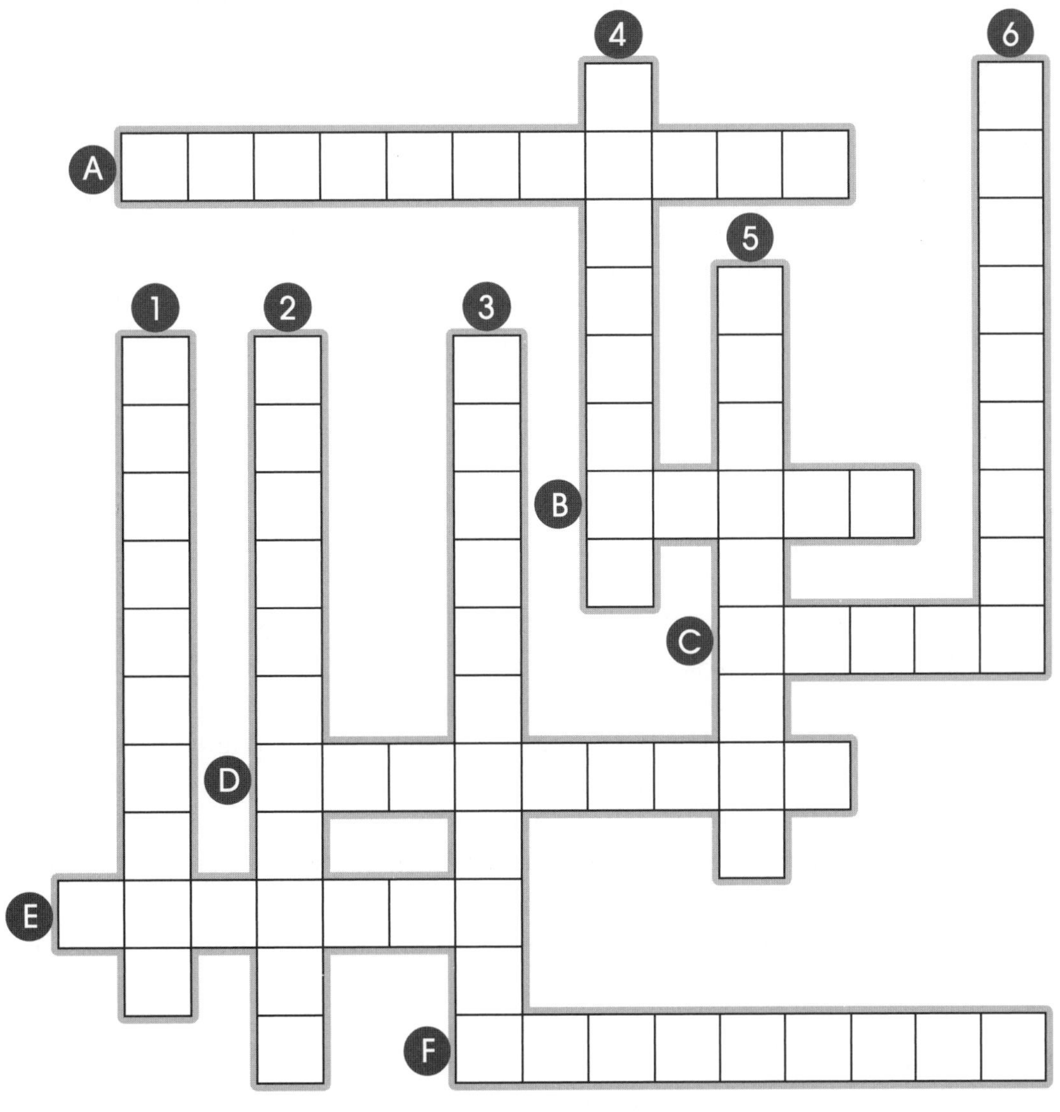

From St. Laurent to the Smithsonian

The tiny town of St. Laurent, Manitoba, is located approximately 80 kilometres north of Winnipeg, and sits at the south-east corner of Lake Manitoba. It has its share of local folklore including the following: the lake monster Manipogo, sightings of which date back as far as 1908; a legendary white horse, brought from Mexico by a Cree Chief as a gift to the local Assiniboine Chief in return for his beautiful daughter's hand in marriage; even stories of UFO sightings by several residents! Past and current residents include a former Lieutenant Governor of the province, a former baseball player for the national baseball team of Australia, several famous fiddlers of all ages, and a renowned wildlife photographer. This is all pretty impressive for a place where there are only 1200 people throughout most of the year – although the population triples during July and August when cottagers from near and far come to spend their summer along the shore of peaceful Lake Manitoba.

However, St. Laurent is a special community in more ways than this: about half of the permanent population of the town is of aboriginal or Métis descent, and it is one of the few places in the world where the Métis culture is still very active, as shown in the way people earn their livelihoods, and in their festivals and music. The language of the Métis people (called Mitchif), which is a mixture of Cree or Salteaux, French, and English, is spoken here, too. For this reason, the town received a visit by two representatives of the famed Smithsonian Institution in Washington D.C., the United States. Founded in 1846, the Smithsonian Institution is a research and education centre and the largest museum in the world. The Institution had been planning to build a new museum, called the National Museum of the American Indian, and curators wanted St. Laurent to be included in an exhibit.

Some of the items provided by the townspeople to the National Museum of the American Indian include: several historical photos, an ice chisel and ice augur, nylon fishing nets and hooks, a muskrat trap hook, a chair made of willow branches, and even an old Bombardier snowmobile! These items reflect the fact that hunting, trapping, and fishing had been the mainstay of the community for generations, and are an important part of Métis history and culture. The museum also took a CD of songs written by a popular local band called Coulee which, according to lead vocalist Serge Carriere, "reflect the great spirit of Lake Manitoba that weaves us together as a community... [and] celebrate the Métis language, and other aspects of Métis culture such as our relationships to nature and to each other, and how we fit in the world." The exhibit opened in the fall of 2004, thereby enshrining a part of Métis culture for all to see in one of the most visited, and most revered, places of learning. Plans are now underway for a Métis Interpretive Centre to be built in St. Laurent, pending government support.

So, if you cannot make it to Washington, D.C., to learn more about a culture that has so much to do with Canada's history, then why not come to Manitoba, to the little town nestled in the south-east corner of peaceful Lake Manitoba? See for yourself what the unique, and very Canadian, Métis culture has to offer!

A. Complete the following information about St. Laurent.

1. Location:

   ____

   ____

2. Local folklore:

   ____

   ____

   ____

3. Average population:

   ____

4. Language of the Métis people:

   ______________ (a mixture of ______________

   ______________________________)

5. Name of a popular local band:

   ____

Avoiding Repetition

To make our writing more interesting to read, we have to avoid repeating the same words. We can do so by using synonyms or words with similar meanings. A thesaurus would be helpful.

Examples: several famous fiddlers

a renowned wildlife photographer

the famed Smithsonian Institution

B. Complete the crossword puzzle with synonyms of the clue words.

Across

A. placid
B. abandon
C. homesick
D. apparent
E. endure

Down

1. hygienic
2. scarce
3. moan
4. concede
5. frightening

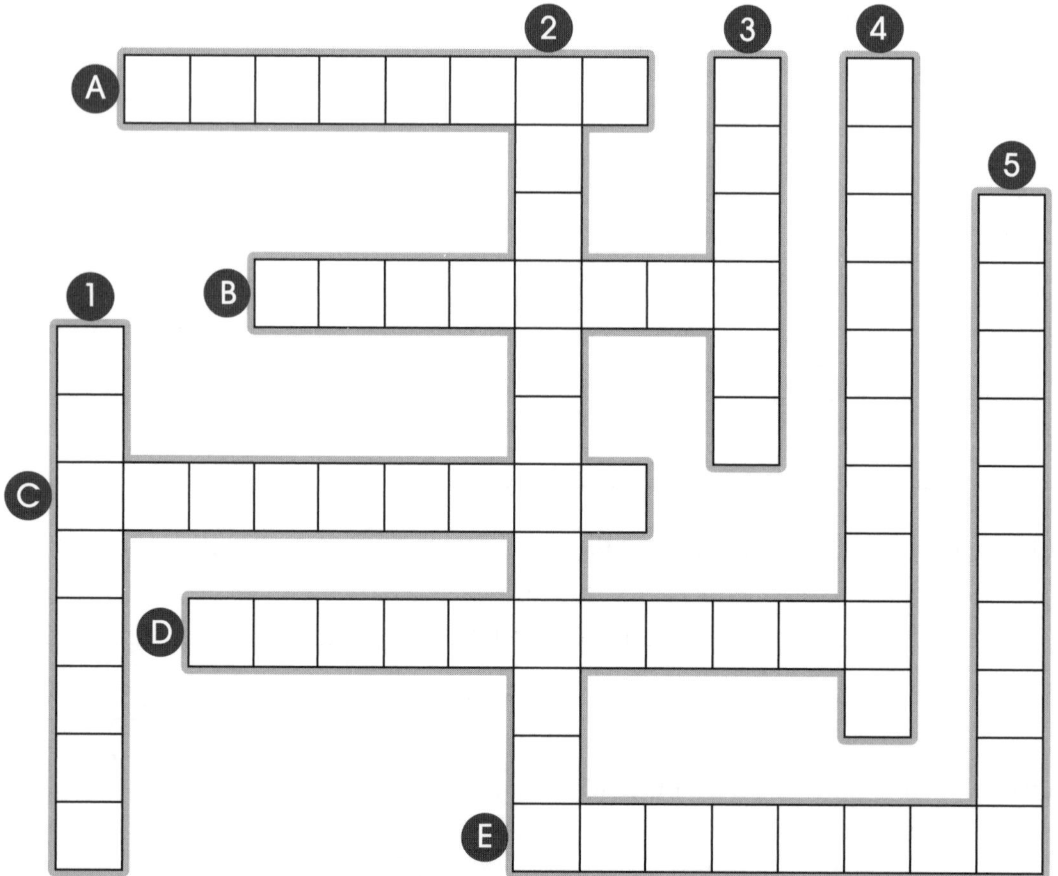

C. For each of the following words, write three words that have similar meanings.

1. brave ______ ______ ______
2. restrict ______ ______ ______
3. ring ______ ______ ______
4. shiver ______ ______ ______
5. amazing ______ ______ ______
6. cease ______ ______ ______

D. Rewrite the following paragraph by replacing the underlined words with words that have similar meanings to avoid repetition.

Manipogo is a legendary creature that lives in Lake Manitoba. Those who claimed to have seen it described it as a huge snake-like creature that swims fast. Some people believe it to be a living dinosaur that <u>lives</u> in the lake. Every year, tourists flock to Lake Manitoba hoping to have a chance to <u>see</u> this <u>huge</u>, <u>legendary</u> creature with a body that resembles a <u>snake</u>.

The Making of a *Sea-faring* Legend

The world of sea-faring has been rich with legend and superstition for centuries. Deep-sea fishing and ocean explorations through the ages have meant that the brave souls lucky enough to return to shore have told of their adventures – and who could dispute what they have said? These stories have inspired great literary works. For example, famed poet Samuel Taylor Coleridge's *The Rime of the Ancient Mariner*, which mentions frightening sea creatures, was said to be inspired by the exploratory South Pacific voyage of Captain James Cook. Herman Melville's classic novel *Moby Dick*, published in 1851, is about an encounter with a long and "pulpy" sea creature. Another poet, Alfred Lord Tennyson, also wrote about a sea monster in his poem, *The Kraken.*

The Kraken - *Alfred Lord Tennyson*

Below the thunders of the upper deep;
Far, far beneath in the abysmal sea,
His ancient, dreamless, uninvaded sleep
The Kraken sleepeth: faintest sunlights flee
About his shadowy sides; above him swell
Huge sponges of millennial growth and height;
And far away into the sickly light,
From many a wondrous grot and secret cell
Unnumber'd and enormous polypi
Winnow with giant arms the slumbering green.
There hath he lain for ages, and will lie
Battening upon huge seaworms in his sleep,
Until the latter fire shall heat the deep;
Then once by man and angels to be seen,
In roaring he shall rise and on the surface die.

This poem later influenced novelist Jules Verne's classic, *Twenty Thousand Leagues Under the Sea*, published in 1870. In fact, stories of such sea monsters have appeared as far back as the Norse Sagas and as recently as C.S. Lewis's "Narnia" books and J.R.R. Tolkien's *The Fellowship of the Ring*. Scandinavian children have long heard legends of the Kraken – told by parents who wish to keep them wary of wading too far off the beach. The word "Kraken" is derived from their word *krake*, meaning "something that is twisted", or otherwise "an unhealthy animal". In the German language, the word for "sick" is *krank*, and the word *krake* means "octopus" – and herein lies the answer to what exactly was scaring sailors in far-off waters all those years!

Recent marine explorations, which incorporate the use of deep-sea roaming cameras, as well as rare catches by fishing boats much better-equipped than the wooden sailing ships of yore, have resulted in the discovery of the real-life inspiration for all these myths and legends about sea monsters. While the general consensus had been for ages that these stories were based on encounters with large octopuses, it is now believed that the Kraken is actually the elusive giant squid, with its torpedo-shaped mantle, eight enormous arms, and two even longer tentacles!

A. Answer these questions.

1. People who returned from ocean explorations have told of their adventures, and the writer of "The Making of a Sea-Faring Legend" says "...and who could dispute what they have said?" Why do you think the writer says so?

   ____

   ____

   ____

2. What do literary works such as *The Rime of the Ancient Mariner, The Kraken,* and *Twenty Thousand Leagues Under the Sea* have in common?

   ____

   ____

   ____

3. Find an example of a sea-faring superstition from the library or the Internet. Do you believe in it? Why or why not?

   ____

   ____

   ____

Creating Images with Precise Words

In writing, we **create images** to arouse the reader's interest and imagination. This can be achieved by using precise words instead of more common and general words to create vivid images in the reader's mind.

Example: The giant squid has a triangular mantle, eight big arms, and two even longer tentacles. (general)

The giant squid has a torpedo-shaped mantle, eight enormous arms, and two even longer tentacles. (more precise)

B. Rewrite the sentences by replacing the underlined words with more precise ones.

1. For many years, the sea creature Kraken has appeared in stories told by sailors.

   ____

2. The Kraken was believed to have strong arms that could break a large ship.

   ____

3. Returning from the trip, the man wrote a book about his story.

   ____

4. Last night, I had a dream. I was chased by an ugly monster.

   ____

5. The animal we saw was small but it was fierce.

   ____

6. Do you see a weak light moving in the thick fog?

   ____

7. You can find more information about what this creature is from the book.

   ____

Creating Images with Literary Devices

Literary devices like personification, similes, and metaphors are also employed to create vivid images in writing.

Personification is the attribution of human qualities to inanimate objects.

A **simile** is a descriptive comparison of two things that have some characteristics in common using "as" or "like".

A **metaphor** is a comparison of two things without using "as" or "like". We describe something as though it were something else.

C. Identify the literary devices used in the sentences below. Write "P" for personification, "S" for similes, and "M" for metaphors.

1. According to some stories, the Kraken was the king of the ocean. ______
2. The creature swam past the cruiser as fast as a speedboat. ______
3. Deep under the sea, it is dark like a black hole. ______
4. The giant ray dances gracefully in the water. ______
5. The sea monster was as tall as the mast of a large ship. ______

D. Imagine you saw a sea monster on a voyage. Describe the sea monster using the three literary devices you have learned in this unit.

Who is Oscar? And why do people always talk about him on the night of the Academy Awards? Oscar is the nickname of the gold-plated statuette, officially called the Academy Award of Merit, that winners receive on this special night when the Academy of Motion Picture Arts and Sciences rewards its top achievers of the year.

Outside the Kodak Theatre in Los Angeles, where the Academy Awards ceremony is held, and before the ceremony starts, another very important show is going on. People who registered months in advance to sit on bleachers outside the theatre watch the stars exit their limousines and walk the red carpet to the theatre entrance. Here, the stars chat with celebrity interviewers and have their pictures taken.

These interviewers will ask, "Who are you wearing?" No, their grammar is not wrong. They are asking the stars who designed their clothes because fashion is a very important part of being a star. Maybe the interviewers will ask, "Who do you think has a shot at the (Best Picture) Oscar?" The stars are happy to talk about who designed the clothes they are wearing, but they will only smile when asked for their Oscar predictions.

The Academy Awards: **Oscar's Big Night**

The opening ceremony usually includes a big musical number. Then we may hear, "Ladies and gentlemen, your host for the evening is..." The host, the Master of Ceremonies, is usually a famous comedian. Soon it is time for the first Oscar to be awarded, and the first pair in a long line of celebrity presenters will come on stage. They will joke with each other, talk about the Oscar category, and then say, "And the nominees are..." After the nominees are shown, we hear, "And the Oscar goes to..." It's all very exciting! The winners come on stage and give a short speech, usually starting with, "I'd like to thank..." They will want to thank everyone they can think of!

Oscars are given in a variety of categories, such as screenwriting, costume design, makeup, cinematography, film editing, animation, documentary filmmaking, sound editing and mixing, as well as special visual effects. But perhaps the presentations that viewers are most eager to see are the ones for best foreign language film, best song, best supporting actor/

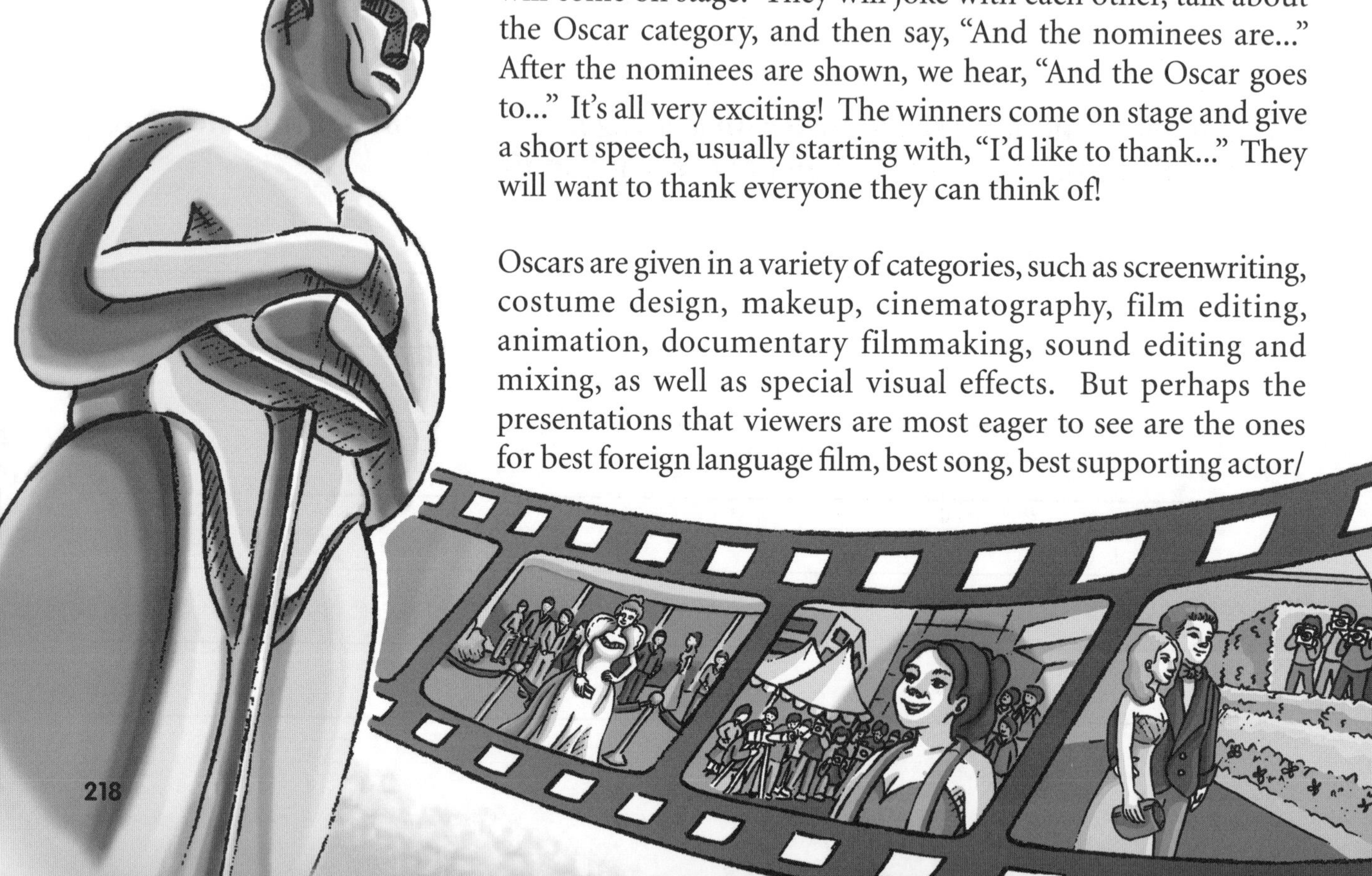

actress, best actor/actress, best director, and best picture. Of course, the Oscar for best picture of the year is given at the end.

By now, if you are watching an evening telecast of the show, it may be quite late, especially if the winners have taken more than their two minutes each for their "thank-you" speeches. For us, when the show is over, we go to bed. But once the show is over in Los Angeles, it is time for everyone, winners and losers, to celebrate at an after party. They will party until dawn and enjoy the greatest night in show business: the Oscars.

A. Answer these questions.

1. "Fashion is a very important part of being a star." Do you agree with what the writer thinks? Why or why not?

   ____

   ____

   ____

2. Why will the stars only smile when interviewers ask about their predictions of Oscar winners? Give your opinion.

   ____

   ____

   ____

3. Why do you think the host of the Academy Awards is usually a famous comedian?

   ____

   ____

   ____

4. Name three presentations of Oscars that you are most eager to see. Give reasons for your choices.

   ____

   ____

   ____

Using Phrases to Begin Sentences

To make our writing more interesting to read, we can vary the construction of sentences. One way to do so is to start a sentence with a phrase instead of the subject.

Examples: Outside the Kodak Theatre, another very important show is going on. (prepositional phrase)

To watch the entire show, we have to stay up late. (infinitive phrase)

Not knowing who will win, the nominees wait anxiously. (gerund phrase)

Surprised with the result, the winner forgot whom to thank. (participle phrase)

B. Rewrite each of the following sentences by starting it with a phrase.

1. The winner held the Oscar in his hands, and he was too excited to say a word.

____

____

2. The people got excited when they saw the celebrity exiting the limousine.

____

____

3. The presenter paused before announcing the winner to create suspense.

____

____

4. People registered for the bleacher seats outside the theatre months in advance.

____

____

Using Appositives

Combining simple sentences can make our writing more concise and stylish. One way to do so is to use appositives. An **appositive** is the renaming of a word that immediately precedes it. It is set off from the rest of the sentence with commas.

Example: The host is the Master of Ceremonies. The host is usually a famous comedian.

The host, the Master of Ceremonies, is usually a famous comedian.

C. Use an appositive to combine each pair of sentences below.

1. The Academy Awards ceremony is the greatest event in show business. It is held annually.

____

____

2. The Oscar is a gold-plated statuette. It is presented to every Academy Award winner.

____

____

3. James Cameron is a Canadian-American director and screenwriter. He won the Best Director Award for *Titanic,* released in 1997.

____

____

4. The Oscar is one of the most recognized awards in the world. It is a symbol of achievement in the film industry.

____

____

22

A Story of **What Kids Can Do**

Have you ever heard of the global organization, Free The Children? Ontario native Craig Kielburger founded the organization in 1995, when he was just 12 years old. It is now the world's largest network of children helping children. And it all began one day when Craig was reading the local newspaper.

The article Craig read was about another 12-year-old boy named Iqbal Masih who lived in Pakistan. The boy had been murdered after speaking out about the terrible conditions he and other child-labourers had to endure while working in the carpet-making industry. Craig was determined to do something. He convinced his parents to let him accompany Alam Rahman, a Canadian human rights worker, to various South Asian countries. He wrote about the terrible injustices against children he saw on that trip in his first book *Free the Children.*

Craig had only just begun. He founded Free The Children with his 12-year-old friends. The group started petitioning governments, demanding that they stop child labour. Craig would meet with world leaders and tell them in person, sometimes when he wasn't invited to do so! Even though Craig's cause was a good one, some adults felt that he, as a child and also as a person from North America, had no right to tell adults and politicians what they should or shouldn't do. But this did not stop Craig.

Since those early years, Craig, along with his elder brother Marc, has founded a youth leadership training organization called "Leaders Today" and has written several books. In 2007, Craig was awarded the Order of Canada medal by the Governor General, Canada's top civilian honour. Craig has also won a variety of distinctions from around the world, including: The Reebok Human Rights Award, The Roosevelt Freedom Medal, The 2005 Kiwanis World Service Medal, The Nelson Mandela Human Rights Award, The Community of Christ International Peace Award, and The World Economic Forum GLT Award. He has been awarded an honorary degree in law from the University of Guelph, and a Doctorate in Education from Nipissing University. He has

appeared on *CNN*, *60 Minutes*, and *The Oprah Winfrey Show*.

Of course, Craig Kielburger is deserving of these accolades, but do you think they are what motivate him to do what he does? Do you think Craig works towards the goal of freeing children around the world from enslavement because he can meet celebrities and world leaders? Surely not. Craig Kielburger's commitment to children is clearly stated in one of his founding mottos: "If we are to achieve true peace in this world, it shall have to begin with the children."

We would be lucky if all world leaders felt this way and followed Craig's example of positive action. Check out www.freethechildren.com to learn more about what this great organization is doing and how you can be a part of it!

A. Check the true statements. Rewrite the false ones to make them true.

1. Free the Children is a global organization founded by Craig Kielburger. ☐

   ____

2. In his first book, Craig Kielburger wrote about the injustices against children in Pakistan. ☐

   ____

3. Craig founded "Leaders Today" with his elder brother Marc and his 12-year-old friends. ☐

   ____

4. "Leaders Today" runs leadership training programs for young people. ☐

   ____

5. Craig received an honorary degree in education from Nipissing University. ☐

   ____

6. Craig Kielburger believes that world peace has to begin with world leaders. ☐

   ____

Omitting Superfluous Words and Phrases

Clear and concise writing makes it easier for the reader to follow your ideas. To write concisely, we have to avoid using superfluous words or phrases. Replace these words or phrases with fewer words that mean the same or simply delete them without affecting the meaning.

Example: Free The Children is <u>at this point in time</u> the world's largest network of children helping children. (✘)

Free The Children is <u>now</u> the world's largest network of children helping children. (✔)

B. Replace each of the superfluous phrases below with a word.

1. in the absence of ____________
2. in light of ____________
3. in order to ____________
4. on account of the fact that ____________
5. despite the fact that ____________
6. prior to the time of ____________
7. subsequent to ____________
8. in conjunction with ____________
9. am in the opinion that ____________
10. with the exception of ____________
11. in the event that ____________
12. in spite of the fact that ____________
13. owing to the fact that ____________

C. Cross out the superfluous words and phrases in the following sentences.

1. Craig Kielburger is the kind of person who always thinks of freeing children around the world from enslavement.
2. Craig Kielburger's successful achievements in fighting for child rights can be proven by the various distinctions he has received.
3. "Leaders Today" organizes programs that are intended to train young people as leaders.
4. You don't need to have any past volunteer experiences to join the group.
5. All new volunteers will have to attend the orientation tomorrow at 12 o'clock noon.

D. Rewrite the following sentences by deleting the superfluous phrases or replacing them with fewer words.

1. Child labour has existed in some countries for a very long period of time.

   ____

2. Despite the fact that he was not invited, Craig would meet with world leaders and demand that they stop child labour.

   ____

3. In order to achieve world peace, it is absolutely essential to ensure children's rights.

   ____

4. In my opinion, I think that young people have the power to change the world into a better one.

   ____

5. Free The Children has built more than 500 schools in China, Kenya, Sri Lanka, and etc.

   ____

The Truth about CARBS

Carbohydrates – nicknamed "carbs" – have become an increasingly popular topic of discussion. Usually this discussion is about obesity and the increasing levels of it, especially among young people. This fact has given rise to all sorts of diets and books about diets, which some people get wealthy writing and publishing. Some of the most popular weight-loss regimes, such as the Atkin's Diet, the Scarsdale Diet, or the High Protein Diet, are "low-carb" or even "no-carb" diets. In such regimes, one cuts out all carbohydrates – pasta, bread, rice – and eats very few fruits and vegetables. However, dieters can eat all the fats and proteins, such as meat, butter, and cheese, they wish. Although weight will come off quickly this way, it never stays off once a dieter stops dieting. Moreover, most people who adhere to a diet made up mostly of proteins and fats will eventually suffer ill health. The truth is, we need carbohydrates in our diet.

Carbohydrates are, in fact, our most important and readily available energy source. The energy is formed through a complex chemical process in our bodies. Broken down into simple sugars, all carbohydrates are absorbed into our bloodstream. As our blood sugar level rises, a hormone called insulin is released by the pancreas, which moves the sugar into the cells. The cells then use that sugar as their energy source. This energy gives us the "get-up-and-go" feeling we need to work and play all day long. When we are more energetic, we use up more of this energy source, which we measure in calories.

It is important to know that there are different kinds of carbohydrates. First of all, there are two main forms: simple carbs and complex carbs. Simple carbs are also referred to as simple sugars, such as the lactose we find in dairy products, the fructose we find in nutritious fruits, and the glucose we find in natural sweets such as maple sugar and honey. Complex carbs are starches found in vegetables such as potatoes, as well as in grains, rice, bread, and cereals.

These simple and complex carbohydrates are all good, but modern food manufacturing has also created "bad" carbs – those found in "refined" foods such as candy, soft drinks, white sugar, white flour in pastas and white bread, and many things we love to eat like doughnuts, cakes, and pastries. Because of the widespread availability and marketing of these types of products, they are being consumed in larger quantities than ever before. This, and more affordable and common home entertainment systems and computers which lead to more sedentary lifestyles, has helped create the high levels of obesity and obesity-related illnesses, such as diabetes, among young people.

Doctors recommend that up to 60% of the diet of young people should be comprised of carbohydrates. Make sure that your 60% comes in the form of the "good" carbs, found in food items such as whole-grain cereals, brown rice, whole-grain breads, fruits, vegetables, and low-fat dairy products, which are available everywhere. And along with a healthy diet, stay active!

A. Based on the information in the passage, explain the cause or effect of the following.

1. Cause: A person cuts out all carbohydrates and adheres to a diet rich in proteins and fats.

   Effect: ______________________________

   ____

2. Cause: ______________________________

   ____

   Effect: The pancreas releases a hormone called insulin, which moves the sugar into the cells.

3. Cause: Sugar is moved into the cells.

   Effect: ______________________________

   ____

4. Cause: ______________________________

   ____

   Effect: Bad carbs are being consumed in large quantities.

5. Cause: ______________________________

   ____

   Effect: Young people are leading more sedentary lifestyles.

Faulty Parallels

Coordinate elements in a sentence must be parallel in structure. A **faulty parallel** occurs when these elements do not have a consistent grammatical construction.

Example: Some people cut out all carbohydrates and very few fruits and vegetables are eaten. (✗)

Some people cut out all carbohydrates and eat very few fruits and vegetables. (✓)

Remember not to omit necessary words in the parallels.

Example: Starches found and extracted from potatoes are complex carbs. (✗)

Starches found in and extracted from potatoes are complex carbs. (✓)

B. Rewrite the following sentences to correct the faulty parallels.

1. To live healthy lives, we must choose our food wisely and working out regularly.

____

____

2. Carbohydrates provide the energy we need to work and for playing in our everyday lives.

____

____

3. This book focuses and gives detailed explanations of the benefits of low-carb diets.

____

____

4. Dietitians promote proper eating habits and participation in research.

____

____

Dangling Modifiers

A **dangling modifier** refers to a modifier that modifies something that it should not be modifying. When constructing a sentence, we need to keep the modifier close to the words it modifies to avoid confusion in meaning.

Example: Broken down into simple sugars, our bloodstream absorbs all carbohydrates. (✘)

Broken down into simple sugars, all carbohydrates are absorbed into our bloodstream. (✔)

(It should be "all carbohydrates", not "our bloodstream", that are broken down into simple sugars.)

C. Rewrite the following sentences so that they do not have dangling modifiers.

1. Classified as a simple carb, we find lactose mainly in dairy products.

___

___

2. Although easily digested, dietitians do not recommend the carbs from refined foods.

___

___

3. As a carbohydrate found in plants, our bodies do not digest fibre.

___

___

4. Like a sponge, water is absorbed by insoluble fibre to help move solid waste out of our bodies.

___

___

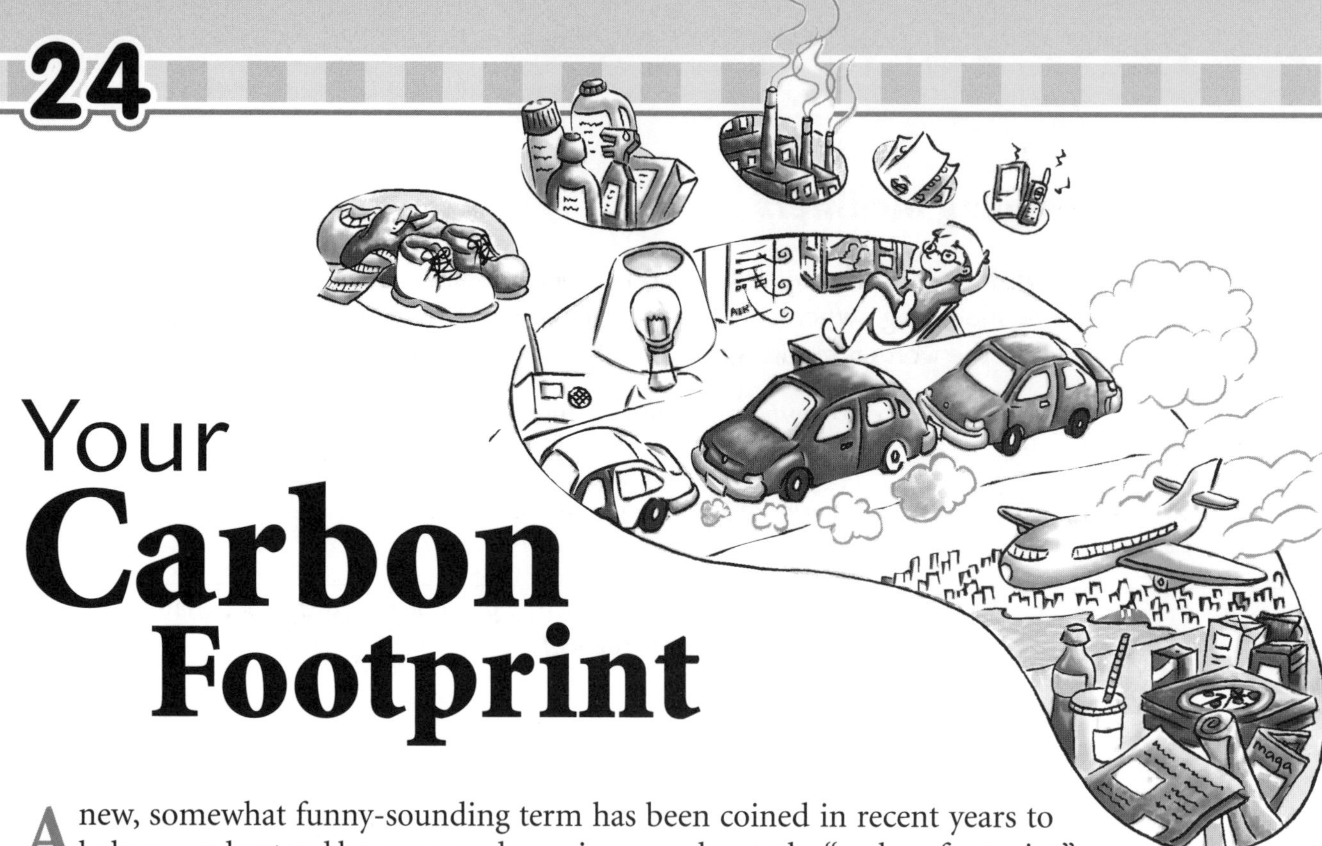

Your Carbon Footprint

A new, somewhat funny-sounding term has been coined in recent years to help us understand how we are damaging our planet: the "carbon footprint". According to carbonfootprint.com, a carbon footprint is "a measure of the impact human activities have on the environment in terms of the amount of greenhouse gases produced, measured in units of carbon dioxide".

Why must we be aware of how our activities factor into the creation of greenhouse gases, which include, in order of abundance, water vapour, carbon dioxide, methane, nitrous oxide, and ozone? The answer is clear, and is also contained in two other relatively new terms: global warming and global climate change. We need these "greenhouse gases" to help keep our Earth warm, but too much of them, in particular carbon dioxide, causes the planet's atmosphere to heat up, with catastrophic effects ranging from melting glaciers to poleward spreading of tropical diseases to extreme weather.

There are two types of carbon footprint. The primary footprint is a measure of direct carbon dioxide emissions created by the burning of fossil fuels such as oil, coal, and natural gas. Domestic energy consumption, automobile, and air transportation account for a great percentage of this "footprint". The secondary footprint measures indirect carbon dioxide emissions based on the manufacturing and eventual disposal and breakdown of the products we use. In fact, the breakdown of the average person's carbon footprint shows us the following: electricity consumption – 12%, private transport – 10%, public transport – 3%, holiday flights – 6%, food and drink – 5%, clothes and personal effects – 4%, carbon in car manufacturing – 7%, household – 9%, recreation and leisure – 14%, financial services – 3%, gas, oil, and coal – 15%, and a person's share of public services – 12%.

So, how can we reduce our carbon footprint? According to carbonfootprint.com, the five best ways to reduce our primary footprint are: (1) avoid air travel for the holidays; (2) sign up for a renewable energy source of electricity; (3) use solar heating instead of gas for heating water; (4) use public transportation; (5) participate in carpools.

Then what can we do to reduce our secondary footprint? We should avoid drinking bottled water, reduce our meat consumption, avoid buying food, drinks, and clothes from far-off countries, and avoid buying goods with a lot of unnecessary packaging. But there are so many other things we can do! We can become more energy efficient in many ways: take shorter showers, bike to school, switch to compact fluorescent light bulbs, and buy foods and clothing with fair-trade labels.

There are even carbon "offset" schemes that allow people to "cancel out" the carbon dioxide creating effects in their everyday lives. For example, if you are taking a long-haul flight for your next holiday, you can go to the website of a carbon-offsetting organization and use their carbon calculator to find out the amount of emissions the flight would create. This will be worked out to a fee. In turn, the organization uses the money you pay to fund projects such as reforestation or the distribution of energy-efficient light bulbs. A flight from Toronto to London, UK, might cost you about $25 to "neutralize". The purchase of carbon offsets is becoming increasingly popular with both individuals and corporations who are eager to live – another new term – "carbon neutral" lives.

A. Write the main idea of each paragraph.

Paragraph 1: ____________________

____

Paragraph 2: ____________________

____

Paragraph 3: ____________________

____

Paragraph 4: ____________________

____

Paragraph 5: ____________________

____

Paragraph 6: ____________________

____

Developing Paragraphs

A **paragraph** consists of a group of sentences with a common topic. It is made up of a topic sentence and supporting sentences. The topic sentence states the main idea of the paragraph. It is usually the first sentence of a paragraph. The supporting sentences explain the main idea further or add details to it. A paragraph may end with a closing sentence that restates the main idea, gives a conclusion, or leads on to the paragraph that follows.

B. Write a topic sentence for each of the following groups of sentences.

1. ____

____

One of them is the more frequent occurrence of heat waves. The excessive heat, usually accompanied by high humidity, leads to heat-related illnesses such as heat stroke and heat rash, and even death. Heat waves that occur in dry areas or during drought may cause wildfires, which may burn down massive areas of forests and agricultural lands. Scientists warn that global warming will continue to have disastrous effects on our planet.

2. ____

____

Take a shower instead of a bath. Never leave the light on when nobody is in a room. Think carefully of what you want to get before you open the fridge door. Walk or bike to school if possible. These are just a few among the many easy ways to save energy in our everyday lives.

3. ____

____

First, we can put a composter in our backyard. Through composting, organic material is converted into a soil-like material called humus, which can be used to nourish the plants in the garden. Another way is to separate organic waste like fruit and vegetable scraps, coffee grinds, and egg shells from garbage and recyclable material, and put it in the green bin. With these two ways, the amount of household waste that goes to landfills will be greatly reduced.

C. Develop a paragraph with each of the topic sentences below.

1. Yesterday was Plant a Tree Day at my school. ____________________

2. I read an interesting story about how an alien helped a little girl save some endangered animal species on Earth. ____________________

25

The Biofuel Controversy

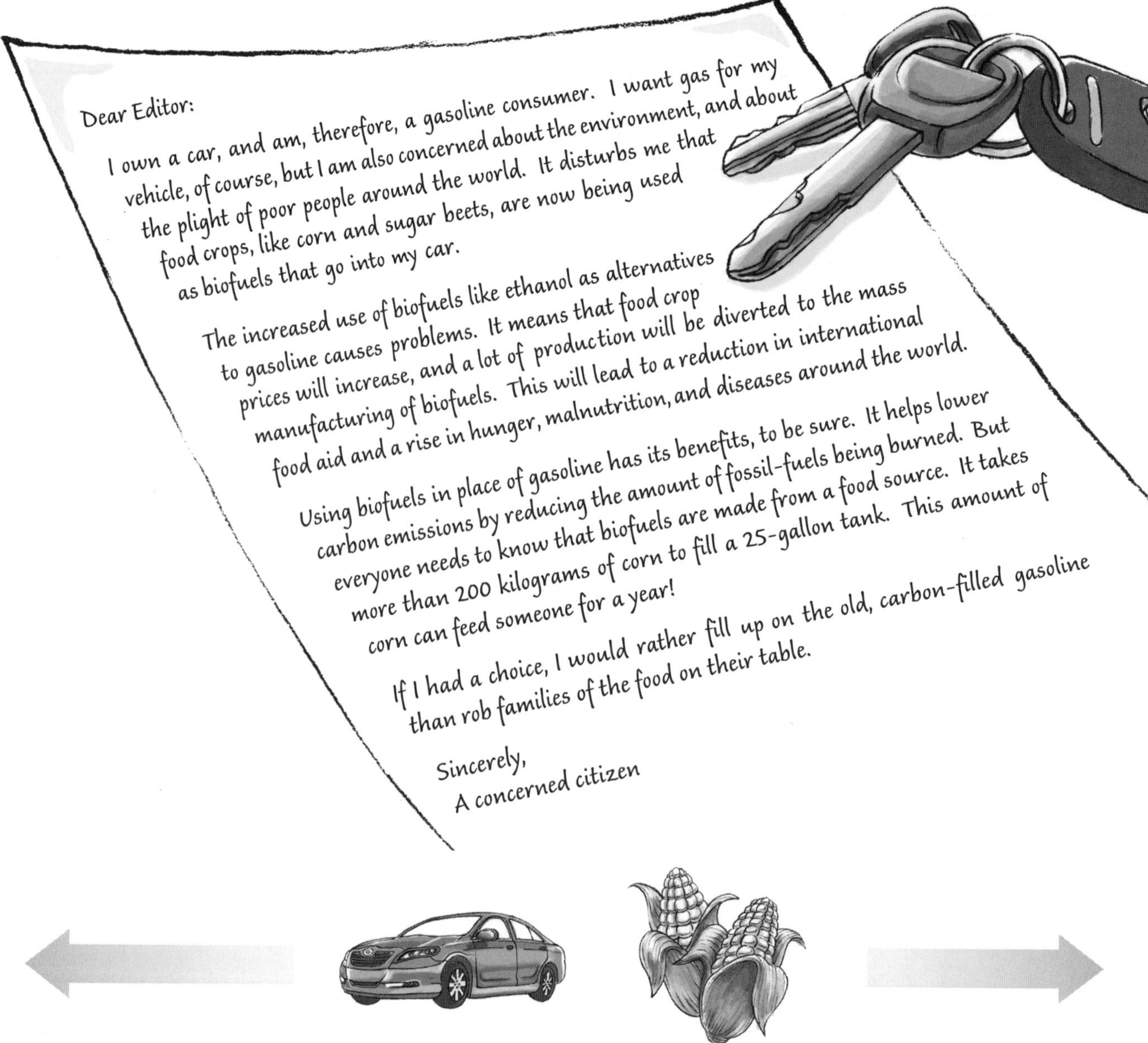

Dear Editor:

I own a car, and am, therefore, a gasoline consumer. I want gas for my vehicle, of course, but I am also concerned about the environment, and about the plight of poor people around the world. It disturbs me that food crops, like corn and sugar beets, are now being used as biofuels that go into my car.

The increased use of biofuels like ethanol as alternatives to gasoline causes problems. It means that food crop prices will increase, and a lot of production will be diverted to the mass manufacturing of biofuels. This will lead to a reduction in international food aid and a rise in hunger, malnutrition, and diseases around the world.

Using biofuels in place of gasoline has its benefits, to be sure. It helps lower carbon emissions by reducing the amount of fossil-fuels being burned. But everyone needs to know that biofuels are made from a food source. It takes more than 200 kilograms of corn to fill a 25-gallon tank. This amount of corn can feed someone for a year!

If I had a choice, I would rather fill up on the old, carbon-filled gasoline than rob families of the food on their table.

Sincerely,
A concerned citizen

What do you think of this letter to the editor? Do you agree or disagree with the writer? The growing use of food for fuel is becoming a serious controversy. While it seems that biofuels are part of an answer to the huge issue of global warming, the reasons for the biofuel controversy are as much environmental as they are economic and political.

People will not stop buying cars. In fact, Tata Motors in India unveiled a new car there in 2008, the Tata Nano, which can be purchased for the same price as a fancy laptop computer. This car is not a hybrid vehicle, nor one powered purely by non-carbon fuels. The existence of such an inexpensive car has come at precisely the time when governments need to be improving public transit systems and encouraging people to give up their "love of the open road" to a more collective mentality for the common good.

Moreover, if global mass motorization becomes that much more common, it means that the production of biofuels is going to increase. We already know that this will lead to increased commodity prices, such as the prices of corn, sugar beets, sugar cane, soybeans, palm-oil, and rapeseed, making it more difficult for people to buy those products to eat. It will also mean that forests will be cut down even more in order to provide the land needed to increase the production of these plants for biofuels. We have already seen this happen in the case of removing forests for raising cattle to supply the fast food restaurants of the world.

There are groups in society, such as agro-industrial corporations, that say biofuels are the way to move forward. What do you think?

A. Rewrite the false statements below to make them true.

1. Gasoline is used in place of biofuels to reduce carbon emissions.

___

___

2. Mass production of biofuels will result in a decrease in food crop prices.

___

___

3. 200 kilograms of corn can feed a family for a year.

___

___

4. The Tata Nano is powered by non-carbon fuels.

___

___

5. Forests will be cut down for the construction of biofuel production plants.

___

___

Formal Writing – a Letter to the Editor

A letter to the editor serves the purpose of expressing one's opinion with the public as audience. It usually contains the following:

- **Introduction**: states clearly the issue that you are concerned about
- **Body**: gives details about the issue; builds up evidence to support your opinion
- **Conclusion**: restates your opinion or offers a solution

As a letter to the editor is a type of formal writing, complete sentences should be used throughout, and contractions and informal language should be avoided.

Pay attention to the following when writing a letter to the editor:

- stick to only one topic
- keep your letter brief
- use facts and figures to support your arguments

B. Read the letter to the editor on page 234 again. Name the different parts with the given words. You may use the words more than once.

body **closing** **introduction** **salutation** **conclusion**

Dear Editor: ________

Paragraph 1 ________

Paragraph 2 ________

Paragraph 3 ________

Paragraph 4 ________

Sincerely, ________

C. Suppose you read the letter to the editor on page 234 in a newspaper. Write your response to that letter to the editor, expressing your view on the biofuel controversy.

When you're writing in response to a letter to the editor, be specific by stating the date that letter was published.

26

A Letter from Sammy in Mali

Hi Kiyoka,

I hope you're doing well. I still think a lot about my visit to your home in Japan a few years ago. I'll never forget it. In fact, I'll always remember Japan as the place that made me realize that I wanted to see the world! See the postmark on this letter? I'm on another big adventure right now, as a member of a Canada World Youth delegation. I'm so excited!

When I returned to Canada from Japan, I started to look in my school's guidance office and browse online to find ways to achieve my goal of seeing the world. My guidance counsellor at school told me that the Canadian government has programs for young people that might interest me. Since I was going to graduate soon from high school, I decided to apply for Canada World Youth. They've been organizing educational exchanges for more than 30 years.

After talking with my parents and grandparents, I sent in my application, and was selected to attend a day-long seminar in which other candidates and I learned about the program. We were told that it wouldn't be easy to go to a foreign country for three months, and then live with our "counterpart" in another part of Canada for an additional three months. We would need to handle things like culture shock and would have to do things like eat strange foods so as not to be disrespectful to our host families. Several weeks after the seminar, I got the call – they wanted to send me to Mali in West Africa!

So, Kiyoka, I'm writing to you from a place called Gao, not too far from the famed city of Timbuktu. We live and work as a group here, helping build heat-efficient ovens from clay. We also help out with AIDS awareness programs. My Malian counterpart is a nice girl my age named Worokia. She speaks both French and her local language. I'm glad that my own French is going to get much better by the time this exchange is over. That's because when Worokia and I and the rest of the team head back to Canada, we'll be living in rural Quebec! Worokia and I will be living with a farming family, so we'll probably be helping out with the harvest.

I'm so thrilled about this experience, and thrilled with myself. If you asked me if I ever thought I would live and work in Africa, I would have said "No". But here I am, and even though there are challenges (like scorpions, sometimes), I'm proud to stick them out, and grateful for this opportunity. Can't wait to show Worokia my own country.

Enclosed is a photo of me and Worokia in Gao. Take care, Kiyoka. Will write again.

Love,
Sammy

A. Read the clues and complete the crossword puzzle with words from the letter.

Across

A. chance
B. adviser
C. having knowledge of
D. group of representatives
E. well-known
F. very excited

Down

1. gain or reach
2. people who are considered for something
3. appreciative of something received
4. of the countryside
5. meeting to discuss a particular topic

Informal Writing

Informal writing is a casual way of communicating with our family and friends. It does not have to follow precise rules of grammar, and the sentence structure can be casual, which often include contractions, utterances, or brief sentences. Friendly letters or e-mail, notes, postcards, and greeting cards are examples of informal writing.

B. Read "A Letter from Sammy in Mali" again and complete the following activity.

1. What is the informal salutation in this letter?

 ____

2. What is the casual closing?

 ____

3. Find three sentences that contain contractions from the letter. Circle the contractions.

 a. ______________________________

 b. ______________________________

 c. ______________________________

4. Find three sentences that are not grammatically correct in the letter.

 a. ______________________________

 b. ______________________________

 c. ______________________________

5. Why are the sentences you gave above not grammatical?

 a. ______________________________

 b. ______________________________

 c. ______________________________

C. **Imagine you volunteered to help at a summer camp and have just returned home. Write an e-mail to your friend telling him/her about the summer camp.**

Everyone can and does write! But if you want to write captivating stories, and deliver them with prose that shines, and in a style that is uniquely yours, there are things you must consider. Below are the main concepts integral to writing good fiction.

Plot is the story you wish to tell, and it should answer the question, "What's happening?" Novels usually include subplots, which are inner "stories" connected to the main plot and are less important than the main plot. Short stories usually do not have subplots. In terms of plot structure, a story usually starts with a situation and a problem, or conflict. What follows is a rising action, followed by a climax and the resulting dénouement, or resolution, and a conclusion. Another, less common form of story is in the picaresque style, where the plot is simply a series of adventures without a clear "resolution", since one is not called for. Most stories are structured in chronological order, although many have been written out of order, or even backwards! Flashbacks, time-lapse, and flashforwards are literary devices of structure that you can use to create a story that is unique.

The Elements of Fiction

Conflict is the struggle between two people or between a person and something. Conflict is essential in a story. It would be a boring story indeed if the characters encountered no problems. Conflict can come in different forms, such as a person against another person, against nature, against himself/herself, against fate, and against society.

Characters are the people who act out the plot. The central character is the protagonist, and the antagonist is the force providing conflict for the central character. Some stories include a character foil, which is someone whose traits are meant to highlight the traits of the protagonist. Minor characters may be employed to help further the story quickly if necessary. Main characters need to be fully developed, with good and bad qualities. They must also be dynamic, that is, they must change over the course of the story.

Setting refers to the place and the time in which the plot takes place. The setting may be an important part of the plot or conflict, or it can simply act as a backdrop to the story, with no effect on outcomes.

Theme refers to the underlying meaning of the story: the reason for writing the story and what the writer expects the reader may learn. The theme can be explicit (stated openly in the story) or implicit (implied by the plot, the characters' actions, etc.).

Point-of-view refers to the way a story is narrated. A "first-person" point of view means that the main character is telling the story, so we read about "I". A story can be narrated in the "third person", in which case we read about "he" or "she". The narrator may be "omniscient" (meaning that he/she knows everything about the story and the characters), "limited-omniscient", or "objective" (in which case he/she knows nothing more than the reader).

Style refers to the language the author uses to deliver the story. The style can be conversational, unusual, and can include the use of dialect. Related to style is tone, which reflects the author's (or character's) attitude towards the story as well.

Give these things the consideration they deserve, and you, too, can be a great writer!

A. Briefly explain what each of the following terms means.

1. Plot ____________________

2. Conflict ____________________

3. Characters ____________________

4. Setting ____________________

5. Theme ____________________

6. Point-of-view ____________________

7. Style ____________________

Descriptive Writing

When writing fiction, we can draw the reader into the world of our story by using descriptive language. Many plain and common words can be replaced with more descriptive words to create vivid images and enhance the reader's visual experience. Descriptive adjectives, adverbs, and phrases that appeal to the five senses add details to our descriptions, making our story more interesting to read.

B. Think of the setting and characters for the story below. Write as many descriptive words and phrases as you can for each of them.

A Day with Rudolph the Reindeer

Setting: ______________________________

Descriptive words and phrases for the setting:

____

____

____

Character 1: ______________________________

Descriptive words and phrases for this character:

____

____

____

Character 2: ______________________________

Descriptive words and phrases for this character:

____

____

____

C. Based on the setting and characters you have created in (B), develop a descriptive story "A Day with Rudolph the Reindeer".

A Day with Rudolph the Reindeer

28

Who Will Be the Next Man on the Moon?

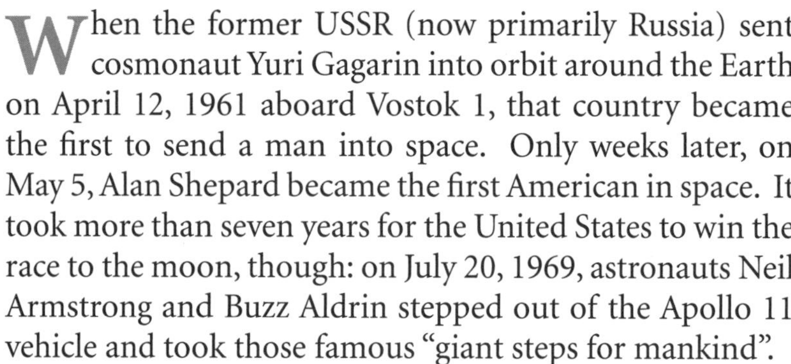

When the former USSR (now primarily Russia) sent cosmonaut Yuri Gagarin into orbit around the Earth on April 12, 1961 aboard Vostok 1, that country became the first to send a man into space. Only weeks later, on May 5, Alan Shepard became the first American in space. It took more than seven years for the United States to win the race to the moon, though: on July 20, 1969, astronauts Neil Armstrong and Buzz Aldrin stepped out of the Apollo 11 vehicle and took those famous "giant steps for mankind".

Despite the significance of this achievement, no other country can claim to have sent a space traveller to the moon in the 40 years since. The American and Russian Shuttle programs have resulted in astronauts from other countries (such as Canada and Japan) orbiting the Earth and spending time at the International Space Station, and many countries have sent un-manned spacecraft and satellites into space for decades (Canada sent Anik 1, the world's first domestic communications satellite, into space way back in 1972). However, no countries other than the U.S.A. and Russia have been able to send their own personnel into orbit, and only the U.S.A. has sent anyone to the moon. It may surprise you then that the next person to land on the moon may be neither American nor Russian – but Chinese!

On October 15, 2003, China launched its Long March rocket in the Gobi Desert, carrying Chinese astronaut Yang Liwei on board the Shenzhou 5 spacecraft, becoming the third country to send a manned vehicle into space. He orbited Earth 14 times during his 21-hour flight. In 2005, the country completed its second manned mission. As awesome as the achievement seems – to be the third country to send a human into space – it is only the beginning of China's ambitious space program, which is geared towards placing a human on the moon once again.

The Chinese Lunar Exploration Program is being carried out by the China National Space Administration, China's space agency, and includes both explorations by un-manned robotic vehicles as well as by human missions. The first lunar orbiter, Chang'e 1, was the first phase of this project and was launched on October 24, 2007 at the Xichang Satellite Launch Centre in Sichuan province. It took 12 days to reach the moon and began its orbit of the moon on November 5. It stayed in orbit around the moon for a year, at about 200 kilometres above the moon's surface, to undertake analyses of the moon's geology and chemistry. Further plans in the program include the launch of Chang'e 2, and the deployment of a lunar rover for limited surface exploration sometime in 2009. A program designed to return un-manned lunar vehicles will commence in 2012 and last until the manned space program commences in 2017. This may seem like a long time for a young student, but now there are millions of young students in China who can share the dream of becoming an astronaut, and of walking on the moon.

A. Write 1 to 6 to put the events in order.

☐ The first domestic communications satellite was sent into space.

☐ Neil Armstrong and Buzz Aldrin stepped on the moon.

☐ Yuri Gagarin was sent into orbit around the Earth.

☐ Yang Liwei orbited the Earth on Shenzou 5.

☐ Alan Shepard was sent into space.

☐ Chang'e 1 orbited the moon.

B. Answer these questions.

1. What do you think "giant steps for mankind" means?

____

____

2. Why do you think the writer describes China's space program as an "ambitious" one?

____

____

3. Describe briefly the Chinese Lunar Exploration Program.

____

____

Expository Writing

Expository writing is frequently used by students, especially when we write for school projects. The purpose of expository writing is to inform, describe, explain, define, or instruct. We have to assume that the reader has no prior knowledge of the topic. A good piece of expository writing should remain focused on its topic, be clear and logical, and have strong organization. To achieve this, we can organize facts according to their common topics, list events in chronological order, analyze cause and effect relationships, and compare objects to show their similarities and differences.

C. Organize the facts about Chinese astronaut Yang Liwei below and compose an expository composition about him.

- dreamed of flying at a young age
- an astronaut of the China National Space Administration (CNSA)
- selected as an astronaut candidate in 1998
- born in Liaoning, China
- promoted to colonel after his first mission
- joined the Chinese People's Liberation Army (PLA) in September 1983
- born on June 21, 1965
- was a lieutenant colonel at the time of his first mission in space
- excelled in sciences when studied at school
- first Chinese citizen in space on board China's first manned spacecraft Shenzhou 5
- promoted to major general on July 2, 2008
- graduated from the No. 8 Aviation College of the PLA Air Force in 1987 and became a fighter pilot
- underwent five years of training at the Astronaut Training Base in Beijing with 13 other candidates since 1998
- launched into space aboard the Shenzhou 5 spacecraft on October 15, 2003
- received the title of "Space Hero" from the chairman of the Central Military Commission of China on November 7, 2007
- participated in the screening process for astronauts in 1996

Title

Opening Paragraph (state the subject of your composition, make it interesting to read)

Body Paragraphs (organize the facts and put them into paragraphs, each with a common topic)

Concluding Paragraph (summarize your writing or lead the reader to think further about the topic)

Review 2

A. Proofread the passage for errors in spelling, punctuation, and capitalization. Underline the errors and make the corrections above them.

winterlude, a winter celebration hostted by canada's Capitol Region, attracts thousands of visitors to Ottawa in Feburary every year.

The ice hog family the mascots of winterlude consists of; Papa Ice Hog, Mama Ice Hog, and their twin children noumi and nouma. You can meet them and play with them at sun life snowflake kingdom, the largest slow playground in north america. They bring happyness to children and adults alike. They even have a family song called the ice hogs' song.

Activities of winterlude take place over three weekends. There is an astounishing sound and light show called ukiuk ukiuk means winter in inuktitut presented at the american express Snowbowl on the rideau canal skateway, the ice-carving masters showcase organized at rogers crystal garden in confederation park with numerus giant and marvellous masterpeices which demonstrate the skills and createivity of the sculptors; and Ice Fishing for All at sun life snowflake kingdom in jacques-cartier park where visitors can try to fish for rainbow trout in the chili winter of Canada.

B. Rewrite the following sentences to avoid repetition of words.

1. The smart professor is talking with his smart student.

2. This city is famous for its great scenery and great hotels.

3. Mom has put the small figurine on the small table.

4. I had a delicious dinner with my family tonight, and tomorrow, I will have another delicious dinner with my friends.

C. Replace the underlined words with more precise words. Add descriptive adjectives, adverbs, or phrases to the sentences.

1. The girl ran into the shop.

2. The man planted a tree in the garden.

3. There is a restaurant in this building.

4. The car is parked outside the house.

D. Check the sentences that make use of personification.

1. The moonlight embraced the lonely tree. ☐
2. The stream flows gently in the light breeze. ☐
3. The giant pumpkin is as heavy as a man of medium build. ☐
4. The hyenas laughed loudly on seeing their prey. ☐
5. The flowers welcome spring by putting on their most colourful clothes. ☐
6. The dog barked ferociously as the stranger approached. ☐

E. Rewrite the similes as metaphors and the metaphors as similes.

1. The lake water shines like crystals in the sun.

   ____

2. The amusement park is a paradise for children.

   ____

3. The capital city of the country is as important as the heart.

   ____

4. For every athlete, medals are precious like jewels.

   ____

5. Emmy is the princess of her family.

   ____

6. Larry is an eagle. He has very keen eyesight.

   ____

F. Rewrite each of the following sentences by beginning it with a phrase.

1. People like strolling leisurely along the river bank after dinner.

   ____

2. Ginny left home two hours earlier to avoid being late.

   ____

3. Kelly let out a shrill cry when she saw the sudden movement under the tablecloth.

   ____

4. The team practised every day as they were determined to win the game.

   ____

G. Combine each pair of sentences with an appositive.

1. Samuel is the tallest boy in our class. He can easily reach that clock on the wall.

   ____

2. The Mariana Trench is located in the Pacific Ocean. It is the deepest place on Earth.

   ____

3. *Ratatouille* is Wilson's favourite DVD. It was a Christmas gift from Grandma.

   ____

   ____

4. *The Starry Night* is one of Vincent van Gogh's most renowned works. It was painted by the great artist in 1889.

   ____

   ____

H. Rewrite the paragraph below by deleting the superfluous words or phrases or replacing them with fewer words.

In my opinion, I think that nothing is more important than my family. Despite the fact that my little sister is in favour of bossing me around, and my elder brother always wears strange clothing he calls fashion, I love them to the utmost depth of my heart. Mom and Dad are of the opinion that at times I may probably be even bossier than my sister and my clothes are much stranger than my brother's clothes. However, they all have no problems tolerating all the imperfections of mine owing to the fact that I am one among the family.

I. The following sentences contain faulty parallels or dangling modifiers. Rewrite them so they are correct.

1. Yoga is a great way to relax, improving flexibility, and relieve stress.
2. Being the coach, everyone on the basketball team respects him.
3. Out of the corner of her eye, a tiny mouse scurried into a crack in the wall of her kitchen.
4. The doors opened and the athletes were filing into the stadium.
5. The Wellings checked and stayed at the Grand Hill Hotel.

J. You have just read a magazine article about the increased number of pet owners who abandon their dogs or cats. Write a letter to the editor expressing your view on this issue.

Remember to avoid using contractions and informal language in the letter.

HISTORY

1

Settlement of New France

In the early 1600s, French settlers started a colony in the New World. They did this to ensure that France would have a share in the profitable fur trade and that missionaries could be sent to convert the Aboriginal peoples to Christianity.

A. Label the map. Then use yellow to colour the area that shows the colony of New France in 1645. Use blue to show the bodies of water that serve New France.

Tadoussac **Trois-Rivières** **Montreal** **Gaspé** **Quebec**

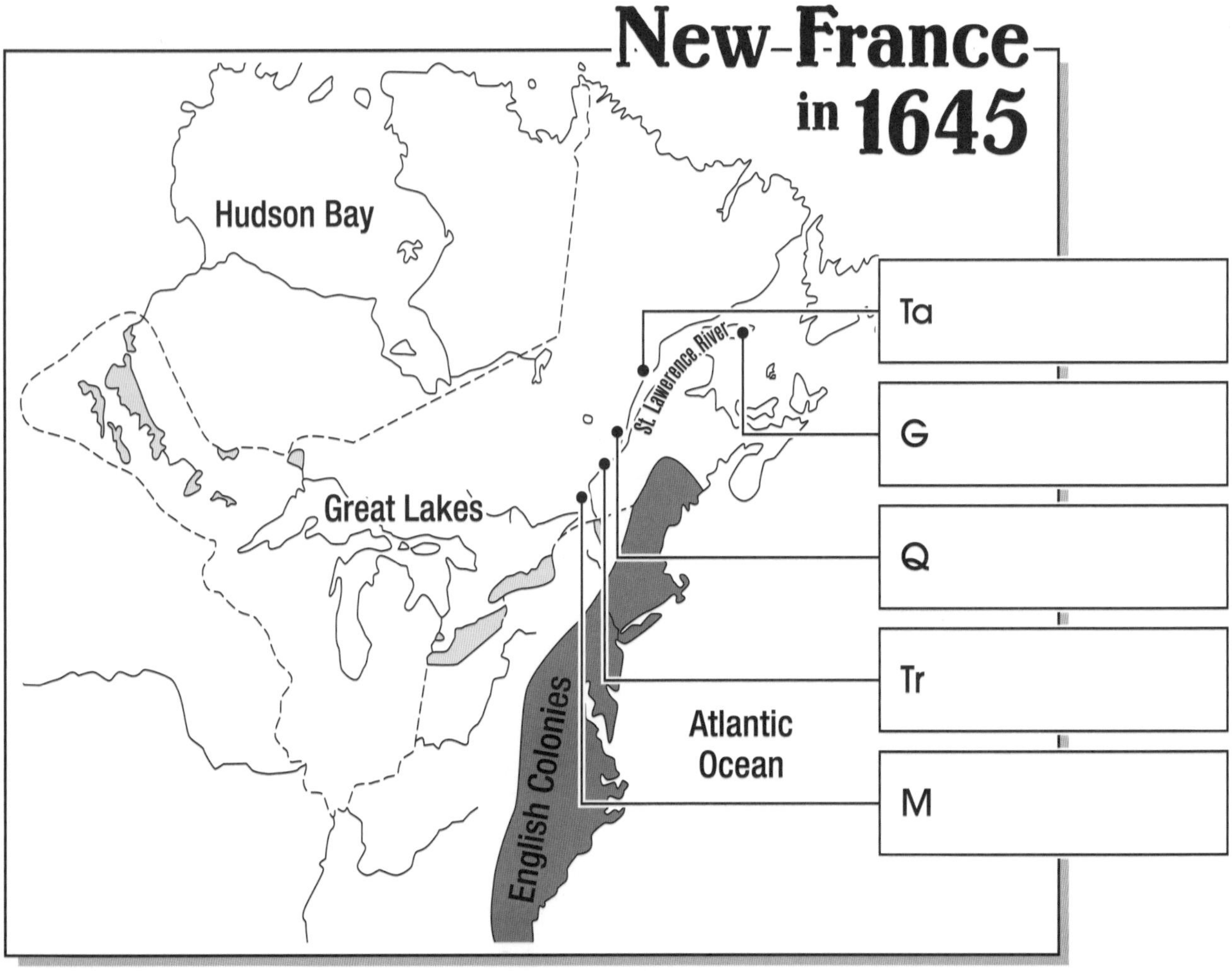

New France in 1645

Hudson Bay

Great Lakes

St. Lawerence River

English Colonies

Atlantic Ocean

Ta

G

Q

Tr

M

B. The children are role-playing French settlers. Help them find their lines. Write the names of the settlers on the lines.

1. "I work the land. It is difficult during these first few years, but soon I will have a harvest to share with my landlord." ________________

2. "I came with other orphan girls to marry and start a family with a settler. Who paid for our passage? The King of France!" ________________

3. "My aristocratic background landed me here. Sure, I was given the land, but I am responsible for many families on my seigneury." ________________

4. "I was one of the first to come, with the hope of finding riches and adventure to take back to France. I never thought I would stay for good." ________________

5. "I left my comfortable parish in Paris to convert the Aboriginal peoples to Catholicism." ________________

6. "I came, on orders from my superiors, to help protect the new colony. The offer of free land enticed me to stay. I even married one of the filles du roi." ________________

2

New France – Economic and Political Life

New France was created to provide riches and power to its parent country, France. The King of France was at the top of New France's hierarchy, even though he never visited the colony.

A. Read the paragraph. Circle the correct answers.

New France was forbidden by the King of France to sell its resources to anyone other than its parent country and other French colonies, and the colony was required to purchase all supplies needed from outside the colony from France. This economic system is called ***mercantilism****.*

Mercantilism

Fur, fish, wood

France

New France

manufactured goods

1. What was France's main motivation for starting the colony of New France?

   A. to accumulate more wealth

   B. to learn more about Aboriginal peoples

2. What did New France export to France or other French colonies?

   A. sugar, coffee

   B. fur, fish, wood

3. What effect did the mercantile economic system have on the beaver population of the New World?

   A. Beaver population increased.

   B. Beaver population decreased.

4. Who benefited the most from the mercantile system of New France?

   A. the homeland, France

   B. the colony, New France

B. Read about the basic political structure of New France. Write the words in bold in the boxes. Then list the responsibilities for each of the specified positions.

New France was ruled by the ***King*** *of France. No king ever visited the colony, but the* ***governor*** *permanently resided there and represented him. The governor commanded soldiers, dealt with other colonies and Aboriginal nations, and otherwise behaved like royalty.*

The ***intendant*** *was positioned below the governor yet reported directly to the king. His duties involved the financial, legal, and economic concerns of the colony. The intendant and governor were a part of the* ***sovereign*** *council. The governor appointed others to the council, which made laws and set taxes for the colony's citizens.*

Although the ***bishop*** *was an official of the church, he held an important position in the sovereign council. His responsibilities included overseeing the hospitals, schools, missions, and churches.*

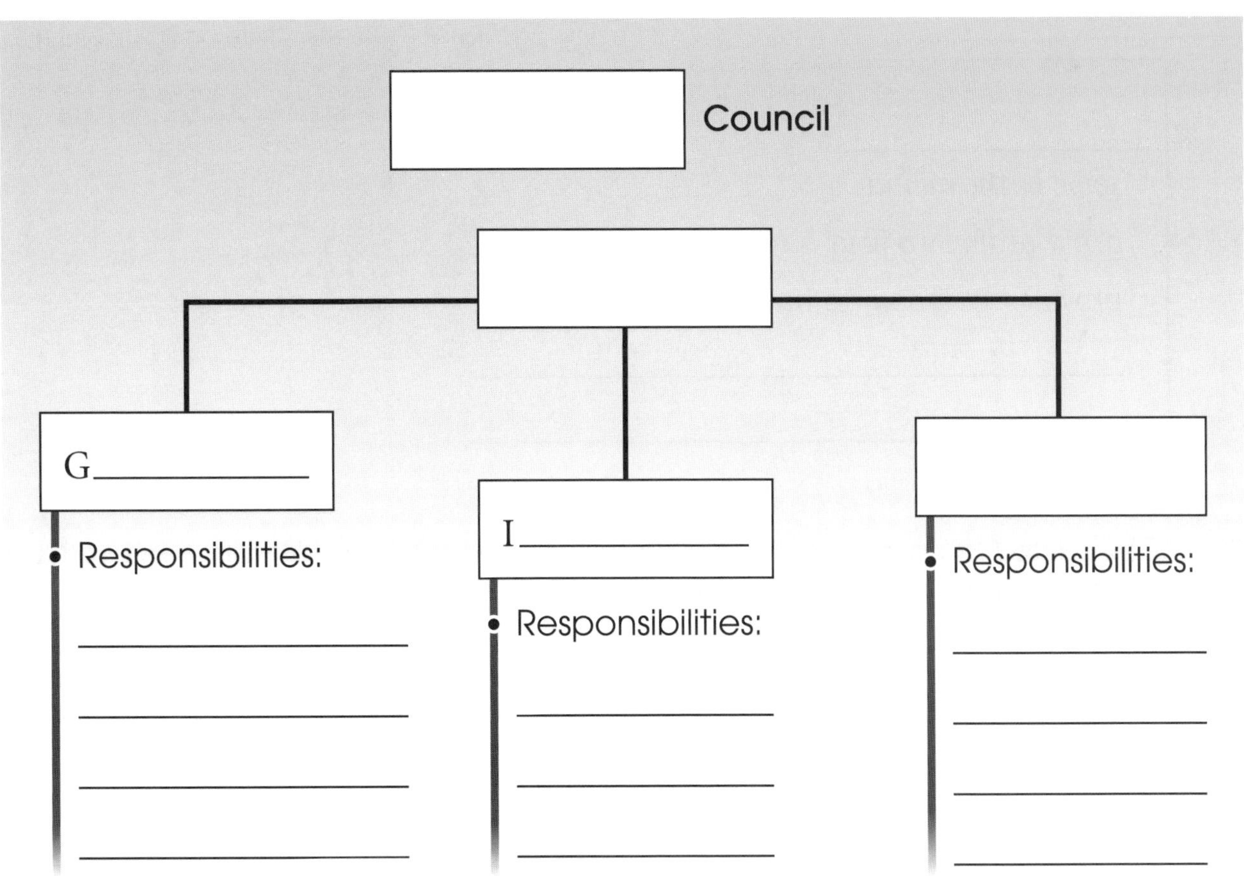

3

New France – Social Life

Rural New France operated using a seigneurial system. The seigneur, usually a man of nobility, owned land on which the habitants lived and worked. He also had responsibilities to the habitants.

A. Look at the duties or responsibilities of a seigneur or a habitant. Write "Seigneurs" or "Habitants" in the boxes. Then list the given duties or responsibilities on the lines.

- **build a mill**
- **pay rent**
- **attract settlers**
- **work the land**

1. [ ]

- *build their own manors*
- *resolve conflicts within the seigneurie*
- *defend the seigneurie from outside attack*
- ____________________
- ____________________

2. [ ]

- *serve in the militia*
- *grind grain into flour*
- *provide free labour to build a church*
- ____________________
- ____________________

B. If you lived in rural New France in the mid-1600s, would you want to be a seigneur or a habitant? Explain your choice.

____

____

____

____

C. Miranda is researching information on the social life of New France. Help her organize the data to indicate whether each piece of information comes from a primary or secondary source. Write "P" for primary source or "S" for secondary source in the circle.

We use primary sources and secondary sources to learn about history. A primary source is first-hand information that is recorded during or shortly after an event. It could be an interview with someone who was there, or a newspaper article from the time it happened. A secondary source often uses a primary source. It may be an encyclopedia article, or information found on a website.

1. census data from the office of Statistics Canada that says there were 5 surgeons and 36 carpenters in the French colony in 1665

2. information in a textbook that tells us that French thieves were often given the choice to serve their sentence in France, or become a colonist in New France

3. the journal of a wealthy merchant's daughter that mentions the different domestic chores of the slaves her father brought from the Caribbean

4. a CD-ROM that shows how the daily life of the habitants changed with the seasons: harvest in the fall, planting crops and tapping sugar maples in the spring

5. a letter from a habitant woman in New France describing her difficult life on the farm and announcing the home-birth of her sixth child

6. an illustration in a modern storybook depicting the busy comings and goings of people in Montreal

New France – Cooperation and Conflict

The fur trade ignited cooperation between the French and First Nations peoples. However, it increased competition for global power between the French and the British.

A. Choose the correct words to complete the sentences about the cooperation and conflict between New France and Britain.

1. The final battle between the French and the British on North American soil took place on the ____________, a field near the city of Quebec.

2. At the entrance of the St. Lawrence River, ____________ was surrounded by thick walls. This ____________ was New France's first line of defence from British ships wanting entrance.

3. The capture of Louisbourg by the ____________ marked the beginning of the ____________________ in North America.

4. The Seven Years' War ended with the warring ____________ signing a ____________.

5. The British and French took advantage of ____________ between different Iroquoian and Huron nations to form their ____________.

6. Throughout the Seven Years' War, both the British and the French had ____________ in Aboriginal nations.

B. Read the passages about the wars of New France. State whether each is a "fact" or an "opinion".

In a treaty that followed one of the wars between Britain and France, Britain offered to return either Acadia or the sugar-producing islands of Martinique and Guadeloupe.

1.

France sent far fewer troops to the New World than Britain did.

2.

The British won the Battle of the Plains of Abraham because they had more troops than the French.

3.

France was wrong to believe its troops would do better to fight the enemy closer to home than in the New World.

4.

"The Death of General Wolfe"

Both commanders of the warring armies met their demise at the Battle of the Plains of Abraham: British Major General Wolfe died on the battlefield, while French General Montcalm was mortally wounded.

6.

France cared little about the colony that was to be Canada; it chose two small Caribbean islands over the portion of New France called Acadia.

5.

5

The Settlement of British North America

After the Treaty of Paris signalled the end of the formal conflict between Britain and France, the Royal Proclamation and the Quebec Act were set up to appease the French.

A. Fill in the blanks to complete the details of the key events in the settlement of British North America. Then answer the questions.

Treaty of Paris — At the end of the Seven Years' War, fought between Britain and France on North American soil, the Treaty of Paris was signed in 1763.

Outcomes of the signing of the Treaty of Paris:

- The ________________ came to a formal end.
- France gave up any ________________ it had to North America, except for fishing rights to two islands off ________________ .
- New France fell into ________________ hands.

Newfoundland
rights
British
Seven Years' War

Royal Proclamation — The Royal Proclamation of 1763 indirectly led to the creation of the United States of America.

Outcomes of the creation of the Royal Proclamation:

- Colonial use of lands west of the ________________ Mountains was restricted.
- British colonists felt that Britain made the Royal Proclamation to benefit ________________ , not the colonists.
- The dissatisfaction of the colonists with Britain started the ________________ Revolution.

American
Britain
Appalachian

Quebec Act Along with the Royal Proclamation, the Quebec Act was designed to please the French in Quebec, as well as the Aboriginal peoples who were worried about losing the rights to their land and its resources.

Outcomes of the Quebec Act:

Aboriginal
Roman
seigneurial
French

- Allowed the ______________ system to continue.
- Discouraged entry to traditional ______________ lands to the west.
- Permitted ______________ civil law to continue.
- Recognized the importance of the ______________ Catholic Church.

Why do you think the British colonists would not be happy with the Royal Proclamation and the Quebec Act?

____

____

B. Read the paragraph. Complete the legend to reflect North America in 1763.

With the Treaty of Paris in 1763, the British claim to North America spread into the west. Spain was granted Louisiana, and Russia had a claim to land in the northwest of the continent.

Spanish **British** **Russian**

- ______________ claims
- ______________ claims
- French claims
- ______________ claims

6

The Causes and Effects of the American Revolution

Many American colonists were ready for more independence, but Britain was moving in the opposite direction, offering less independence. By 1775, the American Revolution had begun.

A. Determine whether each was a cause or effect of the American Revolution. Then complete the summary table with the words in bold.

1. The colonists who wanted a less restrictive economic system found they were stuck with **mercantilism** under British rule. ____________

2. The **United States of America** was the name given to the newly independent American colonies. ____________

3. Some British officials trying to enforce the **new tax laws** were tarred and feathered by unruly crowds. ____________

4. The **Invasion of Quebec** was an attempt by American rebels to get Quebec to join their side. ____________

5. The **Stamp Act** of 1765 was imposed on the colonies by the British to help pay for the expense of defending it. This enraged most colonists, and the law was repealed the following year. ____________

6. **British North America** was the name of the remaining colonies controlled by Britain after the American Revolution. ____________

American Revolution

Causes	Effects
•	•
•	•
•	•

B. Read what Peter says. Choose sides. Indicate who each person was likely to side with in the American Revolution by writing the paragraph letters in the boxes.

A. A seigneur from Quebec whose privileged position was respected by the British government

B. A person who sympathized with the rebel cause, but did not agree with the extreme punishments used by the rebels

C. A Mohawk who had a protected land claim under British rule

D. A black slave who had the promise of freedom if he or she remained loyal to Britain

E. A land speculator who had hoped that the British conquest of New France would make it easier for American colonists to move to fertile inland valleys

F. A man who, with his wife and children, emigrated from England two years before and still had family and friends in the homeland

*Colonists everywhere were under pressure to choose sides in the American Revolution. Those for the continuation of British rule were called **loyalists**; those against were **rebels**.*

Loyalists	Rebels

C. Write a paragraph that supports the position you have taken in the revolution.

American Revolution

The Loyalists and British North America

By the beginning of the 1800s, British North America was split into distinct regions. Immigrant populations grew with Loyalists arriving from the south and others arriving from overseas.

A. Fill in the blanks to complete the paragraph. Outline the borders of Upper Canada in red and the borders of Lower Canada in blue. Then label both sections.

The Constitutional Act of 1791 saw the division of Quebec into ____________________ (on the upper end of the St. Lawrence River) and ____________________ . These two colonies joined Nova Scotia, New Brunswick, Prince Edward Island, and Newfoundland.

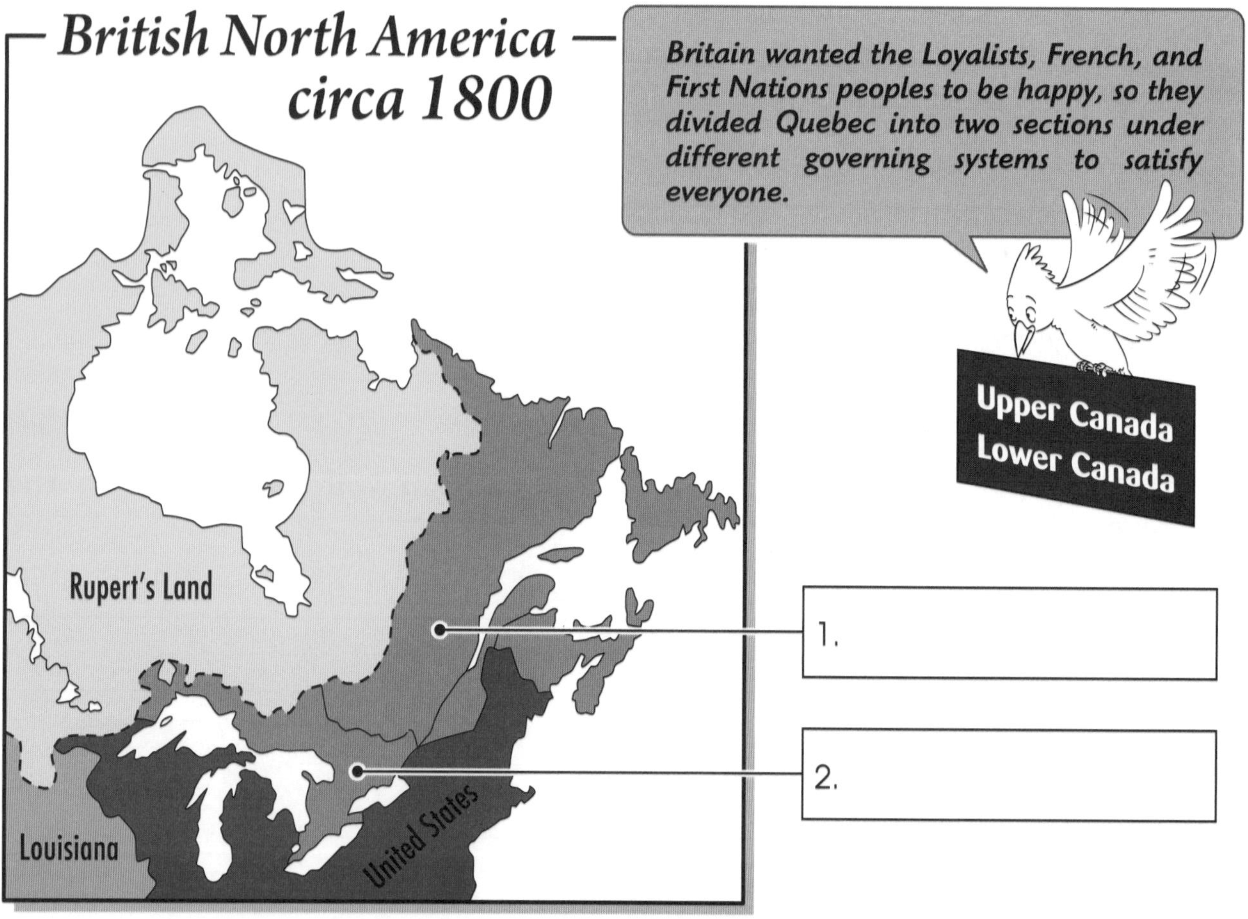

British North America – circa 1800

Britain wanted the Loyalists, French, and First Nations peoples to be happy, so they divided Quebec into two sections under different governing systems to satisfy everyone.

Upper Canada
Lower Canada

Rupert's Land

Louisiana

United States

1. ____________________

2. ____________________

B. Read what Jason says and the descriptions of the British North Americans. Then unscramble the letters to write the names.

British North America continued to grow after the American Revolution. Loyalists (Americans who were loyal to the British monarchy) and others increased its population to about half a million.

British North American People

Many came from the southern colonies because they were promised freedom from slavery.

A ______________________

klBac syoLalits

Some Aboriginal peoples were already in Upper Canada.

B ______________________

agusisMissa , wiChppea

Poverty drove these people from their homes in the British Isles to Upper Canada.

C ______________________

tcSoisth

More than 40 000, particularly farmers, went to the Maritimes, helping to create the province of New Brunswick.

D ______________________

hWiet iloLyasts

These businessmen lived in cities among the French of Lower Canada, although they were usually Protestant and English speaking. They were favoured by the governing British and quickly dominated the local economy.

E ______________________

sirBith temrcahns

Poor British citizens would not have had enough money to pay their passage to North America. Their only route to emigration was to promise several years of service to wealthy families in return for the fare.

F ______________________

dedlnenrtu esrnvtas

Some pacifist religious groups (those who did not believe in war) were welcomed to Upper Canada from the United States by Lieutenant Governor Simcoe.

G ______________________

nestMenoin nda seukQar

The War of 1812

Several events conspired to cause relations between British North America and the United States to sour. The hostilities that ensued are known as the War of 1812.

A. Fill in the blanks to complete the sentences about the War of 1812.

Events of the War of 1812

Queenston Heights **Treaty of Ghent** **North American** **October** **Louisiana** **Laura Secord**

A The United States and Britain fought a battle in ____________ in 1815 because news of the peace treaty signed overseas had not yet reached them.

B In 1814, the ____________ officially ended the war. British North America had successfully avoided being conquered.

C Shawnee Chief Tecumseh joined the British in their defence of Canada when the war broke out. He had bravely led many successful battles when he was killed in ____________ of 1813.

D In August of 1812, under Major General Isaac Brock, the British won the first battle of the war in Upper Canada. A couple of months later, a second battle was won at ____________, but Brock was killed.

E From 1812 to 1813, Britain was so embroiled in the war with France that very few resources were sent to help fight the American/British ____________ war.

F In June of 1813, ____________ made a 30-kilometre trek on foot to warn a British officer of an impending American attack.

B. Put the events of the war recounted in part A in order by writing the letters in the circles. Then fill in the blanks to complete the sentences.

The War of 1812

France British west Britain

1812 ◯
◯
1813 ◯
◯
1814 ◯
1815 ◯

The United States believed the __________ were preventing them from expanding to the __________ by supplying weapons to the resident Aboriginal nations.

The British navy disrupted trade between the United States and __________ by searching ships on the high seas, even though the U.S. was neutral in the war between France and __________ .

C. Use the information on page 272 and above to answer the questions.

1. Give one reason why the United States declared war on British North America.

____

2. Name two major figures of the War of 1812.

____

3. Why did the last battle occur after the war had ended?

____

9

Conflict and Resolution

Conflict has been a part of human history for as long as records have been kept. Throughout the ages, we have tried to resolve conflict in many different ways.

A. Fill in the blanks with words from the word bank to complete the sentences.

strike conflict protest war rebellion

1. ______________ is a resistance, either violent or non-violent, against a ruler or government.

2. ______________ can occur when the needs and wants of one group of people are different from another.

3. The first known ______________ was staged under an Egyptian Pharaoh when workers of the Royal necropolis refused to do work.

4. An armed conflict between different groups of people is called a ______________ .

5. A ______________ is an organized public demonstration that voices an objection toward something a government wants to do.

B. Read the newspaper headlines and identify the types of conflict. Then choose the correct words from part A and write them on the lines.

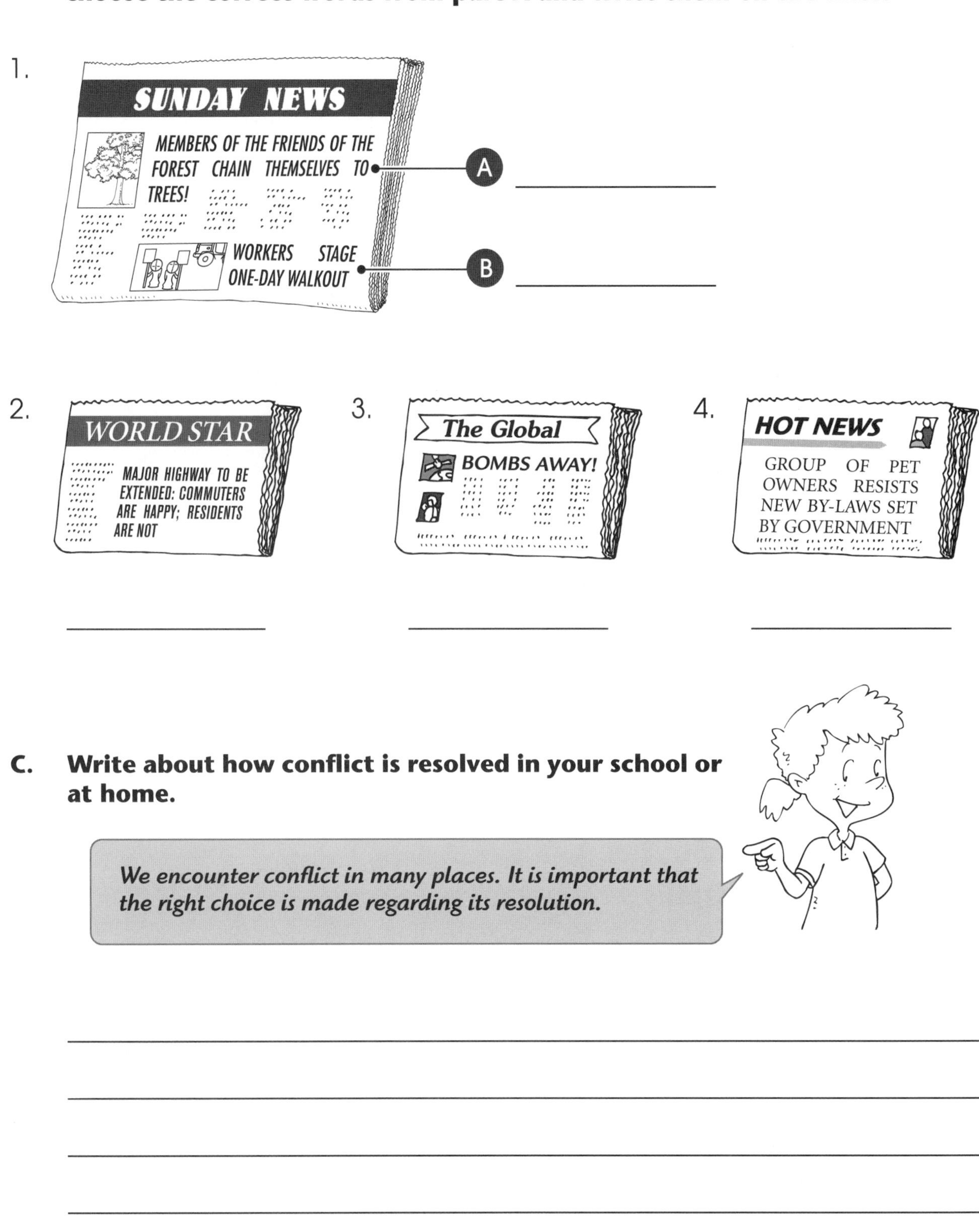

1.
SUNDAY NEWS
MEMBERS OF THE FRIENDS OF THE FOREST CHAIN THEMSELVES TO TREES!
WORKERS STAGE ONE-DAY WALKOUT
A
B
2.
WORLD STAR
MAJOR HIGHWAY TO BE EXTENDED: COMMUTERS ARE HAPPY; RESIDENTS ARE NOT
3.
The Global
BOMBS AWAY!
4.
HOT NEWS
GROUP OF PET OWNERS RESISTS NEW BY-LAWS SET BY GOVERNMENT

C. Write about how conflict is resolved in your school or at home.

We encounter conflict in many places. It is important that the right choice is made regarding its resolution.

The Rebellions of 1837 - 1838: Causes

The rebellions that occurred in Lower and Upper Canada in 1837 and 1838 were caused by a number of factors. In each case, the colonists felt they were not being treated fairly.

A. Use words from the word bank to complete the signs addressing some of the issues that caused the rebellions.

responsible French crown family compact farmers oligarchy rebel

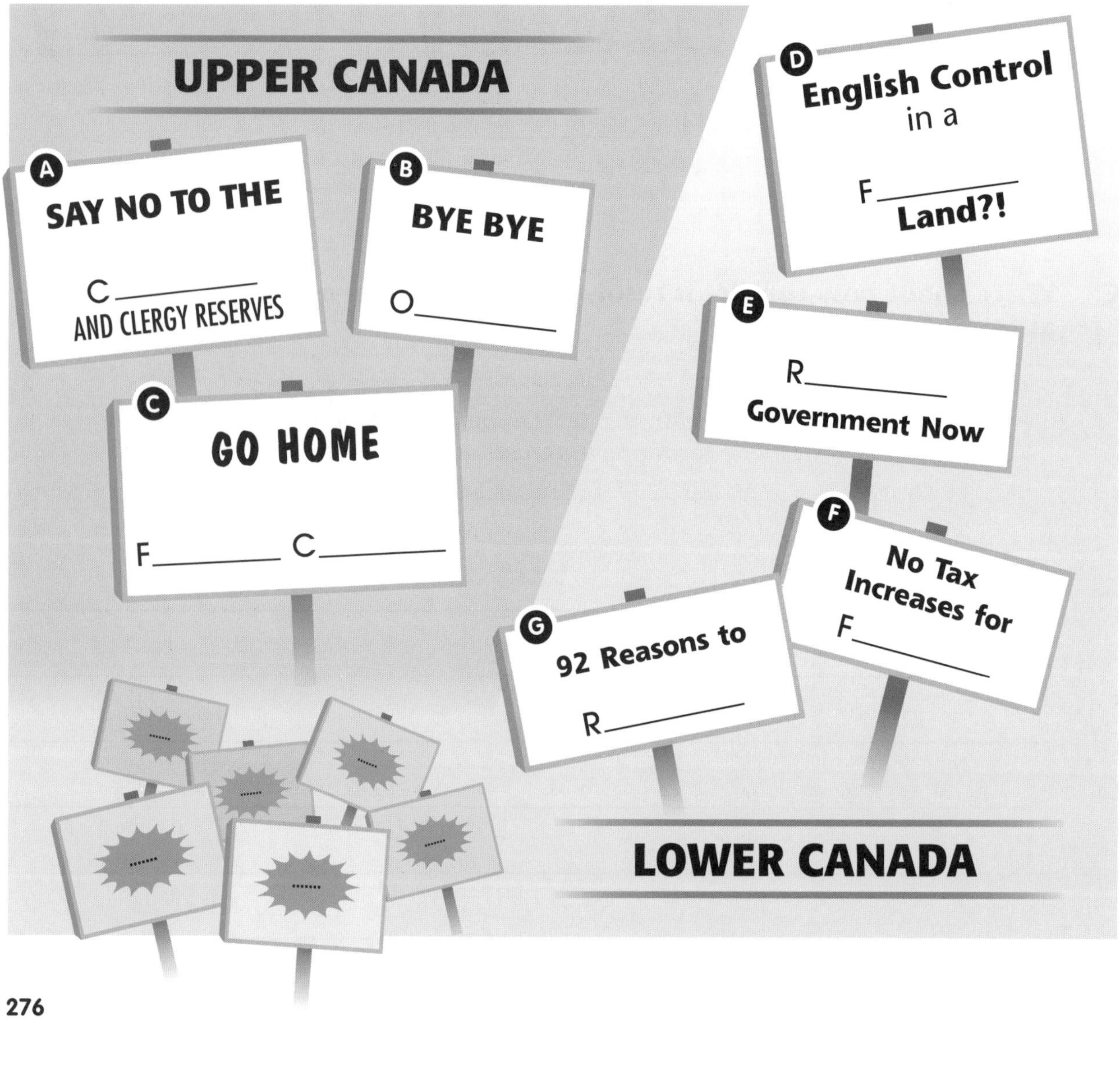

UPPER CANADA

A. SAY NO TO THE C________ AND CLERGY RESERVES

B. BYE BYE O________

C. GO HOME F________ C________

LOWER CANADA

D. English Control in a F________ Land?!

E. R________ Government Now

F. No Tax Increases for F________

G. 92 Reasons to R________

B. Match the signs in part A with the issues below. Place the letters of the signs in the circles.

1. The elected assembly in Lower Canada was mostly French, while the governor's appointed council was mostly English. The French could not control anything, and this seemed unfair to them.

2. A responsible government is accountable to the representatives of the people. For example, the votes of the people make up the Members of Parliament.

3. Large blocks of land set aside for clergy and crown made straight-line travel difficult for colonists. These sections of land also forced the price of the surrounding lands to increase.

4. The Family Compact was a small group of people of loyalist settler descent who had a lot of control over the Upper Canada government's decisions. This type of government is called "oligarchy".

5. Farmers resented British attempts to raise their taxes while business taxes remained untouched.

6. The Legislative Council was made up of the family compact, and it controlled a lot of what happened in Upper Canada. The elected members of the Legislative Assembly thought this was unfair.

7. The British government said "no" to a list of grievances called the "92 Resolutions". Assembled by the reform group – the Parti patriote – the "92 Resolutions" outlined what they believed the government should do.

Personalities and Events of the Rebellions

Rebellions do not happen by themselves. Real people and key personalities were involved in the events that led to the formation of the political system that we have in Canada today.

A. Match the names and descriptions with the pictures of the key figures of the rebellions.

Louis-Joseph Papineau
Roman Catholic Church
William Lyon Mackenzie
Parti patriote
Francis Bond Head

(A) Lieutenant Governor of Upper Canada in 1836

(B) a radical group of young French Canadian elites that gained control of the elected assembly

(C) instructed its parishioners not to support the rebellion in Lower Canada

(D)
- main author of the "92 Resolutions"
- aristocratic reformer and leader of the Parti patriote

(E)
- was the mayor of Toronto in 1834
- came from Scotland, a poor son of a widow, went on to lead the rebellion in Upper Canada

1. ____________ ( )

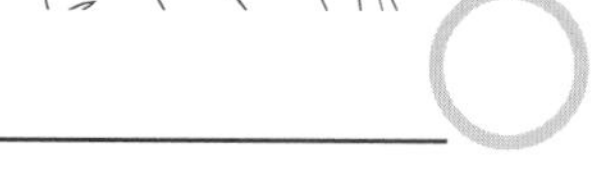

2. ____________ ( )

3. ____________ ( )

4. ____________ ( )

5. ____________ ( )

B. Complete the sentences about the events of the rebellions.

patriotes | Bond Head | British | William Lyon Mackenzie | Caroline | defeated | Fils de la Liberté | Louis-Joseph Papineau | church | Montgomery's Tavern

Lower Canada

1. Rebellion activity first erupted in Lower Canada in the form of a brawl involving the ________________ and the English speaking Doric Club.
2. ________________ leaders advised their parishioners to stay loyal to Britain.
3. An attempted arrest of ________________ resulted in his fleeing Montreal.
4. Dr. Wolfred Nelson led the ________________ to their only victory at St. Denis.
5. At St. Charles, the ________________ defeated the rebels.

Upper Canada

6. ________________ did not like the "clergy reserves" (large tracts of land set aside for clergy and crown) or the Family Compact. He would have liked to see a more American-style democracy being exercised in the colonies.
7. Mackenzie planned on taking ________________ prisoner and setting up a new government.
8. Mackenzie met with his rebels at ________________ on Yonge Street. They marched down Yonge Street and exchanged shots with a group of British militia. Confusion ensued, and Mackenzie's men returned to the tavern where they were ________________ .
9. The Canadians burned and sank the rebel boat ________________ , during which an American citizen was killed.

12

Impact of the Rebellions

For every action, there is a reaction. Some historians say that the Rebellions of 1837-1838 were just a series of little skirmishes that had no real effect, while others maintain that they were integral to the formation of a responsible government.

A. Some of the immediate results of the Rebellions of 1837-1838 are stated below. Use words from the word bank to complete the passage.

rebels economy 300 rebellions soldiers Australia hanging civil rights poverty

By 1839, the 1. __________ were over. However, the 2. __________ was in bad shape and many farmers were living in 3. __________ due to poor harvests. In Lower Canada, 27 4. __________ and 5. __________ French Canadians had lost their lives. The British government punished the 6. __________ by 7. __________, jailing, or exiling them. Boats transported the 92 English and 58 French rebels to the harsh penal colonies that Britain had set up in 8. __________. Great Britain shelved 9. __________ and dissolved the assemblies of Upper and Lower Canada.

CANADA

AUSTRALIA

B. Read what Jacob says. Then circle the correct answers for the questions about Lord Durham's recommendations.

Britain sent John George Lambton, the 1st Earl of Durham, to the colonies to report on the causes of the rebellions. His report, known as Lord Durham's Report, recommended that some changes be made.

1. Upper and Lower Canada should

   A. be combined under one government.

   B. remain separate with two opposing governments.

2. The colonies should have control

   A. over their own internal affairs.

   B. over Britain's affairs.

3. People from Britain should

   A. go to live in France.

   B. come to live in Canada.

4. Responsible government should be set up, where the leaders of the elected legislative assembly

   A. are named as the governor general's advisers.

   B. do not advise anyone.

5. The freedoms that the French received under the Royal Proclamation of 1763 and the Quebec Act of 1774 should

   A. be increased.

   B. be taken away.

Review

A. Sophie and George are preparing a presentation about the beginnings of Canada. Help them complete the information about the settlement of New France.

missionaries	fur
wealth	Aboriginal
soldiers	habitants
seigneurs	mercantilist
power	filles du roi

France created New France to increase its 1. ____________ and 2. ____________ . This was achieved primarily through the 3. ____________ trade, which was even more profitable because the French used the 4. ____________ system. Also, the 5. ____________ had an interest in converting 6. ____________ peoples to Christianity. 7. ____________ also came because New France used a seigneurial system with many 8. ____________ working the land. Other settlers came as well, including the 9. ____________ and 10. ____________ .

B. Name the settlers with the help of the information above.

1. ____________ 2. ____________ 3. ____________ 4. ____________

C. Sophie is working on a section about the Seven Years' War. Help her write "T" for the true statements and "F" for the false ones.

1. Britain and France were competing for global power. ☐
2. Britain entered New France via Hudson Bay. ☐
3. The Seven Years' War was marked in North America by Britain's capture of Louisbourg. ☐
4. The final battle at the Plains of Abraham ended with the Treaty of Ghent. ☐

D. Look at the information about the aftermath of the Seven Years' War. Write the letters in the circles and answer the question.

- **A** *British colonists were upset, leading them to start the American Revolution.*
- **B** *Put an official end to the Seven Years' War.*
- **C** *Restrictions were made to the colonial use of land.*
- **D** *New France was placed under British rule.*
- **E** *Seigneurial system was allowed to continue.*
- **F** *French civil law was permitted.*

1. ◯◯ Treaty of Paris

   ◯◯ The Quebec Act

   ◯◯ The Royal Proclamation of 1763

2. *Who were the Royal Proclamation and the Quebec Act designed to please?*

   ____

E. Sophie and George divided a display board into three parts. There is a theme for each part. Help them complete the information.

Part I: American Revolution (write "loyalist" or "rebel")

1. "As a black slave, I'm motivated by the promise of freedom." ____________
2. "I'm upset that the French have been looked after so well. I'm ready for more independence." ____________
3. "I chose this side because I don't like mercantilism and want a less restrictive economic system." ____________

Part II: War of 1812 (write the effects)

1. Cause: The British gave weapons to resident Aboriginal nations.

   Effect: ____________________________
   (What did the United States think?)

2. Cause: The British went to battle at Queenston Heights.

   Effect: ____________________________
   (What happened to the British Major General? Who won the battle?)

Part III: British North America (write "First Nations", "Quebec", or "Newfoundland")

1. The Constitutional Act of 1791 divided ______________ into Upper Canada and Lower Canada. This division was made to satisfy the Loyalists, the French, and the ______________ peoples.

2. The colony united Nova Scotia, New Brunswick, Prince Edward Island, and ______________ as part of British North America.

F. Read the quiz that Sophie and George prepared about the Rebellions of 1837-1838. Circle the correct answers.

Test Yourself

Name: ____________

The Rebellions of 1837-1838

1. The Rebellions occurred because the colonists
   A. missed their homeland.
   B. wanted to join the United States.
   C. felt they weren't being treated properly.

2. In Lower Canada, the French thought it was unfair that
   A. they could not control anything in their government.
   B. more and more British people were immigrating.
   C. more loyalists were coming up from the U.S.

3. Most of the decisions of the Upper Canada government were controlled by
   A. William Lyon Mackenzie.
   B. The Roman Catholic Church.
   C. the Family Compact.

4. After the rebellions, the British government punished the rebels by
   A. raising their taxes.
   B. jailing, exiling, or hanging them.
   C. making them march down Yonge Street.

5. The recommendation that Upper and Lower Canada be united under one government came from
   A. John George Lambton (Lord Durham).
   B. the King of France.
   C. Louis-Joseph Papineau.

GEOGRAPHY

1

Themes of Geographic Inquiry: Location/Place

There are different ways to describe a specific place. We can use maps to tell its location and to describe its characteristics.

A. Identify the axis gradation used for each map. Write the answers in the boxes. Then write which map you should use to answer the questions.

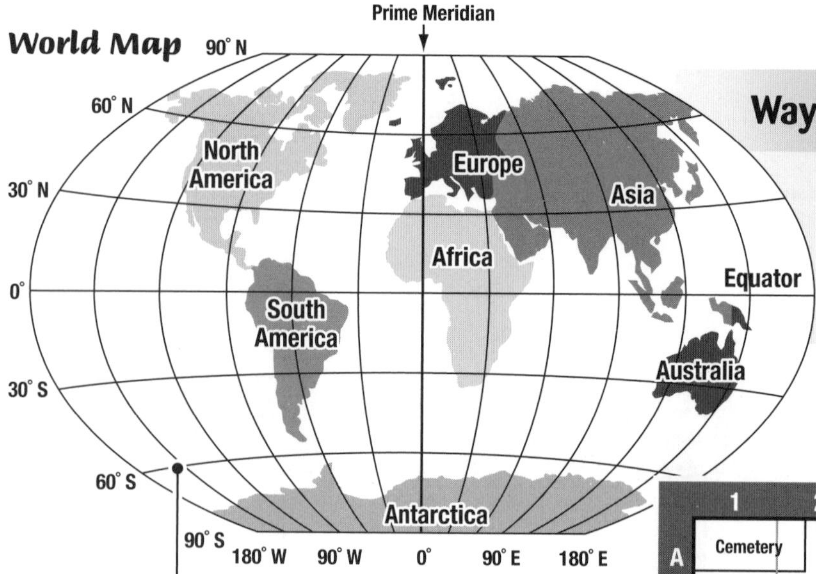

World Map

Ways to Make Maps:

- the imaginary lines of latitude and longitude
- an alphanumeric grid

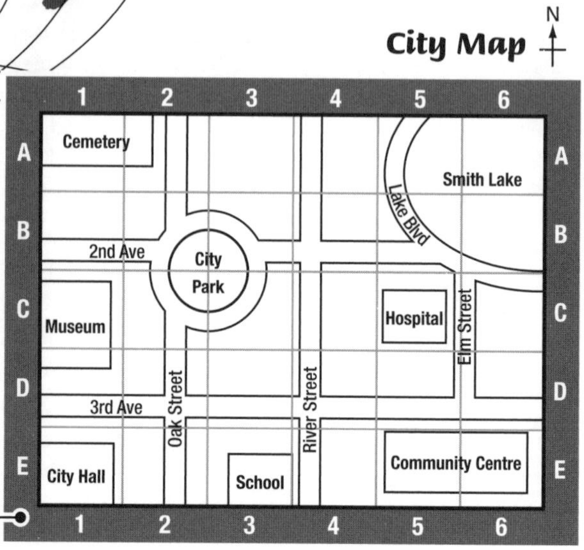

City Map

1. using

2. using

3. Which continents have land below the 30° S latitude line?

(__________ map) ____________________

4. Name one continent that has the equator or 0° latitude run through it.

(__________ map) ____________________

5. Name two roads found in the coordinates D2.

   (____________ map) ______________________________

6. In which coordinates would City Park be found?

   (____________ map) ______________________________

7. In which continent are the coordinates 60° N, 120° W?

   (____________ map) ______________________________

8. What buildings are west of the community centre? What are their coordinates?

   (____________ map) ______________________________

B. Check the circle if the sentence gives directions that are a relative location. Then write a sentence in your own words, giving a relative location.

A relative location tells us where a place is in relation to something else.

1. The lost sailors were found at 53° N, 129° W.
2. The dog was last seen two blocks north of the airport.
3. ✔ ______________________________

C. Match the descriptions with the correct places. Then underline the physical characteristics.

Northern Canada **Montreal** **Tropical rainforest**

1. ____________	2. ____________	3. ____________
• majority speak French • small island • tall buildings	• wet and warm climate • many different species of animals and plants • wooden bridge spans a river	• permafrost • travel by snowmobile • low-growing plants with short life cycles

2

Themes of Geographic Inquiry: Environment

The environment is our physical surrounding. We can describe its characteristics, and we can also use thematic maps to illustrate certain aspects of the environment.

A. Read what Cayden says. Then fill in the blanks with one of the five characteristics of the environment.

When we talk about environment, we could be referring to any one of these five different characteristics: ***landform, climate, water, soils,*** *and* ***natural vegetation.***

1. The ______________ of an area is a good clue of which animal species call it home.

2. All through history, human settlement has depended on the availability of ______________ .

3. The form of transportation for our trip, whether it is ferry, foot, car, or canoe, will depend on the ______________ we travel across.

4. ______________ can make a place more or less desirable as a habitat, though humans and animals have adapted to almost any kind.

5. We rely on healthy, unpolluted ______________ to provide us with most of our food.

B. Describe your natural environment using the five characteristics in part A. Which parts of your environment have been altered by humans?

____

____

____

C. Thematic maps tell us more about a place than simply its location. Identify the types of thematic maps. Then choose the correct map for each situation.

population density **climate regions** **contour** **active volcano**

Types of Thematic Maps:

1.

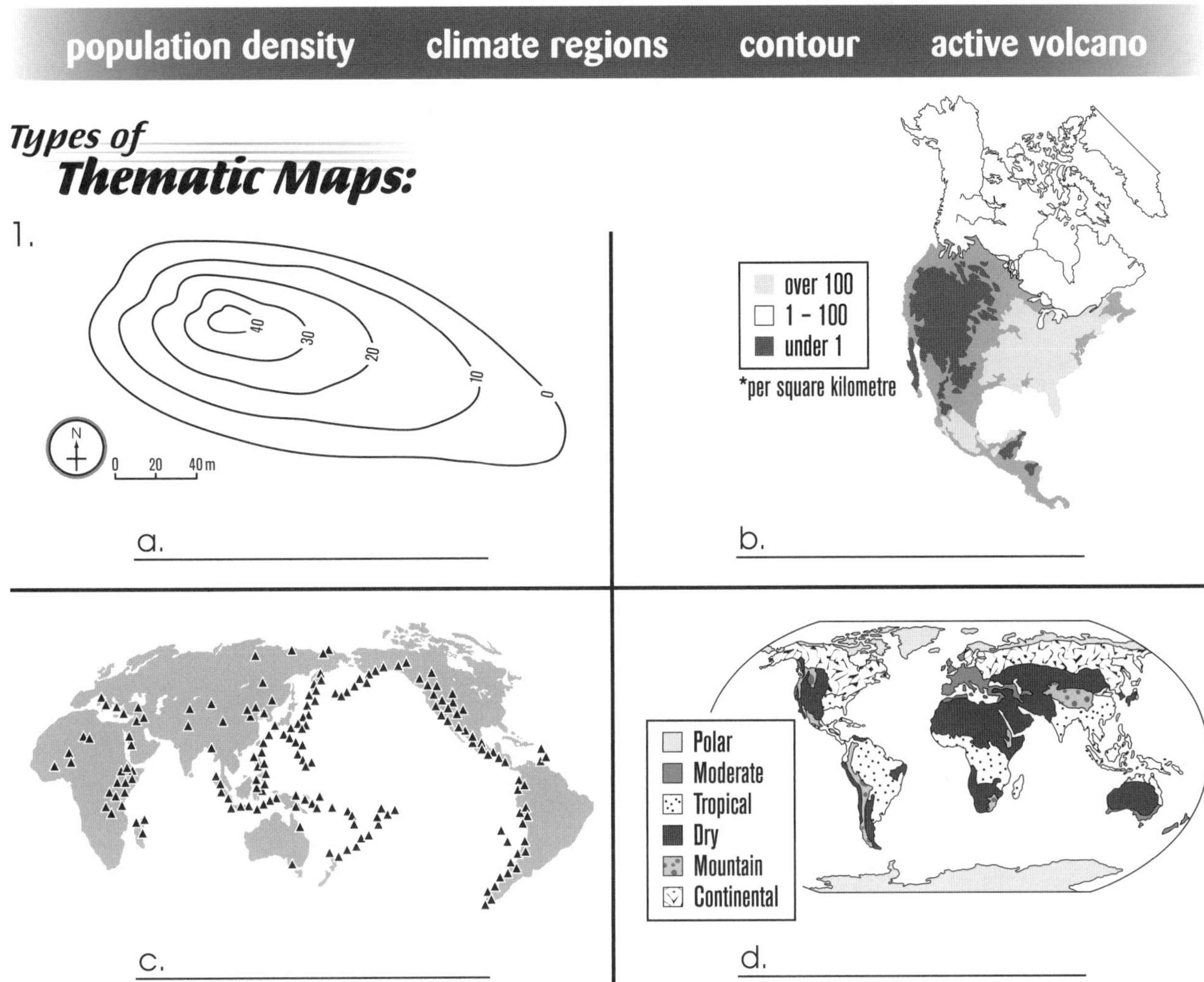

a. ____________________

b. ____________________

c. ____________________

d. ____________________

Which thematic map would you use for the following situations?

2. A museum display demonstrates current volcanic activity. ____________________

3. A teacher wants her class to find out where human population is distributed within a country. ____________________

4. A grade seven class is comparing climates of the world. ____________________

5. A mountain climber is planning out how long it should take him to reach the top of a mountain. ____________________

3

Themes of Geographic Inquiry: Region

A region is a section of the Earth's surface that has some unifying characteristics.

A. Compare contrasting regions. See which regional characteristics are being compared, what the theme is, and decide whether the characteristics are human or physical. Fill in the blanks.

human English/French physical landforms climate purpose of buildings

1. Characteristics of the region:

   Desert/Rainforest (physical)

   Theme: ________________

2. Characteristics of the region:

   ________________ (human)

   Theme: language

3. Characteristics of the region:

   Commercial/Residential (____________)

   Theme: ________________

4. Characteristics of the region:

   Canyon/Badlands (____________)

   Theme: ________________

B. Look at the map of Canada that shows the country's physical regions. List the physical regions.

____

____

____

____

____

____

____

Innuitian Region

Arctic Region

Cordilleran Region

Canadian Shield

Interior Plains

Appalachian Region

Great Lakes-St. Lawrence Lowlands

C. Look at the map of Canada that shows the political boundaries. Name any five of the regions.

Yukon
Northwest Territories
Nunavut
Newfoundland and Labrador
Quebec
British Columbia
Alberta
Saskatchewan
Manitoba
Ontario
Prince Edward Island
New Brunswick
Nova Scotia

____

____

____

____

____

D. Look at the maps of Canada in parts B and C. Answer the questions.

1. Most physical regions have transition areas where one region turns into another. How are the boundaries between Canada's physical regions different from the boundaries between the political regions (provinces, territories, countries)?

____

____

2. How were Canada's political boundaries drawn? Use the map to explain how they coincide with imaginary lines or physical characteristics.

____

____

E. Divide your city or town into different regions. How many different regions can you list? What is the unifying characteristic of each region?

____

____

____

____

Themes of Geographic Inquiry: Interaction

Our environment provides us with food, clothing, and shelter, as well as many other things we need and want. Often, the environment is altered as a result of our interaction with it.

A. We alter the environment for many reasons, and there is a possible effect of each alteration. Fill in the blanks to reveal the environmental consequences of our actions.

restricts | erosion | habitats | pollutes | deforests

1. **We need:** Housing

   We do: Clear forests

   Environmental Consequence:

   destroys animal ______________

2. **We need:** Power/Energy

   We do: Burn coal

   Environmental Consequence:

   ______________ air

3. **We need:** Transportation

   We do: Build highways

   Environmental Consequence:

   ______________ animal movement

4. **We need:** Recreation/Sports

   We do: Build ski resorts

   Environmental Consequence:

   ______________ mountainsides

5. **We need:** Entertainment/Shopping

   We do: Pave ground for enormous parking lots

   Environmental Consequence:

   prevents the soaking of water into the ground, causing ______________

B. Read the example to see what reasons the transport developer has to alter the environment and what concerns the representative has to oppose the alteration. Then give an example.

The new highway will take traffic away from the old highway. It won't take people as long to travel, and there will be fewer traffic jams, so vehicles will cause less pollution than if we don't build the new highway.
I have two questions:
1. The new highway crosses the frog migration route. How will the frogs get across the highway safely?
2. How can you be sure the new highway will not encourage more people to drive rather than use public transit, or even better, ride a bike?

Your Turn

Suppose you are in charge of providing one of the needs/wants in part A. Give reasons for altering the environment.

___

___

___

Some people have come to you with concerns about how you are interacting with the environment. Write a question they might ask you.

___

___

C. Write a paragraph that describes a change you would like to make in your interaction with the environment. Explain how the environment is affected by your interaction before and after the change.

___

___

___

5

Themes of Geographic Inquiry: Movement

All sorts of things can move from one place to another: information and ideas, people and animals, and goods and all their parts. This flow is the theme of movement in geography.

A. Can you find eight things in the picture that are evidence of movement? List them on the lines.

B. Use the map to plot the places you and your belongings have come from.

You:

- use yellow to plot where you have travelled to, where you were born, and where you live

Belongings:

- use red to plot where your clothing has come from (hint: look at your clothing tags to see where they were made)
- use blue to plot where other belongings have come from

C. Fill in the blanks with the given words. Then take the letters in bold from each of the seven words and write them in the order of the statements they complete to see how the kinds of movement described are connected.

The geographic theme of movement doesn't just describe the way we move ourselves and things.

e**r**osion migratio**n** c**l**ouds gl**a**ciers
circ**u**latory p**a**ssengers diges**t**ive

1. It is believed that Pacific salmon use their sense of smell to find their way to their spawning grounds in their final ______________ .

2. The slow movement of mighty ______________ can form whole valleys over hundreds of thousands of years.

3. The human ______________ system carries nutrients from the food we eat to all the cells in our body.

4. Blood moves through the ______________ system of our body.

5. Wind and rain cause the movement of rock and soil, resulting in ______________ .

6. Seeds and pollen can be ______________ of the wind, streams, or even the tide.

7. In ______________ we see the movement of water around the atmosphere.

What kind of movement or movement systems are all of the above a part of?

8. ______________

Patterns in Physical Geography: Landforms

The Earth is made up of various landforms. The landforms determine where different types of work and recreation can be performed.

A. Look at the map showing the world's physical geography. Complete the legend and answer the questions.

1.

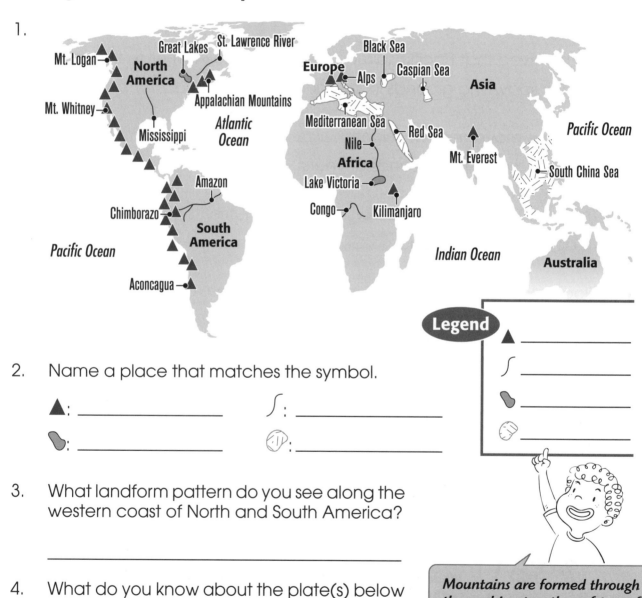

2. Name a place that matches the symbol.

▲: ____________ ∫: ____________

(lake symbol): ____________ (sea symbol): ____________

3. What landform pattern do you see along the western coast of North and South America?

____

4. What do you know about the plate(s) below the west coastline of the Americas?

____

Mountains are formed through the pushing together of two of the constantly moving plates that form the Earth's crust.

B. Describe the landforms shown in the pictures. Then match the people with the correct places to perform their duties.

- *coastal region*
- *mountainous region*
- *rocky, mineral-rich region*
- *flat plains region with rich soil*

Before performing an activity in a region, the landform must be considered.

miner fisher
farmer skier

1.

2.

3.

4.

C. Describe a landform in your region of Canada.

____

____

____

____

____

Things to Consider:

- Is it a part of a larger landform pattern?
- How does the landform pattern affect what people do for a living in your region?
- What do people do for recreation?

7

Patterns in Physical Geography: Climate

Climate, or the general weather condition of an area, is due to many different things. However, a location's latitude, or distance from the equator, is probably the most important determiner of climate.

A. Colour the map and fill in the blanks to show the Earth's major climate patterns, which are due to latitude.

Tropic of Capricorn driest
Antarctic Circle
equator wettest

Climate Map

3. blue — The coldest parts of the Earth are at the North and South Poles, above the Arctic Circle and below the Antarctic Circle.

4. red — The Earth is warmest around the equator, between the Tropic of Cancer and the Tropic of Capricorn.

5. Tropical rainforests are found in areas of land near the ______________ . They are the Earth's ______________ regions.

6. Deserts are the ______________ areas on the planet. They are usually found in the more temperate parts of the world, away from the equator.

B. Different things can influence the climate of a location. Match the definition with the climate-influencing element.

Climate-influencing Element

- Altitude
- Latitude
- Air masses
- Ocean currents
- Global wind systems
- Proximity to ocean, sea, or large lake

1. ______________________ :

The warm Gulf Stream, which flows from the tropics northward, has a moderating effect on otherwise colder, drier climate locations.

2. ______________________ :

There are large bodies of air of the same temperature and water content. They form over a period of days, creating weather events as they move through the atmosphere.

3. ______________________ :

Places near the poles have the coldest climates, while places near the equator have the warmest.

4. ______________________ :

A mountain, if it is tall enough, will have snow at its peak even if it is near the equator. The farther up you go, the colder the air gets.

5. ______________________ :

Because water absorbs and loses heat much more slowly than land, coastal regions tend to have milder climates than continental interiors.

6. ______________________ :

In the same way ocean currents move streams of warm or cold water, air currents move streams of warm or cold air. Both have an effect on the climate of areas they regularly reach.

8

Patterns in Physical Geography: Rivers

Rivers are important resources, and there are many elements that make up the river systems of the world.

A. Look at the diagram showing a river system from source to mouth. Then match each term in the diagram with its definition.

1. water that comes to the surface

   ____

2. the place where two rivers become one

   ____

3. a large turn in a river

   ____

4. an area that is drained by a particular river system

   ____

5. the place where a river or stream begins

   ____

6. the smaller creeks and rivers that contribute water to a larger water system

   ____

7. a lake formed from a bend in a river being cut off from the rest of the river

   ____

8. mud and silt deposits at the mouth of a river, named for its triangular shape resembling the fourth letter of the Greek alphabet

   ____

9. the part of the river that empties into an ocean or a lake

   ____

A River System

drainage basin
source
confluence
oxbow lake
tributaries
meander
mouth
delta
ground water

B. The map includes some of the major rivers of the world. Use the clues to label the rivers.

Clues

- The **Amazon** runs almost across the entire continent.
- The **Nile** runs mainly north/south.
- The **St. Lawrence** cuts a path from Lake Ontario to the Atlantic Ocean.
- The **Mississippi** runs north/south, draining in the Gulf of Mexico.
- The **Yangtze** is the third longest river in the world and drains near Shanghai.
- The **Ganges** is in Asia.
- The **Congo** is in Africa, southwest of the Nile.

Major Rivers of the World

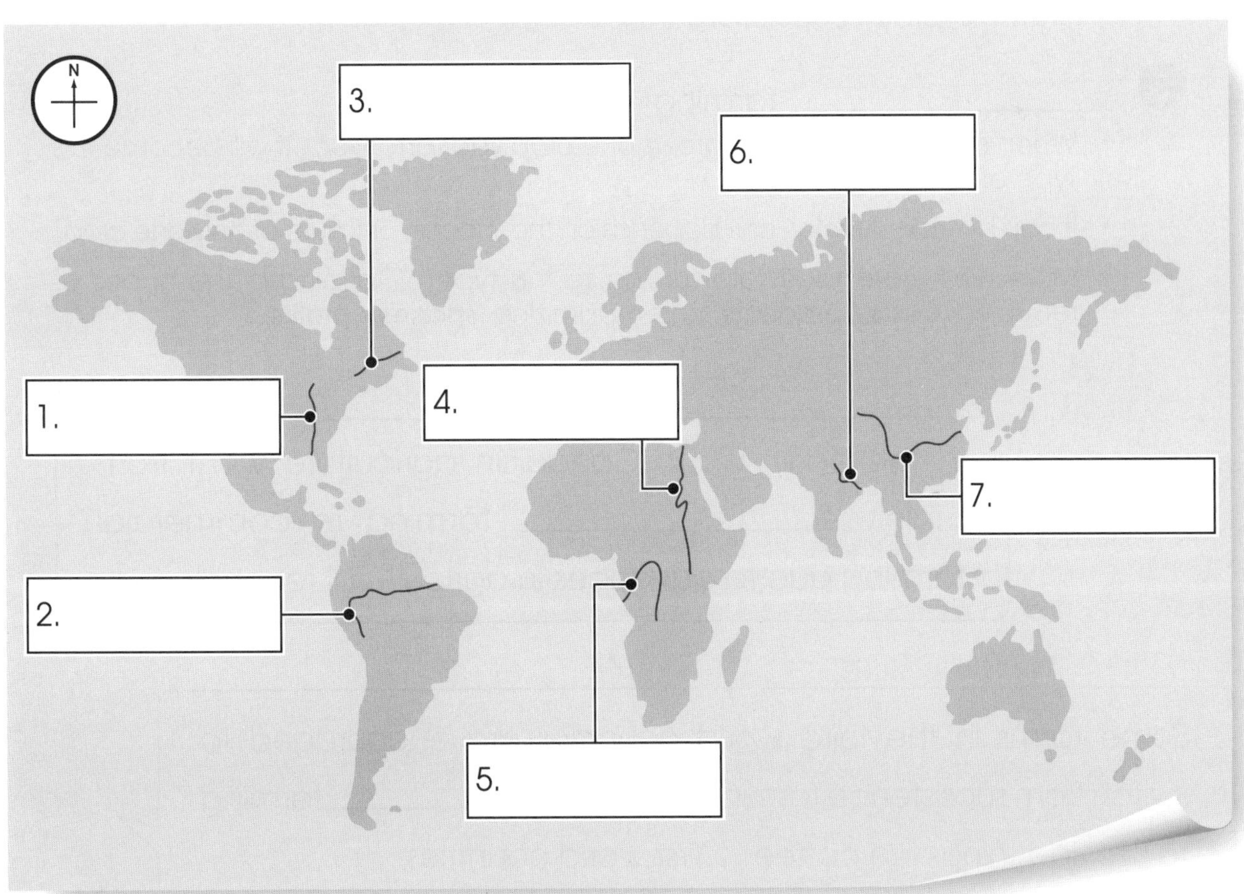

9

Patterns in Physical Geography: Agriculture

There are three types of agriculture: subsistence, commercial, and specialized. The crops that are grown depend on the conditions of the environment.

A. Identify three different types of agriculture. Fill in the blanks with "subsistence", "commercial", or "specialized" and circle the correct words.

Three Types of Agriculture

1. ____________________ farming
   - Farmers grow just enough to provide food for themselves and their families.

2. ____________________ farming
   - Farmers grow enough food to match the demand that comes with the growth of urban populations.

3. ____________________ farming
   - When a commercial farm grows one crop year after year, it will become this type of farm.
   - It can be **risky / lucky** as it depends on the success or failure of only one crop.
   - More and more farms are turning to this type of farming in the hopes of reducing **costs / products** and maximizing **spaces / profits** .

In the early 1900s, Canadian agriculture went from mainly 4. ____________________ farming to commercial farming due to advances in agricultural technology.

Some farms in the third world countries are encouraged to switch from subsistence farming to 5. ____________________ farming to provide things like coffee to first world countries.

B. Identify the types of conditions by writing "climate", "landforms", or "soil" on the lines. Then write the correct agricultural product next to its favourable condition.

Around the world, agricultural success depends on conditions such as climate, landforms, and soil conditions.

potatoes bananas rice
beef cotton salmon

		Type of Condition:	Agricultural Product:
1.	coastal waters	____________	____________
2.	tropical	____________	____________
3.	rolling grassland	____________	____________
4.	rich, fertile soil	____________	____________
5.	high rainfall	____________	____________
6.	long, hot growing season	____________	____________

C. Unscramble the words to discover some of Canada's agricultural products. Then write the shaded letters in order to see what type of agriculture they all have in common.

1. ronc ____
2. stopotae ________
3. shummoors _________
4. febe ____
5. rdaiy _____
6. bnrcaeerirs ___________
7. epmal ysurp _____ _____

8. We are ____________ agricultural products.

Natural Resources: Origins and Uses

Canada's many natural resources are spread out across the country. Some of these resources are available in a number of provinces and territories, while others are only found in one specific region.

A. See where many of Canada's natural resources are. Complete the words with the help of the word bank. Then answer the question.

wheat	**gravel**	**grain**	**potash**	**copper**	**oil**	**natural gas**
salt	**gold**	**salmon**	**nickel**	**sand**	**coal**	**harp seals**
timber	**asbestos**	**tin**	**zinc**	**lead**	**iron ore**	**maple syrup**

Natural Resources

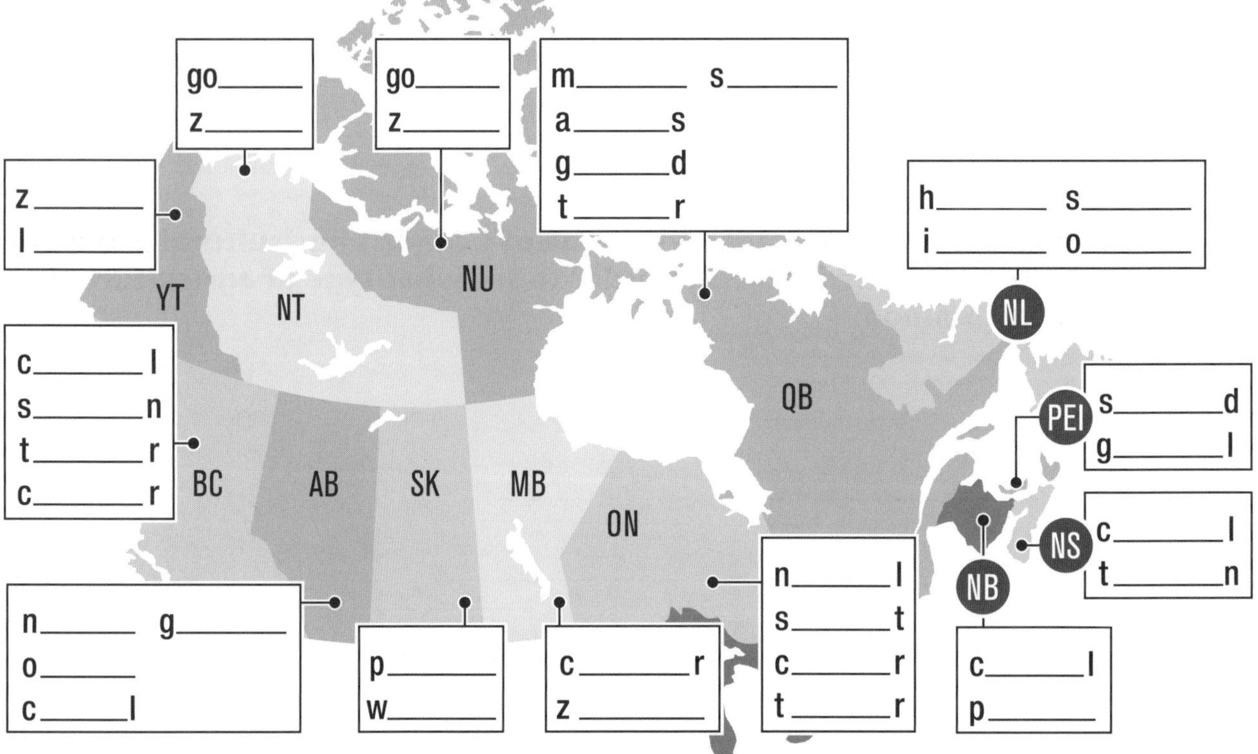

Which provinces or territories are abundant in zinc?

____

B. Match the resources with their end products.

oil timber sand nickel salt tin wheat gold coal

1. ____________________

Usage: stainless steel, magnets, coinage

2. ____________________

Usage: concrete, glass

3. ____________________

Usage: cans, solder

4. ____________________

Usage: flour, bread, pasta, beer

5. ____________________

Usage: chemicals, ice control, food processing

6. ____________________

Usage: diesel, kerosene, gasoline

7. ____________________

Usage: paper, furniture, flooring

8. ____________________

Usage: electricity, coke (for steel-making)

9. ____________________

Usage: jewellery, electronics, dentistry

Natural resources are used for food, fuels, or goods.

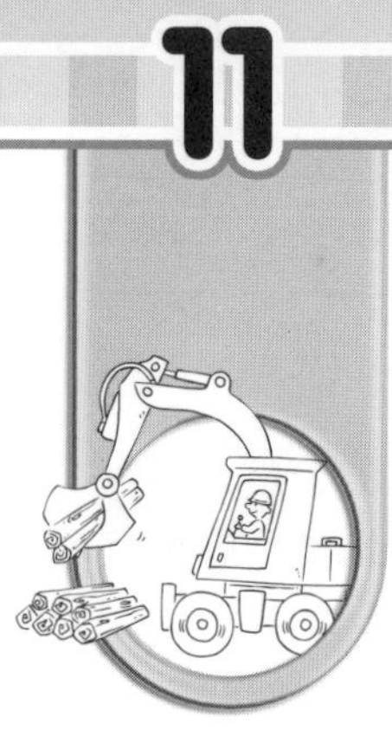

Natural Resources: Technology

Technology helps us discover, extract, and use more and more natural resources. Over time, new technologies have developed out of old ones, making resources even more available to us.

A. Match the old technology with the new one. Write the words. Then write a sentence to describe how our use of a natural resource has changed with the new technology.

New Technology vs. Old Technology

1. Fishing

   seine boat: ________________

   change: More / Fewer fish are caught.

2. Forestry

   chain saw: ________________

   change: ____________________________

3. Mining

   explosives/drills/loaders: ________________

   change: ____________________________

4. Forestry

   logging truck: ________________

   change: ____________________________

B. Write which part of the process technology is used for.

Technology is used from the discovery of natural resources to the marketing of the final product.

discovery management extraction processing marketing

1. Percussive drilling, a method of drilling which employed repeated pounding of the earth, gave way to the more efficient rotary drilling that is most often used today.

   ____

2. Solar energy production has become much more efficient with the advent of new technologies.

   ____

3. Fish farms vaccinate their fish to protect their product from disease.

   ____

4. Seismographs give scientists data for geological research.

   ____

5. Satellites help identify areas of the Earth that may be suitable for gold mining.

   ____

6. The Internet has increased the flow of information from producer to consumer about various types of natural resources.

   ____

Natural Resources: Sustainable Development

Not all natural resources are able to replenish themselves. We need to use them responsibly so that they will continue to be available to us.

A. Identify each type of resource. Then put each natural resource in the correct group.

Flow

Non-renewable

Renewable

wind energy   codfish   ocean currents
marble   timber   natural gas   oysters   coal
gold   aluminum   tidal energy   copper
wheat   oil   solar energy   oranges
cucumbers   diamonds   rivers   lamb

Types of Resources:

1. ____________________ resources
   - take millions of years to replace and are therefore unavailable for everyday human purposes
   - e.g. ____________________

2. ____________________ resources
   - can be replenished within our lifetime if consumed responsibly
   - e.g. ____________________

3. ____________________ resources
   - whether used or not, are frequently and naturally replaced
   - e.g. ____________________

B. Read what the children say. Answer the questions.

Forests are valuable to us as a renewable resource.

1. Why is it important to use this renewable resource responsibly?

____

____

____

____

____

2. Give an example of responsible use of a renewable resource.

____

____

People in most societies are extremely dependent on oil, a non-renewable resource.

3. Why is it important to use this non-renewable resource responsibly?

____

____

____

____

____

4. Give an example of responsible use of a non-renewable resource.

____

____

Review

A. Look at the map and fill in the blanks. Then help Jack the Pilot complete his flight schedule and finish his speech.

1.

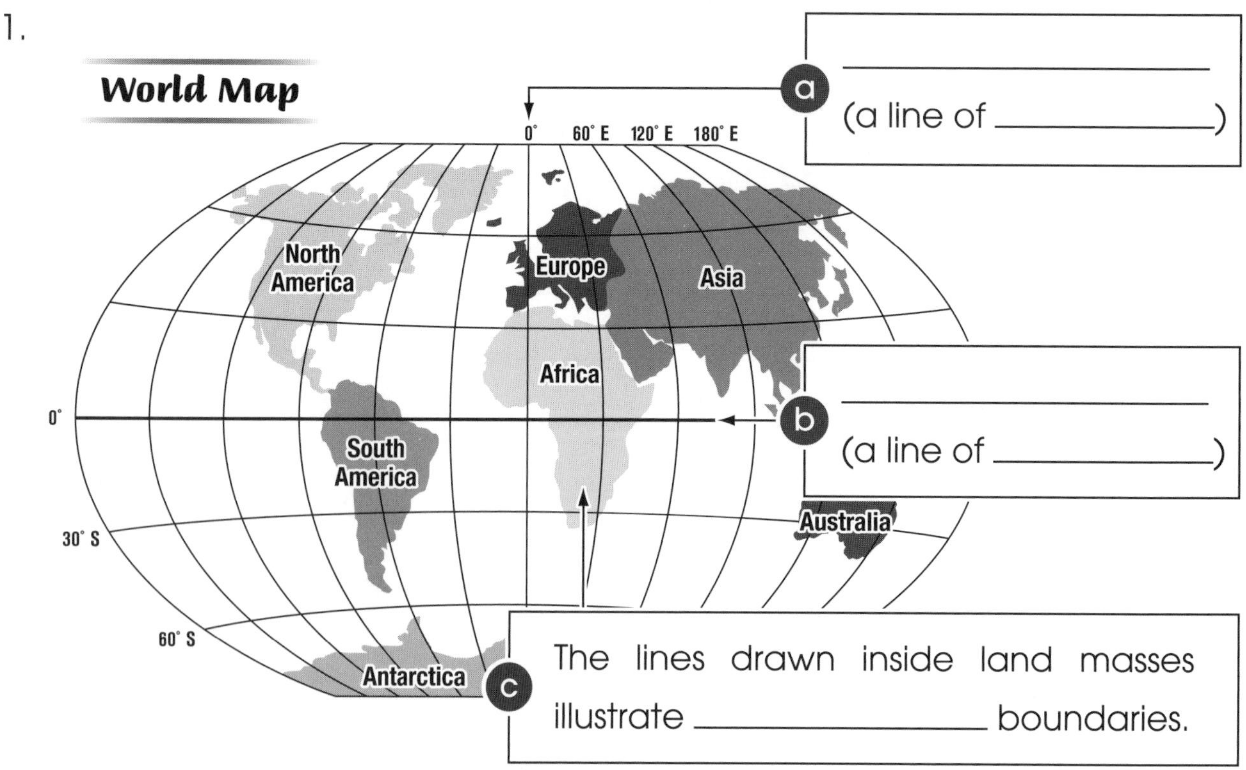

The lines drawn inside land masses illustrate ________ boundaries.

2.

Date	From (coordinates/continent)	To (coordinates/continent)
May 25	30° S, 150° E / ________	40° N, 100° E / ________
May 30	________ / Europe	________ / Canada

3.

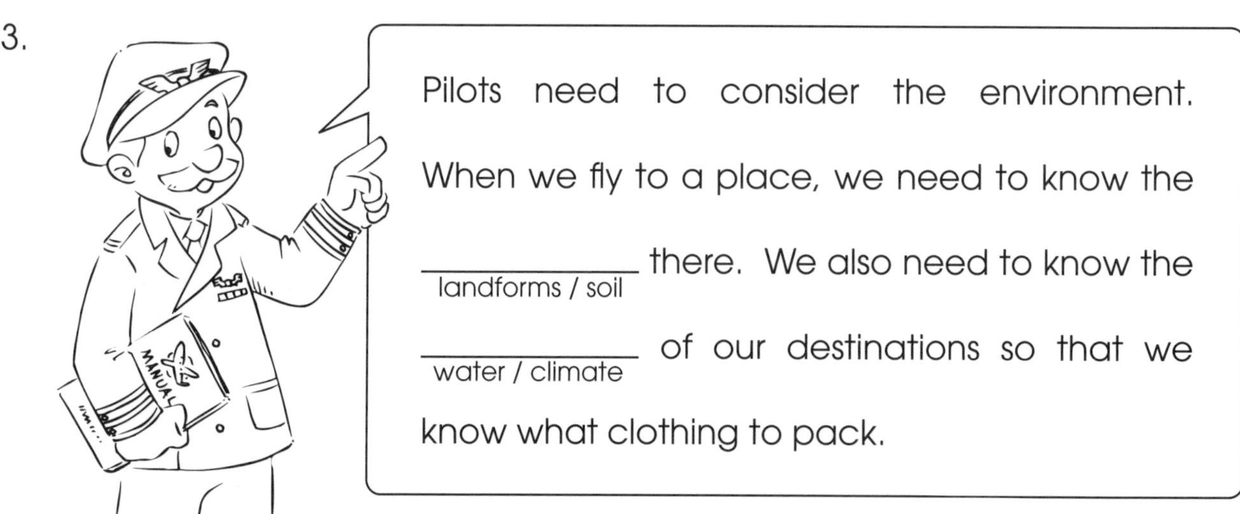

MANUAL
Pilots need to consider the environment. When we fly to a place, we need to know the ________ (landforms / soil) there. We also need to know the ________ (water / climate) of our destinations so that we know what clothing to pack.

B. Jack is flying to an airport in Manitoba, Canada. He wants to introduce Manitoba to his passengers. Complete the labels with "Lake" or "River". Then answer the questions.

1. **Map of Manitoba**

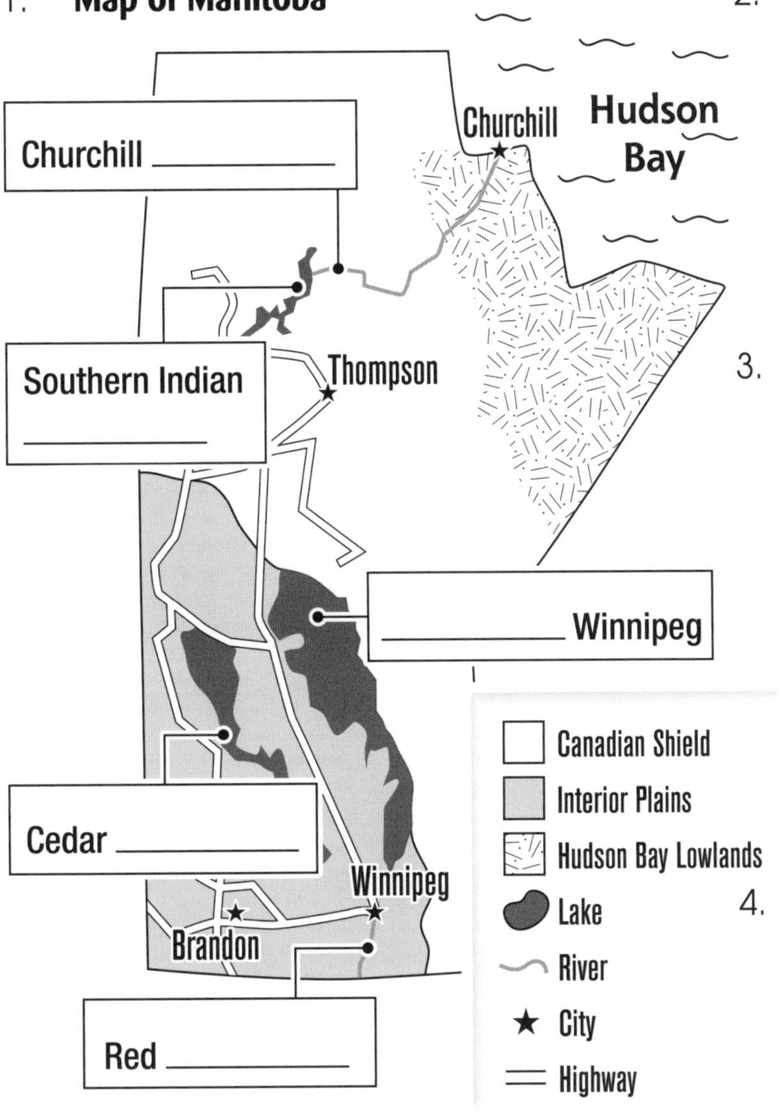

2. Write the physical regions in Manitoba:

____

____

____

3. Give examples of the following landforms:

(Lake): ________________________

____

____

(River): ________________________

____

4. Name two different types of movement on the map.

____

5. *A transport developer proposes to build a highway between Thompson and Churchill. What are some concerns people might have regarding the proposal?*

____

____

____

C. **At the airport, Jack has taken a map of a Manitoba town. Look at the map. Answer the questions.**

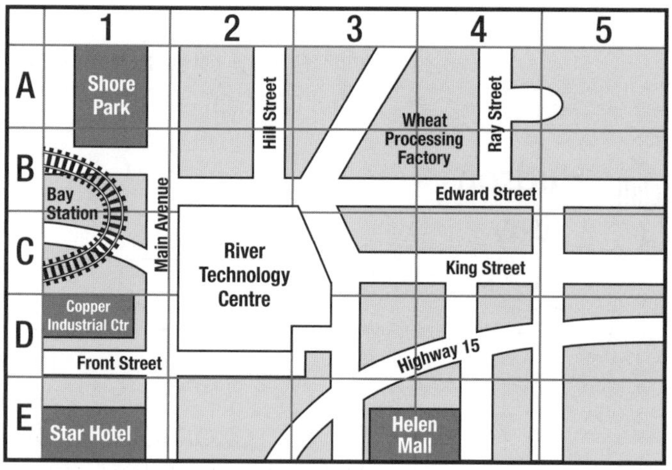

1. This map uses an ____________________ grid.
2. The coordinates of the places:
   a. River Technology Centre ____________________
   b. Copper Industrial Centre ____________________
   c. Bay Station ____________________
   d. Wheat Processing Factory ____________________
3. Give an example of a natural resource that can be found in Manitoba. Then give an example of its end product.

   ____

4. Give an example of an agricultural product in Manitoba. Then describe it.

Product	***End Product(s)***	***Sustainability***
	____________	A. Renewable
	____________	B. Non-renewable
	____________	C. Flow

5. Jack will go to Star Hotel for accommodation. Then he wants to go to River Technology Centre. Describe the relative location of these two places.

   ____

D. Look at the model of the river system displayed at River Technology Centre. Complete the diagram and match the terms with the definitions. Then answer the questions.

1. ground water – water that comes to the surface

drainage basin – an area that is drained by a particular river system

confluence – the place where two rivers become one

oxbow lake – a lake formed from a bend in a river being cut off from the rest of the river

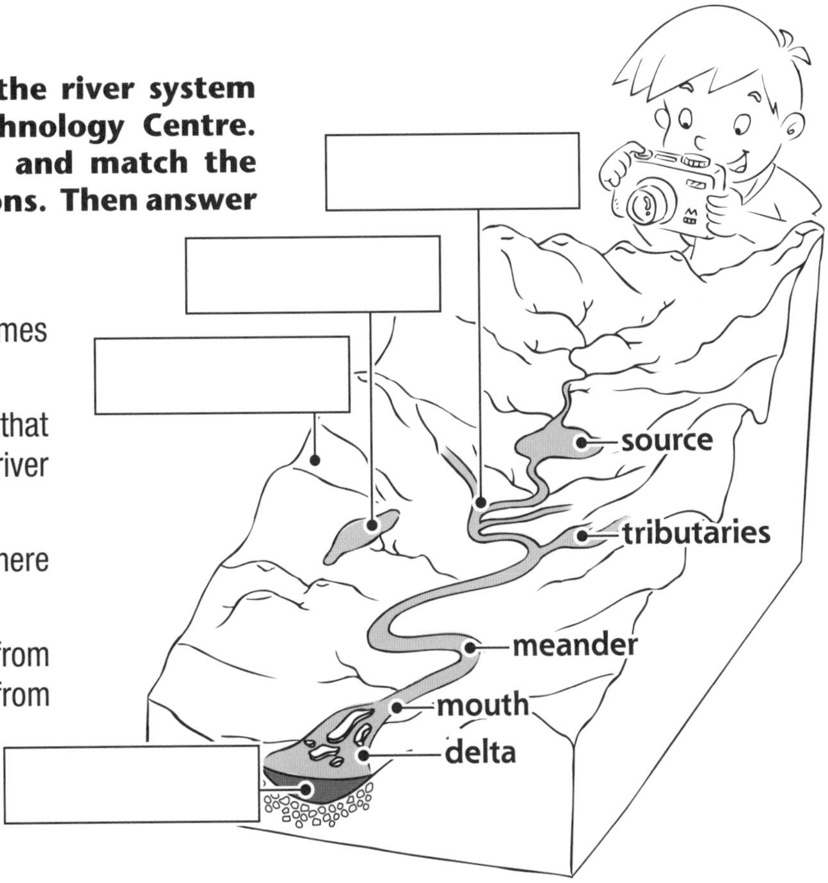

source
tributaries
meander
mouth
delta

_______________: the smaller creeks and rivers that contribute water to a larger water system

_______________: the place where a river or stream begins

_______________: a large turn in a river

_______________: the part of the river that empties into an ocean or a lake

_______________: mud and silt deposits at the mouth of a river, named for its triangular shape

2. Rivers are important resources. Are they renewable, non-renewable, or flow resources? Why is it important to use this kind of resource responsibly? Give an example of responsible use of this kind of resource.

___

___

___

___

SCIENCE

Ecosystems

- *The system of interaction between living and non-living things in an area is called an ecosystem.*
- *Ecosystems can be any size, with smaller ecosystems found inside larger ones.*

The dry weather, the soil, the plants, and the animals here, including myself, are the components of a desert ecosystem.

A. Read the paragraph. Then match the words in bold with their meanings.

An **ecosystem** is a natural area where living and non-living things interact with each other. For the living members of the ecosystem, or **community**, it is their **habitat**, providing everything they need to live. Many different **species** of **organisms** can live in an ecosystem, but their **populations** vary, depending on their role.

1. The number of members of a species within an ecosystem __________
2. A particular type of organism __________
3. A living thing __________
4. The natural home of an organism __________
5. A place where organisms interact with each other and their environment __________
6. The organisms, both animal and plant, within an ecosystem __________

B. Fill in the blanks to complete the definitions. Fill in the missing letters and check the correct answer to complete the diagram of interactive ecosystems. Then draw a representative picture in each circle.

animals landforms ecosystem atmosphere

Biosphere: the 1.______________ that encompasses the entire Earth, including the land surface, water, and 2.______________, as well as the living things within it

Biome: a large area of Earth defined by similar plants, 3.______________, weather patterns, and 4.______________, such as a **tropical rainforest**

5.

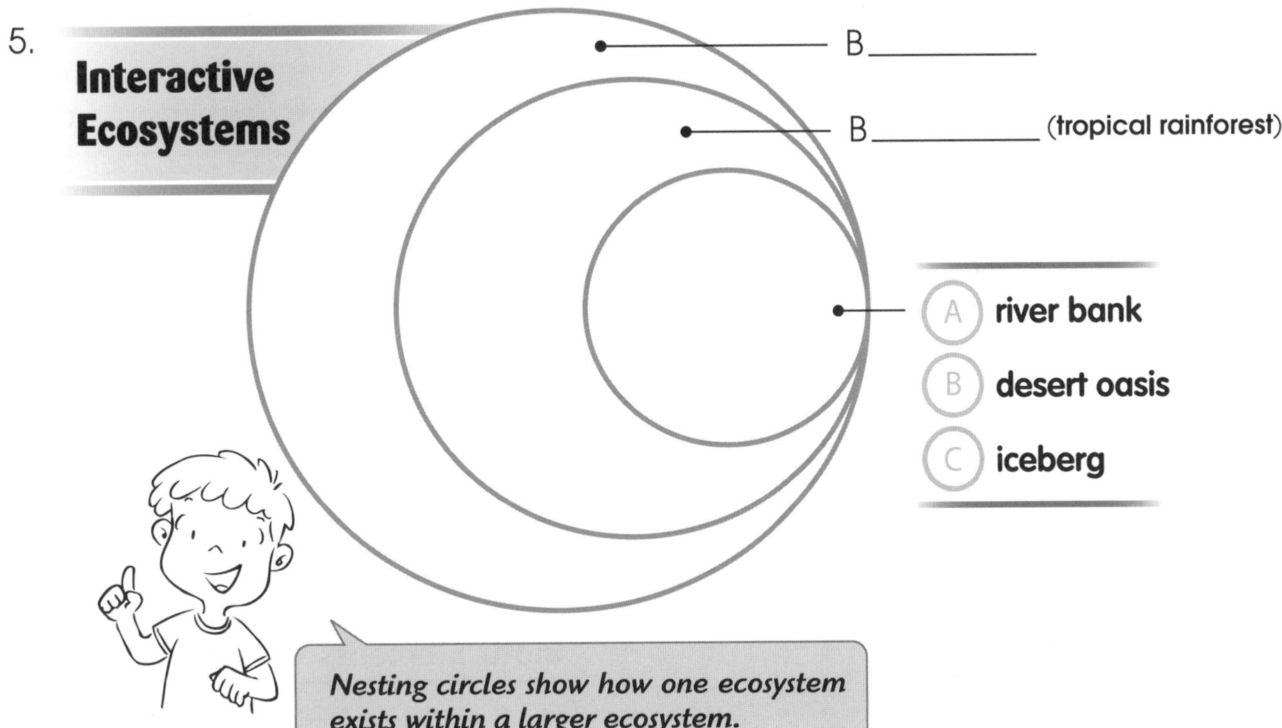

Science Fact

Humans, like all other animals, are home to hundreds of different kinds of bacteria and other microorganisms. We are walking ecosystems.

Biotic and Abiotic Elements in Ecosystems

- *Living or having lived members of an ecosystem are called biotic, and non-living or never having lived members are called abiotic.*
- *Biotic or abiotic members of an ecosystem affect each other.*

I'm a member of biotic.
I'm a member of abiotic.
We live well with each other.

A. Fill in the blanks. Then identify five biotic and five abiotic elements of the ecosystem shown.

abiotic | water | ecosystem | microorganisms | biotic

1. ______________ : a habitat in which plants, animals, and microorganisms interact with one another and their surroundings

2. ______________ : the living elements of an ecosystem, such as plants, animals, and ______________

3. ______________ : the non-living elements of an ecosystem, such as soil, air, and ______________

4.

Biotic Elements	Abiotic Elements

B. Each sentence describes a relationship between two elements of an ecosystem. Highlight the biotic elements blue and the abiotic elements yellow. Then describe their relationships.

1. Humans cannot live more than three or four days without water.

   Relationship: ____________________

2. Tiny wild berries are a major food source for the lumbering black bear.

   Relationship: ____________________

3. Wind is one of the forces responsible for soil erosion.

   Relationship: ____________________

4. The beaver builds its shelter, a partially submerged lodge, out of logs harvested from trees in its own habitat.

   Relationship: ____________________

5. Snakes and other reptiles use the warmth of the sun to raise their body temperatures after a cool night.

   Relationship: ____________________

6. For a typical meal, the "cleaner fish" cleans the gills and teeth of other bigger fish, which, in turn, become cleaner.

   Relationship: ____________________

The most unique animals and plants on Earth are found in ecosystems that developed far from neighbouring ecosystems, such as the Galapagos Islands.

3

Food Cycle

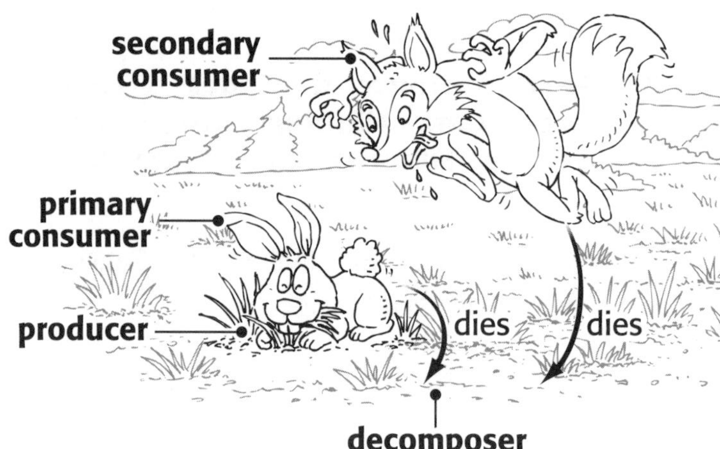

- *The food cycle is made up of producers, consumers, and decomposers.*
- *Different models have different ways of showing relationships within the food cycle.*

A. Trace the arrows to complete the food cycle. Then fill in the blanks with the given words.

fungi decomposer nutrients omnivore plant primary consumer herbivore producer food

Food Cycle

1.

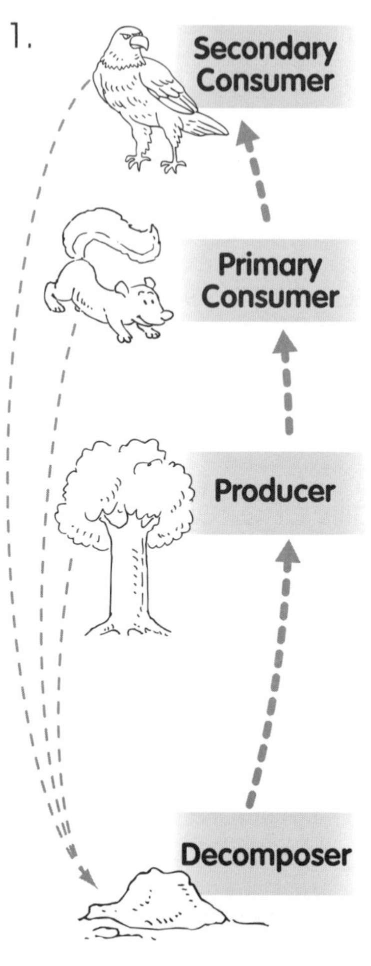

A secondary consumer consumes a primary consumer that has consumed a 2. ______________ .

A primary consumer eats plants. It can be a 3. ______________ or an 4. ______________ .

A producer is a 5. ______________ . It uses the sun's energy to make its own 6. ______________ .

A decomposer causes the decomposition of anything that was once living. It converts all organic matter into carbon dioxide and 7. ______________ . These nutrients become part of the soil. More plants can grow as a result. Bacteria and 8. ______________ are primary decomposers.

B. Construct a food cycle with one of the food chains below. Check the food chain. Then add a decomposer to complete the cycle.

Ⓐ zooplankon ⟶ krill ⟶ seals

Ⓑ grass ⟶ zebra ⟶ lion

Ⓒ leaf ⟶ dragonfly ⟶ frog ⟶ snake

Food Cycle

C. Match each model with its name. Write the letters. Then answer the questions.

1.

- Ⓐ **food web**
- Ⓑ **food cycle**
- Ⓒ **food chain**
- Ⓓ **energy pyramid**

a.

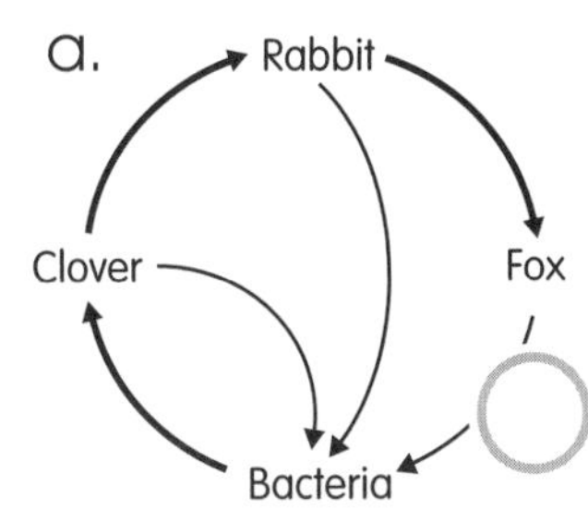

b.

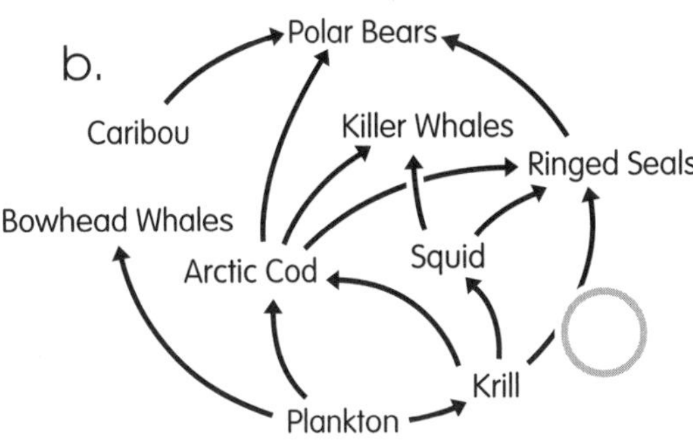

c.

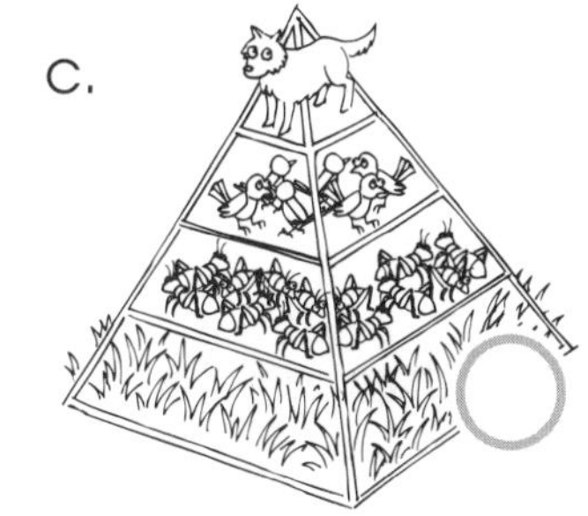

d.

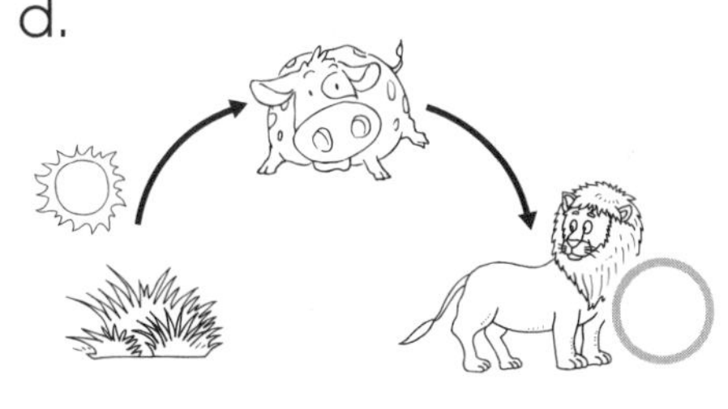

2. Which model would you use to show

   a. a straight-line relationship from the food source to the food consumer? __________

   b. how members of different food chains depend on each other? __________

Science Fact

Food chains are usually not very long because some of the food energy is lost from one link to another.

4

Natural Cycles

- *Every ecosystem depends on the water cycle, which affects both biotic and abiotic elements.*
- *The carbon cycle is a major part of every ecosystem.*

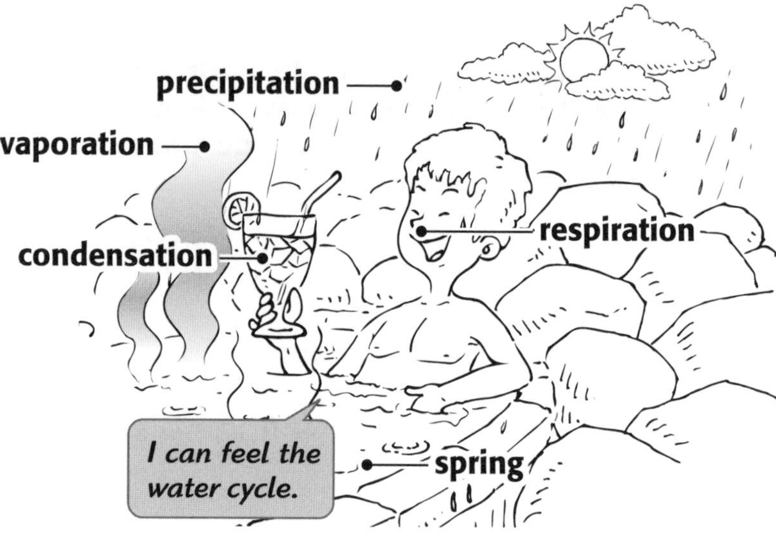

A. Look at the diagram. Answer the questions.

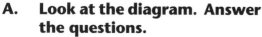

Water Cycle

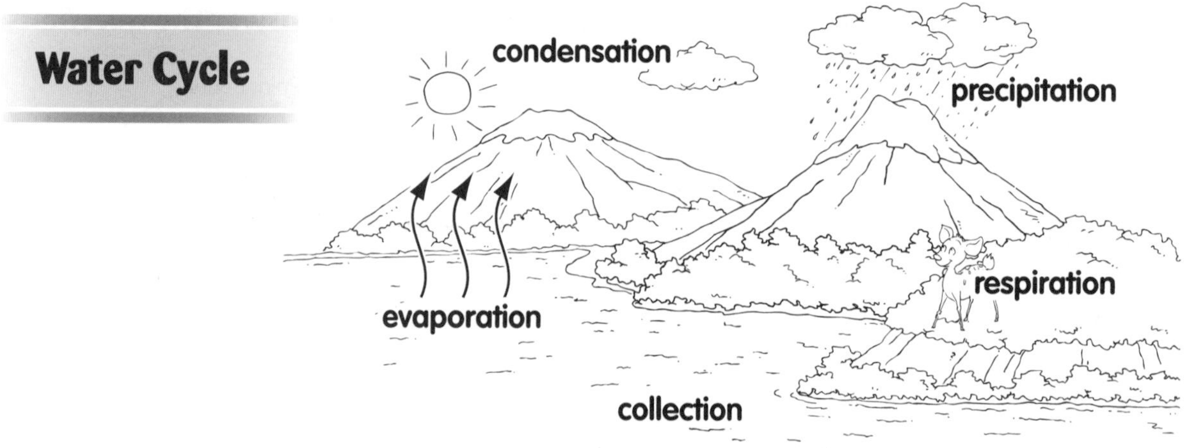

1. What powers the water cycle? ____________

2. Which process causes water to change to vapour? ____________

3. Which process causes animals and plants to release water into the atmosphere? ____________

4. Give three examples of precipitation. ____________

5. Give three major reservoirs of water. ____________

6. Complete the example of biotic and abiotic interaction that involves the water cycle. Then give one more example.

   - Plants take up water from the soil and release it during ____________ .
   - ____________

B. Read the passage and complete the carbon cycle with the words in bold.

Carbon, the fourth most common element on Earth, is found within every cell of every living thing, as well as water, rocks, soil, and air. Pairing up with oxygen, it cycles through the ecosystem in a number of ways.

Animals release carbon dioxide into the atmosphere through **respiration**. Plants use this carbon dioxide during **photosynthesis**; it helps them make food for themselves. Forests of trees use so much carbon dioxide that they are known as **carbon sinks**, as are oceans, which use up far more carbon dioxide than they release.

The carbon from dead animals and plants is released into the earth through **decomposition**. They may be stored there for millions of years, when they may be released as carbon dioxide from a volcano. The coal, oil, and natural gas we extract from the earth is millions-of-years-old carbon. Lots of carbon dioxide is released during the **combustion** of **fossil fuels**.

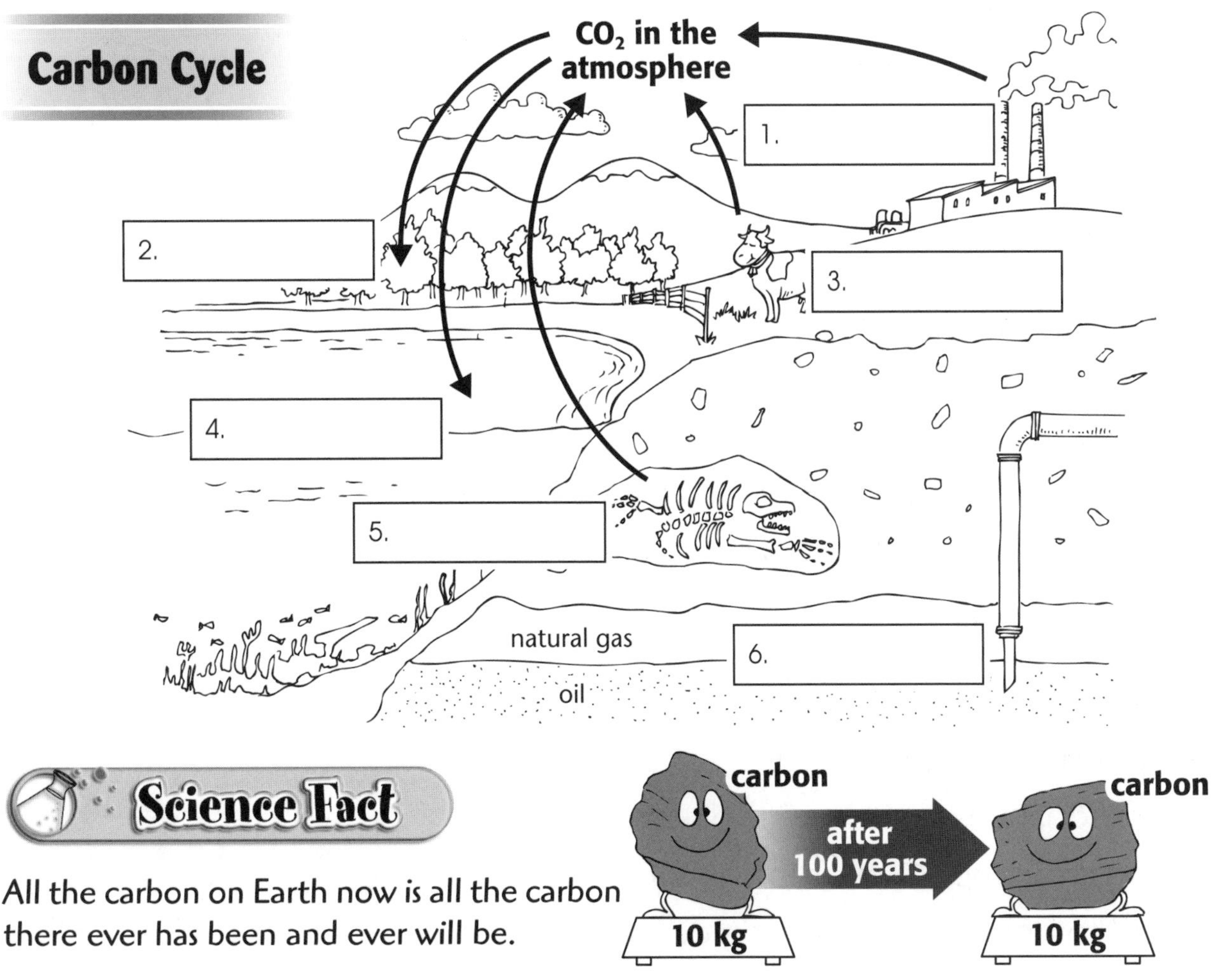

All the carbon on Earth now is all the carbon there ever has been and ever will be.

5

Succession and Adaptation

- *Succession is the change that happens when one habitat is replaced by another.*
- *Adaptation is the ability of plants or animals to change to better suit their environment.*

I'm sure there was a pond here before.

A. Read the paragraph. Complete the descriptions with the given words and draw lines to match them with the pictures.

Pond Succesion

Sometimes succession is quickened by events, either natural or human-caused, such as drought, floods, and fires. Succession can cause habitat loss for animals and plants.

debris emergent marsh inhabit

As a pond develops, animals come to 1.__________ the pond. •

As more creatures arrive, the 2.__________ on the bottom increases. Some submergent vegetation appears. •

3.__________ plants appear on the edges of the pond. As pond plants grow, die, and decompose, layers of debris build up to raise the pond. •

Emergent plants grow across the floor. Then the pond becomes a 4.__________ . The marsh continues to fill in with dirt and debris to form a swamp. Over time, the swamp may dry out to become a forest or grasslands. •

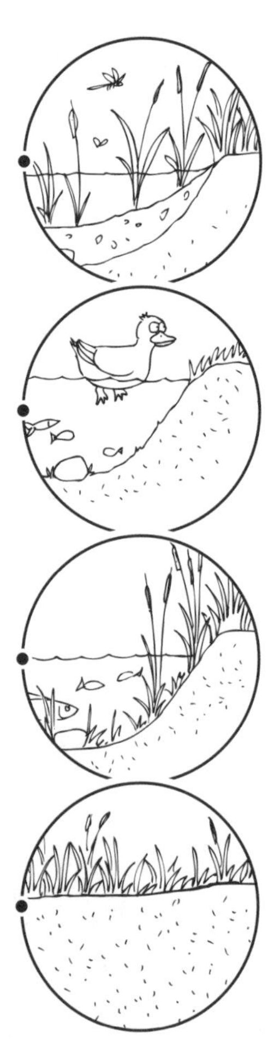

B. Match each term with its definition. Write the word on the line.

succession adaptation extinction competition species diversity

1. ______________ the most drastic event to happen when a species cannot adapt to a changed environment and cannot survive

2. ______________ this is when two or more species put pressure on the same limited elements of an ecosystem to fulfil their needs for living

3. ______________ where, through change in an ecosystem, one habitat is replaced by another

4. ______________ the assortment of different species of organisms in an ecosystem, which goes up and down with the process of succession

5. ______________ this must take place in order for an organism to stay in an environment that is changing

C. Try the experiment showing fast-motion succession.

Experiment – Fast-Motion Succession

Materials

- *a tray with high edges*
- *soil*
- *water*

Steps:

1. Pat the soil into the tray, leaving depressions for a small pond and adjoining streams.
2. Slowly sprinkle water over the soil. Let the "rain" fall, filling up the streams and pond.
3. Continue to sprinkle even after they are full. "Sediment" from run-off and erosion will gradually fill the pond.

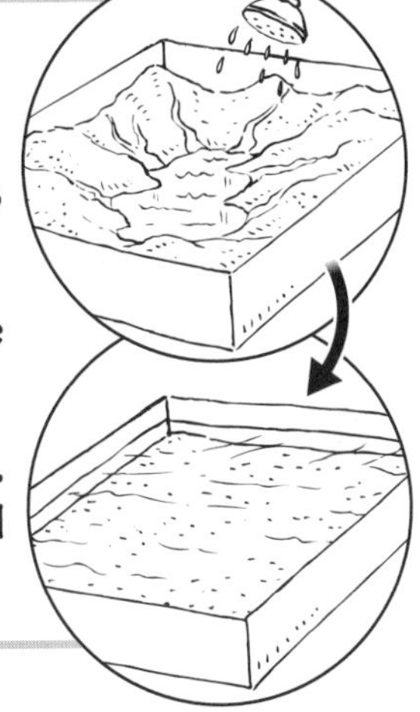

Geological time is much slower than the time we are used to. Your lifetime is but a wink in the time an ecosystem might go through one succession.

6

Human Activity

- *Human activity can negatively impact ecosystems.*
- *There are things we can do to reduce, and even reverse, negative impacts on ecosystems.*

A. Underline the factors involved in harming the ecosystems.

Problems

Ⓐ Air pollution from factories and cars causes acid rain, a form of precipitation that harms forests and other plants.

Ⓑ Construction and logging practices can increase sediment in nearby streams, suffocating fish and destroying spawning grounds.

Ⓒ It may take hundreds of years to replace groundwater that has been depleted due to overuse.

Ⓓ Chemical fertilizers from agriculture may leach into lakes and rivers.

Ⓔ A dam built along a river drastically changes the ecosystem, flooding large areas of land and forcing its inhabitants to leave or die off.

Ⓕ Non-native species introduced into an ecosystem can become invasive species, where native plants or animals cannot compete with the newcomer.

Ⓖ The manufacturing of goods creates industrial waste that is difficult to dispose of.

Ⓗ Transportation pollution is a serious problem. Most of the food we eat has been transported hundreds of kilometres to reach us.

B. Match the solutions with the problems mentioned in part A. Write the letters on the lines.

Solutions

There are alternatives to activities that cause ecosystem destruction. We have to solve the problems creatively.

1. The town of Remington passed a law restricting construction and protecting vegetation near stream banks. ______
2. BeeCome Farms adopts organic farming practices now. Their eco-friendly ways attract more pollinating bees and have less of an impact on the natural ecosystem. ______
3. The West family do most of their grocery shopping at the local farmer's market, and find out where other things they buy come from. ______
4. Margaret always uses recycled items, and her friends enjoy her homemade gifts. ______
5. Sand City is doing environmental impact studies on all possibilities before deciding how to provide power for its growing population. ______
6. The Forest family are using a water-saving device after they found out how much water was used every time the toilet was flushed. ______
7. A&M Company gives staff a reward if they walk to work or take environmentally friendly modes of transport. ______
8. Lydia puts a collar with a bell on her outdoor cat because it was bringing home songbirds it had caught. ______

Land conservation is one way of protecting ecosystems from human activities.

7

Structures

Stop copying my design!
PRO

- Structures are things with a definite size and shape. Human-made structures are based on structures found in nature.
- Structures can be made of one or many parts, and can be classified as being solid, frame, or shell.

A. Find the similarities between the natural and human-made structures. Match the structures that are similar. Then give one more example.

Natural Structures	Human-made Structures
mosquito mouthpart •	• fishing net
spiderweb •	• needle
kangaroo pouch •	• bowl
honeycomb •	• baby frontpack
tooth •	• brick wall
bird wings •	• spear
nest •	• airplane wings
________________ •———————•	________________

B. Write whether each of the following is a solid, a frame, or a shell structure.

1. ________________ is a framework that supports other parts of the structure. A skeleton is a framework.

2. ________________ is protective; it blocks entry or exit.

3. *________________ is mostly matter. If it is made of more than one part, the parts are stacked or piled close together.*

C. **Determine whether the objects are solid, frame, or shell structures.**

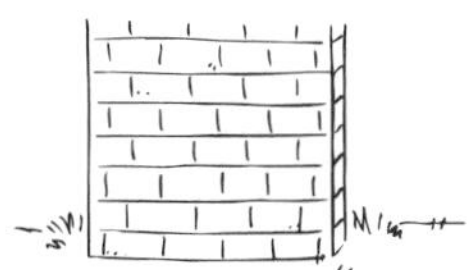

iceberg egg ladder bike helmet
house cap paperweight loaf of bread

Solid Structures: ______________________

Frame Structures: ______________________

Shell Structures: ______________________

D. **For each box, think of an object that is created by combining the two structures.**

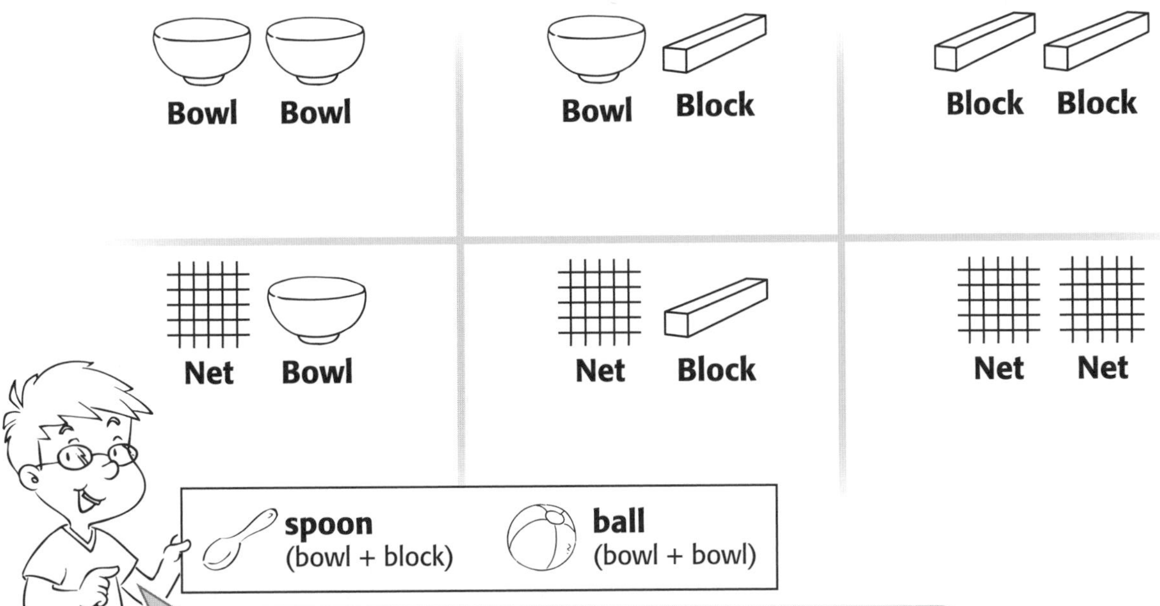

Many structures are made of more than one part. Some objects have different shapes, but they may have the same basic structures.

Science Fact

At more than 6000 kilometres long, the Great Wall of China is the world's largest human-made structure.

Centre of Gravity and Stability

- *Stability is the capacity a structure has for staying upright.*
- *The stability of a structure depends largely on its centre of gravity.*

A. Check the correct definition. Label each picture as stable or unstable. Then mark the centre of gravity on each picture.

1. Centre of Gravity:

It is the balancing point in a structure, or the place that has the most mass.

(B) It is the balancing point in a structure, or the place that has the least mass.

2. a.

__________ __________

b.

__________ __________

c.

__________ __________

d.

__________ __________

B. Redesign these structures so that they have better stability. Draw the new structures.

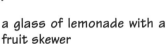

A structure performs its function best if it is stable.

a glass of lemonade with a fruit skewer

a triple-decker bus

C. Do the experiment about the centre of gravity. Then answer the question.

Experiment – Finding Changes in the Centre of Gravity

Materials

- *a cereal box*
- *scissors*
- *marker*
- *paperclips*

Steps:

1. Cut out a big circle from the cereal box.
2. Find the point at which it will balance on your fingertip. Mark it with an X.
3. Attach a paperclip to the edge of the circle.
4. Find the point at which it will balance on your fingertip. Mark it with another X. Can you see that the centre of gravity changes?

What happens if you add another paperclip right beside the first one?

____

____

Science Fact

It is a fact that when we walk, we are starting out by "falling". That is, we become unstable with the first movement of our foot, and then adjust our centre of gravity as we move our body over our foot.

9

Forces on Stable and Unstable Structures

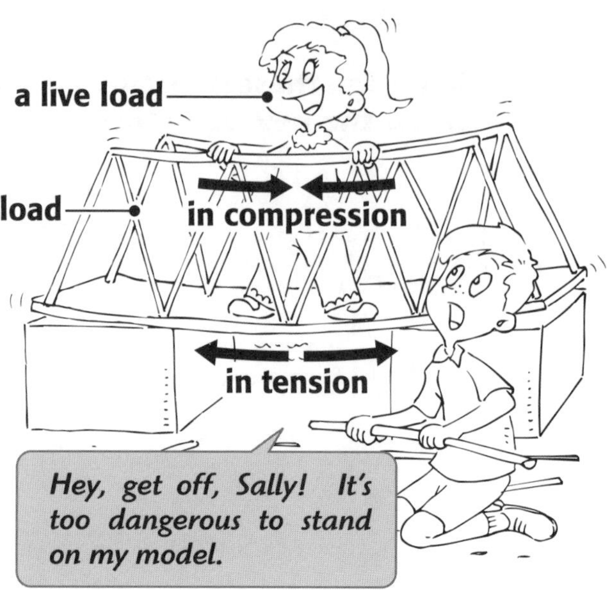

- *Different types of forces act upon structures.*
- *A force can be applied to a structure at different magnitudes and from different directions.*
- *The point of application of a force on a structure is the point of contact.*

A. Complete the passage about forces that act upon structures.

live torsion shear dead
compressive load tensile

Structures are made to withstand many kinds of forces, or stresses.

External Force

A 1. ______________ is an external force of weight upon a structure. A 2. ______________ load is one that is not part of the structure itself, like the weight of a person riding a bicycle. A 3. ______________ load is the weight of the structure itself, in this case, a bicycle.

Internal Force

An internal force can be one that pushes or pulls. A compression force occurs when a load, either live or dead, pushes upon a structure. The structure's ability to carry a load is its 4. ______________ strength. A train track must have enough compressive strength to withstand a train's weight as well as its own. A pull is called a tension force. A rope swing is a structure that must have the 5. ______________ strength to withstand the pull of a child's weight on the end.

Two other internal forces are shear and torsion. 6. ______________ force is where different parts of the structure press in opposite directions, while 7. ______________ force is the twisting of an object in opposite directions.

B. Read the following sentences. Circle the correct words.

1. Baby Bear's chair did not have enough compressive / tensile strength to hold Goldilocks.

2. Goldilocks was a live / dead load on the Three Bears' chairs.

3. Goldilocks was a tension / compressive force on both their chairs and their beds.

4. Rapunzel let down her long, braided hair, and then the Prince applied tension / compressive force as he climbed up her tower.

5. The old witch used torsion / shear force to punish Rapunzel by cutting her hair short.

C. Draw an arrow at the point of application to indicate the direction and magnitude of force.

Drawing Arrows to Indicate Force

Direction: The arrows show the direction of force.

Size: The larger magnitude of force, the larger the arrows.

Placement: The arrows are placed at the point of application of force.

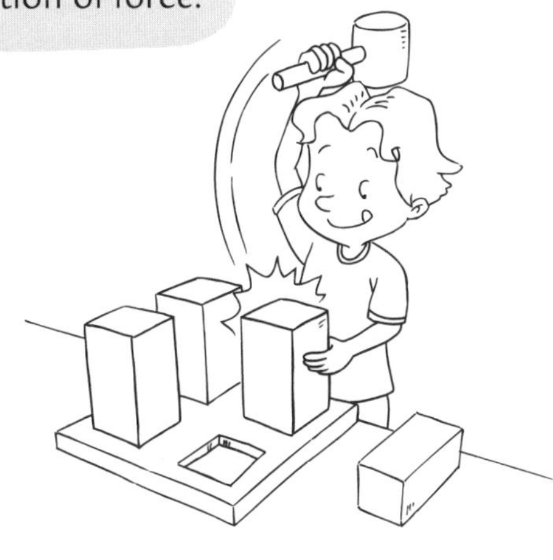

An eggshell is surprisingly indestructible when compressive force is applied to the ends. Humans have imitated this shape in the architectural arch, which holds up many bridges and buildings.

10

Materials and Design

- Every structure has a function, and the materials used to make a structure affect its ability to perform its function.
- Certain factors must be considered in choosing materials to build a structure.

Mom, let's buy this wool scarf for Grandma. Wool is soft and has good insulating properties. It'll keep Grandma warm all winter.

A. Timothy is the producer of a play. What properties should he look for in the materials for making the props below? Help him check the correct properties.

1. **sunset**
   - (A) colour
   - (B) water resistance
   - (C) strength

2. **staircase**
   - (A) elasticity
   - (B) environmental impact
   - (C) strength

3. **stage make-up**
   - (A) flexibility
   - (B) water resistance
   - (C) energy efficiency

4. **fake sword**
   - (A) elasticity
   - (B) fire resistance
   - (C) hardness

5. **costumes**
   - (A) hardness
   - (B) decomposability
   - (C) appearance

6. **hose**
   - (A) flexibility
   - (B) colour
   - (C) environmental impact

B. Fill in the blanks with the correct words.

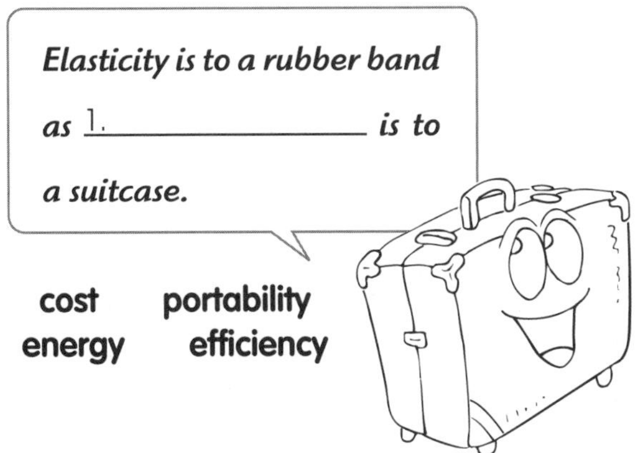

Elasticity is to a rubber band as 1. ________________ *is to a suitcase.*
cost portability
energy efficiency

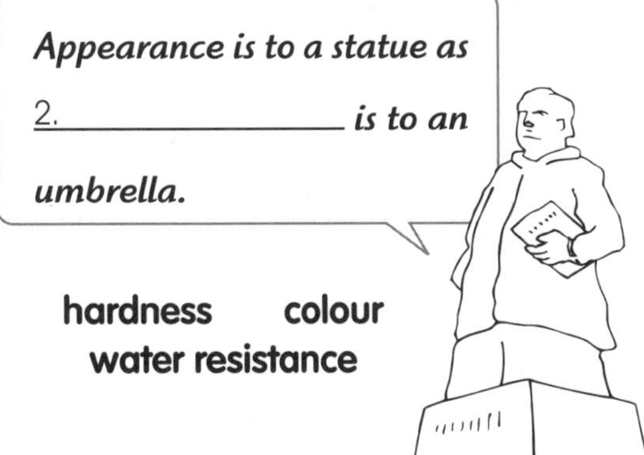

Appearance is to a statue as 2. ________________ *is to an umbrella.*
hardness colour
water resistance

C. Complete the chart by writing what materials would be used to make these human-built structures. Then write one factor that would be considered by the builder when choosing the materials.

Building	Material	Factor Considered
skyscraper	concrete	strength
tree house		
hamster cage		
bus shelter		
tent		
laptop		

Materials

e.g. plastic
glass
concrete
metal
wood

Factors Considered

e.g. flexibility
hardness
energy efficiency
cost
portability
strength
water resistance

Science Fact

The silk of a tiny spider is one of the strongest materials in the world. For its diameter and weight, it is stronger than steel. For general toughness and elasticity, it beats out anything humans have made.

The Particle Theory of Matter

- *The particle theory of matter describes what makes up all matter.*
- *Particles of matter behave in different ways, depending on the state of the matter.*

gas
Particles can move from place to place.
liquid
solid
Particles are densely packed together.
Particles of liquids can move freely but are confined to a container.

A. Unscramble the letters to complete the statements about the Particle Theory of Matter. Then write "true" or "false" for each statement.

1. **Particle Theory of Matter**

   - All matter is made up of ____________ particles.
     itny
   - The particles are always ____________ .
     ivmong
   - There are ____________ between the particles.
     sscape
   - ____________ causes the particles to move faster.
     ahet

2. Particles are the building blocks of all matter. ____________
3. The particles of matter move only when heat is applied. ____________
4. There are no spaces between particles. ____________
5. Temperature affects the particles' speed of movement. ____________
6. Particles at a lower temperature move faster. ____________

B. Read about the behaviour of the particles in different states of matter. Write what state the matter is in. Then continue the pattern by drawing the particles to complete the diagrams.

______________	______________	______________
The particles are so close together that they can barely move.	The particles are spread farthest apart and move in all directions, filling any container they are in.	The particles remain together, though they are far enough apart to slip past each other.
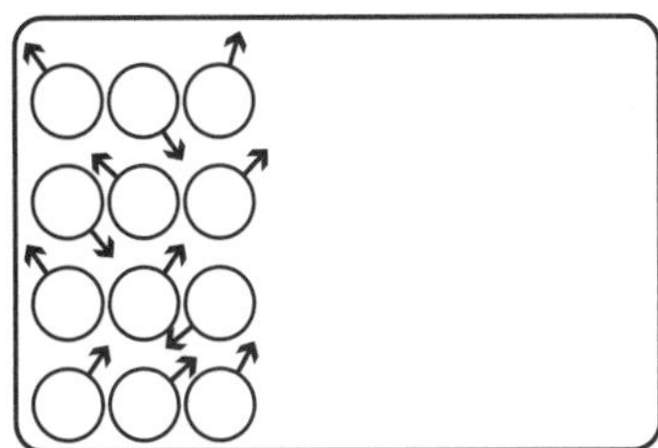	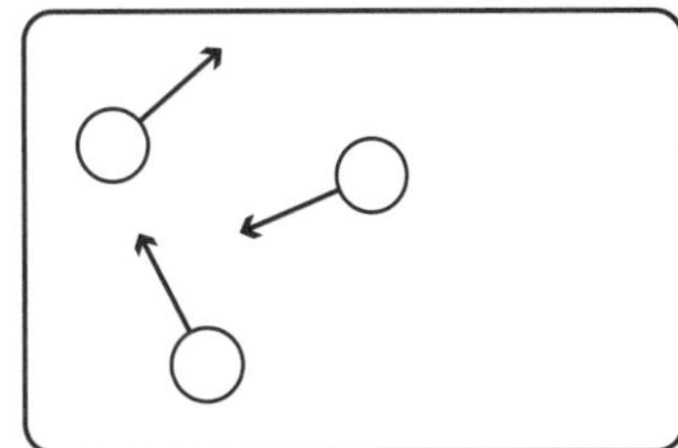	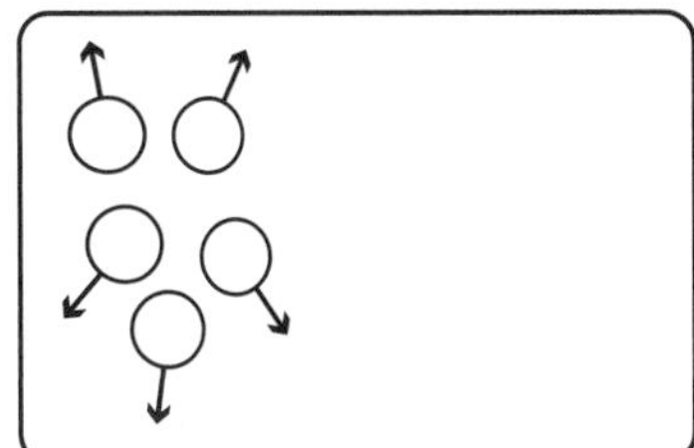

C. What happens to particles of water in different states? Complete the diagram by drawing the missing particles. Then fill in the blanks.

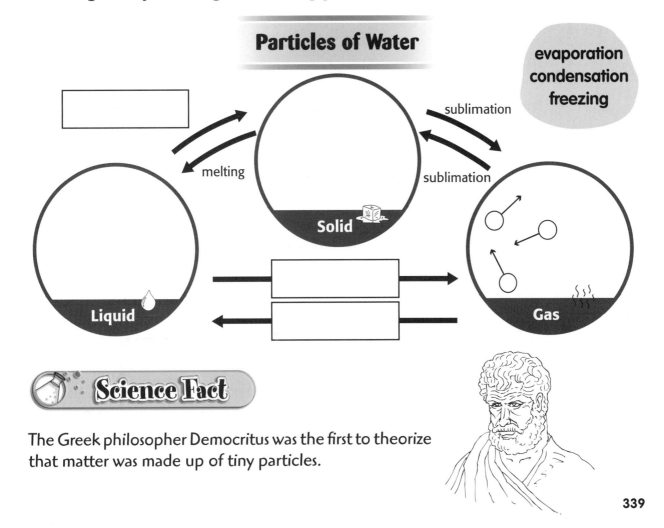

Particles of Water

evaporation
condensation
freezing

melting

sublimation

sublimation

Solid

Liquid

Gas

Science Fact

The Greek philosopher Democritus was the first to theorize that matter was made up of tiny particles.

Pure Substances and Mixtures

- *All matter is either a pure substance or a mixture.*
- *Most matter is either a mechanical mixture or a solution.*

A. Circle the correct words to complete the sentences giving the facts about the two different types of matter. Then complete the chart with the words in bold.

1. A **pure substance** is matter that is made up of identical / different particles.

2. A **mixture** is matter that contains particles from two / twenty or more pure substances. It is either a **mechanical mixture** or a **solution**.

Classification of Matter

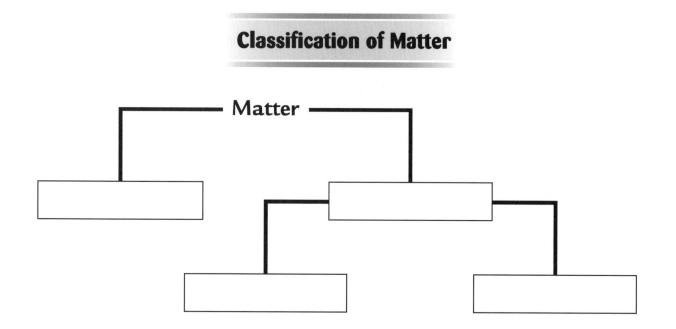

Matter

B. Identify whether each is an example of a pure substance or a mixture. Write "ps" or "m" on the line.

1. Cocoa is made from more than one kind of particle. ______
2. All particles that make a diamond are identical. ______
3. Regardless of where it is found, the melting point of carbon is 4000°C. ______
4. Oxygen, nitrogen, and a few other substances make up air. ______
5. Milk is made up of fat, and many other components. ______
6. Aluminum is a solid with a shiny, silvery appearance. ______
7. Brass is made from copper and zinc. ______

C. Label each substance as being a mechanical mixture (mm) or a solution (s).

Juice
Vinegar
Window cleaner
Party Mix
Substances joined together but still individually recognizable are called mechanical mixtures. A mixture that appears to be a single substance is a solution.

Science Fact

Pure
Honey

In ordinary language many things are called pure. Pure honey! Pure soap! Pure silk! In chemistry, though, scientists use the definition of "pure" that is explained by the particle theory of matter. So, to a chemist, there is no pure soap, honey, or silk.

13

All about Solutions

- A solution is a substance formed when one substance (solute) has been dissolved in another (solvent).
- A solute is the part of a solution that is dissolved in another substance.
- A solvent is the part of a solution that dissolves another substance.

Can I have a glass of solution made of carbon dioxide and water?
MENU
Pop = Solution
Solute
carbon dioxide
Solvent
water
Do you mean you want a glass of pop?

A. Fill in the blanks to complete the descriptions. Identify the missing solute or solvent of each solution with the help of the given substances. Then write the solution type.

1. **Making a Solution**

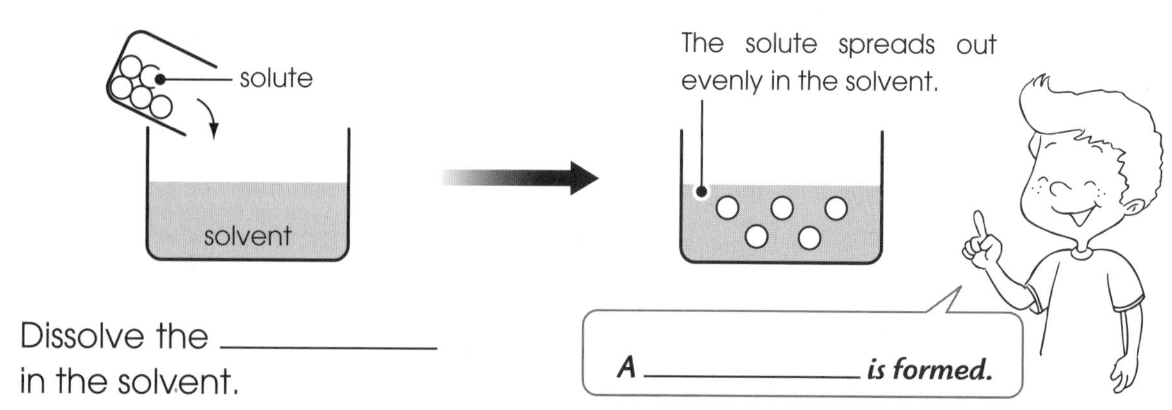
solute
solvent
The solute spreads out evenly in the solvent.
A ____________ is formed.

Dissolve the ____________ in the solvent.

2.

oxygen sugar water salt zinc water

Solution	Solute	Solvent	Solution Type
pop	carbon dioxide (gas)		gas – liquid
salt water		water (liquid)	solid – liquid
vinegar	acetic acid (liquid)		liquid – liquid
brass		copper (solid)	
air	nitrogen (gas)		
maple tree sap		water (liquid)	solid – liquid

B. Fill in the blanks and label the diagrams with "saturated" or "unsaturated".

When a solvent has dissolved the greatest amount of solute that it can, it is a 1.______________ solution. An 2.______________ solution is one that is capable of dissolving more solute.

3. ______________

4. ______________

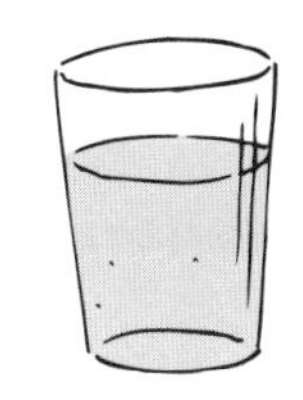

5. ______________

6. ______________

C. Match each definition with the correct word.

concentration •	• a low concentration of dissolved substance in a solvent
dilute •	• a solution that can still dissolve more solute
solvent •	• a solvent that has dissolved all the solute it can
solute •	• ability to dissolve
solubility •	• unable to dissolve
insoluble •	• amount of solute dissolved in a solution
saturated •	• substance that dissolves in a solution
unsaturated •	• dissolves another substance

Science Fact

Water is known as the universal solvent, as it is capable of dissolving more solutes than any other substances.

14

Separating Mixtures

- *Mixtures can be separated into their different substances by using different methods.*
- *The physical properties of substances in a mixture determine how they can be separated.*

I know! You separate the nails from the sand by magnetism!
A Mixture of Sand and Nails

A. Name each method of separation. Then match it with its definition. Write the letter in the circle.

filtration magnetism distillation evaporation density

1. ____________ ◯
2. ____________ ◯
3. ____________ ◯
4. ____________ ◯
5. ____________ ◯

Ⓐ the evaporation, and then condensation, of a liquid in order to separate the substances of a solution

Ⓑ turning a liquid into a gas to separate it from another substance in the mixture

Ⓒ the use of a substance's greater mass per volume to separate it from other substances in a mixture

Ⓓ the separation of a larger substance from a smaller one using a filter that does not allow the larger substance to pass through

Ⓔ the use of a magnet to attract a substance, separating it from other substances in a mixture that are not attracted to a magnet

B. Look at each mixture. Name a physical property that can help determine a method of separation.

1. 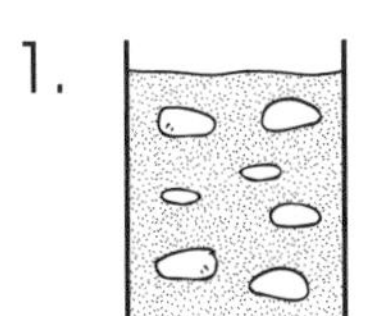 pebbles + sand ____________

2. 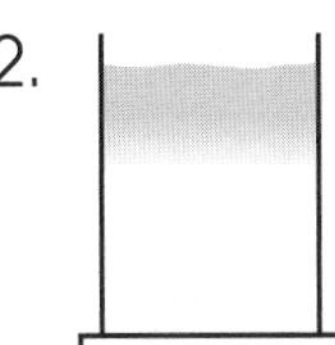 oil + water ____________

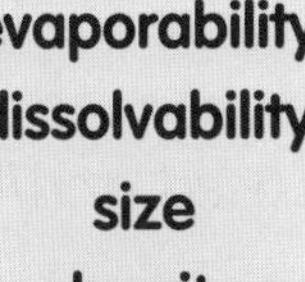

3. pieces of glass + sugar ____________

4. 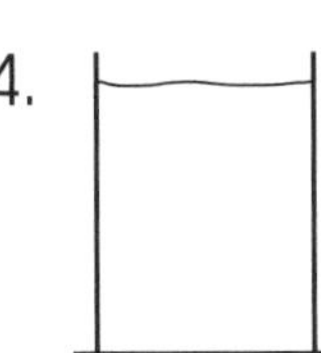 water + salt ____________

C. Write the method of separation that is being used for each mixture.

1. 

____

2. *Let me spoon the fat off the top.*

____

4. 

____

3. 

____

Science Fact

When evaporation is used to separate water from a dissolved solid, such as salt or sugar, the solid substance often appears in the form of a crystal. Each crystallized solid has its own unique geometrical shape, which helps scientists identify it.

Solutions, Mixtures, the Environment, and You

- *Negative impacts on the environment occur when certain solutions and mixtures are used and/or disposed of improperly.*
- *Some solutions and mixtures being created are harmful to the environment.*

BLEACH
SUN
Sally, this is a useful solution, but it's extremely dangerous. We have to handle it carefully.

A. Match the descriptions with the solutions and mixtures that are found in the house. Write the letters in the circles.

1.

A. This may contain turpentine, which helps remove oil-based materials.

B. This contains solutions that make it one of the most hazardous household products that can be bought at the supermarket.

C. This solution is used to whiten things, but it is extremely dangerous and should not be mixed with other chemicals.

2.

P. This solution lowers the freezing point of water. It turns into an acid in the body; drinking even a small amount of it could be fatal.

Q. This may contain mixtures and solutions that are able to help control pests in a garden and should be chosen on the basis of their toxicity.

R. Made from tree resins, this dangerous fluid is used as a solvent to break down oil-based paint. It must be deposed of at an authorized facility.

S. Companies are beginning to produce these decorative products with low volatile organic compounds, and they should be chosen over those that are more toxic.

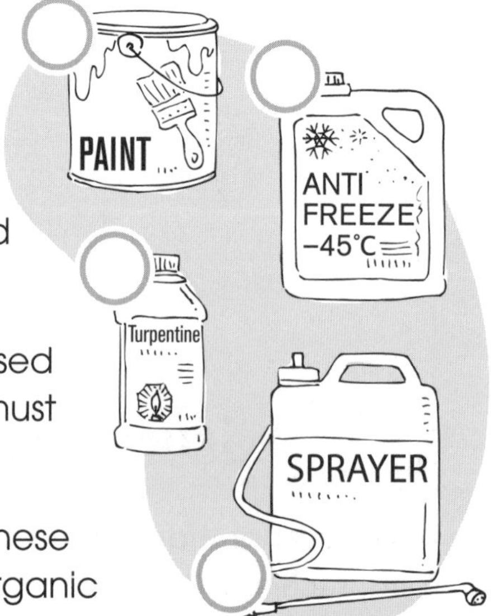

B. Fill in the blanks with the words in the diagram to complete the passage. Then answer the questions.

Acid Rain Formation

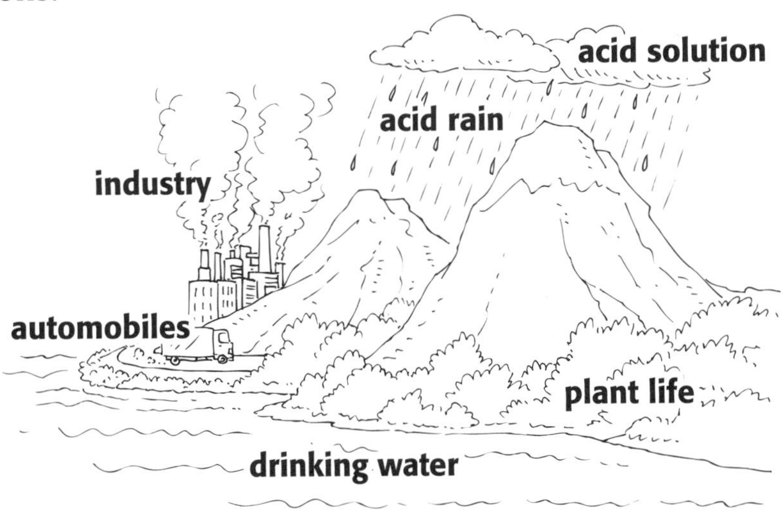

Many of the things that we find ourselves doing on this planet leave an environmental "footprint". One of the more serious "footprints" is 1. ______________ . Polluting gases from 2. ______________ and 3. ______________ dissolve into the water of clouds creating an 4. ______________ that kills aquatic and 5. ______________ , damages buildings and cars, and contaminates 6. ______________ .

7. *How does our consumer-based lifestyle contribute to acid rain?*

____

____

8. How can you reduce acid rain?

____

____

Science Fact

Being an environmentally friendly person, you may use lemon juice – a natural cleaning substance – to clean your house. Lemon juice can be used to dissolve soap scum and hard-water deposits. The lemon peel can be placed in the garbage disposal to freshen the drain and the kitchen.

16

Heat and the Particle Theory of Matter

- *Heat, also called thermal energy, is the energy in the particles of a substance.*
- *Temperature is a measurement of the heat energy of an object at a given time.*
- *We use the particle theory of matter to explain heat energy.*

You can feel the heat on my surface because I'm full of thermal energy.

A. Fill in the blanks with the help of the clues. Then colour the thermometers and draw particles in the beakers.

1. **The Particle Theory of Matter**

   - All substances are made of ______________ (not big) particles.
   - The particles are always ______________ (going everywhere).
   - The more heat energy a substance has, the ______________ (not slower) the particles' motion.

2. *Beaker A contains a liquid that has more heat energy than the liquid in beaker B. The temperature of the liquid in beaker B is 20°C.*

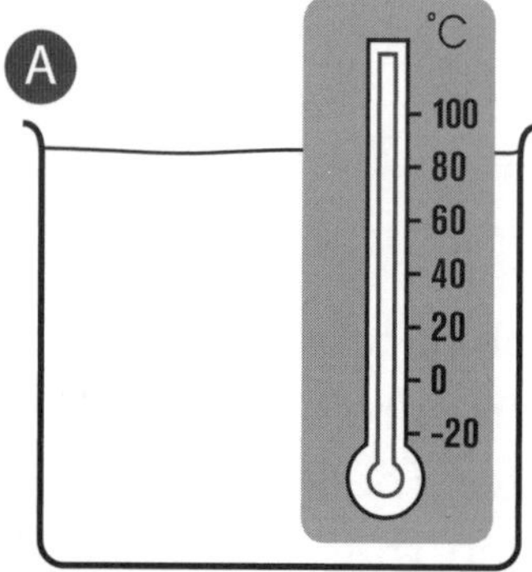

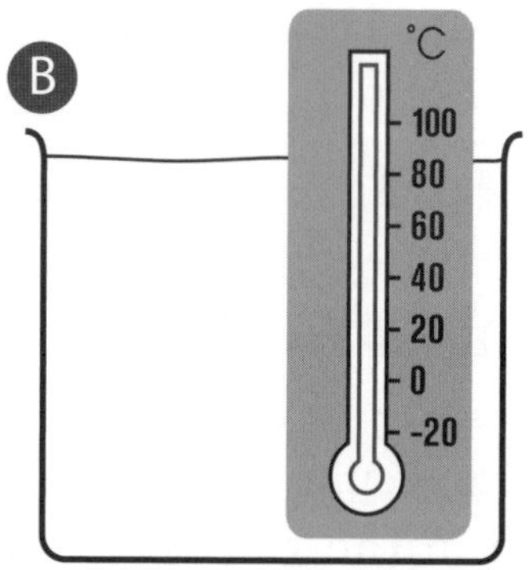

B. Put the substances in order from the one that has the most heat energy per cubic centimetre to the one that has the least. Write 1 to 5.

C. Check the correct endings to complete the sentences.

Heat is

1. (A) a form of energy.
   (B) a form of light.

2. (A) a result of the growth of particles in a substance.
   (B) a result of the vibration of particles in a substance.

3. (A) measured with a thermometer.
   (B) measured with a spring scale.
   (C) measured with an equal arm.

4. (A) never transferred from one substance to another.
   (B) something that is transferred from one substance to another.
   (C) sometimes transferred from one substance to another.

Science Fact

Heat energy always flows from the substance with more heat energy to the substance with less heat energy.

Heat and Volume

- *Most substances that gain heat expand in volume, while substances that lose heat contract.*
- *Unlike any other substances, when water changes state to become ice, it expands.*

Look! The crack is much bigger than before!
July
Sam, don't worry. In winter, the concrete contracts, moving the edges slightly further apart. When it is summer, the crack will not be as big.

A. Fill in the blanks with "more" or "less".

1. A particle of liquid water has ____________ energy than a particle of evaporated water.

2. Fast-moving particles take up ____________ space than slow-moving particles.

3. Particles in a hot liquid take up ____________ space than the particles of the same liquid when it is cold.

4. Particles of evaporated water take up ____________ space than particles of liquid water.

5. The particles of a solid have little energy and require ____________ space than a liquid with more energy.

B. Decide whether each picture is an example of substance expanding or contracting. Write "expand" or "contract" on the line.

1.

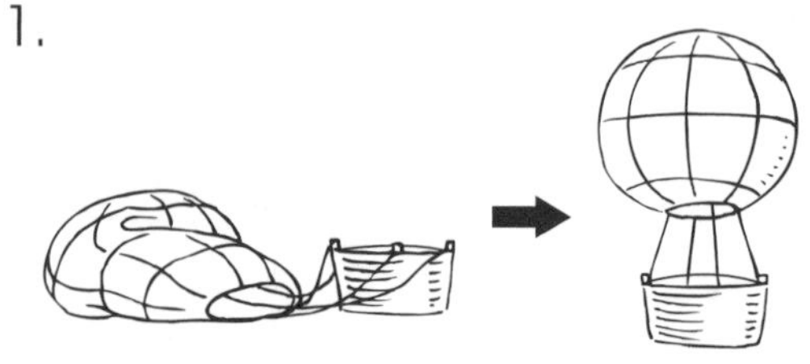

____

2.

____

C. Help Mr. Cowan label the models of the water's particles to show their unique response to freezing. Write "water" or "ice" on the lines.

There is an exception to the rule that when heat is taken away from liquids, less space is taken up. Unlike any other substance, when water changes state to become ice, it expands.

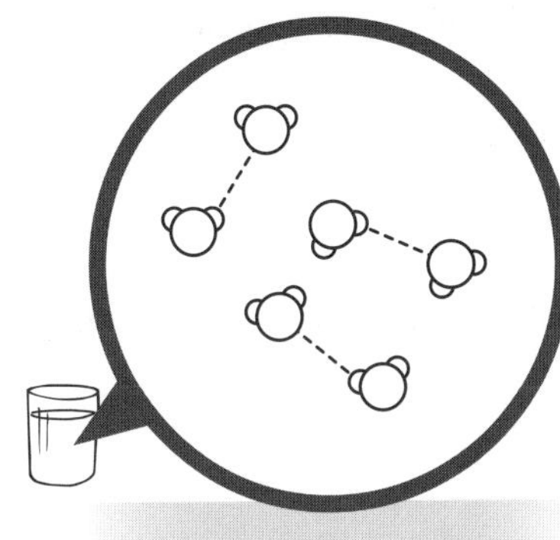

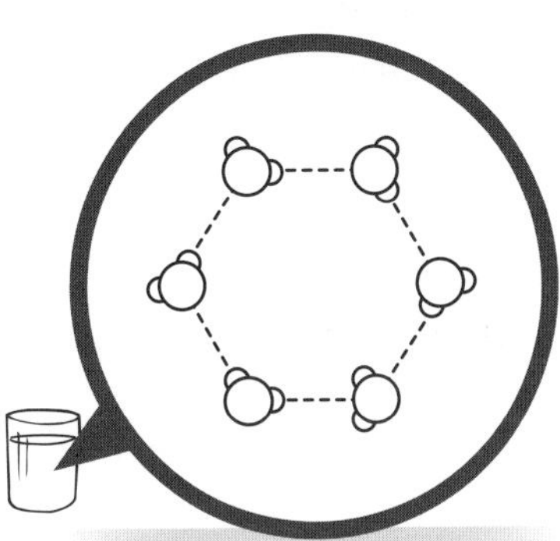

____________________ ____________________

D. Use the particle theory to explain why a tightened lid on a jar is easier to remove when heated.

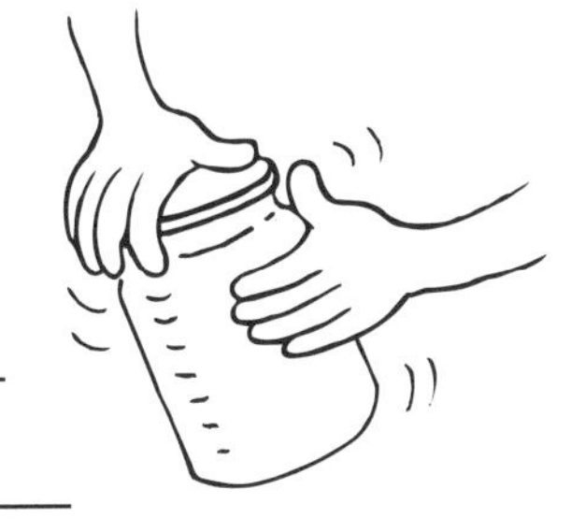

____

____

____

____

____

Can you guess why popcorn pops? A kernel pops when heated because the liquid inside the kernel turns to gas. The gas particles take up more space than the liquid particles do.

18

The Transmission of Heat

- *There are three ways heat flows from one substance to another: conduction, radiation, and convection.*
- *A thermal insulator is a substance that has low heat conductivity, and a thermal conductor has high heat conductivity.*

A. Match the words with the definitions. Then check the correct examples.

radiation convection conduction

1. 

____

Heat is transferred from one substance to another through direct physical contact when both substances are conductors of heat.

(A) a hot pan on the oven

(B) a wet shirt under the sun

2. 

____

Heat is transferred when warm and less dense gas or liquid moves upward to make way for cold and denser gas or fluid.

(A) a spoon in a cup of hot chocolate

(B) the vegetable drawers at the bottom in the refrigerator

3. 

____

Heat travels through air (or space), from an object that radiates heat to another that absorbs it.

(A) food heated in a microwave

(B) hot water in a kettle

B. Decide whether the method of heat transfer is conduction, radiation, or convection.

1. A metal spoon used to stir a hot mixture becomes hot itself. ______________

2. A campfire warms campers even though they sit three metres away from it. ______________

3. Eric must use an oven mitt to hold the handle of his cast iron pot. ______________

4. Emperor penguins huddle to stay warm in some of the coldest weather conditions on Earth. ______________

5. The hot water in a kettle rises to the top, only to cool and sink once more. ______________

C. For each object, write whether the material it is made with should be a thermal insulator (TI) or thermal conductor (TC).

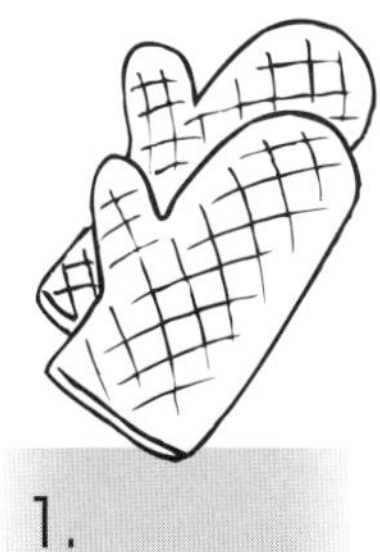

1.

2.

3.

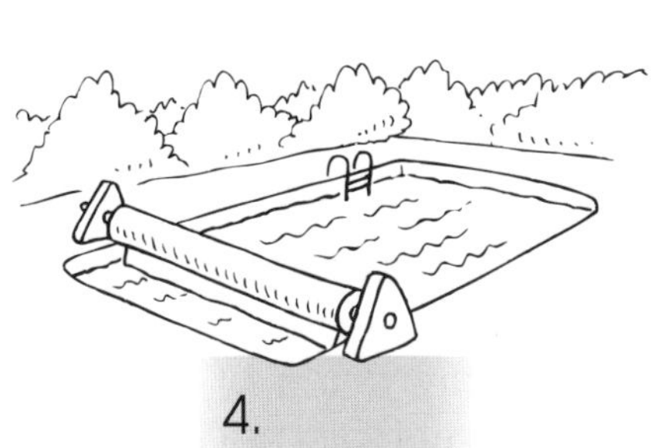

4.

Snow is an excellent thermal insulator. A blanket of snow can protect tender plants, as well as buried pipes, against harsh winter temperatures.

19

Heat and How It Is Produced

- *There are many different sources of heat energy available.*
- *Some sources are non-renewable, meaning they can be used up, while others are renewable.*

During digestion, the chemical energy stored in food is released into my body. I can use the energy to stay warm, to grow, or to move my muscles.

A. Name the major heat producers.

Major Heat Producers

Chemical Energy **Mechanical Force** **Electrical Energy**
Nuclear Energy **Solar Energy** **Geothermal Energy**

1. ____________________

   This produces heat through the push or pull that can cause friction and results in faster-moving particles.

2. ____________________

   Coal-burning and hydroelectric generating stations are major producers of one of our main sources of heat: electricity.

3. ____________________

   It takes advantage of the intense heat found within the Earth. Some parts of the world use this renewable heat source more than other parts of the world.

4. ____________________

   When atoms are split, energy is released. While there are many advantages to use this source of heat energy, there are many unsolved, and perhaps, unsolvable disadvantages.

5. ____________________

   This form of energy is released when fuel such as wood is burned. The same thing happens when we eat food, an important fuel for our bodies. But in this case, the heat is produced through the process of digestion.

6. ____________________

   A form of radiant energy, this is one of the most obvious natural sources of heat available to us. Electromagnetic waves carry this heat source the great distance it needs to travel to reach Earth.

B. Write which type of energy produces the heat in each of the following.

1. 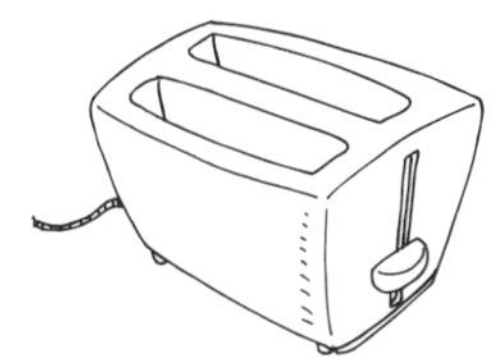

____

2. 

____

3. 

____

4. 

____

5. 

____

C. Write "T" for the true sentences and "F" for the false ones.

1. Chemical energy is non-renewable. ______
2. Food is a source of heat only when it is cooked before eating. ______
3. Geothermal heat originates in the Earth's oceans. ______
4. Radiant energy travels by electromagnetic waves. ______
5. The sun is a form of electrical energy. ______
6. A geyser, a heat source coming from the Earth, is a source of geothermal energy. ______
7. Friction, from a mechanical force, can be a source of heat energy. ______

I'm an example of unintended heat producer.

Electrical energy is one of the largest producers of heat in our homes, and the sources of heat are usually intended for something else!

The Greenhouse Effect

- *The greenhouse effect occurs naturally – the Earth's atmosphere capturing the sun's heat and warming the land and air within.*
- *The greenhouse effect is intensified when more greenhouse gases are released into the atmosphere. This can cause the unnatural rise in temperature on Earth.*

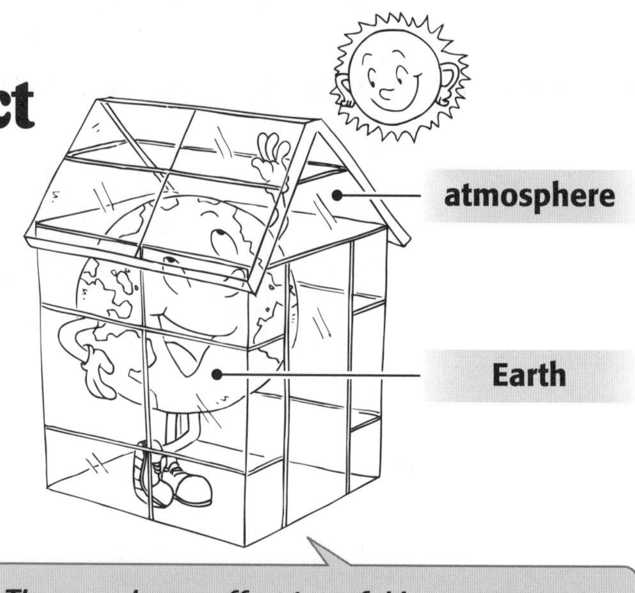

The greenhouse effect is useful because trapping some energy keeps the temperatures on our planet mild and suitable for living things.

A. Fill in the blanks to complete the diagram.

The Greenhouse Effect

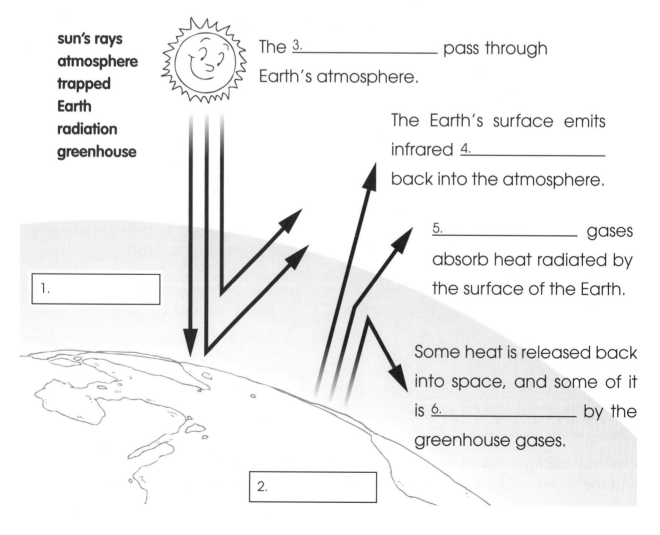

sun's rays
atmosphere
trapped
Earth
radiation
greenhouse

The 3. ____________ pass through Earth's atmosphere.

The Earth's surface emits infrared 4. ____________ back into the atmosphere.

5. ____________ gases absorb heat radiated by the surface of the Earth.

Some heat is released back into space, and some of it is 6. ____________ by the greenhouse gases.

1. ____________

2. ____________

B. Fill in the missing letters to complete the names of the greenhouse gases. Then check the sources of the greenhouse gases.

water vapour ozone methane carbon dioxide nitrous oxide

Common Greenhouse Gases

- c__________ d__________
  - produced naturally when animals breathe
  - product of fossil fuel combustion
  - product of forest fires
- m__________
  - produced when garbage decays
  - product of the digestive process of livestock and manure
- o__________
  - occurs naturally
- n__________ o__________
  - product of fossil fuel combustion
  - emitted through the use of certain fertilizers and industrial processes
- w__________ v__________
  - occurs naturally

Sources of Greenhouse Gases

- (A) cooking
- (B) burning fossil fuels
- (C) decaying organic matter
- (D) agricultural livestock
- (E) during the process of photosynthesis
- (F) plant and animal respiration
- (G) volcanoes
- (H) deforestation
- (I) watering lawns

C. Write the correct answers.

1. *The increase in greenhouse gases in the atmosphere causes Earth's average temperature to __________ (rise / fall).*

2. ________________ (Ozone / Methane) is a greenhouse gas emitted by agricultural livestock.

3. A significant amount of water vapour is released into the atmosphere through plant and animal ________________ (respiration / decomposition).

Science Fact

Methane, the second most important greenhouse gas, can be used as a fuel to generate electricity through a gas recovery system.

Methane

Review

A. Write the meaning of each term. Circle the biotic elements and underline the abiotic elements in the given sentences. Then draw lines to describe their relationships.

1. Ecosystem: ______________________

   Biotic elements: ______________________

   Abiotic elements: ______________________

2. **Relationship**

- biotic & biotic •
- biotic & abiotic •
- abiotic & abiotic •

- • It doesn't take long for a shallow puddle of water to evaporate in the sun.
- • Frogs, toads, and salamanders all begin life in water.
- • For a typical meal, the "cleaner fish" cleans the gills and teeth of other bigger fish which, in turn, become cleaner.

B. Complete the food cycle with the given words. Then write the importance of a decomposer in a food cycle.

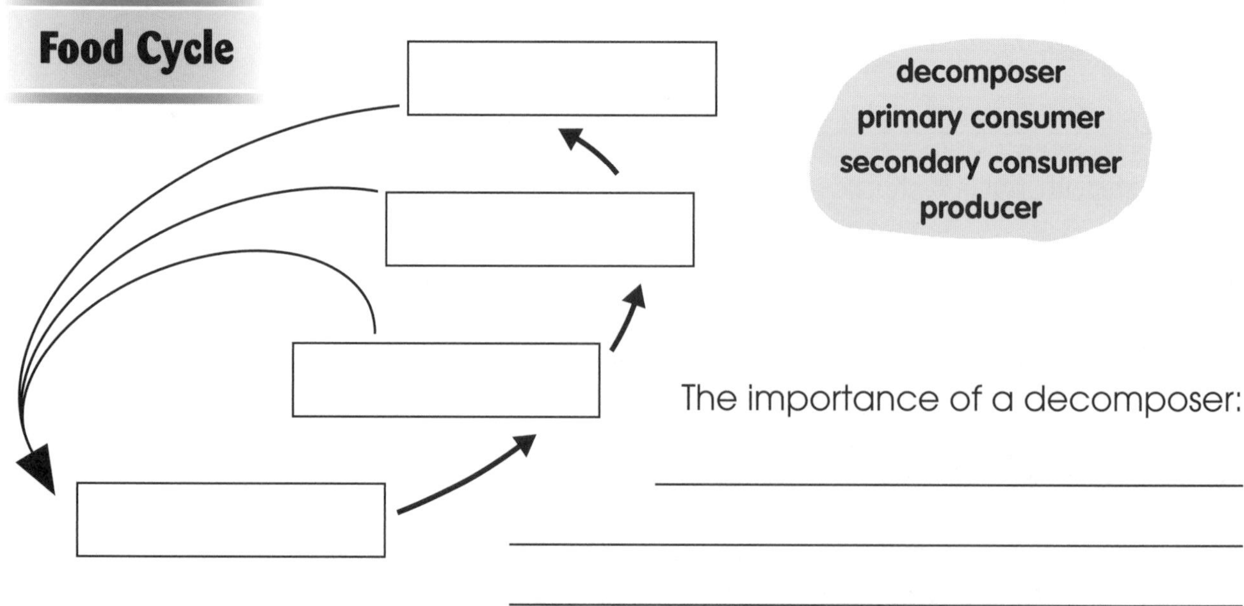

The importance of a decomposer: ______________________

____

____

C. Write sentences about pond succession with the help of the pictures and given words.

Pond Succession

debris
inhabit
emergent plants
marsh
grassland

____

____

____

____

____

D. Fill in the blanks to complete the passage and the diagram. You may use the words more than once.

compressive compression tension tensile live dead

A 1. ______________ load is one that is not part of the structure itself, like the weight of a person on a swing. A 2. ______________ load is the weight of the structure itself, in this case, a seat. The seat has enough 3. ______________ strength to hold the child sitting on it. The swing rope has a strong 4. ______________ strength to withstand the pull of the weight of the child.

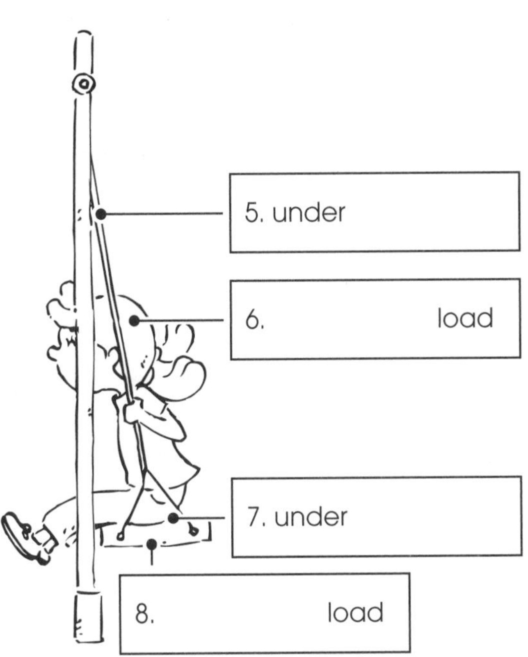

E. Use the particle theory of matter to explain the changes of state of water. Draw diagrams to show the particles in different states.

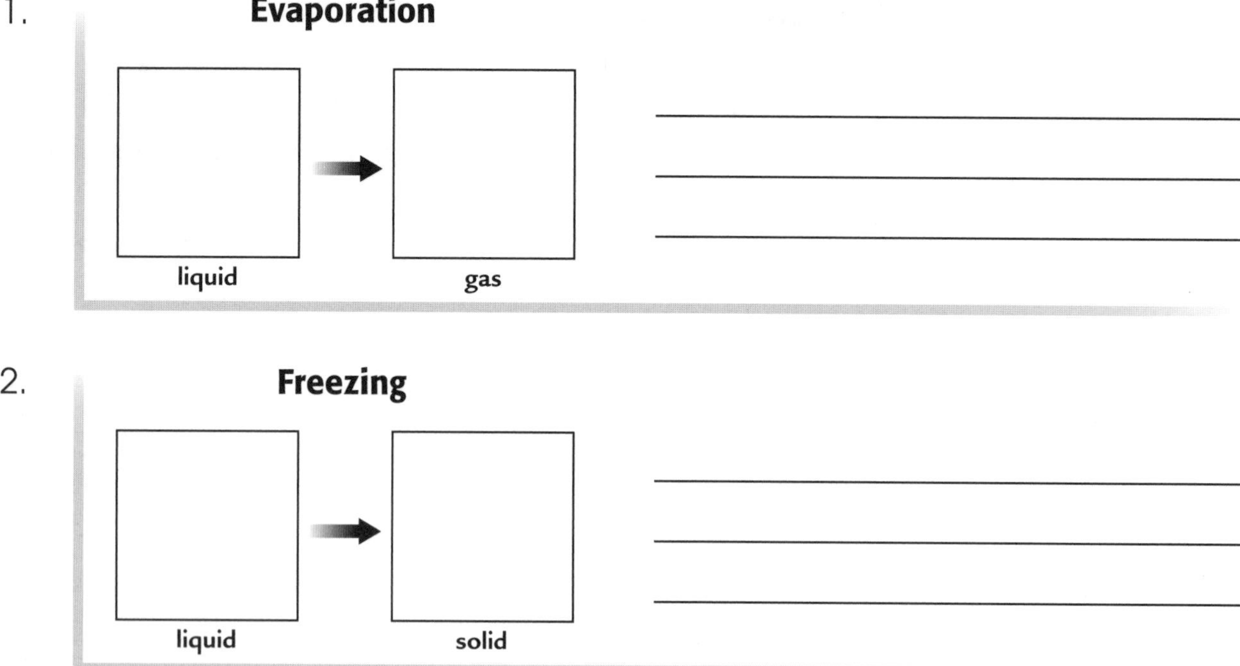

F. Complete the diagram of classification of matter. Then put the correct example into each type of matter. Write the letters in the circles.

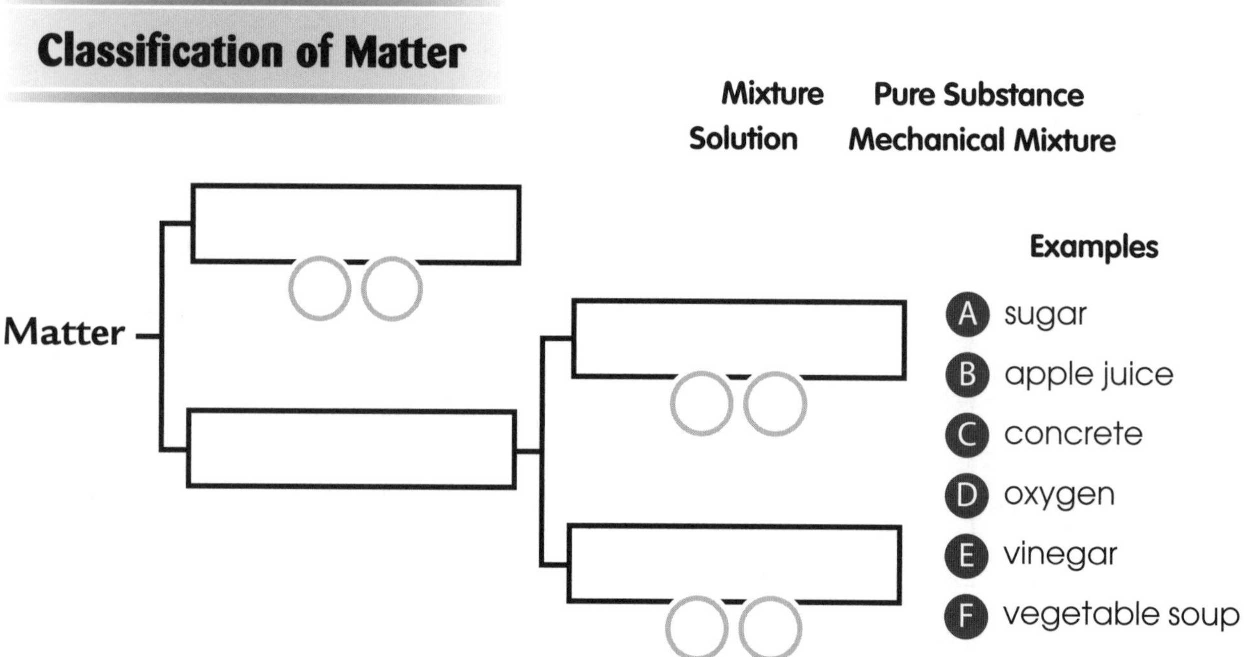

G. Write a possible way to separate the given mixture by using some of the suggested methods of separation.

Method of Separation: filtration, evaporation, density, magnetism, distillation

Mixture

- sand
- salt
- water
- iron

H. Explain the formation of acid rain with the help of the diagram and the given words. Then answer the questions.

1. Formation of acid rain:

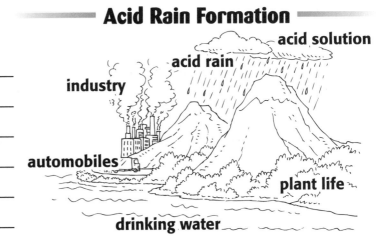

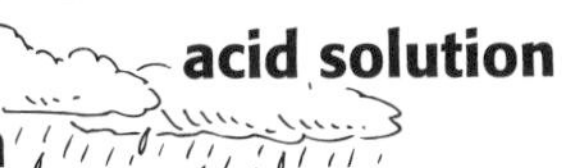
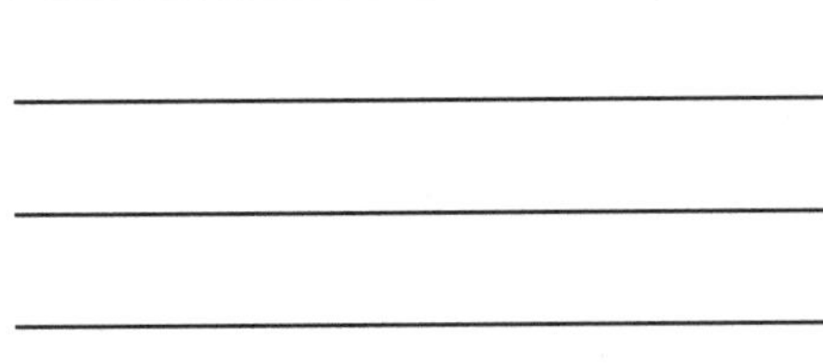

2. Why is acid rain harmful to the environment?

3. Check the activities that can help reduce acid rain.

(A) Use less electricity and transportation.

(B) Leave the lights on even when not in use.

(C) Run the washing machine only when needed.

(D) Use natural gas as an alternative fuel.

Review

I. Decide whether each picture is an example of a substance expanding or contracting. Write "expand" or "contract" in the box. Then complete the description.

1.

a.

b. volume change: ________ → ________

c. energy change: ________ → ________

d. space occupied: ________ → ________

2.

a.

b. volume change: ________ → ________

c. energy change: ________ → ________

d. space occupied: ________ → ________

J. Name the heat transmission that matches each description. Give one example of each type of heat transmission. Then answer the question.

1. ________________: Heat is transferred when warm and less dense gas or liquid moves upward to make way for cold and denser gas or fluid.

For example: ________________________________

2. ________________: Heat is transferred from one substance to another through direct physical contact when both substances are conductors of heat.

For example: ________________________________

3. ________________: Heat travels through air (or space), from an object that radiates heat to another that absorbs it.

For example: ________________________________

4. Do you think that food warms faster in a convection oven than in a regular oven? Why?

____

____

K. Check the correct answers.

1. Which object is a shell structure?

   (A) cap (B) spiderweb (C) pyramid

2. What is heat?

   (A) a form of light (B) a form of energy (C) a form of gas

3. Which picture shows the centre of gravity (•) correctly?

   (A) 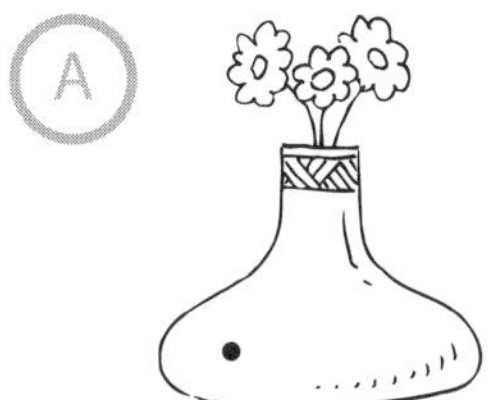 (B) 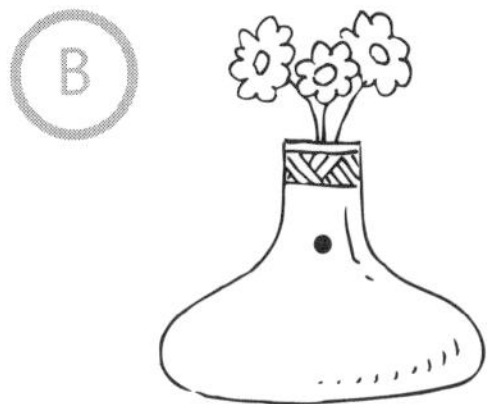 (C) 

4. What is a solvent?

   (A) the part of a solution that is dissolved in another substance

   (B) the part of a solution that dissolves another substance

   (C) a chemical substance that can be dissolved

5. What are the common greenhouse gases?

   (A) methane, oxygen, nitrogen, ozone, water vapour

   (B) carbon dioxide, methane, ozone, nitrous oxide, water vapour

   (C) nitrous oxide, oxygen, water vapour, methane, hydrogen

6. ***Which heat producer gives us heat in the form of radiant energy?***

   (A) solar energy

   (B) geothermal energy

   (C) mechanical force

ANSWERS

1 Exponents

1. 3 x 3 x 3 x 3 x 3 x 3 x 3 x 3
2. 4 x 4 x 4 x 4 x 4
3. 8 x 8 x 8 x 8 x 8 x 8 x 8
4. 12 x 12 x 12 x 12
5. 9 x 9 x 9 x 9 x 9 x 9
6. 7 x 7 x 7 x 7 x 7 x 7 x 7 x 7

7. 3 8. 6 9. 2 ; 2 ; 2
10. 7 11. 4 12. 8
13. 11 ; 11 ; 11 ; 11
14. 3 15. 5 ; 3 16. 7 ; 5
17. 22 ; 10 18. 13 ; 6 19. 39 ; 2
20. 1 ; 100 21. 64 22. 3^4 ; 81
23. 7^3 ; 343 24. 5^5 ; 3125 25. 9^3 ; 729
26. 2^6 ; 64 27. 1^8 ; 1
28. 5^4 ; 5 x 5 x 5 x 5 ; 625
29. 7^6 ; 7 x 7 x 7 x 7 x 7 x 7 ; 117 649
30. 2^8 ; 2 x 2 x 2 x 2 x 2 x 2 x 2 x 2 ; 256
31. $2^2 \times 5^3$ 32. $4^3 \times 6^2$ 33. 5×9^4
34. $1^2 \times 8^4$ 35. $2^4 \times 7^5$ 36. $3^6 \times 8^3$
37. 27 ; 1296 a. >
    125 ; 32 b. <
    1024 ; 343 c. >
    729 ; 4096 d. >
38. > 39. < 40. <
41. > 42. < 43. >
44. 5 ; 25 ; 2 ; 625 ; 625 ; perfect square
45. 8 x 8 ; 64 ; 64 ; 3 ; 262 144 ; 262 144 ; perfect cube
46. 2 ; 2401 ; 2401 ; perfect square
47. 3 ; 19 683 ; 19 683 ; perfect cube
48. A: 8 ; 15 ; 415 ; 67
    itself
    B: 1 ; 1 ; 1 ; 1
    If the exponent of a power is 0, then the answer will be 1.

2 Squares and Square Roots

1. From 1^2 to 10^2: 1, 4, 9, 16, 25, 36, 49, 64, 81, 100
2. 7 3. 6 4. 9
5. 2 6. 10 7. 4
8. 1 9. 9 10. 6
11. 9 12. 4 13. 5
14. 4 15. 9 16. 1
17. 4 18. 4 ; 4
19. 7 ; $49 = 7^2$ 20. 64 ; $8^2 = 64$
21. 625 ; $25^2 = 625$ 22. 49 ; $7^2 = 49$
23. 81 ; $9^2 = 81$ 24. 100 ; $100 = 10^2$
25. 12 ; $144 = 12^2$ 26. 15 ; 225
27. 20 ; $20^2 = 400$ 28. 11 ; $11^2 = 121$
29. 256 ; $\sqrt{256} = 16$ 30. 289 ; $\sqrt{289} = 17$
31. 21 ; $21^2 = 441$ 32. 8 ; $\sqrt{64} = 8$
33. 400 ; $20^2 = 400$ 34. 6 ; 36
35. 3^2 ; 9 36. 8^2 ; 64 (square units)
37. 256 ; 16 38. $\sqrt{144}$; 12 (units)
39. 289 ; 576
    17 ; 24
40. 64 ; 225
    8 ; 15
41.

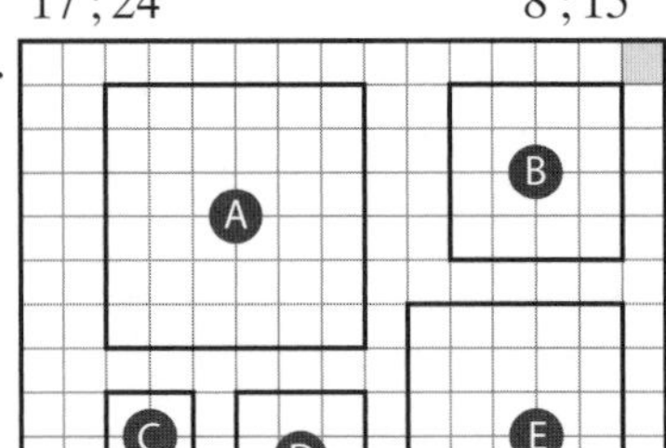

42a. Side length of big square: $\sqrt{169} = 13$ (cm)
    Side length of small square: $\sqrt{49} = 7$ (cm)
    13 cm and 7 cm
b. $y = 13 - 7 = 6$
    6
43. Area of a small square: $576 \div 4 = 144$ (cm^2)
    Side length of small square: $\sqrt{144} = 12$ (cm)
    12

3 Factors and Multiples

1. ①②③⑥
   ①②③ 4, ⑥ 12
   6
2. ①③ 5, 15
   ① 2, ③ 4, 6, 8, 12, 24
   3
3. ① 2, ⑦ 14
   ① 3, ⑦ 21
   7
4. ①②③④⑥⑫
   ①②③④⑥ 9, ⑫ 18, 36
   12
5. ①②④ 8
   ①②④ 5, 10, 20
   ①②④ 7, 14, 28
   4
6. ①②③④⑥ 8, ⑫ 16, 24, 48
   ①②③④ 5, ⑥ 10, ⑫ 15, 20, 30, 60
   ①②③④⑥ 8, ⑫ 16, 24, 32, 48, 96
   12
7. 1, 2, 4, 8 ; 8 8. 1, 2, 4, 5, 10, 20 ; 20
9. 1, 2, 3, 4, 6, 12 ; 12 10. 1, 2, 4 ; 4
11. 5 10 15 30 | 1 2 3 6 | 7 14 21 42 ; 6
12. Factors of 28 Factors of 35
    2 4 14 28 | 1 7 | 5 35 ; 7
13. Factors of 12 Factors of 20

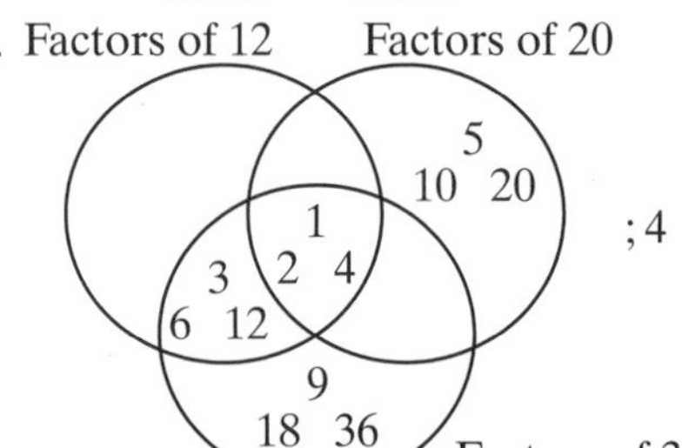

; 4

14. Factors of 10 Factors of 45

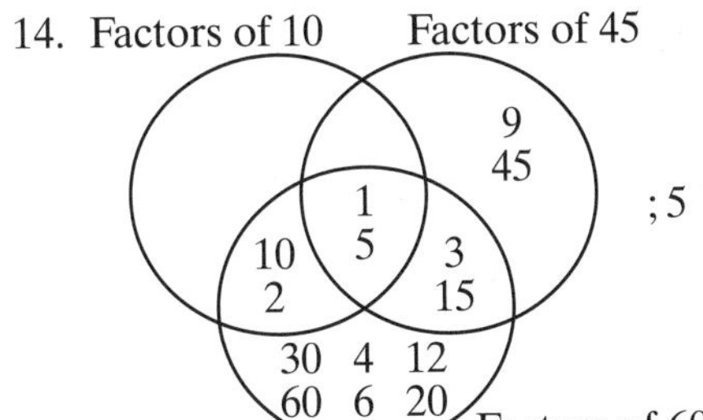

; 5

15. Make a legend to mark the multiples of the numbers.
 a. 30, 60, 90 ; 30
 b. 12, 24, 36, 48, 60, 72, 84, 96 ; 12
 c. 20, 40, 60, 80, 100 ; 20

16a. 10, 20, 30, 40, 50, 60, 70, 80, 90, 100
 b. Each multiple goes up by 10 each time.
 c. 110, 120, 130, 140, 150

17. 4, 8, (12), 16, 20, (24), 28, 32, (36), 40, 44, (48)
 6, (12), 18, (24), 30, (36), 42, (48), 54, 60, 66, 72
 12
 12, 24, 36, 48

18. 3, 6, 9, 12, 15, 18, 21, 24, 27, 30, 33, 36
 4, 8, 12, 16, 20, 24, 28, 32, 36, 40, 44, 48
 5, 10, 15, 20, 25, 30, 35, 40, 45, 50, 55, 60
 6, 12, 18, 24, 30, 36, 42, 48, 54, 60, 66, 72
 7, 14, 21, 28, 35, 42, 49, 56, 63, 70, 77, 84
 L.C.M.: 12 ; 30 ; 42 ; 35

19. 4, 8, 12, 16, 20, 24
 6, 12, 18, 24
 12

20. 1, 2, 3, 6, 9, 18
 1, 2, 3, 4, 6, 12
 6 ; 3 ; 2

4 Integers

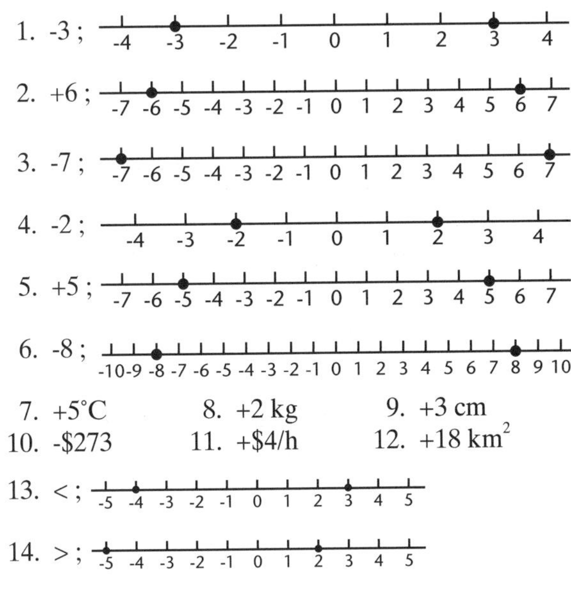

17. +5
18. -3
19. -2
20. 0
21. -4, -2, +6, +8
22. -5, -3, +2, +5
23. -9, -7, -1, 0
24. -11, -8, +3, +12
25. -4, -2, 0, 4
26. -15, -9, -6, -3
27. 7
28. -1 ; (5 units)
29. 3 ; (5 units)
30. 4
31. -12
32. -9
33. 6
34. -1
35. -6
36. -7
37. -3
38a. 5 b. 2 points c. -1 point
39. No. The team needs 4 more points.
40. -4
41. 6
42. 11
43. -5
44. 9
45. -3
46. -8
47. 0
48. -6
49. 5
50. Wednesday: 4°C ; 1°C ; -3°C
 Thursday: -6°C ; -11°C ; -3°C

5 Ratios and Rates

1a. 2 ; 5 b. 2:10 c. 5:10
 d. 10:17
2a. 7:6 b. 8:7 c. 5:16
3. Colour 5 circles green and 6 rectangles red.
 5:6
4. Colour 3 triangles and 3 squares red, 3 stars blue, and 2 stars yellow.
 3:3
5.

Marbles	Ratio	Ratio (New)
green : blue	3:2	3:6
red : green	4:3	5:3
blue : all	2:9	6:14
red : all	4:9	5:14

6. 6 ; 10
7. 8 ; 28
8. $\frac{4}{3}$
9. $\frac{3}{5}$

(Suggested answers for questions 10 to 19)

10. 2:6
11. 2:4
12. 15:4
13. 2:5
14. 3:2, 12:8
15. 2:5, 8:20
16. 16:10, 32:20
17. 2:5, 20:50
18. 4:5, 24:30
19. 2:14, 6:42
20. 9
21. 2
22. 1
23. 2
24. 6
25. 18
26. 1:3 ; 9
27. 2:5 ; 9
28. 5:2 ; 7
29. 5:3 ; 6
30. 5:8 ; 3
31. 7:3 ; 6
32. height:base = 2:3
 2:3 = 18:27
 The length of the base is 27 cm.

33. Tom's candies:my candies = 4:5
    4:5 = 28:35
    Tom has 28 candies.
34. 13.73 km/h
35. $0.59/chicken ball
36. 9 pages/day
37. 5 bicycles/h
38. 42 ; 66 words/min ; Check B
39. 76.52 km/h ; 64.88 km/h ; Check A
40. 81.5 g/day ; 78.5 g/day ; Check A

6 Fractions

1a. $\frac{15}{35}$ b. $3 ; \frac{6}{15}$ c. $4 ; \frac{20}{24}$

2a. $\frac{4}{5}$ b. $2 ; \frac{4}{5}$ c. $5 ; \frac{1}{4}$

(Suggested answers for questions 3 to 6)

3. $\frac{1}{3}$
4. $\frac{2}{8}$
5. $\frac{8}{15}$
6. $\frac{2}{5}$
7. $10 ; \frac{5}{10} ; \frac{4}{10}$

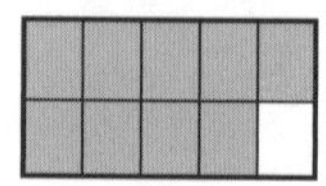

$; \frac{9}{10}$

8. $20 ; \frac{15}{20} ; \frac{2}{20}$; $\frac{17}{20}$
9. $\frac{6}{10} ; \frac{7}{10}$
10. $15 ; \frac{4}{20} ; \frac{19}{20}$
11. $9 ; \frac{16}{30} ; \frac{25}{30} ; \frac{5}{6}$
12. $\frac{20}{36} + \frac{7}{36} ; \frac{3}{4}$
13. $\frac{4}{14} + \frac{5}{14} ; \frac{9}{14}$
14. $\frac{15}{20} + \frac{16}{20} ; 1\frac{11}{20}$
15. $\frac{9}{18} + \frac{17}{18} ; 1\frac{4}{9}$
16. $\frac{1}{2} + \frac{7}{10} ; 1\frac{1}{5} ; 1\frac{1}{5}$ kg
17. $\frac{5}{6} + \frac{1}{2} ; 1\frac{1}{3} ; 1\frac{1}{3}$ kg
18. $10 ; \frac{5}{10} ; \frac{2}{5}$
19. $30 ; \frac{25}{30} ; \frac{22}{30} ; \frac{1}{10}$
20. $\frac{1}{2}$
21. $\frac{1}{6}$
22. $\frac{1}{3}$
23. $\frac{1}{2}$
24. $\frac{1}{4}$
25. $\frac{1}{5}$
26. $\frac{9}{10} - \frac{1}{2} ; \frac{2}{5} ; \frac{2}{5}$ km
27. $\frac{9}{10} - \frac{1}{6} ; \frac{11}{15} ; \frac{11}{15}$ km/min
28. $\frac{5}{8} ; \frac{5}{8} ; 15 ; 1\frac{7}{8}$
29. $\frac{5}{6} + \frac{5}{6} + \frac{5}{6} ; 20 ; 3\frac{1}{3}$
30. $2\frac{2}{3}$
31. $\frac{6}{7}$
32. $2\frac{2}{5}$
33. $1\frac{1}{3}$
34. $2\frac{1}{4}$
35. $2\frac{6}{7}$
36. $3\frac{1}{2}$
37. $1\frac{3}{4}$
38. $\frac{3}{5} \times 7 ; 4\frac{1}{5} ; 4\frac{1}{5}$ L
39. $\frac{11}{12} \times 8 ; 7\frac{1}{3} ; 7\frac{1}{3}$ kg
40. $\frac{5}{6} \times 8 ; 6\frac{2}{3} ; 6\frac{2}{3}$ h

7 Decimals

1. 3 ; 2.8 ; 2.8 ; 2.804
2. 12 ; 11.5 ; 11.55 ; 11.549
3. 4 ; 4.1 ; 4.07 ; 4.068
4. 26 ; 25.8 ; 25.8 ; 25.802
5. sum: 18 + 8 = 26; difference: 18 − 8 = 10; sum: 17.620 + 8.193 = 25.813; difference: 17.620 − 8.193 = 9.427
6. sum: 24 + 9 = 33; difference: 24 − 9 = 15; sum: 24.300 + 9.087 = 33.387; difference: 24.300 − 9.087 = 15.213
7. 13.0 ; 5 ; 15
8. 8.76 ; 4 x 2 = 8
9. 3.24 ; 5 x 1 = 5
10. 18.17 ; 8 x 2 = 16
11. 22.4 x 1.8: 1792; 2240; 40.32
12. 1.76 x 3.7: 1232; 5280; 6.512
13. 8.7 x 3.1: 87; 2610; 26.97
14. 14.6 x 0.5: 7.30
15. 1.06 x 4.3: 318; 4240; 4.558
16. 13.4 x 0.8: 10.72

17a. 82.46 x 1.6 ; 131.936 (km)
b. 82.46 x 2.3 ; 189.658 (km)
c. 82.46 x 3.5 ; 288.61 (km)
d. 82.46 x 4.7 ; 387.562 (km)

18. 7.2 ; 6 ; 7
    58 ⟌ 417.6 = 7.2: 406; 116; 116
19. 15.5 ; 32 ÷ 2 = 16
    208 ⟌ 3224.0 = 15.5: 208; 1144; 1040; 1040; 1040
20. 1.92 ; 12 ÷ 6 = 2
    625 ⟌ 1200.00 = 1.92: 625; 5750; 5625; 1250; 1250
21. 14.4 ; 22 ÷ 2 = 11
    15 ⟌ 216.0 = 14.4: 15; 66; 60; 60; 60
22. 24.7
23. 5.37
24. 4.2
25. 5.48
26. 6.5
27. 8.56
28. = 3.9 x 4
    = 15.6
29. = 7.5 − 2.5
    = 5
30. = 5.98 − 2.1
    = 3.88
31. 10.5
32. 6.25
33. 9.28
34. 7.68
35. 6.3
36. 47.882

37. Check A ; 1.65
38. Check B ; 28.35
His average speed was 28.35 km/h.

8 Fractions, Decimals, and Percents

1. $\frac{35}{100}$; 0.35 ; 35% 2. $\frac{28}{100}$; 0.28 ; 28%
3. $\frac{52}{100}$; 0.52 ; 52% 4. $\frac{66}{100}$; 0.66 ; 66%
5. $\frac{42}{100}$; 0.42 ; 42% 6. $\frac{50}{100}$; 0.5 ; 50%
7. 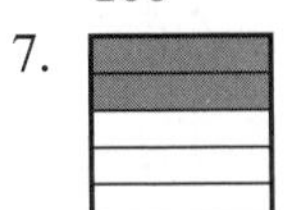 8.  9. 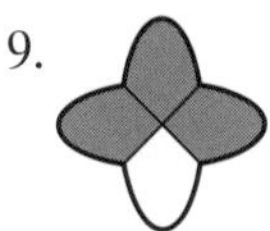

10a. 48% b. 80% c. 215%
d. 27.9% e. 8.2% f. 105%
11a. 0.52 b. 0.154 c. 2
d. 0.005 e. 0.089 f. 0.07
12. 0.3 ; 30% 13. 0.5 ; 50% 14. 0.75 ; 75%
15. 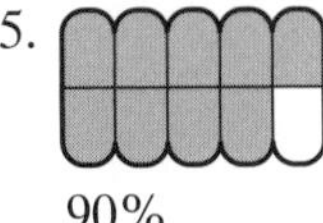
90%
16. 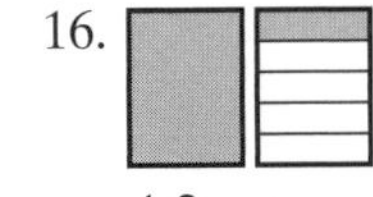
1.2
17. 30 ; 30 18. $\frac{18}{100}$; 18% 19. $\frac{64}{100}$; 64%
20. $\frac{75}{100}$; 75% 21. $\frac{95}{100}$; 95% 22. $\frac{60}{100}$; 60%
23. 0.16 ; 16 ;
$$\begin{array}{r} 0.16 \\ 50\,\overline{)8.00} \\ \underline{50} \\ 300 \\ \underline{300} \end{array}$$
24. 0.36 = 36% ;
$$\begin{array}{r} 0.36 \\ 25\,\overline{)9.00} \\ \underline{75} \\ 150 \\ \underline{150} \end{array}$$
25. 0.85 = 85% ;
$$\begin{array}{r} 0.85 \\ 20\,\overline{)17.00} \\ \underline{160} \\ 100 \\ \underline{100} \end{array}$$
26. $\frac{6}{25}$
27. $\frac{13}{25}$ 28. $\frac{39}{50}$ 29. $\frac{83}{100}$
30. $\frac{9}{25}$ 31. $\frac{31}{50}$
32.

	Fraction	Decimal	Percent
circle	$\frac{3}{10}$	0.3	30%
parallelogram	$\frac{2}{5}$	0.4	40%
triangle	$\frac{3}{4}$	0.75	75%
square	$\frac{7}{20}$	0.35	35%
rectangle	$\frac{9}{25}$	0.36	36%

33. Jason's cup: $\frac{4}{5}$ = 80%
George's cup: 0.7 = 70%
Tim's cup: 75% ; Jason
34. 1 – 0.25 – 0.1 = 0.65
0.65 of the buttons are red.
35. English: $\frac{19}{20}$ = 95% ; Math: 89% ;
History: 0.92 = 92% ; Science: $\frac{23}{25}$ = 92% ;
He did the best in English.

9 Percents

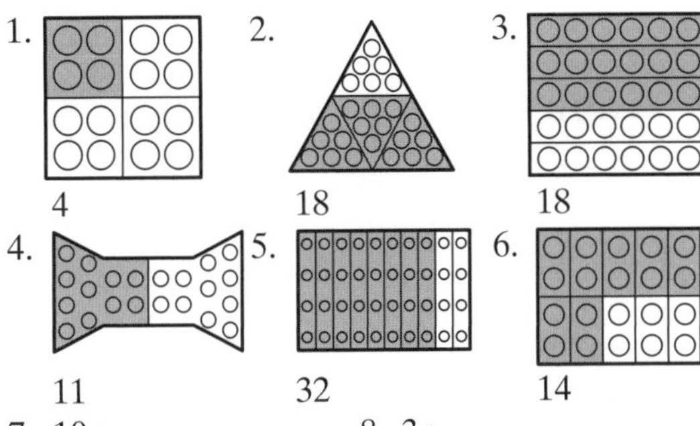

7. 10 ; 8. 3 ;
9. 15 ; 0.15 ; 3
10. = 30% x 90
= 0.3 x 90
= 27
11. = 10% x 27
= 0.1 x 27
= 2.7
12. = 7.5% x 360
= 0.075 x 360
= 27
13. = 35% x 60
= 0.35 x 60
= 21
14. = 3.2% x 50
= 0.032 x 50
= 1.6
15. Yellow: 20% x 80 = 16
Green: 25% x 80 = 20
Blue: 30% x 80 = 24
Red: 10% x 80 = 8
Orange: 15% x 80 = 12
16. 70% x 20 = 14 ; 14 boys like green.
17. 18 ; 6 ; 600 ; 600 18. 24 ; 2 ; 200 ; 200
19. 125 20. 70 21. 64
22. 28% → 140 ;
1% → 5 ;
100% → 500 ; The capacity of the jar is 500 mL.
23. 25% → 24 ;
1% → 0.96 ;
100% → 96 ; Jane's savings were $96.
24. Judy:
160 x 20% + 30 x (1 – 40%) = 32 + 18 = 50
Judy has 50 marbles.
Ken:
30 x 40% + 50 x 20% = 12 + 10 = 22
Ken has 22 marbles.

Sam:
160 x 45% + 50 x 48% = 72 + 24 = 96
Sam has 96 marbles.
Tina:
160 x (1 – 20% – 45%) + 50 x (1 – 48% – 20%)
= 56 + 16 = 72
Tina has 72 marbles.

25. 96 x 25% = 24
Pamela will get 24 marbles from Sam.
26. No. of red marbles Judy has:
50 x 70% = 35
No. of red marbles Erica gets from Judy:
35 x 80% = 28
Erica gets 28 red marbles from Judy.

10 Angles

1a. ℓ_1 and ℓ_2

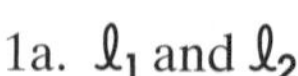

b. ℓ_5 and ℓ_6

c. ℓ_3 and ℓ_4

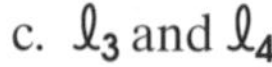

d. ℓ_7 and ℓ_8

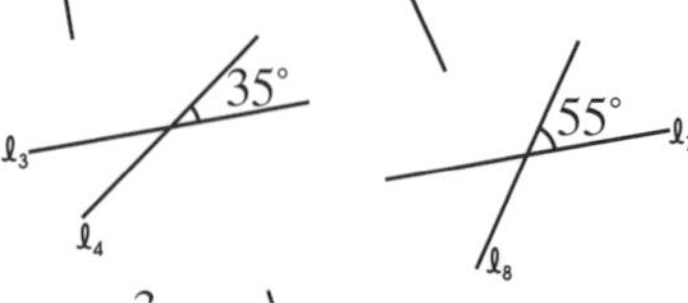

2.

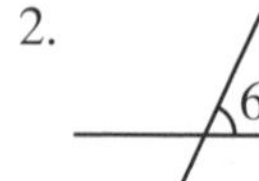

3.

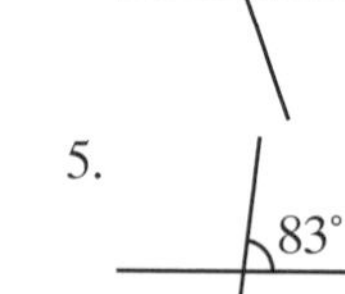

4.

5.

6. IJ ; w ; y
7. QR ; a and e ; d and f
8. AB ; m and p ; o and q

9.

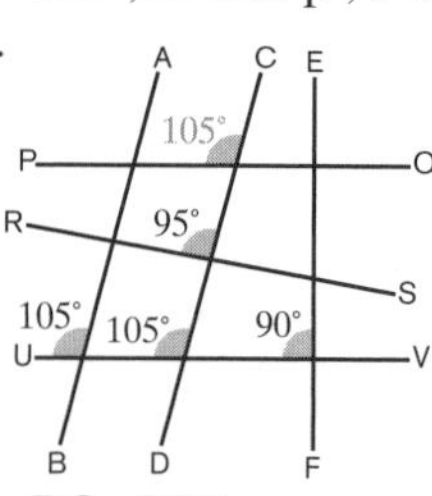

PQ ; UV
AB ; CD

10.

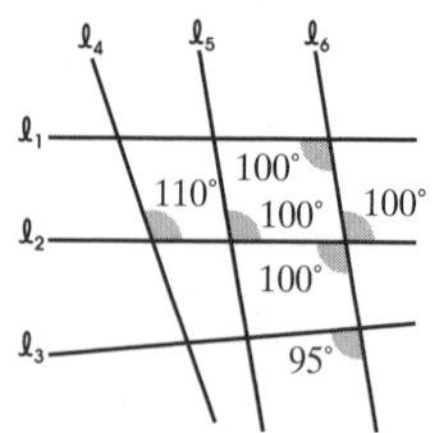

$\ell_1 // \ell_2$
$\ell_5 // \ell_6$

(Suggested answers for questions 11 to 13)

11.

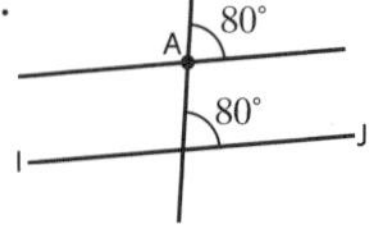

80°

12.

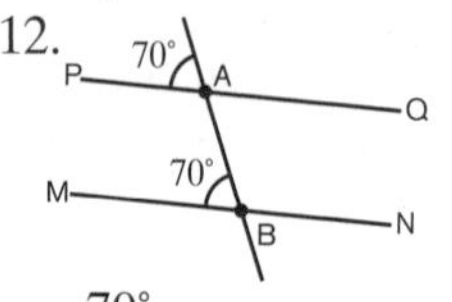

70°

13.

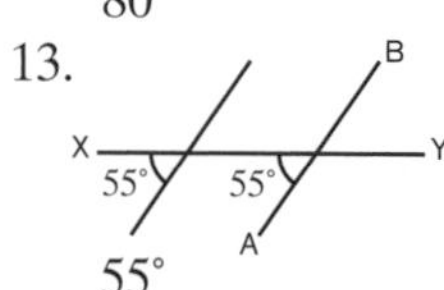

55°

14. perpendicular

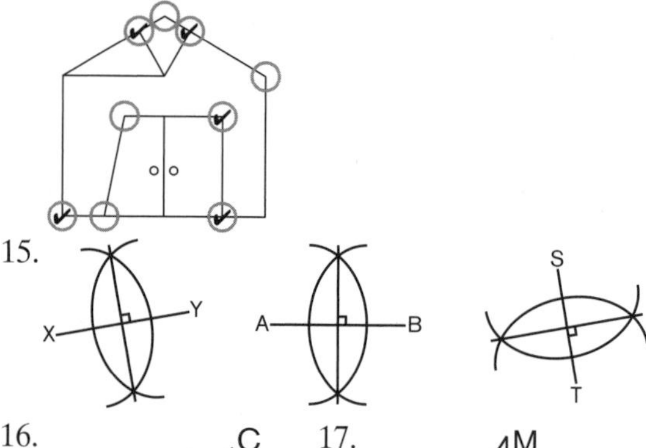

15.

16.

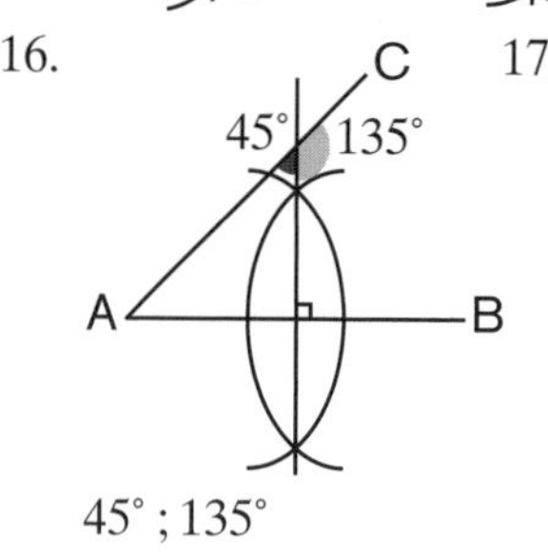

45° ; 135°

17.

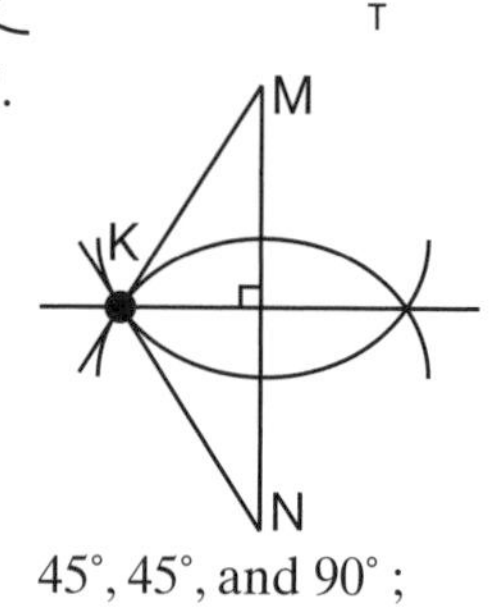

45°, 45°, and 90° ; isosceles

11 Angles and Lines in Shapes

1. F
2. F
3. F
4. T
5. F
6.

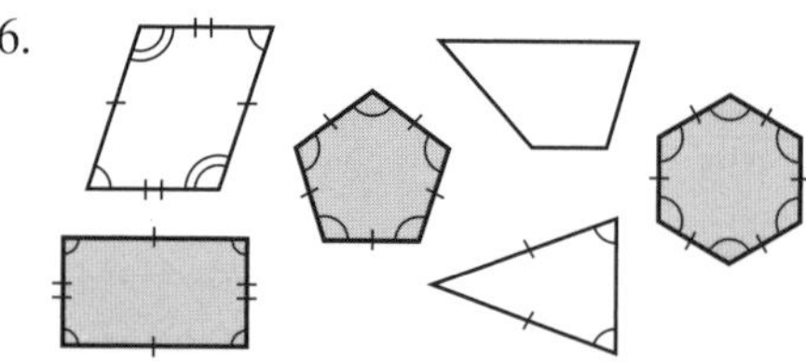

7.

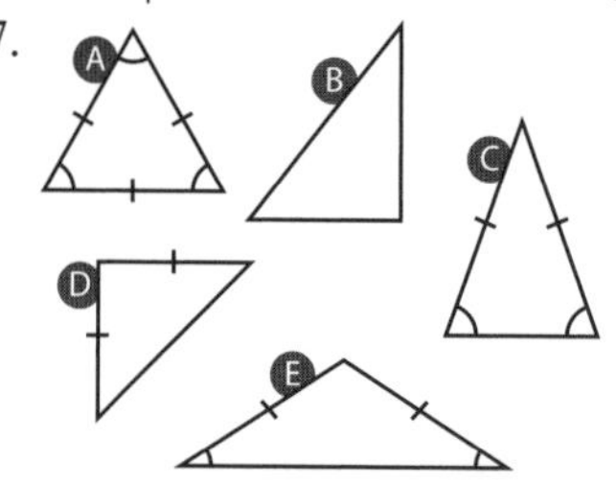

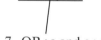

A: acute triangle, equilateral triangle
B: right triangle, scalene triangle
C: acute triangle, isosceles triangle
D: right triangle, isosceles triangle
E: obtuse triangle, isosceles triangle

8. R – red ; Y – yellow

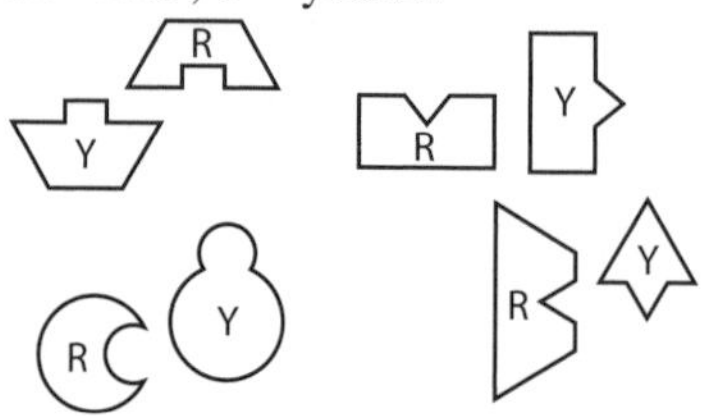

9. ✘ 10. ✘ 11. ✔
12. ✔ 13. ✘ 14. ✔

15. $a + 60° + 65° = 180°$
$a = 55°$

16. $m + 30° + 90° = 180°$
$m = 60°$

17. $3y = 180°$
$y = 60°$

18. $2r + 38° = 180°$
$2r = 142°$
$r = 71°$

19. $a + 57° + 90° = 180°$
$a = 33°$
$b = 67°$ (isos. △)
$c + 67° + 67° = 180°$
$c = 46°$

20. $3a = 180°$ (equil. △)
$a = 60°$
$42° + 100° + b = 180°$
$b = 38°$

21.  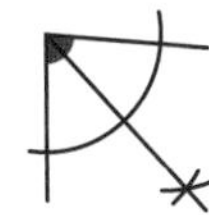 

22. (Suggested answer)
 ; acute triangle, isosceles triangle

23. 70° and 70°

12 Congruent and Similar Figures

1. Sides: PQ ; QR ; PR
Angles: ∠P ; ∠Q ; ∠R
≅
2. Sides: DE ; BC = EF ; AC = DF
Angles: ∠D ; ∠B = ∠E ; ∠C = ∠F
≅ △DEF
3. Sides: AB = XW ; BC = WY ; AC = XY
Angles: ∠A = ∠X ; ∠B = ∠W ; ∠C = ∠Y
≅ △XWY
4. side-angle-side
5. angle-angle-side
6. side-side-side
7. angle-angle-side
8. side-angle-side
9. angle-side-angle
10. 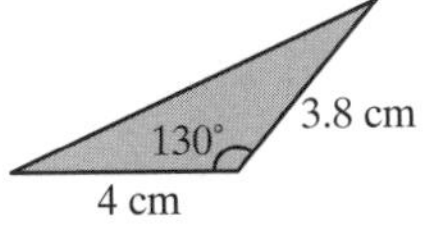

side-angle-side
11. 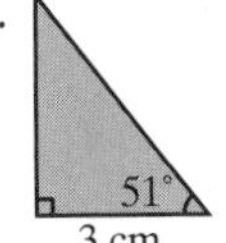

angle-side-angle
12. 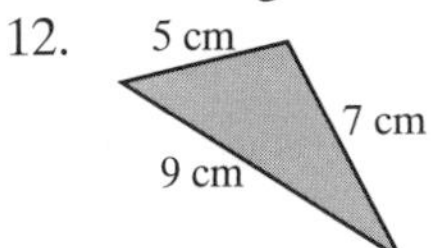

side-side-side
13. DE ; ∠E ; 68° ; EF ; 4 units ;
△DEF ; angle ; side
14. IJ = LM = 6 cm ; IK = LN = 8 cm ;
JK = MN = 11 cm ;
So, △IJK ≅ △LMN by side-side-side.
15. PQ = ST = 7 cm ; ∠P = ∠S = 90° ;
∠Q = ∠T = 44° ;
So, △PQR ≅ △STU by angle-side-angle.
16. Circle △ABC and △LMN.
∠B = ∠M = 65° ; ∠C = ∠N = 48° ;
BC = MN = 6 units ;
△ABC ≅ △LMN ; angle-side-angle
17. 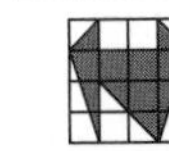 18. 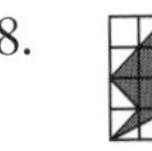 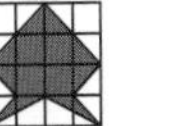 19. 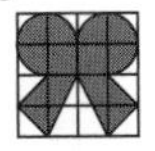

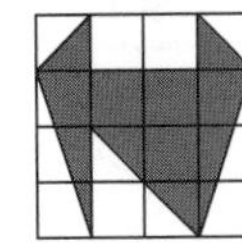 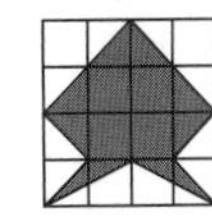 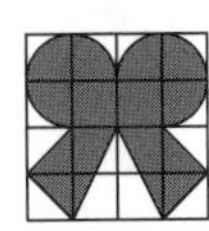

20. 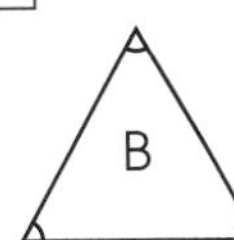

△A and △B are similar.

13 Solids

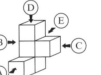

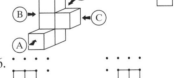

1. 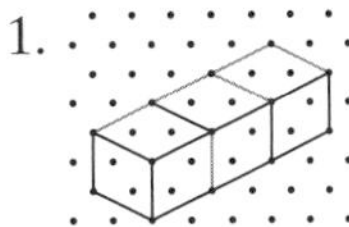
2. 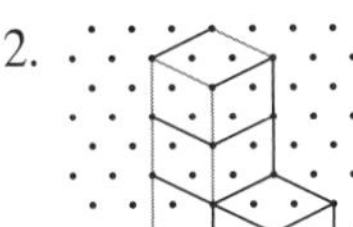
3. 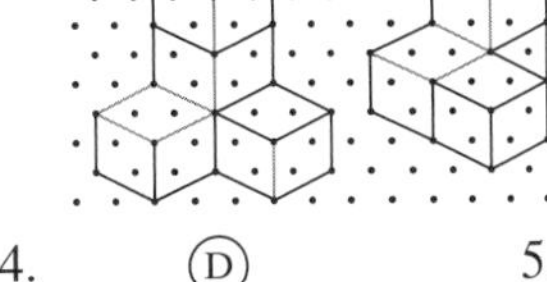
4. (D) (E) (B) (C) (A)
5. 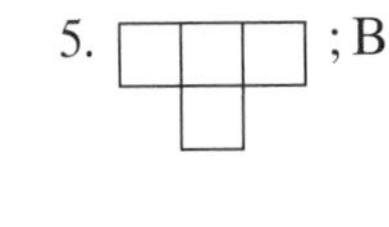 ; B
6. 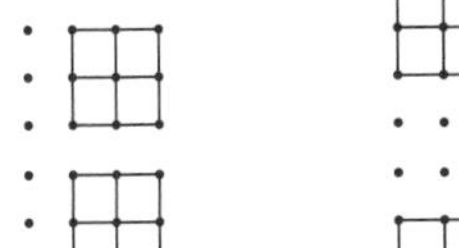 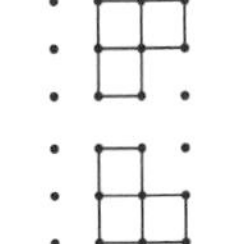 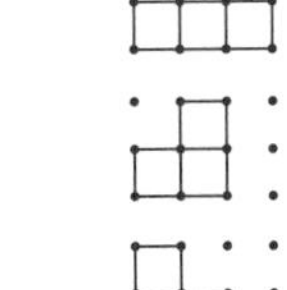
7. 8. 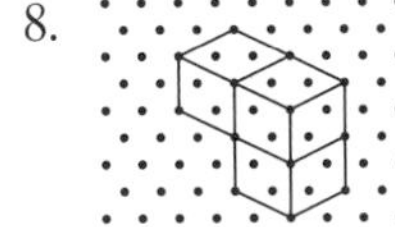
9. 10. 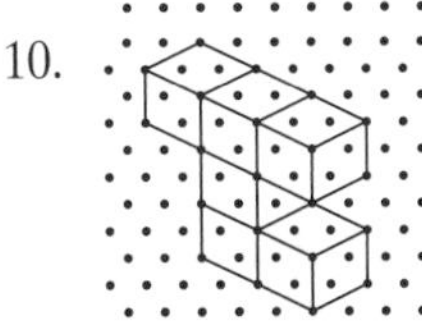
11. A: tetrahedron B: pentagonal prism
C: triangular prism D: hexagonal pyramid

12. 8 ; 18 ; 12 ; 2 ; 6 ; hexagonal prism

13. 9 ; 16 ; 9 ; 1 ; 8 ; octagonal pyramid

14.

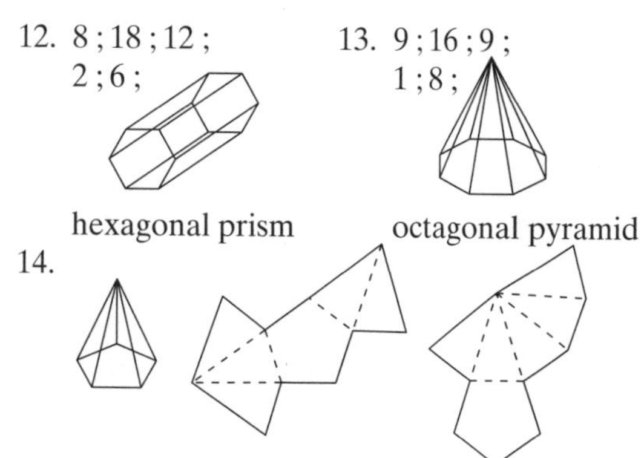

14 Area

1. b = 23 cm ; h = 15 cm
   23 ; 15 ; 345
2. b = 16 cm ; h = 13 cm
   16 x 13 = 208 (cm^2)
3. 6 x 6 ; 36 (km^2)
4. 12 x 8 ; 96 (m^2)
5. 3 x 10 ; 30 (m^2)

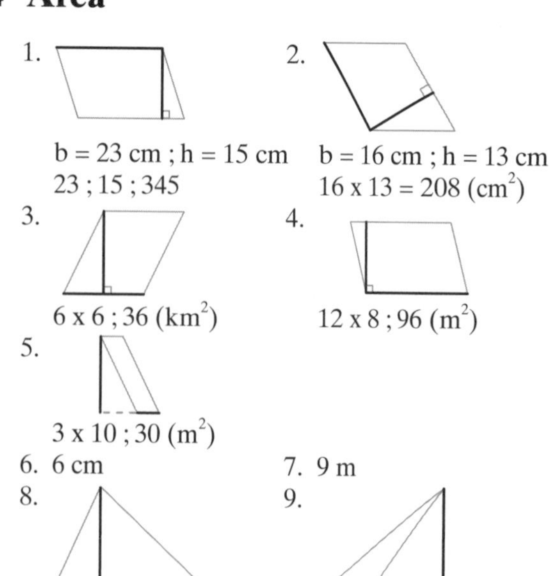

6. 6 cm
7. 9 m
8. b = 7 m ; h = 4 m
   7 ; 4 ; 14
9. b = 5 km ; h = 12 km
   (5 x 12) ÷ 2 = 30 (km^2)

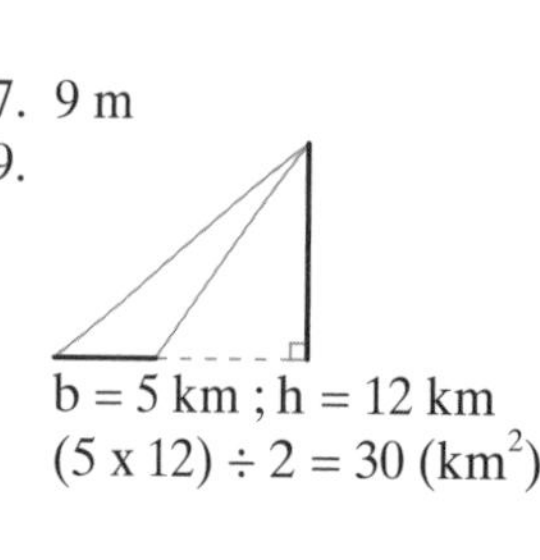

10. A: (7 x 9) ÷ 2 = 31.5 (cm^2)
    B: (12 x 10) ÷ 2 = 60 (m^2)
    C: (14 x 11) ÷ 2 = 77 (m^2)

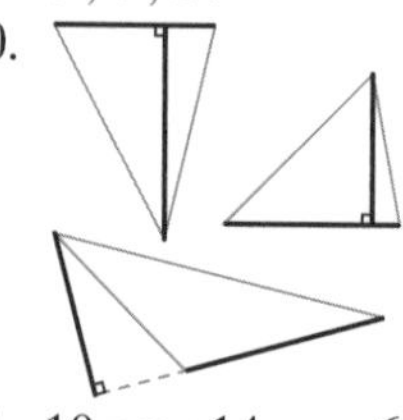

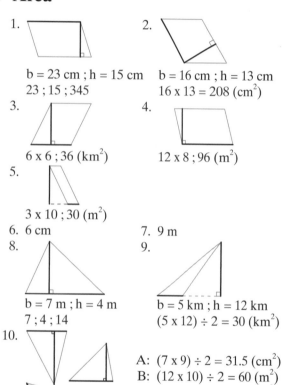

11. 10 cm ; 14 cm ; 6 m
12. 8 cm ; 3.9 m ; 28 m
13. Area of A: (8 x 7) ÷ 2 = 28 (cm^2)
    Area of B: (14 x 7) ÷ 2 = 49 (cm^2)
    Area of trapezoid: 28 + 49 = 77 (cm^2)
14. Area of triangle:
    (5.5 x 9) ÷ 2 = 24.75 (m^2)
    Area of parallelogram: 12.5 x 9 = 112.5 (m^2)
    Area of trapezoid: 24.75 + 112.5 = 137.25 (m^2)
15. A: 56 cm^2 B: 45 km^2 C: 88 m^2
    D: 40 m^2 E: 119 cm^2
    (Trace the dotted lines for questions 16 and 17)
16. Area of triangle: (12 x 3) ÷ 2 = 18 (cm^2)
    Area of rectangle: 12 x 5 = 60 (cm^2)
    Area of figure: 18 + 60 = 78 (cm^2)
17. Area of trapezoid:
    (6 x 7) ÷ 2 + (3 x 7) ÷ 2 = 31.5 (m^2)
    Area of parallelogram: 6 x 2 = 12 (m^2)
    Area of figure: 31.5 + 12 = 43.5 (m^2)
18. A: 93 m^2 B: 162 m^2
    C: 32.5 m^2 D: 52 m^2
19. Area of A: (4 x 4) ÷ 2 = 8 (cm^2)
    Area of B: (4 x 2) ÷ 2 = 4 (cm^2)
    Area of C: (2 x 4) ÷ 2 = 4 (cm^2)
    Area of D: (6 x 6) ÷ 2 = 18 (cm^2)
    Area of trapezoid:
    8 x 8 – (8 + 4 + 4 + 18) = 30 (cm^2)

Review 1

1. 3 ; 216
2. 3 ; 243
3. 3 ; 18
4. 5 ; 2000
5. 0 ; 2000
6. 11 ; 8800
7. Side length of small squares: $\sqrt{25}$ = 5 (m)
   Length of rectangle: 50 ÷ 5 = 10 (m)
   Side length of big square: 10 + 5 = 15 (m)
   Area of big square: 15 x 15 = 225 (m^2)
8. Side length of square: $\sqrt{36}$ = 6 (cm)
   Area of trapezoid:
   (10 x 6) ÷ 2 + (6 x 6) ÷ 2 = 48 (cm^2)
   Area of polygon: 36 + 48 = 84 (cm^2)
9. Side length of square: $\sqrt{256}$ = 16 (m)
   Area of parallelogram: 16 x 7 = 112 (m^2)
   Area of polygon: 256 + 112 = 368 (m^2)
10. Area of triangle: 13 x 6 ÷ 2 = 39 (m^2)
    Area of trapezoid:
    (7 x 6) ÷ 2 + (13 x 6) ÷ 2 = 60 (m^2)
    Area of polygon: 39 + 60 = 99 (m^2)

11a. $\sqrt{400}$ = 20 ; The side length is 20 cm.
  b. Side length of small square: 8 cm
     Area of small square: 8^2 = 64 (cm^2)
     The ratio is 4:25.

12. 2:3 ; 2
13. 4:3 ; 3
14. 8:1:4 ; 2
15. 2:5 ; 5
16. 7:15 ; 2
17. 3:4:1 ; 7

18a. G.C.F. of 27 and 21: 3
     There will be 3 teams.
  b. No. of boys: 27 ÷ 3 = 9
     No. of girls: 21 ÷ 3 = 7
     There will be 9 boys and 7 girls on each team.

19. 3: 3, 6, 9, 12, 15, 18, 21, 24, 27, 30
    4: 4, 8, 12, 16, 20, 24, 28, 32, 36, 40
    5: 5, 10, 15, 20, 25, 30, 35, 40, 45, 50
    6: 6, 12, 18, 24, 30, 36, 42, 48, 54, 60
    7: 7, 14, 21, 28, 35, 42, 49, 56, 63, 70
    8: 8, 16, 24, 32, 40, 48, 56, 64, 72, 80
    L.C.M.: 30 ; 56 ; 20 ; 12 ; 30
20. 30 gumballs

21. Check A ; 3 lemon pies/h ; 2.5 lemon pies/h
In 12 hours,
Katie makes: 3 x 12 = 36 (lemon pies)
Jane makes: 2.5 x 12 = 30 (lemon pies)
They make a total of 66 lemon pies.

22. Check B ; 1.5 patios/day ; 2 patios/day
To build 15 patios,
Jack needs: 15 ÷ 1.5 = 10 (days)
Tom needs: 15 ÷ 2 = 7.5 (days)
Jack needs 2.5 more days than Tom.

23. $1\frac{1}{2}$ 24. $\frac{1}{2}$ 25. 12

26. 13 27. $\frac{1}{6}$ 28. 6

29. $\frac{19}{24}$ 30. 1 31. 1

32. Marco gives: 40 x $\frac{2}{5}$ = 16 (marbles)
No. of marbles left: 40 – 16 = 24
Marco will have 24 marbles left.

33. 72.16 ;
17.6
x 4.1
176
7040
72.16

34. 3.6 ;
3.6
25 ⟌ 90.0
75
150
150

35. 2.5 ;
2.5
73 ⟌ 182.5
146
365
365

36. 20.3 ;
13.53
x 1.5
6765
13530
20.295

37. 3.5 ;
3.5
526 ⟌ 1841.0
1578
2630
2630

38. 68.85 ;
6.75
x 10.2
1350
67500
68.850

39. $\frac{9}{50}$; 0.18 40. 0.625 ; 62.5%

41. 0.4 ; 40% 42. 250% ; $2\frac{1}{2}$

43a. Sally spent 45% of her savings.
b. 1% ➔ $1 ; 100% ➔ $100
Her savings was $100.

44.
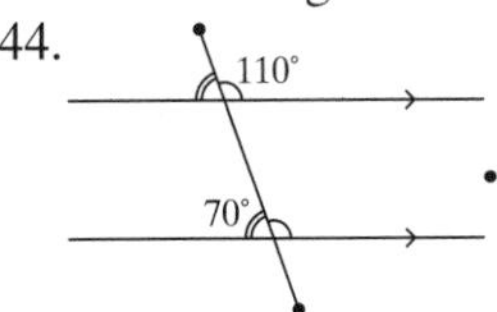

45.
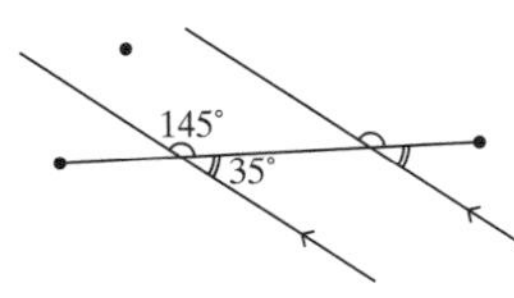

46.
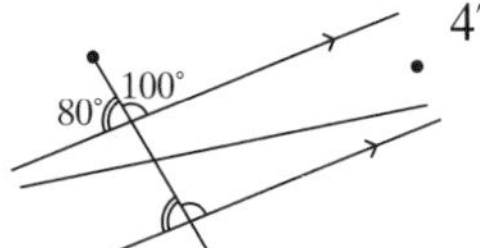

47.
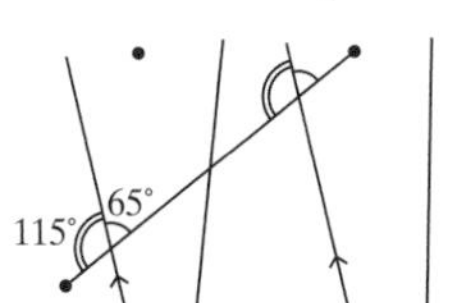

48.
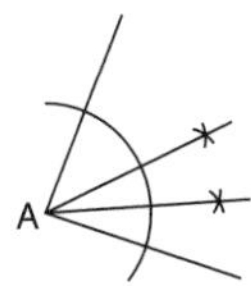

The measure of one of the smallest angles is one fourth of A.

49.
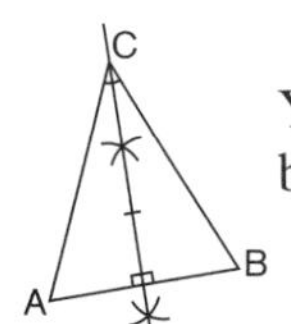

Yes. The triangles are congruent by angle-side-angle.

50. angle ; side 51. side-side-side

52. angle-angle-side

53. Circle △DEF. ;
∠E ; BC = EF = 10 cm ; ∠C = ∠F = 35°
△DEF ; angle-side-angle

54. 55.
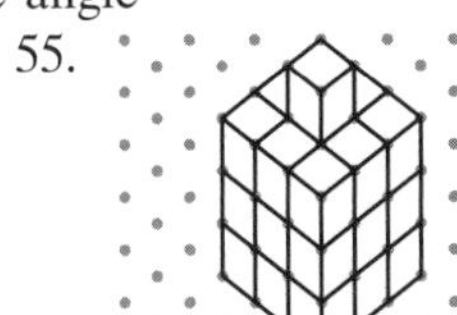

15 Surface Area

1. A: 8 x 3 ; 8 x 12 ; 3 x 12 ;
48 ; 192 ; 72 ;
312

B: 2 x 7 x 2 + 2 x 7 x 10 + 2 x 2 x 10
= 28 + 140 + 40
= 208 (m^2)

C: 2 x 20 x 4 + 2 x 20 x 50 +2 x 4 x 50
= 160 + 2000 + 400
= 2560 (cm^2)

D: 2 x 11 x 6 + 2 x 11 x 5 + 2 x 6 x 5
= 132 + 110 + 60
= 302 (cm^2)

2.
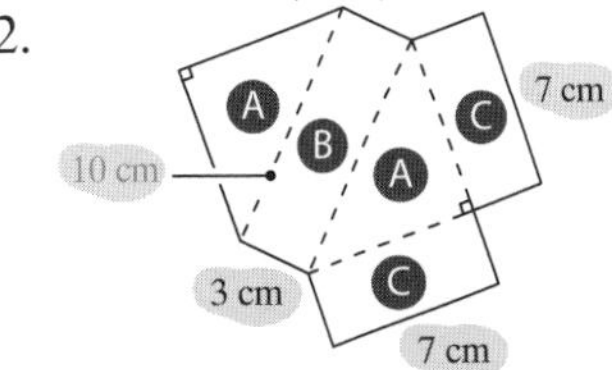

2Ⓐ = (7 x 7) ÷ 2 x 2 = 49 (cm^2) ;
1Ⓑ = 10 x 3 = 30 (cm^2) ;
2Ⓒ = (7 x 3) x 2 = 42 (cm^2) ;
49 + 30 + 42 = 121 (cm^2)

3.
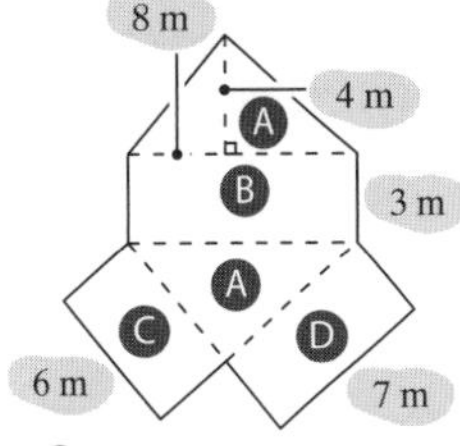

2Ⓐ = (8 x 4) ÷ 2 x 2 = 32 (m^2)
1Ⓑ = 8 x 3 = 24 (m^2)
1Ⓒ = 6 x 3 = 18 (m^2)
1Ⓓ = 7 x 3 = 21 (m^2)
32 + 24 + 18 + 21 = 95 (m^2)

4.

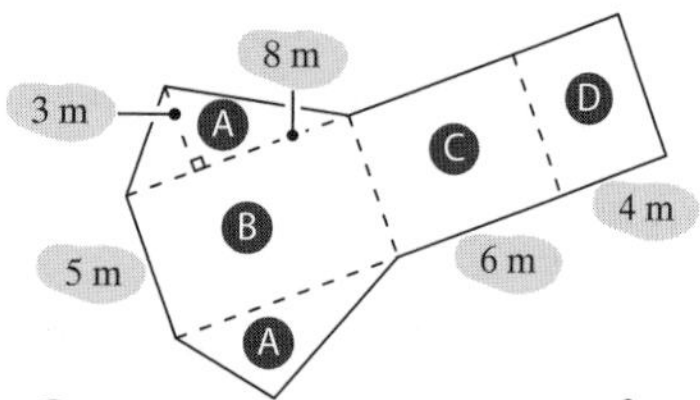

2Ⓐ = (8 x 3) ÷ 2 x 2 = 24 (m^2)
1Ⓑ = 8 x 5 = 40 (m^2)
1Ⓒ = 6 x 5 = 30 (m^2)
1Ⓓ = 4 x 5 = 20 (m^2)
24 + 40 + 30 + 20 = 114 (m^2)

5. 9 x 5 + 6 x 2 + 9 x 2 + 10 x 2
= 45 + 12 + 18 + 20
= 95 (cm^2)

6. 12 x 3 + 4 x 5 + 12 x 5 + 10 x 5
= 36 + 20 + 60 + 50
= 166 (m^2)

7a. 1625 cm^2 ; A b. 518.4 cm^2 ; C

8.

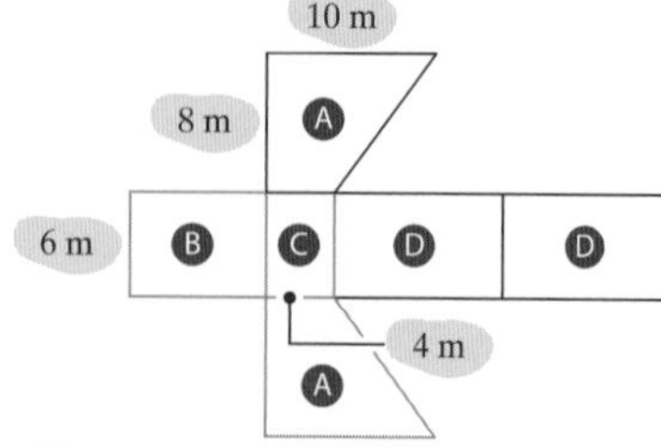

2Ⓐ = (4 x 8 ÷ 2 + 10 x 8 ÷ 2) x 2 = 112 (m^2)
1Ⓑ = 8 x 6 = 48 (m^2)
1Ⓒ = 6 x 4 = 24 (m^2)
2Ⓓ = (10 x 6) x 2 = 120 (m^2)
Total: 112 + 48 + 24 + 120 = 304 (m^2)

9.

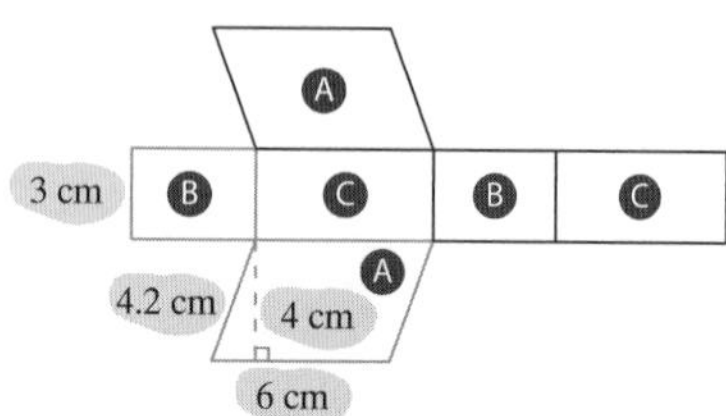

2Ⓐ = (6 x 4) x 2 = 48 (cm^2)
2Ⓑ = (4.2 x 3) x 2 = 25.2 (cm^2)
2Ⓒ = (6 x 3) x 2 = 36 (cm^2)
Total: 48 + 25.2 + 36 = 109.2 (cm^2)

10. A: 324 cm^2 B: 344 cm^2 ; A

16 Volume

1. 20 ; 6 ; 120
2. 63 x 12 ; 756 (cm^3)
3. 150 x 6 ; 900 (cm^3)
4. 1050 x 12 ; 12 600 (cm^3)
5. A: 60 x 11 ; 660 (cm^3)
B: 500 x 18 ; 9000 (cm^3)
C: 3.15 x 4.2 ; 13.23 (m^3)
D: 2.16 x 0.5 ; 1.08 (m^3)
6. 3.67 m 7. 3.6 cm 8. 2.37 m
9. A: 27 B: 0.2
C: 12.5 D: 0.5
10. A: 108 cubes B: 360 cubes
C: 200 cubes D: 16 896 cubes
11. Area of base: (3 x 5) ÷ 2 + (7 x 5) ÷ 2 = 25 (m^2)
Volume: 25 x 2 = 50 (m^3)
12. Area of base: 8 x 15 = 120 (cm^2)
Volume: 120 x 6 = 720 (cm^3)
13. Area of base:
(0.5 x 0.9) ÷ 2 + (1.3 x 0.9) ÷ 2 = 0.81 (m^2)
Volume: 0.81 x 0.5 = 0.405 (m^3)
14. Area of base: (10 x 8.7) ÷ 2 x 6 = 261 (cm^2)
Volume: 261 x 10 = 2610 (cm^3)
15. Area of base:
(2 x 4) ÷ 2 + (5 x 4) ÷ 2 + 4 x 2 = 22 (cm^2)
Volume: 22 x 3 = 66 (cm^3)
16. Area of base:
(12 x 3) ÷ 2 + (12 x 8) ÷ 2 + (6 x 8) ÷ 2 = 90 (cm^2)
Volume: 90 x 5 = 450 (cm^3)

17A: 6000 B: 6510 mL C: 5250 mL
18A: 6 B: 7 bottles C: 6 bottles

19. Volume of 40 pebbles: 3.6 x 40 = 144 (cm^3)
Vase A holds: 6000 – 144 = 5856 (mL)
Vase A can now hold 5856 mL of water.
20. Volume of gift box:
6000 + 6510 + 5250 = 17 760 (cm^3)
Thickness of gift box:
17 760 ÷ (40 x 40 ÷ 2) = 22.2 (cm)
The thickness of the gift box is 22.2 cm.

17 Coordinates

1.

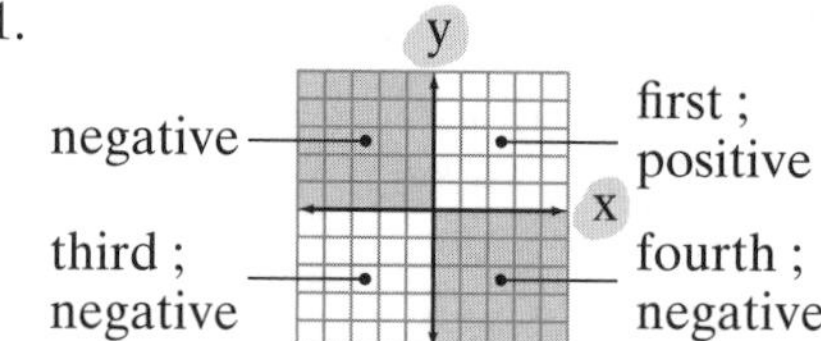

2.

(-8,7) (-2,13) (-20,28) $(-0.8,\frac{1}{3})$	(6,4) (19,2) (14,5) (16,4)
(-7,-9) (-15,-1) (-6,-3.5) (-2.7,-4)	(8,-2) (5,-3) (10,-11) $(\frac{1}{2},-1)$

3.

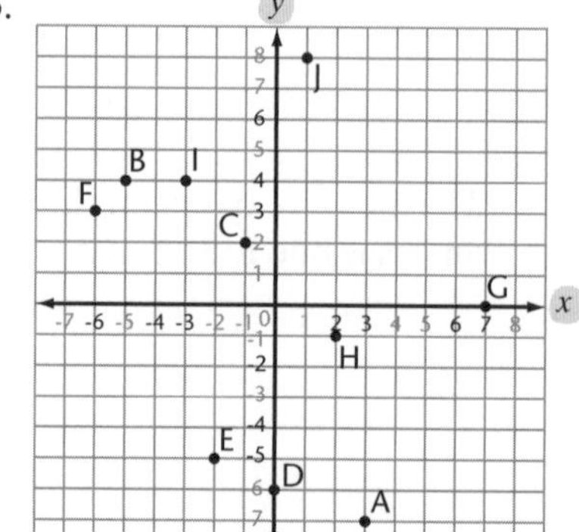

4. M(-3,4) ; N(0,4) ; O(0,-2) ; P(4,-4) ; Q(-1,-6) ; R(-5,-4) ; S(3,3) ; T(6,2) ; U(-7,1) ; V(6,-2)
5. (-3,-2) 6. parallelogram
7. (0,-2) ; (0,-4) ; (3,-6)

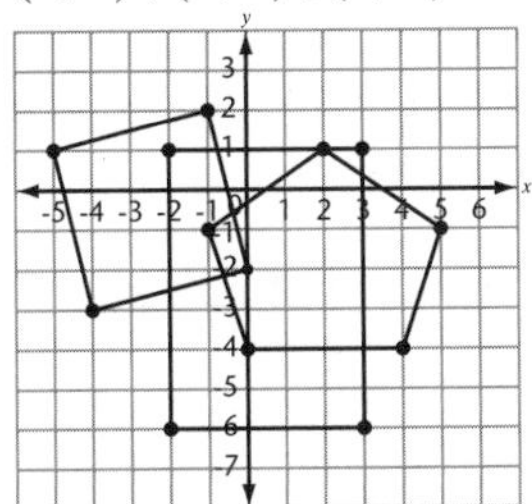

8.

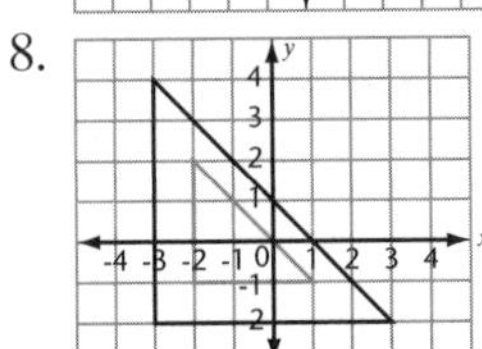

enlarge ; (-3,4), (3,-2), (-3,-2)

9.

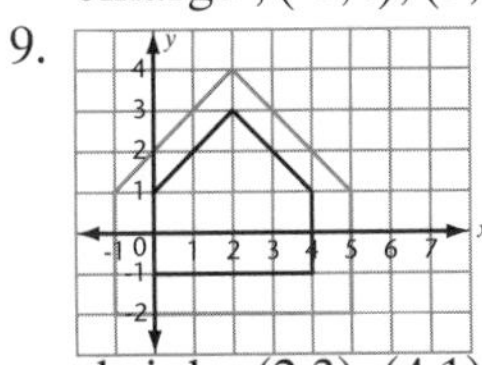

shrink ; (2,3), (4,1), (4,-1), (0,-1), (0,1)

10.

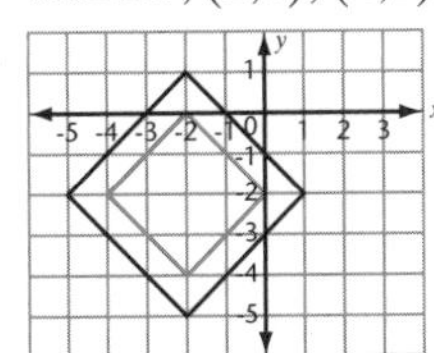

enlarge ; (-2,1), (1,-2), (-2,-5), (-5,-2)

11-12.

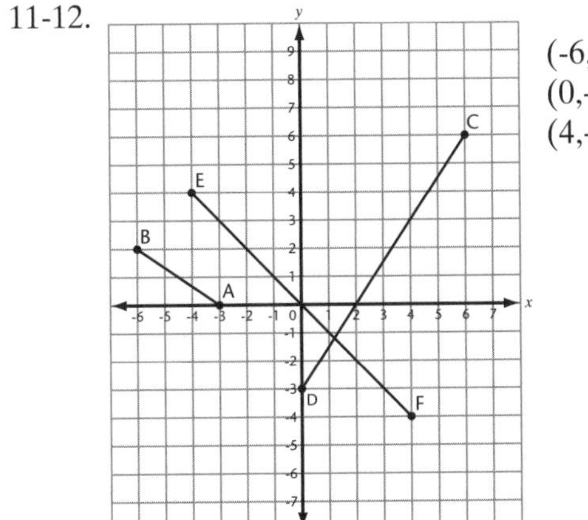

(-6,2) ; (0,-3) ; (4,-4)

13. No 14. Yes
15. (Suggested answer) (0,-3), (2,0), (4,3)
16. The point on the line EF are (-4,4), (-3,3), (-2,2). The x and y values of each coordinate is the opposite of each other.

18 Transformations

1a. translation b. rotation c. reflection
d. rotation e. translation
2. Translation Image: D, E, H
Reflection Image: A, C
Rotation Image: B, F, G

3.

4.

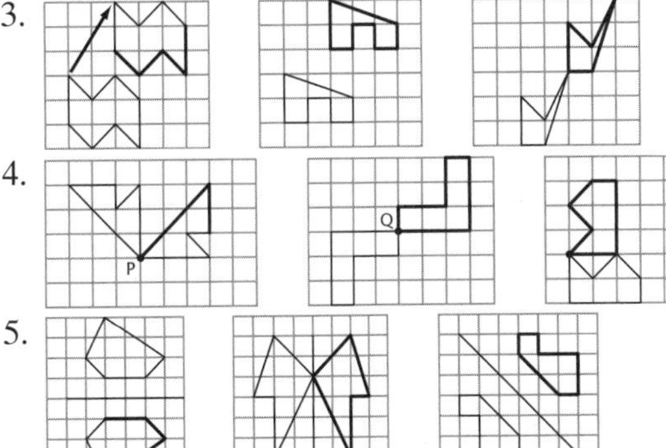

5.

6.

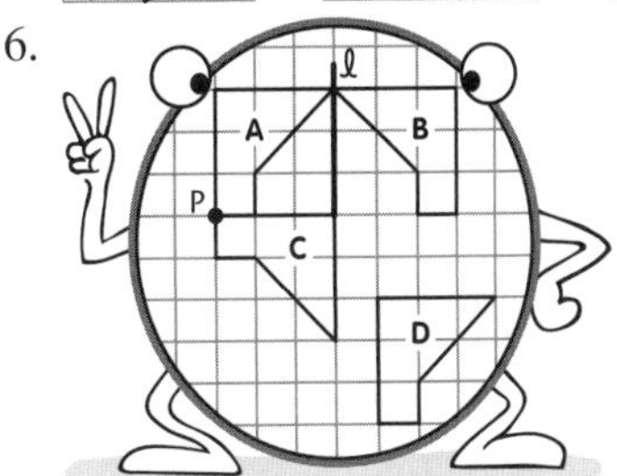

Flip figure A in line ℓ to get image B. ;
Rotate figure A 90° at point P to get image C. ;
Translate figure A 4 units right and 5 units down to get image D.

7.

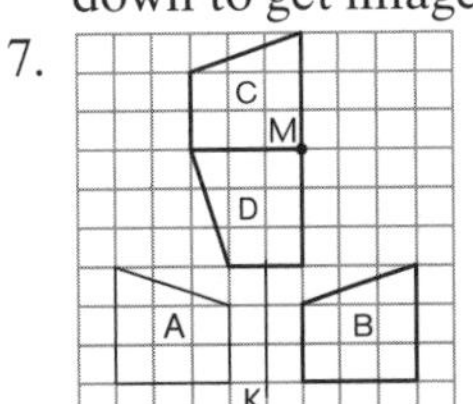

8.

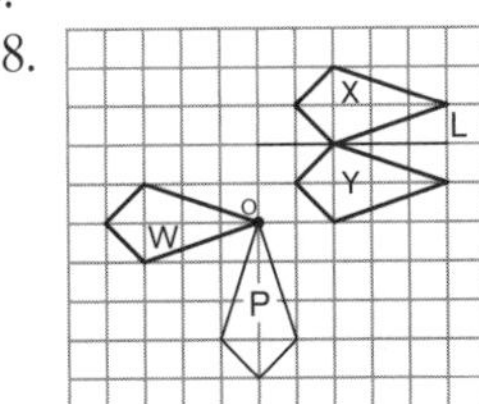

9. Translate A 1 unit right and 4 units up. Then reflect it in line ℓ. ;
Reflect A in line ℓ. Then translate it 1 unit left and 4 units up.
10. Rotate M $\frac{1}{4}$ clockwise at point K. Then translate it 1 unit left and 5 units up. ;
Translate M 5 units right and 1 unit down. Then rotate it $\frac{1}{4}$ clockwise at point K.

11. ✔ 12. ✘ 13. ✘

14. 15.

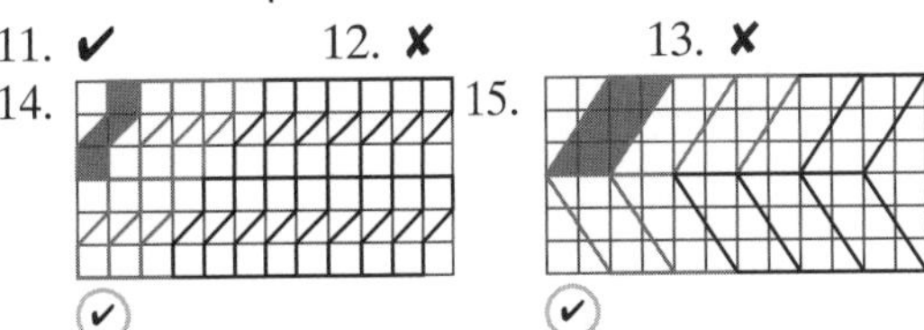

16. 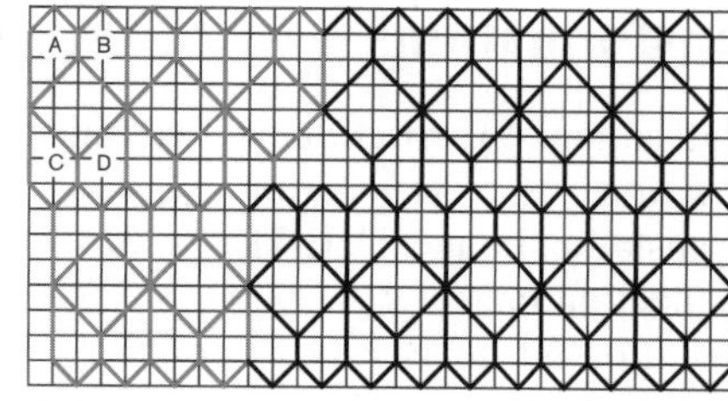

right ;
A & B is reflected in a horizontal line along the bottom to make C & D. ;
Figure A, B, C, D, and the square forms a decagon. The decagon is translated 4 units right to make its way across and translated 1 unit right and 7 units down to make its way down.

19 Patterning

1. Circle the first three terms.
   a. 3 b. 3 c. ;
2. Circle the first four terms.
   a. 4 b. 2 c. ;
3. 4AKM ; 4 ; 4, 8, 12, 16, 20... ; 4 ; M ; K ; M ; 4
4. ; 2 ; 2 ; 2, 4, 6, 8, 10... ; 2 ;

5. ;
   5 ; 5 ; 5, 10, 15, 20, 25... ; 5 ;
   ; ;
6. Descriptions: 1 ; 1 ; 3 ; 8 ; 5 ; 8 ;
   Multiples of 8: 16 ; 24 ; 32 ; 40 ; 48 ;
   8 ; 5 ; 8 ; 5
7. Number of Cookies Made
   (Number of Cookies vs. Time (min))
8. 59 ; 75 ; 115
9. 9 min ; 11 min

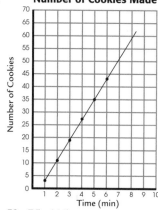

10a. Output: 16 ; 19
Descriptions: increases ; 3 ; 3 ; 1 ; 3
Pattern rule: 3 ; 1
b. 46 ; 58 ; 73 ; 106

11a. Output: 19 ; 23
Descriptions:
- Each output number increases by 4 each time.
- Compare the output number with multiples of 4. Each output number is 1 less than 4 times the input number.

Pattern rule:
Output number = 4 x Input number – 1
b. 79 bones

20 Algebraic Expressions (1)

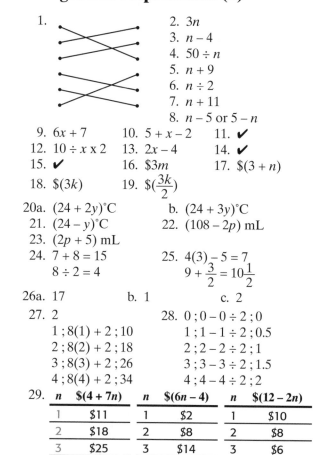

1. 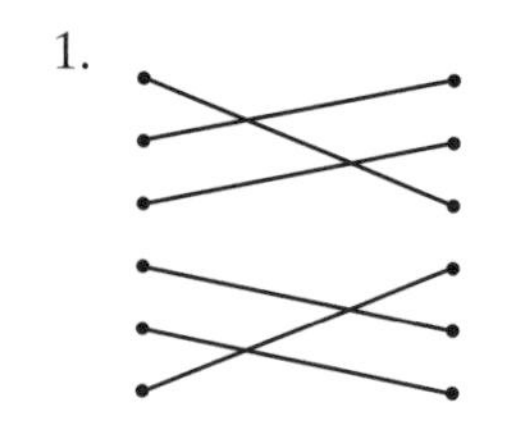
2. $3n$
3. $n - 4$
4. $50 \div n$
5. $n + 9$
6. $n \div 2$
7. $n + 11$
8. $n - 5$ or $5 - n$
9. $6x + 7$
10. $5 + x - 2$
11. ✔
12. $10 \div x \times 2$
13. $2x - 4$
14. ✔
15. ✔
16. $\$3m$
17. $\$(3 + n)$
18. $\$(3k)$
19. $\$(\frac{3k}{2})$

20a. $(24 + 2y)$°C b. $(24 + 3y)$°C
21. $(24 - y)$°C
22. $(108 - 2p)$ mL
23. $(2p + 5)$ mL
24. $7 + 8 = 15$
    $8 \div 2 = 4$
25. $4(3) - 5 = 7$
    $9 + \frac{3}{2} = 10\frac{1}{2}$

26a. 17 b. 1 c. 2
27. 2
    1 ; 8(1) + 2 ; 10
    2 ; 8(2) + 2 ; 18
    3 ; 8(3) + 2 ; 26
    4 ; 8(4) + 2 ; 34
28. 0 ; 0 – 0 ÷ 2 ; 0
    1 ; 1 – 1 ÷ 2 ; 0.5
    2 ; 2 – 2 ÷ 2 ; 1
    3 ; 3 – 3 ÷ 2 ; 1.5
    4 ; 4 – 4 ÷ 2 ; 2
29.

n	$(4 + 7n)	n	$(6n – 4)	n	$(12 – 2n)
1	$11	1	$2	1	$10
2	$18	2	$8	2	$8
3	$25	3	$14	3	$6
4	$32	4	$20	4	$4

30. Jenny's savings increases by $7 each week. ;
    Erica's savings increases by $6 each week. ;
    Stella's savings decreases by $2 each week.
31. $(46 + 53) = $99

21 Algebraic Expressions (2)

1. By car: 50 ; 100 ; 150 ; 200
   By airplane: 120 ; 240 ; 360 ; 480

2.

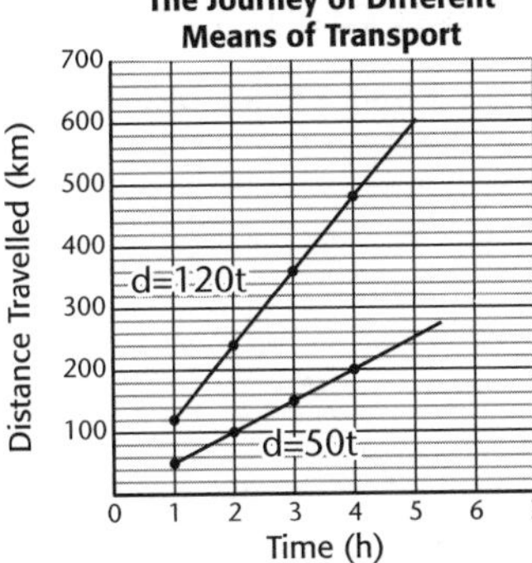

3. 300 km 4. $5\frac{1}{2}$ hours

5. The airplane travels at a constant speed of 120 km per hour.

6. Karen's Earnings: 14 ; 18 ; 22 ; 26 ; 30 Mike's Earnings: 18 ; 20 ; 22 ; 24 ; 26

7.

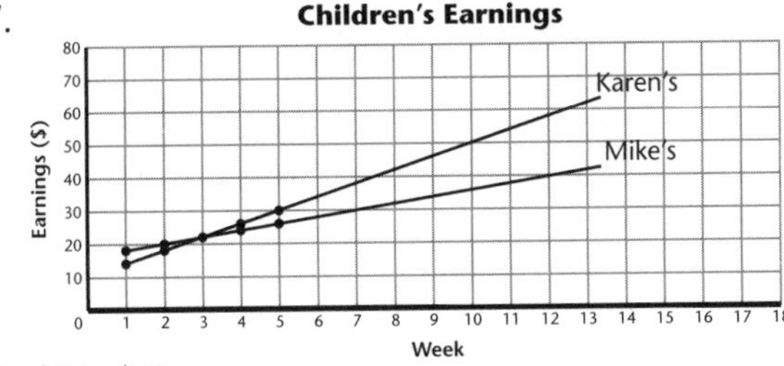

8. \$54 ; \$38

9. Yes. The intersection point means the children have the same earning after 3 weeks.

10. I prefer Karen's earning pattern. Because her earning is always greater than Mike's after 3 weeks.

11. 4 ; $(4(s + 200))$ m ;

s	A $(4s)$	B $(4(s + 200))$
400	1600	2400
500	2000	2800
600	2400	3200
700	2800	3600

12a.

y	A $(480 + 2400y)$	B $(480 + 3200y)$
3	7680	10 080
4	10 080	13 280
5	12 480	16 480
6	14 880	19 680

b.

y	A $(480 + 2000y)$	B $(480 + 2800y)$
3	6480	8880
4	8480	11 680
5	10 480	14 480
6	12 480	17 280

13. $20m$; $\$(6 + 90\% \times 20m)$; $\$(16 + 80\% \times 20m)$

14.

Number of Visits	General $\$(20m)$	Silver $\$(6 + 90\% \times 20m)$	Gold $\$(16 + 80\% \times 20m)$
1	\$20	\$24	\$32
2	\$40	\$42	\$48
3	\$60	\$60	\$64
4	\$80	\$78	\$80

15.

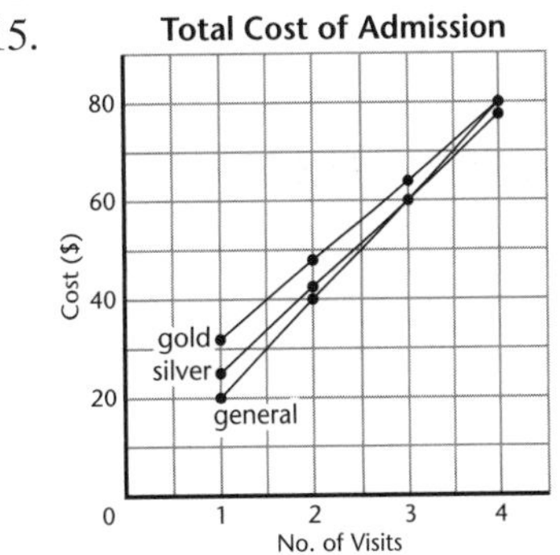

16. Jane should choose the silver membership because it has the lowest total cost.

22 Equations

1. 2. 3.

4. $\div$; y ; 3 5. $-$; 21 ; 20 6. y ; $+$; 34

7. $3y = 18$ 8. $\frac{1}{6}y = 9$ 9. 4

10. 36 11. 7 12. 40

13. 2 14. 35

15-18. (Individual checking)

15. 7 ; 7 ; 14

16. $t \div 2 \times 2 = 15 \times 2$; $t = 30$

17. 4 ; 4 ; 14 ; 14 ; 7

18. $3m + 2 - 2 = 8 - 2$; $3m = 6$; $3m \div 3 = 6 \div 3$; $m = 2$

19. Check B ; $7x = 546$; $\frac{7x}{7} = \frac{546}{7}$; $x = 78$; 78

20. Check C ; $4x + 20 = 68$; $4x + 20 - 20 = 68 - 20$; $\frac{4x}{4} = \frac{48}{4}$; $x = 12$; 12

21. Check A ; $2x + 17 = 89$; $2x + 17 - 17 = 89 - 17$; $\frac{2x}{2} = \frac{72}{2}$; $x = 36$; 36

22. Check A ; $6(y - 1) = 54$; $\frac{6(y-1)}{6} = \frac{54}{6}$; $y - 1 + 1 = 9 + 1$; $y = 10$; \$10

23-24. (Individual answers)

25. x ; x ; 3 ; 25; $2x + 3 - 3 = 25 - 3$; $\frac{2x}{2} = \frac{22}{2}$; $x = 11$; \$11

26. Let y be the number of treats in a small tub.

$$\frac{y+112}{2} = 92$$

$$\frac{y+112}{2} \times 2 = 92 \times 2$$

$$y + 112 - 112 = 184 - 112$$

$$y = 72$$

There are 72 treats in a small tub.

23 Data Management (1)

1. discrete 2. continuous 3. continuous
4. continuous 5. discrete
6. primary data 7. secondary data
8. primary data
9. biased ; unbiased ; biased
10. unbiased ; biased ; biased
11. census 12. sampling 13. sampling
14. sampling 15. census 16. census
17.

Temperature (°C)	Tally	Frequency
11 – 15	||	2
16 – 20	卌	5
21 – 25	卌 ||	7
26 – 30	卌 ||||	9
31 – 35	卌 ||	7

18.

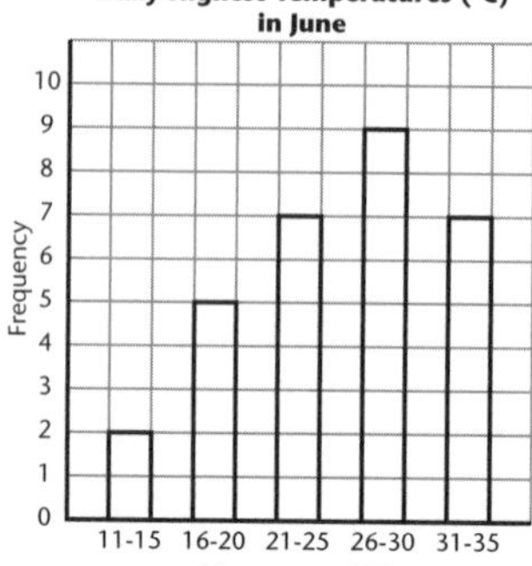

19. It is a set of primary data which is discrete.
20. The range is 26°C – 30°C.
21. No. Because he will get the indoor temperature.

22a. 33 b. 6 c. 18 – 65

23.

Stem	Leaf
13	0 5 6 9 9
14	2 2 7 8 9
15	0 2 3 4 5 5 7 7 7 8 8 8 9 9
16	0 1 1 2 2 4 4 4 4 7
17	0 2

24. 130 – 172 cm 25. 11 children
26. It is a set of secondary data. Because it is collected by someone else other than Daven.

24 Data Management (2)

1.

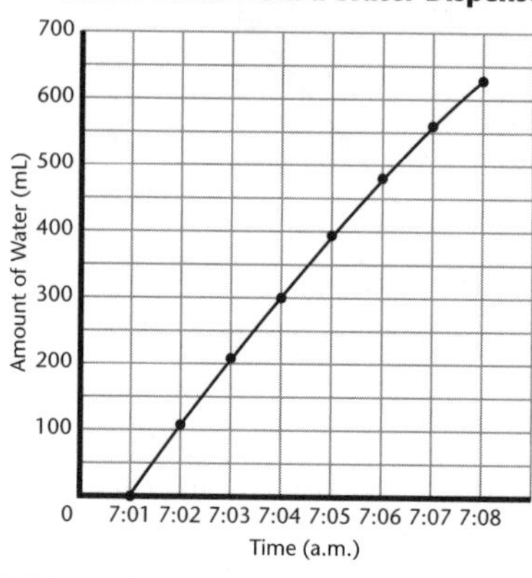

2. 7:01 – 7:02
3. No. The amount of water leaks starts at 105 mL in the first minute and decreases by 5 mL every minute.
4. The amount of water leaks decreases. The amount of water collected at 7:09 a.m. is 700 mL.
5. 132° ;

$\frac{5}{30} \times 360° = 60°$;

$\frac{1}{30} \times 360° = 12°$;

$\frac{2}{30} \times 360° = 24°$;

$\frac{9}{30} \times 360° = 108°$;

$\frac{2}{30} \times 360° = 24°$;

Ways to Come to School

others
on foot
by bus
by car
by bike
by subway

6. 50%
7. (Individual answer)
   (Individual examples for questions 8 to 10)
8. line graph 9. bar graph 10. circle graph
11. Check A
12. He should present graph A. Because it makes the plant seem to have a more dramatic growth.
13. 670 ; 820 ; 970 14. 31 seconds
15. Line graph is the most appropriate to show the data because it is a set of continuous data measured over a period of time.

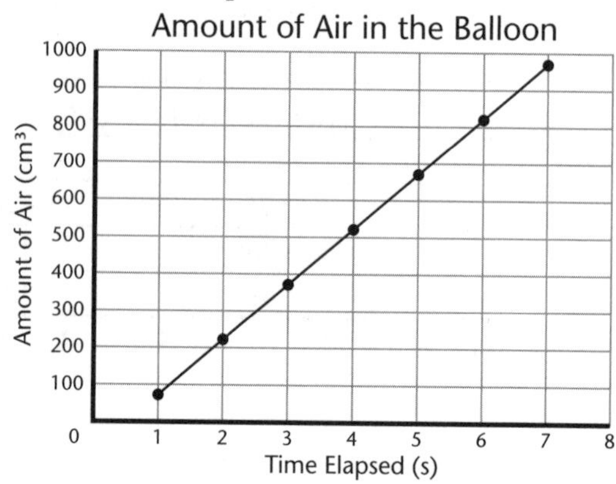

16. (Suggested answer)
The amount of air in the balloon increases as time elapses. Therefore, the line goes upward.

25 Mean, Median, Mode

1. (Suggested answers)
mean: the average of a set of data; add all the values and divide by the number of values
median: the middle value; put the value in order and find the middle value
mode: the value that appears the most
2. mean ; 69
3. mode ; 64 ; median ; 68
4. She should use the median because it is the highest amount.
5. He should use the mode because the value is 20.
6. 11 computers ; 11 computers ; 6 computer and 11 computers
7. 6 ; 10 ; 19
8. 122 ; 123 ; 124
9. 119 ; 116 ; 137
10. Mrs. Jerkin's class
11. the mode
12.

Stem	Leaf
14	0 3 5 6 7
15	0 2 2 4 4 4 8 9
16	2 2 3 3 9
17	0 5

13. 155.9 cm ; 154 cm ; 154 cm
14. 17 ; 18 marbles ; 18 marbles
15. 17 marbles ; 17.5 marbles ; 20 marbles
16. 18 x 8 = 144 ; 144
17. 15.1 x 5 = 75.5 ; 75.5
18. 75.5 – 14.7 x 4 = 16.7 ; 16.7

26 Experimental Probability

1. $\frac{7}{10}$; $\frac{3}{10}$
2. $\frac{22}{50}$; $\frac{28}{50}$
3. 20 ; $\frac{5}{20}$; $\frac{9}{20}$; $\frac{6}{20}$
4. 15 ; $\frac{6}{30}$; $\frac{9}{30}$; $\frac{15}{30}$

5a. $\frac{135}{280}$, 0.48, 48%
b. $\frac{64}{280}$, 0.23, 23%
c. $\frac{199}{280}$, 0.71, 71%

6a. $\frac{15}{85}$, 0.18, 18%
b. $\frac{46}{85}$, 0.54, 54%
c. $\frac{24}{85}$, 0.28, 28%
d. $\frac{40}{85}$, 0.47, 47%

7a. $\frac{5}{25}$; $\frac{6}{25}$
b. 3 ; 5 ; 4 ; 2 ; 5 ; 6
c. $\frac{13}{25}$

8. 87% ; 79% ; 67% ; 82% ; 94%
9. Geography
10. Science
11. Maple: 0.42 ; 0.47 ; 0.12
St. Jacob: 0.44 ; 0.29 ; 0.26
12. St. Jacob
13. Possible relative frequency of winning:
$\frac{19}{48} = 0.4$, $\frac{20}{48} = 0.42$, $\frac{21}{48} = 0.44$, $\frac{22}{48} = 0.46$, $\frac{23}{48} = 0.48$
Maple trees has to win at least 4 more games.
14.

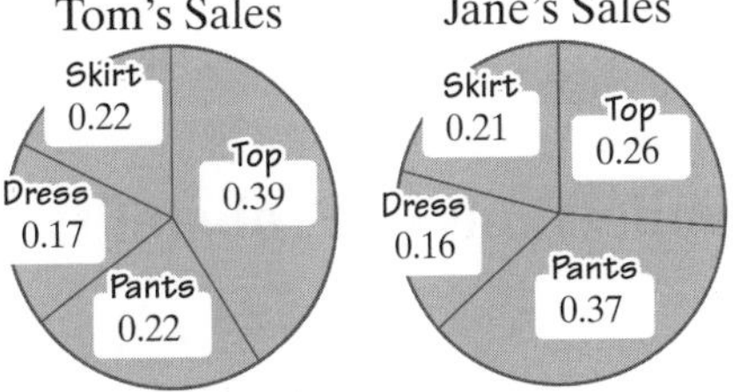

15. 0.29 ; 0.25 ; 0.18 ; 0.29
16. Relative Frequency:
0.46 ; 0.23
Size of Angle:
111.6° ; 165.6° ; 82.8°

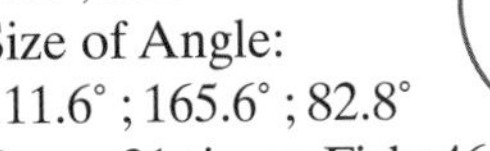

17. Bone: 31 times, Fish: 46 times, Carrot: 23 times

27 Theoretical Probability

1a. 12
b. $\frac{3}{12}$
c. $\frac{2}{12}$
d. $\frac{9}{12}$

2a. 20
b. $\frac{2}{20}$
c. $\frac{15}{20}$
d. $\frac{18}{20}$
e. $\frac{17}{20}$

3a. $\frac{9}{30}$
b. $\frac{8}{30}$
c. $\frac{11}{30}$
d. $\frac{2}{30}$
e. $\frac{11}{30}$
f. $\frac{28}{30}$
g. $\frac{20}{30}$

4a. $\frac{1}{3}$
b. $\frac{2}{3}$
c. $\frac{1}{6}$
d. $\frac{3}{6}$
e. $\frac{3}{6}$

5a. $\frac{1}{26}$
b. 0
c. $\frac{2}{26}$
d. $\frac{1}{26}$

6. Probability: 0.36
Prediction: 10 ; 0.54 x 100 = 54 ; 0.36 x 100 = 36
7a. Box A
b. 6 red balls
8. (Individual answers for tally and relative frequency)
Theoretical Probability: $\frac{1}{8}$; $\frac{3}{8}$; $\frac{1}{4}$; $\frac{1}{4}$
9. (Individual answer)
10. dots: 800 x $\frac{1}{8}$ = 100 (times)
wavy lines: 800 x $\frac{3}{8}$ = 300 (times)
stripes: 800 x $\frac{1}{4}$ = 200 (times)
checkers: 800 x $\frac{1}{4}$ = 200 (times)

It will land on dots 100 times, wavy lines 300 times, stripes 200 times, and checkers 200 times.

11. Let y be the no. of times she needs to swing.
$\frac{3}{8}y = 150$; $y = 400$
She will have to swing the paperclip about 400 times.

28 Applications of Probability

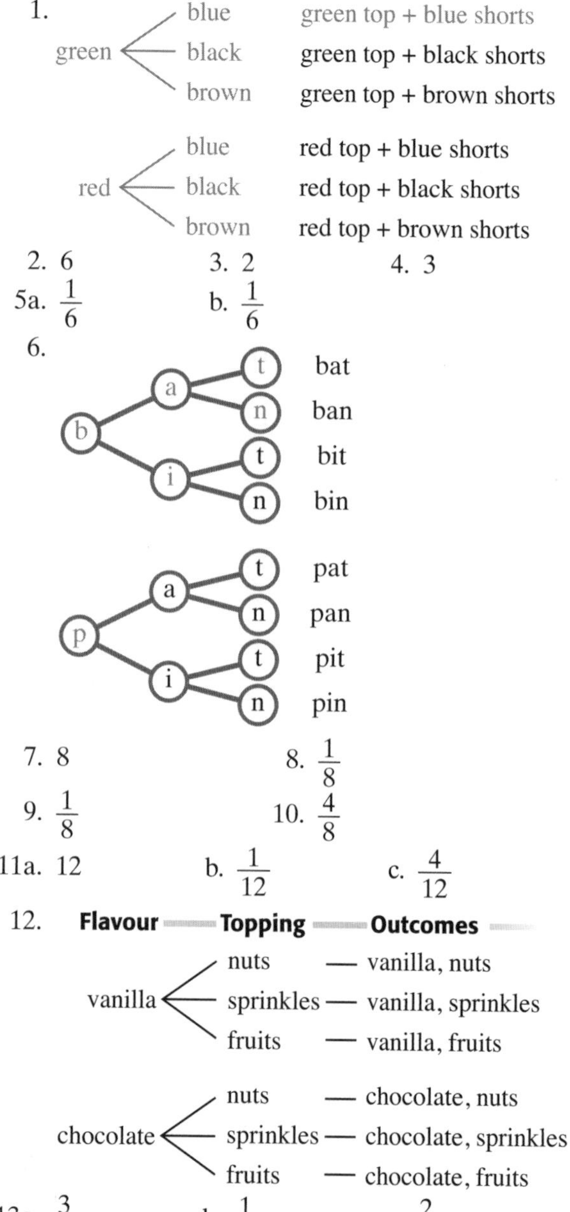

2. 6 3. 2 4. 3

5a. $\frac{1}{6}$ b. $\frac{1}{6}$

7. 8 8. $\frac{1}{8}$

9. $\frac{1}{8}$ 10. $\frac{4}{8}$

11a. 12 b. $\frac{1}{12}$ c. $\frac{4}{12}$

13a. $\frac{3}{6}$ b. $\frac{1}{6}$ c. $\frac{2}{6}$

14. **Flavour** **Topping**

vanilla — nuts
vanilla — sprinkles
chocolate — nuts
chocolate — sprinkles

The probability that each kind of ice cream is chosen is $\frac{1}{4}$. The probability of choosing vanilla ice cream cone with sprinkles will be greater.

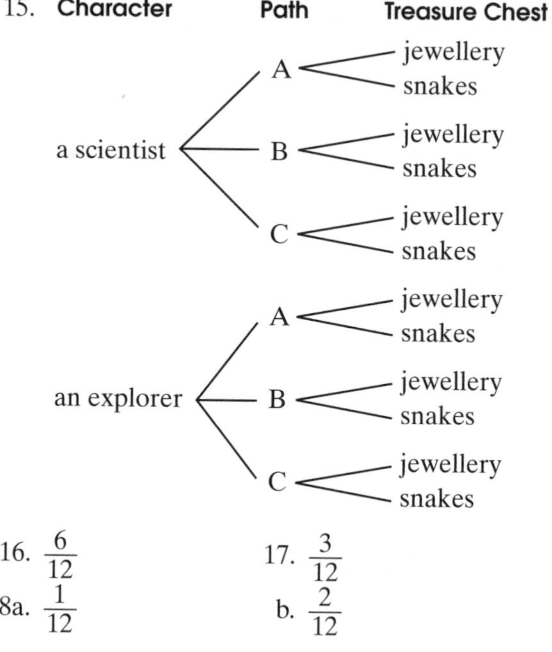

16. $\frac{6}{12}$ 17. $\frac{3}{12}$

18a. $\frac{1}{12}$ b. $\frac{2}{12}$

Review 2

1. A: 12 x 12 x 12 = 1728 (cm^3) ;
(12 x 12) x 6 = 864 (cm^2)
B: (18 x 11) ÷ 2 x 7 = 693 (cm^3) ;
18 x 11 + 21 x 7 + 18 x 7 + 11 x 7 = 548 (cm^2)
C: 21 x 10 x 7 = 1470 (cm^3) ;
(21 x 10 + 10 x 7 + 21 x 7) x 2 = 854 (cm^2)
2. Volume: Check B ; Surface Area: Check A
3. Volume: Check A ; Surface Area: Check B

4&5a.

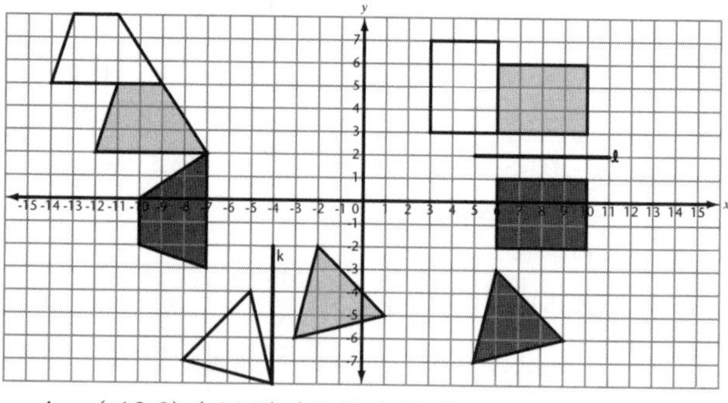

4a. (-13,8) (-11,8) (-9,5) (-14,5)
b. (3,7) (6,7) (6,3) (3,3)
c. (-5,-4) (-4,-8) (-8,-7)

5b. Rotate the trapezoid $\frac{1}{4}$ counterclockwise at (-7,2).
Translate the triangle 8 units right and 1 unit down.
Reflect the rectangle in line ℓ.

6. Y ; K

7. 

8. M A T H

9a. 1 ; increases ; 1

b. 7 and increases by 6 each time

c. 1 ; 6

10. 6 ; 1

11. 55

12. $4m - 8$; $4(5) - 8 = 12$

13. $\frac{m}{2} - 3$; $\frac{8}{2} - 3 = 1$

14. $\frac{m}{3} + 3$; $\frac{24}{3} + 3 = 11$

15. $3m + 6$; $3(12) + 6 = 42$

16a. $0.6c - 300$

b. $0.7c - 550$

17a. store A: \$(0.6 x 2400 – 300) = \$1140
store B: \$(0.7 x 2400 – 550) = \$1130
She should choose store A.

b. store A: \$(0.6 x 3500 – 300) = \$1800
store B: \$(0.7 x 3500 – 550) = \$1900
She should choose store B.

c. store A: \$(0.6 x 5000 – 300) = \$2700
store B: \$(0.7 x 5000 – 550) = \$2950
She should choose store B.

(Individual checkings for questions 18 to 20)

18. $8k + 4 - 4 = 44 - 4$

$\frac{8k}{8} = \frac{40}{8}$

$k = 5$

19. $\frac{m + 7}{2} \times 2 = 13 \times 2$

$m + 7 - 7 = 26 - 7$

$m = 19$

20. $\frac{5(p - 6)}{5} = \frac{15}{5}$

$p - 6 + 6 = 3 + 6$

$p = 9$

21. Let Kay ran l laps.

$5l - 2 = 18$

$5l - 2 + 2 = 18 + 2$

$\frac{5l}{5} = \frac{20}{5}$

$l = 4$

Kay ran 4 laps.

22. Let Josh took m minutes.

$\frac{m}{2} + 1 = 9$

$\frac{m}{2} + 1 - 1 = 9 - 1$

$\frac{m}{2} \times 2 = 8 \times 2$

$m = 16$

Josh ran 16 minutes.

23a. discrete

b. secondary data

24. (1216 x 6) – (1050 + 1154 + 1212 + 1390 + 1245)
= 1245
1245 babies were born in April.

25. 16.5% ; 34% ; 17% ; 15.9% ; 16.6% ; 0%

26. Check B

27. 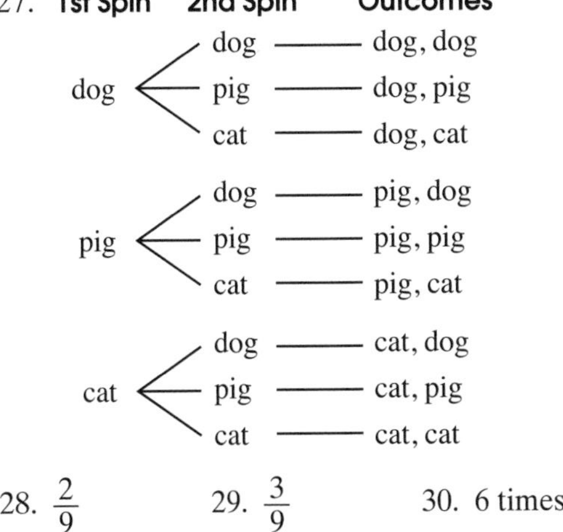

28. $\frac{2}{9}$

29. $\frac{3}{9}$

30. 6 times

1 New Year's Resolutions

A. (Suggested answers)
1. improve
2. promise
3. secular
4. consciously
5. constructive

B. (Individual writing)

C.
1. has
2. represents
3. was
4. has
5. is ; are
6. include
7. want
8. Has
9. makes

D.
1. Either of the two resolutions is made by me.
2. Neither the girls nor Bosco thinks that making resolutions is useless.
3. Working out, as well as reading, is a way to release stress.
4. Mrs. Bauer, together with her students, volunteers to help out after school.
5. Either Angie or Carl is going to be the first to tell us the resolutions.
6. Everybody, including all teachers, is going to the New Year Camp.

2 The Three Roses: a Czech Folktale

A.
1. It was strange for the woman to have found a palace in the woods because she had never heard of any palace in the woods before.
2. (Individual answer)
3. (Suggested answer)
The wizard asked the girl to cut off his head so he might reveal to her his true form as a handsome young man.
4. (Individual answer)
5. (Individual answer)

B.
1. ✘ 2. ✔
3. ✔ 4. ✘
5. ✘ 6. ✔
7. ✔ 8. ✘
9. ✔

C.
1. had heard ; asked ; wanted
2. was not ; had fallen
3. appeared ; had picked
4. had given ; took
5. had cut ; changed

D. (Individual writing)

3 Mythical Creatures from the World of Fantasy

A.
1. half human, half horse
2. human with goat-like features
3. eagle with a lion body
4. part man, part fish, swordfish spear growing out of his head
5. has a lion's head, a turtle's shell, a scorpion's sting, and bear's legs
6. part wolf, part whale

B.
1. active
2. passive
3. passive
4. active
5. passive
6. active
7. active

C.
1. Professor Rayner delivered a lecture on mythical creatures.
2. Nina Kirwan wrote *Exploring the World of Fantasy*.
3. I drew that picture of a unicorn flying in the sky.
4. Mr. Reid's class staged the Inuit legend.
5. The students made all the costumes and props for the play themselves.

D.
1. We were told to do a project on Greek mythology.
2. The famous painting *The Rebirth of the Pheonix* was stolen.
3. A statue of the Ogopogo was built in a park in Kelowna.
4. The island nation of Iceland is inhabited by elves and fairies.
5. A picture of Nessie has been sent to the press.

4 Facebook – Are You Revealing Too Much?

A. 1. F
2. T
3. F
4. F
5. F
6. T

B. (Individual writing)

C. 1. PSP
2. G
3. I
4. G
5. PTP
6. PTP
7. G
8. I
9. PSP

D. 1. to spend ; noun
2. to be put; adjective
3. to read ; noun
4. to find ; adverb
5. to develop ; adverb
6. to have ; noun

E. (Individual sentences)
1. visiting
2. participating
3. written
4. to create
5. to help

5 "My Olympic Hero" Speech Competition

A.

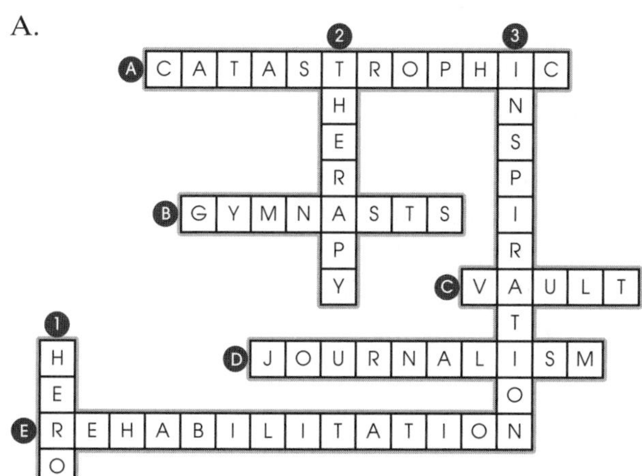

B. 1. COM
2. SUB
3. SUB
4. OBJ
5. OBJ
6. COM
7. SUB
8. COM

C. Sang Lan also began to realize that she could achieve her Olympic dream in other ways. For example, she was part of the Beijing Olympic Games Bid Committee. In 2004, she carried the Olympic torch during the Athens Olympic Games torch relay. She also carried the torch through Beijing during the torch relay leading up to the 2008 games. In addition, she hosted a TV talk show in China about the games, called "Sang Lan Olympics 2008". Sang Lan dreamed of representing China in the 2008 Paralympic Games as a ping-pong player, but this dream was not realized as her hands cannot grasp. Though Sang Lan cannot participate in any Olympic Games as an athlete, she plans to continue to be involved in future Olympics.

D. (Individual writing)

6 Family "Memoirs" – the Gift of a Lifetime

A. (Individual answers)

B. (Individual answer)

C. 1. is making
2. has taken
3. will bind
4. can also be added
5. would be
6. can buy; can think
7. would not have been; had not brainstormed
8. was made; is treasured
9. could not say
10. would be regarded; has ever received

D. (Individual sentences)
1. infinitive
2. gerund phrase
3. past participle phrase
4. gerund phrase
5. infinitive phrase
6. present participle phrase

7 Superstitions around the World

A.

Across: A. ASSIGNING; B. UNDERTAKING; C. ADHERED; D. ORIGINATED; E. OPTIMISTIC; F. MALIGN

Down: 1. PRACTICE; 2. BENEFIT; 3. SUPERSTITION; 4. CONSIDERED

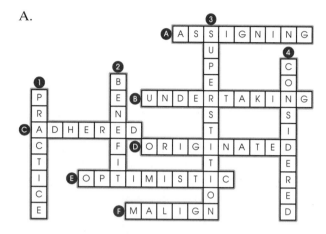

B.
1. very common
2. strange and insulting
3. so superstitious ; somewhat difficult
4. awfully silly
5. quite upset ; big black
6. Objective and scientific

C. (Individual writing)

D.
1. ✔ 2. ✔
3. 4. ✔
5. 6.
7. ✔

E. (Individual writing)

8 Muhammad Yunus and the Grameen Bank

A.
1. F 2. T
3. T 4. F
5. F 6. T
7. T 8. F
9. T

B.
1. P 2. I
3. P 4. P
5. I 6. I
7. P

C. (Suggested answers)
1. The Global Elders consist of a group of very widely respected world leaders.
2. The Global Elders contribute quite greatly to solving some very tough global problems.
3. The Elders are very generously sponsored by a group of founders.
4. Nelson Mandela works quite actively in fighting for freedom and equality in African countries.
5. The Elders respond extremely quickly to conflict situations around the world.

D. (Individual writing)

9 The New 7 Wonders of the World

A. (Suggested examples)

The Seven Wonders of the Ancient World ; the Great Pyramid of Giza
The Seven Natural Wonders of the World ; Mount Everest
The Seven Wonders of the Medieval Mind ; Stonehenge
The Seven Underwater Wonders of the World ; Lake Baikal
The Seven Wonders of the Modern World ; CN Tower
The Seven Forgotten Natural Wonders ; Niagara Falls
The Seven Forgotten Modern Wonders ; the Eiffel Tower
The Seven Forgotten Wonders of the Medieval Mind ; Mont Saint-Michel
The New 7 Wonders of the World ; Machu Picchu

B.
1. ADJ
2. ADV
3. ADV
4. ADV
5. ADV
6. ADJ
7. ADV
8. ADJ

C.
1. of the Mayan culture
2. in the Mayan language
3. at the site
4. at the centre
5. in 2007
6. with 91 steps
7. of its four sides
8. for astronomical purposes

D. (Individual writing)

10 Harmful Microorganisms

A. 1. Pathogens are disease-producing microorganisms.
2. Salmonella is a bacterium that causes food-borne infection.
3. Noroviruses are found in faecal-contaminated water and cause food-borne infection.
4. Staphylococcus aureus are bacteria that produce toxins said to be the most common cause of food poisoning.
5. SARS is a serious and highly infectious form of viral-borne pneumonia.

B. 1. Pathogenic microorganisms are harmful because the diseases they cause may be fatal.
2. When meat is left at room temperature for many hours, the bacteria in it may multiply and contaminate the meat.
3. Illness caused by noroviruses is characterized by nausea, vomiting, and diarrhea.
4. Pathogens can evolve rapidly to avoid being detected by our immune system.
5. Most bacteria are harmless and a few are even beneficial, but some can cause infectious diseases.
6. Although influenza is often confused with the common cold, it is a more severe disease caused by a different kind of virus.
7. At human body temperature, flu viruses can remain infectious for a week but at 0°C, they can last for more than 30 days.
8. When we cough, we have to cover our mouth to avoid the spread of flu viruses.

C. 1. cook food thoroughly to destroy harmful germs
2. If we do not treat food properly
3. food poisoning can still occur

11 The Science of Dreams

A. 1. B
2. B
3. A
4. B

B. 1. ✔
2. ✘
3. ✘
4. ✔
5. ✔
6. ✔
7. ✔
8. ✘
9. ✔
10. ✔
11. ✔

C. Whenever you mention déjà vu to your friends, there will surely be one or two among them that tell you they have had this experience before.

Déjà vu means "already seen" in French. It refers to an uncanny feeling that you have experienced a new situation before.

When I was very young, I had this dream. I came to a temple on a beach. There was an open area built with concrete in front of it. I saw many old people sitting at big round tables. Although they were having a feast, I couldn't hear any sound. Then I saw a Chow-chow tied to a pole. I went over and played with it for a while. After I played with the dog, I turned round and found all the old people gone. I was all alone!

Many years later, I went on a trip with my family to an island in Southeast Asia. The tour guide took us to a beach. There I saw a temple with a concrete open area in front. It gave me the creeps the moment I saw it because it was the first time I had been to that island, but everything was exactly the same as in my dream, even the colours of the temple! The only difference was that there were no old people around. Do you know what the weirdest thing was? There was a Chow-chow tied to a pole near the temple!

12 Chindogu: Weird Inventions We Can Actually Use

A.
- a prototype must have been made
- inventions cannot be for real use
- must be tools for everyday life
- humour must not be the only reason for creating the items
- items must have the inherent spirit of anarchy
- items are not for sale
- items are not propaganda
- items are never taboo
- items cannot be patented
- items must be without prejudice

B. 1. why there are so many inventions
2. that measure when the user has fallen into a deep sleep
3. who may be having a nap during lunchtime
4. whose books have been translated into many different languages

5. to whom the prize was awarded
6. when these two great inventors first met in history
7. in which the design contest is held
8. where the exhibition was held
9. that we encounter in our daily lives
10. that has been voted The Weirdest Invention of the Year

C. (Individual answers)

13 Totem Poles

A. 1. There are very few totem poles built prior to the 1800s still around today.
2. European settlers discouraged aboriginal groups from continuing with their traditions.
3. Trees used for making totem poles on the island of Hokkaido, Japan are smaller in size than those found in the Pacific Northwest.
4. Anthropologists refer to wooden figures found in these places as "ancestor figures", "greet figures", "talismans", or "tikis" instead of totem poles.
5. Totem poles are sacred objects and cannot be made by just anyone.

B. 1. CP
2. CX
3. CX
4. S
5. CPX
6. CP
7. S

C. (Suggested examples)
1. The Royal British Columbia Museum in Victoria, BC has one dated pre-1400s!
2. Totem poles are sacred objects and cannot be made by just anyone.
3. Some totem poles record clan lineage, while others are in fact historical records of the community.
4. Totem poles can also be found in other parts of the world, although they are a little different.
5. Even if you have not had the good fortune of seeing them in person along the Pacific Northwest, you have probably seen them on television.
6. Totem pole construction declined in the early 1900s as European settlers discouraged aboriginal groups from continuing with their traditional ways.
7. Their totem poles are smaller because the sources of wood are much smaller trees than those found along the Pacific Northwest, and they are not painted.

14 One More Reason to Save the Rainforest

A. (Suggested answers)
Paragraph 1: the rainforests' role
Paragraph 2: what rainforests are to animals and what we get from them
Paragraph 3: what "superfoods" are and who uses/wants them
Paragraph 4: what the acai berry is, what it does, and how to consume it
Paragraph 5: what the yerba mate is, what it does, and how to consume it
Paragraph 6: what the cupuassu is, what it does, and how to consume it
Paragraph 7: what we should do to protect these "superfoods", both those that exist and those yet to be discovered

B. 1. majority
2. kilograms
3. derived
4. antioxidants
5. dioxide
6. benefits
7. medicines
8. biodiversity
9. ecosystems
10. popular
11. variety
12. superfoods
13. subtropical
14. contain

C. (Individual sentences)
1. dwellers
2. unknown
3. herbal
4. gentler
5. original
6. discover

Review 1

A. 1. All students gather together every morning to sing the National anthem.
   2. Playing basketball, as well as doing yoga, is among my favourite hobbies.
   3. Whoever makes the most beautiful cake wins the prize.
   4. ✔
   5. Neither of your friends needs a bus ticket to go home.

B. 1. had bought ; celebrated
   2. had not been able ; fell
   3. made ; had turned ; went
   4. hit ; had left

C. 1. Active:
   Daniel cooked a delicious bowl of spaghetti.
   Passive:
   A delicious bowl of spaghetti was cooked by Daniel.
   2. Active:
   Susan donates old toys to charity.
   Passive:
   Old toys are donated to charity by Susan.

D. (Individual sentences)
   1. limiting
   2. to post
   3. fascinating
   4. devoted

E. (Suggested answers)
   1. has remained
   2. busy shoppers
   3. will scramble
   4. very merry holiday
   5. delicate ornaments
   6. big cheerful smile

F. (Individual sentences)
   1. present participle
   2. gerund
   3. past participle
   4. infinitive

G. 1. loud and rowdy ; ADJ
   2. last-minute ; ADL
   3. the fastest ; ADJ
   4. one-year-old ; ADL
   5. brown and white ; ADJ
   6. four-leaf ; ADL
   7. completely hysterical ; ADJ

H. (Individual answers)

I. 1. Let's not be selfish and inconsiderate
   2. If we see our friends waste paper
   3. we are doing enough to help
   4. when we are finished
   5. who inhabit this planet

J. 1. CP
   2. CX
   3. S
   4. CP
   5. CPX

K. (Individual sentences)
   (Suggested answers)
   1. (water) ; hydroelectricity
   2. (earth) ; geography
   3. (not) ; dislike
   4. (small) ; mircoorganism
   5. (between, among) ; Internet

15 The Endangered Tibetan Antelope

A. 1. chiru, tsod, zanglingyang
   2. wild goats and sheep
   3. cold alpine meadows and deserts, mainly the Tibetan Plateau
   4. less than 75 000
   5. 80 to 85 centimetres high at the shoulder
   6. slightly smaller than males
   7. grey to reddish-brown with white underside ; black markings on face and legs in winter (males only)
   8. slender, curving black horns (males only), can survive extremely cold conditions (40 degrees Celsius below zero)
   9. plants and grasses

B. 1. lives
   2. deserts
   3. graze
   4. slender
   5. their
   6. secret
   7. degrees
   8. prices
   9. poachers
   10. sell
   11. despite

C. (Individual writing)

16 One Laptop Per Child

A. 1. Computers can enrich our learning experience by increasing global communication, so we can get more information and learn more.
2. The OLPC project was set back as a result of competition from competitors who, in fear of losing business, started manufacturing their own low-cost computers.
3. (Individual answer)

B. 1. 4
2. 2
3. 2
4. 3 ; 7
5. 2
6. 7
7. 1
8. 5
9. 6

C. 1. XO was unveiled at the World Summit on the Information Society held in Tunisia in November 2005.
2. Inspired by the OLPC project, the Brazilian government started to investigate the use of laptops in education.
3. I came across an article about the features of XO in the computer magazine Today's Technology.
4. Mr. Negroponte aims to eliminate poverty in developing countries through the One Laptop Per Child project.
5. Daisy told me her family has got a new computer, so she can do research on the Internet for our English project.
6. This laptop has a maximum memory capacity of 5 GB.

17 Yummy International Desserts

A. Baklava: Middle-East and Mediterranean countries ; a sweet, sticky dessert made of layers of phyllo pastry, honey, and pistachio nuts
Trifle: England ; custard, fruit, jam, and bits of sponge cake or biscuits thrown in a bowl in layers and topped with whipped cream
Gulab Jamon: South Asian countries ; balls of cake soaked in sweet rose water syrup
Crêpe Suzette: France ; thin pancakes rolled in a sauce of orange juice, sugar, and liqueur

B. (Individual answer)

C. 1. Rachel has a sweet tooth**:** she likes all kinds of desserts.
2. We ordered three desserts**:** cheesecake topped with blueberries, raspberries, and strawberries**;** yogurt parfait with layers of yogurt, fruit, and granola**;** crepe filled with bananas, fresh cream, and chocolate sauce.
3. The world-famous restaurant expects one thing from the new pastry chef**:** creativity.
4. Have you heard of this saying**:** "A world without ice cream is a world in darkness"?
5. The four-judge panel for the dessert competition includes**:** Mrs. Emily Miller, Principal of the French Culinary Academy**;** Mr. Ryan Cann, Executive Chef of North Windsor Hotel**;** Ms. Hannah Evans, Chief Editor of *Fine Cuisine Magazine***;** Mr. Logan Ramos, former winner of the competition.
6. We need these ingredients to make waffles**:** flour, sugar, eggs, milk, and baking powder.
7. This is the first cake I made**:** a chocolate shortcake topped with sweetened strawberries and whipped cream.

D. 1. The souffle at this restaurant **(**I don't remember its name**)** is excellent. You must give it a try.
2. The article **"**How to Make Award-Winning Deserts**"** has given us useful information.
3. Simply Delight **–** a cozy café in downtown Toronto **–** offers a fantastic assortment of desserts and special drinks.
4. **"**Wow, this is the most scrumptious lemon meringue pie I've ever had!**"** exclaimed Josh.
5. Valeria is learning to make chocolate éclair **–** a favourite dessert of everyone in her family.
6. This Japanese chef uses nori **(**dried seaweed**)** in many of his dessert dishes.
7. Tiramisu **–** an Italian dessert made with coffee and mascarpone cheese **–** is loved by many.
8. Elmo gave the brownie a big bite **(**he would have put the whole piece into his mouth if he could**)** and was already reaching for the last piece on the plate.

18 After the "Boom"

A. 1790:
Alexander MacKenzie described the oil sands in his chronicles.
1870:
Fort McMurray was established as a Hudson's Bay Company trading post.
1896:
Gold was discovered in a river near Dawson City.
1930s:
Abasands Oil exploited the oil sand resources.
1960s:
The search for Klondike gold in Dawson City was over.
1967:
The Suncor plant opened in Fort McMurray.
1978:
The Syncrude consortium mine opened in Fort McMurray.

B. (Individual answer)

C.
1. heating
2. stemming
3. worried
4. purposeful
5. hierarchy
6. employed
7. referred
8. visualized
9. speculative
10. terrifying
11. receiver
12. reindeer
13. hurries
14. development

D.
A. JUSTIFIABLE
B. NEIGH
C. YIELD
D. APPEALING
E. AUDITOR
F. DECEITFUL
1. REMORSEFUL
2. ELABORATING
3. TRANSFERRED
4. CATERING
5. PURIFYING
6. SUBMITTED

19 From St. Laurent to the Smithsonian

A.
1. 80 kilometres north of Winnipeg, Manitoba
2. the lake monster Manipogo, a legendary white horse, and UFO sightings
3. 1200 people
4. Mitchif (a mixture of Cree/Salteaux, French, and English)
5. Coulee

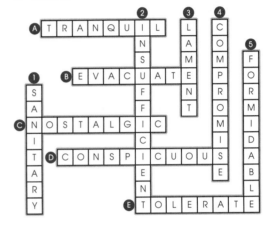

B.
A. TRANQUIL
B. EVACUATE
C. NOSTALGIC
D. CONSPICUOUS
E. TOLERATE
1. SANITARY
2. INSUFFICIENT
3. LAMENT
4. COMPROMISE
5. FORMIDABLE

C. (Suggested answers)
1. courageous ; daring ; fearless
2. limit ; confine ; contain
3. band ; hoop ; circle
4. quiver ; tremble ; shudder
5. astonishing ; marvelous ; wonderful
6. stop ; quit ; end

D. (Suggested words)
lives – resides
see – witness
huge – giant
legendary – mythical
snake – serpent

20 The Making of a Sea-faring Legend

A.
1. (Individual answer)
2. They are about frightening sea creatures.
3. (Individual answer)

B. (Individual writing)

C. 1. M
2. S
3. S
4. P
5. S

D. (Individual writing)

21 The Academy Awards: Oscar's Big Night

A. (Individual answers)

B. (Suggested answers)
1. Holding the Oscar in his hands, the winner was too excited to say a word.
2. Seeing the celebrity exiting the limousine, the people got excited.
3. To create suspense, the presenter paused before announcing the winner.
4. Months in advance, people registered for the bleacher seats outside the theatre.

C. 1. The Academy Awards ceremony, the greatest event in show business, is held annually.
2. The Oscar, a gold-plated statuette, is presented to every Academy Award winner.
3. James Cameron, a Canadian-American director and screenwriter, won the Best Director Award for *Titanic,* released in 1997.
4. The Oscar, one of the most recognized awards in the world, is a symbol of achievement in the film industry.

22 A Story of What Kids Can Do

A. 1. ✔
2. In his first book, Craig Kielburger wrote about the injustices against children in various South Asian countries.
3. Craig founded "Leaders Today" with his elder brother Marc.
4. ✔
5. Craig received a Doctorate in Education from Nipissing University.
6. Craig Kielburger believes that world peace has to begin with the children.

B. 1. without
2. because
3. to
4. because / since
5. although
6. before
7. after
8. and
9. think
10. except
11. if
12. although
13. because / since

C. 1. Craig Kielburger always thinks of freeing children around the world from enslavement.
2. Craig Kielburger's achievements in fighting for child rights can be proven by the distinctions he has received.
3. "Leaders Today" organizes programs to train young people as leaders.
4. You don't need volunteer experiences to join the group.
5. All new volunteers will have to attend the orientation tomorrow at noon.

D. (Suggested answers)
1. Child labour has existed in some countries for a long time.
2. Although not invited, Craig would meet with world leaders and demand that they stop child labour.
3. To achieve world peace, it is essential to ensure children's rights.
4. I think that young people have the power to better the world.
5. Free The Children has built more than 500 schools in China, Kenya, Sri Lanka, etc.

23 The Truth about Carbs

A. (Suggested answers)
1. Weight will be lost quickly but will be regained just as fast. Ill health could also be an effect.
2. Blood sugar levels rise.
3. The cells use the sugar as their energy source.
4. Refined food products containing "bad" carbs are widely marketed and readily available.
5. Home entertainment systems and computers are more affordable and common.

B. 1. To live healthy lives, we must choose our food wisely and work out regularly.
2. Carbohydrates provide the energy we need to work and play in our everyday lives.
3. This book focuses on and gives detailed explanations of the benefits of low-carb diets.
4. Dietitians promote proper eating habits and participate in research.

C. 1. Classified as a simple carb, lactose is found mainly in dairy products.
2. Although easily digested, carbs from refined foods are not recommended by dietitians.
3. As a carbohydrate found in plants, fibre is not digested by our bodies.
4. Like a sponge, insoluble fibre absorbs water to help move solid waste out of our bodies.

24 Your Carbon Footprint

A. Paragraph 1: what a "carbon footprint" is
Paragraph 2: why we must be aware of our "carbon footprint"; effects of one's carbon footprint
Paragraph 3: the two types of carbon footprint
Paragraph 4: five best ways to reduce our carbon footprint
Paragraph 5: ways to reduce our secondary footprint
Paragraph 6: what carbon "offset" schemes are

B. (Suggested writing)
1. Global warming has numerous negative effects.
2. Saving energy in our daily lives is easy.
3. We can all help reduce the amount of waste that goes to landfills.

C. (Individual writing)

25 The Biofuel Controversy

A. 1. Biofuels are used in place of gasoline to reduce carbon emissions.
2. Mass production of biofuels will result in an increase in food crop prices.
3. 200 kilograms of corn can feed someone for a year.
4. The Tata Nano is not powered purely by non-carbon fuels.
5. Forests will be cut down to provide land needed for the production of plants for biofuels.

B. Dear Editor: salutation
Paragraph 1: introduction
Paragraph 2: body
Paragraph 3: body
Paragraph 4: conclusion
Sincerely: closing

C. (Individual writing)

26 A Letter from Sammy in Mali

A.

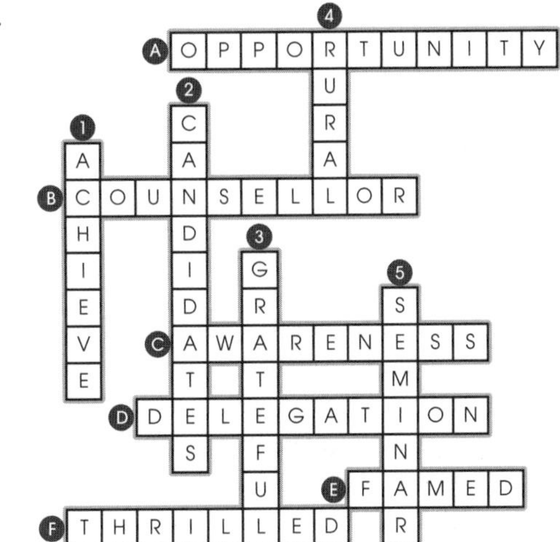

B. 1. Hi Kiyoka
2. Love,
3. (Suggested answers)
a. I hope (you're) doing well.
b. (I'll) never forget it.
c. (I'm) so excited.
4a. See the postmark on this letter?
b. Can't wait to show Worokia my own country.
c. Will write again.
5a-c. There is no subject.

C. (Individual writing)

27 The Elements of Fiction

A. 1. Plot: the story you wish to tell, answers the question, "What's happening?"
2. Conflict: the struggle between two people or between a person and something

3. Characters: the people who act out the plot
4. Setting: the place and the time in which the plot takes place
5. Theme: the underlying meaning of the story
6. Point-of-view: the way the story is narrated
7. Style: the language the author uses to deliver the story

B. (Individual writing)

C. (Individual writing)

28 Who Will Be the Next Man on the Moon?

A. 4
3
1
5
2
6

B. (1 and 2 – Individual answers)

3. (Suggested answers)
The Chinese Lunar Exploration Program is run by China's space agency and involves both explorations by un-manned robotic vehicles and by human missions. Chang'e 1 orbited the moon for a year and analyzed the moon's geology and chemistry. There are plans for the launch of Chang'e 2 and the deployment of a lunar rover for surface exploration in 2009. The program expects the return of the un-manned lunar vehicles in 2012, after which the manned space program will commence sometime in 2017.

C. (Individual writing)

Review 2

A. Winterlude, a winter celebration hosted by Canada's Capital Region, attracts thousands of visitors to Ottawa in February every year.
The Ice Hog Family, the mascots of Winterlude, consists of: Papa Ice Hog, Mama Ice Hog, and their twin children Noumi and Nouma. You can meet them and play with them at Sun Life Snowflake Kingdom, the largest snow playground in North America. They bring happiness to children and adults alike. They even have a family song called "The Ice Hogs' Song".

Activities of Winterlude take place over three weekends. There is an astonishing sound and light show called Ukiuk ("Ukiuk" means winter in Inuktitut) presented at the American Express Snowbowl on the Rideau Canal Skateway; the Ice-carving Masters Showcase organized at Rogers Crystal Garden in Confederation Park with numerous giant and marvellous masterpieces which demonstrate the skills and creativity of the sculptors; and Ice Fishing for All at Sun Life Snowflake Kingdom in Jacques-Cartier Park where visitors can try to fish for rainbow trout in the chilly winter of Canada.

B. (Suggested answers)

1. The intelligent professor is talking with his smart student.
2. This city is famous for its great scenery and fantastic hotels.
3. Mom has put the tiny figurine on the small table.
4. I had a delicious dinner with my family tonight, and tomorrow, I will have another scrumptious dinner with my friends.

C. (Individual writing)

D. 1. ✔
2.
3.
4. ✔
5. ✔
6.

E. (Suggested writing)

1. The lake water is crystals in the sun.
2. The amusement park is like a paradise for children.
3. The capital city of the country is its heart.
4. For every athlete, medals are precious jewels.
5. Emmy is like the princess of her family.
6. Larry's eyesight is as keen as an eagle's.

F. 1. After dinner, people like strolling leisurely along the river bank.
2. To avoid being late, Ginny left home two hours earlier.
3. Seeing the sudden movement under the tablecloth, Kelly let out a shrill cry.
4. Determined to win the game, the team practised every day.

G. 1. Samuel, the tallest boy in our class, can easily reach the clock on the wall.
2. The Mariana Trench, the deepest place on Earth, is located in the Pacific Ocean.
3. *Ratatouille*, Wilson's favourite DVD, was a Christmas gift from Grandma.
4. *The Starry Night*, one of Vincent van Gogh's most renowned works, was painted by the great artist in 1889.

H. (Suggested writing)
I think nothing is more important than my family. Although my little sister likes bossing me around, and my elder brother wears strange clothes, I love them with all my heart. Mom and Dad think that sometimes I'm bossier than my sister and my clothes are much stranger than my brother's. However, they don't have problems tolerating my imperfections because I am part of the family.

I. 1. Yoga is a great way to relax, improve flexibility, and relieve stress.
2. Being the coach, he is respected by everyone on the basketball team.
3. Out of the corner of her eye, she saw a tiny mouse scurry into a crack in the wall of her kitchen.
4. The doors opened and the athletes filed into the stadium.
5. The Wellings checked into and stayed at the Grand Hill Hotel.

J. (Individual writing)

1 Settlement of New France

A.

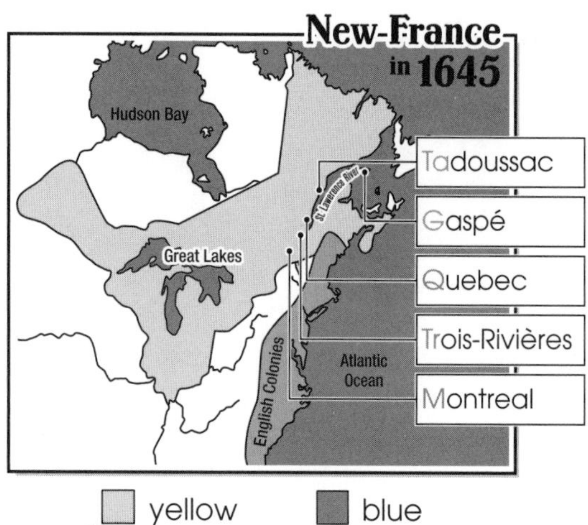

B. 1. Habitant
2. Filles du roi
3. Seigneur
4. Fur trader
5. Missionary
6. Soldier

2 New France – Economic and Political Life

A. 1. A
2. B
3. B
4. A

B. Sovereign ;
King ;
Governor ; Intendant ; Bishop ;
Responsibilities of Governor:
permanently resided there and represented the King, commanded soldiers, and dealt with other colonies and Aboriginal nations
Responsibilities of Intendant:
involved the financial, legal, and economic concerns of the colony
Responsibilities of Bishop:
oversaw the hospitals, schools, missions, and churches

3 New France – Social Life

A. 1. Seigneurs ;
build a mill ;
attract settlers
2. Habitants ;
pay rent ;
work the land

B. (Individual answer)

C. 1. P
2. S
3. P
4. S
5. P
6. S

4 New France – Cooperation and Conflict

A. 1. Plains of Abraham
2. Louisbourg ; fortress
3. British ; Seven Years' War
4. nations ; treaty
5. rivalry ; alliances
6. allies

B. 1. fact
2. fact
3. opinion
4. opinion
5. opinion
6. fact

5 The Settlement of British North America

A. Treaty of Paris:
Seven Years' War ; rights ; Newfoundland ; British
Royal Proclamation:
Appalachian ; Britain ; American
Quebec Act:
seigneurial ; Aboriginal ; French ; Roman
(Individual answer)

B. British ;
Spanish ;
Russian

6 The Causes and Effects of the American Revolution

A. 1. cause
2. effect
3. cause
4. effect
5. cause
6. effect
Causes:
mercantilism ;
new tax laws ;
Stamp Act
Effects:
United States of America ;
Invasion of Quebec ;
British North America

B. Loyalists: A, C, D, F
Rebels: B, E

C. (Individual writing)

7 The Loyalists and British North America

A. Upper Canada ; Lower Canada
(Outline the borders of Upper Canada in red and the borders of Lower Canada in blue.)
1. Lower Canada
2. Upper Canada

B. A. Black Loyalists
B. Mississauga, Chippewa
C. Scottish
D. White Loyalists
E. British merchants
F. Indentured servants
G. Mennonites and Quakers

8 The War of 1812

A. A. Louisiana
B. Treaty of Ghent
C. October
D. Queenston Heights
E. North American
F. Laura Secord

B. D ; E ; F ; C ; B ; A
British ; west
France ; Britain

C. 1. They believed Britain prevented them from expanding to the west.
2. (Suggested answer)
Laura Secord ; Isaac Brock
3. News of the peace treaty signed overseas had not reached them.

9 Conflict and Resolution

A. 1. Rebellion
2. Conflict
3. strike
4. war
5. protest

B. 1. A: protest
B: strike
2. conflict
3. war
4. rebellion

C. (Individual writing)

10 The Rebellions of 1837 - 1838: Causes

A. A. Crown
B. Oligarchy
C. Family Compact
D. French
E. Responsible
F. Farmers
G. Rebel

B. 1. D
2. E
3. A
4. B
5. F
6. C
7. G

11 Personalities and Events of the Rebellions

A. 1. Louis-Joseph Papineau ; D
2. William Lyon Mackenzie ; E
3. Francis Bond Head ; A
4. Roman Catholic Church ; C
5. Parti patriote ; B

B. 1. Fils de la Liberté
2. Church
3. Louis-Joseph Papineau
4. patriotes
5. British
6. William Lyon Mackenzie
7. Bond Head
8. Montgomery's Tavern ; defeated
9. Caroline

12 Impact of the Rebellions

A. 1. rebellions
2. economy
3. poverty
4. soldiers
5. 300
6. rebels
7. hanging
8. Australia
9. civil rights

B. 1. A
2. A
3. B
4. A
5. B

Review

A.
1-2. power / wealth
3. fur
4. mercantilist
5. missionaries
6. Aboriginal
7. Seigneurs
8. habitants
9-10. filles du roi / soldiers

B. 1. habitant
2. seigneur
3. fille du roi
4. missionary

C. 1. T
2. F
3. T
4. F

D. 1. B ; D
E ; F
A ; C
2. The French

E. Part I
1. loyalist
2. rebel
3. rebel

Part II
1. The United States thought the British were preventing their attempts at western expansion.
2. British Major General Isaac Brock was killed but the British won.

Part III
1. Quebec ; First Nations
2. Newfoundland

F. 1. C
2. A
3. C
4. B
5. A

1 Themes of Geographic Inquiry: Location/Place

A. 1. lines of latitude and longitude
   2. an alphanumeric grid
   3. World ; South America, Africa, Australia, and Antarctica
   4. World ; South America / Africa / Asia
   5. City ; Oak Street and 3rd Ave
   6. City ; B2, B3, C2, C3
   7. World ; North America
   8. City ; school, E3 ; City Hall, E1

B. Check 2;
(Individual answer)

C. 1. Montreal ; small island
   2. Tropical rainforest ; wet and warm climate, many different species of animals and plants
   3. Northern Canada ; permafrost ; low-growing plants with short life cycles

2 Themes of Geographic Inquiry: Environment

A. 1. natural vegetation
   2. water
   3. landform
   4. Climate
   5. soils

B. (Individual answer)

C. 1a. contour
   b. population density
   c. active volcano
   d. climate regions
   2. active volcano
   3. population density
   4. climate regions
   5. contour

3 Themes of Geographic Inquiry: Region

A. 1. climate
   2. English/French
   3. human ; purpose of buildings
   4. physical ; landforms

B. Innuitian Region ;
Arctic Region ;
Cordilleran Region ;
Interior Plains ;
Canadian Shield ;
Great Lakes-St. Lawrence Lowlands ;
Appalachian Region

C. (Name any five regions shown on map.)

D. 1. Some of Canada's physical regions continue through a number of provinces or territories which are different than the boundaries between the political regions.
   2. Some areas, like the lower part of British Columbia, were drawn where the physical regions change. And some areas, like Saskatchewan, have the political boundaries follow lines of longitude and latitude.

E. (Individual answer)

4 Themes of Geographic Inquiry: Interaction

A. 1. habitats
   2. pollutes
   3. restricts
   4. deforests
   5. erosion

B. (Individual answer)

C. (Individual answer)

5 Themes of Geographic Inquiry: Movement

A. Write any eight of the following movements: photo store, immigration office, power lines, pizza delivery, the boy using the cell phone, mail carrier, bike rider, people walking on sidewalks, bus, birds flying in the sky

B. (Individual answer)

C. 1. migration
   2. glaciers
   3. digestive
   4. circulatory
   5. erosion
   6. passengers
   7. clouds
   8. natural

6 Patterns in Physical Geography: Landforms

A. 1. mountain ; river ; lake ; sea
2. ▲ : any mountain shown on map
∫ : any river shown on map
: any lake shown on map
: any sea shown on map
3. mountain ranges
4. There are two plates pushing together.

B. 1. mountainous region ; skier
2. flat plains region with rich soil ; farmer
3. coastal region ; fisher
4. rocky, mineral-rich region ; miner

C. (Individual writing)

7 Patterns in Physical Geography: Climate

A. 1. Tropic of Capricorn
2. Antarctic Circle
3. Colour the continents above the Arctic Circle and below the Antarctic Circle blue.
4. Colour the continents between the Tropic of Cancer and the Tropic of Capricorn red.
5. equator ; wettest
6. driest

B. 1. Ocean currents
2. Air masses
3. Latitude
4. Altitude
5. Proximity to ocean, sea, or large lake
6. Global wind systems

8 Patterns in Physical Geography: Rivers

A. 1. ground water
2. confluence
3. meander
4. drainage basin
5. source
6. tributaries
7. oxbow lake
8. delta
9. mouth

B. 1. Mississippi
2. Amazon
3. St. Lawrence
4. Nile
5. Congo
6. Ganges
7. Yangtze

9 Patterns in Physical Geography: Agriculture

A. 1. subsistence
2. commercial
3. specialized ; risky ; costs ; profits
4. subsistence
5. specialized

B. 1. landforms ; salmon
2. climate ; bananas
3. landforms ; beef
4. soil ; potatoes
5. climate ; rice
6. climate ; cotton

C. 1. corn
2. potatoes
3. mushrooms
4. beef
5. dairy
6. cranberries
7. maple syrup
8. commercial

10 Natural Resources: Origins and Uses

A. **YT**: zinc ; lead
NT: gold ; zinc
NU: gold ; zinc
QB: maple syrup ; asbestos ; gold ; timber
BC: coal ; salmon ; timber ; copper
AB: natural gas ; oil ; coal
SK: potash ; wheat
MB: copper ; zinc
ON: nickel ; salt ; copper ; timber
NB: coal ; potash
NS: coal ; tin
PEI: sand ; gravel
NL: harp seals ; iron ore
Nunavut, Northwest Territories, Yukon, and Manitoba

B. 1. nickel
2. sand
3. tin
4. wheat
5. salt
6. oil
7. timber
8. coal
9. gold

11 Natural Resources: Technology

A. 1. spear ; More
2. saw ; More trees are felled.
3. gold pan ; More gold is mined.
4. ox ; Timber travels farther and faster.

B. 1. extraction
2. processing
3. management
4. discovery
5. discovery
6. marketing

12 Natural Resources: Sustainable Development

A. 1. Non-renewable ; marble, natural gas, coal, gold, aluminum, copper, oil, diamonds
2. Renewable ; codfish, timber, oysters, wheat, oranges, cucumbers, lamb
3. Flow ; wind energy, ocean currents, tidal energy, solar energy, rivers

B. 1. We need forests for timber to make paper, furniture, and many other daily necessities. If we do not use forests responsibly, we will not be able to have these items. It will also destroy animal habitats and reduce fresh air.
2. (Individual answer)
3. We use oil to heat our homes, run our cars, and generate electricity. Oil is a non-renewable resource that will run out if we do not use it responsibly.
4. (Individual answer)

Review

A. 1a. Prime Meridian ; longitude
b. equator ; latitude
c. political
2. May 25: Australia ; Asia
(Suggested answers)
May 30: 50° N, 15° E ; 60° N, 120° W
3. landforms ; climate

B. 1. Churchill River ; Southern Indian Lake ; Lake Winnipeg ; Cedar Lake ; Red River
2. Canadian Shield ; Interior Plains ; Hudson Bay Lowlands
3. ●: Southern Indian Lake ; Cedar Lake ; Lake Winnipeg
∽ : Red River ; Churchill River
4. River, Highway
5. (Suggested answer)
More pollution may be produced and also it may cause a loss of animal habitats.

C. 1. alphanumeric
2a. C2, C3, D2, D3
b. D1
c. B1, C1
d. A3, A4, B3, B4
3. copper ; coinage
4. (Suggested answer)
Product: Wheat
End Product(s): bread ; beer ; flour
Sustainability: A. Renewable
5. (Suggested answer)
River Technology Centre is one block north and one block east of Star Hotel.

D. 1.

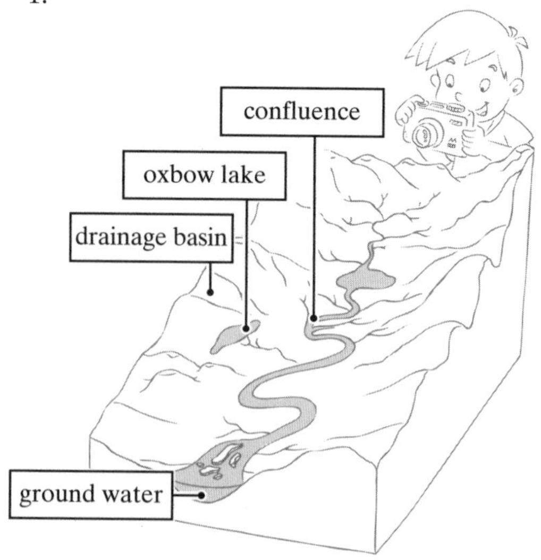

tributaries ; source ; meander ; mouth ; delta

2. (Suggested answer)
   Rivers are flow resources. It is important to use rivers responsibly because polluted water in rivers is harmful for people and animals to consume. One example of responsible use of this resource is not to throw garbage or waste into rivers.

1 Ecosystems

A. 1. population
2. species
3. organism
4. habitat
5. ecosystem
6. community

B. 1. ecosystem
2. atmosphere
3. animals
4. landforms
5. (Suggested drawings)

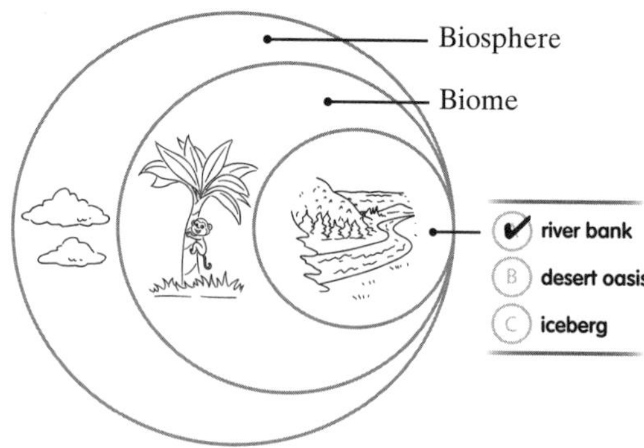

2 Biotic and Abiotic Elements in Ecosystems

A. 1. ecosystem
2. biotic ; microorganisms
3. abiotic ; water
4. (Suggested answers)
Biotic Elements:
tree ; deer ; grass ; fish ; bacteria
Abiotic Elements:
sun ; water ; air ; mountain ; soil

B. Highlight these words blue:
Humans ;
berries ; black bear ;
beaver ; trees ;
Snakes ; other reptiles ;
cleaner fish ; other bigger fish
Highlight these words yellow:
water ;
Wind ; soil ;
sun

1. biotic & abiotic
2. biotic & biotic
3. abiotic & abiotic
4. biotic & biotic
5. biotic & abiotic
6. biotic & biotic

3 Food Cycle

A. 1.

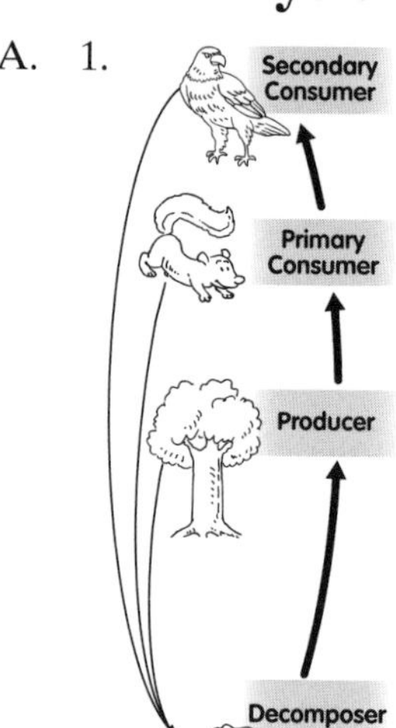

2. producer
3. herbivore
4. omnivore
5. plant
6. food
7. nutrients
8. fungi

B. (Suggested drawing)
C ;

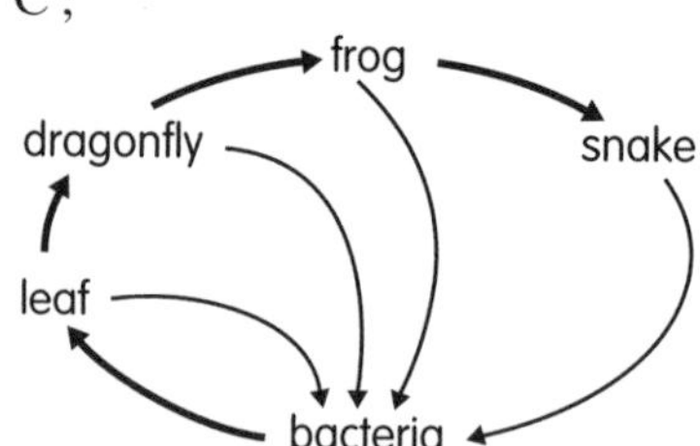

C. 1a. B
b. A
c. D
d. C
2a. food chain
b. food web

4 Natural Cycles

A. 1. the sun
   2. evaporation
   3. respiration
   (Suggested answers for questions 4 and 5)
   4. rain, snow, and hail
   5. oceans, lakes, and rivers
   6. respiration
      (Individual example)

B. 1. combustion
   2. photosynthesis
   3. respiration
   4. carbon sinks
   5. decomposition
   6. fossil fuels

5 Succession and Adaptation

A.

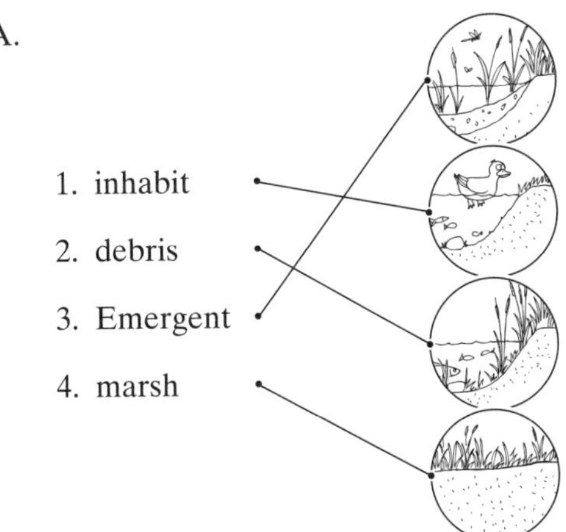

B. 1. extinction
   2. competition
   3. succession
   4. species diversity
   5. adaptation

6 Human Activity

A. (Underline these factors.)
   A. Air pollution ; acid rain
   B. Construction and logging practices
   C. overuse
   D. Chemical fertilizers
   E. A dam ; flooding
   F. Non-native species ; invasive species
   G. manufacturing of goods ; industrial waste
   H. Transportation pollution

B. 1. B
   2. D
   3. H
   4. G
   5. E
   6. C
   7. A or H
   8. F

7 Structures

A.

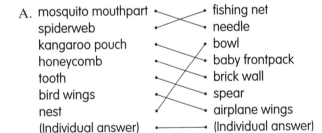

mosquito mouthpart	fishing net
spiderweb	needle
kangaroo pouch	bowl
honeycomb	baby frontpack
tooth	brick wall
bird wings	spear
nest	airplane wings
(Individual answer)	(Individual answer)

B. 1. A frame structure
   2. A shell structure
   3. A solid structure

C. Solid Structure:
   brick wall, iceberg, paperweight, loaf of bread
   Frame Structures:
   spiderweb, umbrella, ladder, house
   Shell Structures:
   soccer ball, egg, bike helmet, cap

D. (Individual answers)

8 Centre of Gravity and Stability

A. 1. A

2a.

unstable ; stable

b.

unstable ; stable

c.

stable ; unstable

d.

stable ; unstable

B. (Individual drawings)

C. The centre of gravity moves closer to the side where the paperclips are placed.

9 Forces on Stable and Unstable Structures

A. 1. load
2. live
3. dead
4. compressive
5. tensile
6. Shear
7. torsion

B. 1. compressive
2. live
3. compressive
4. tension
5. shear

C.

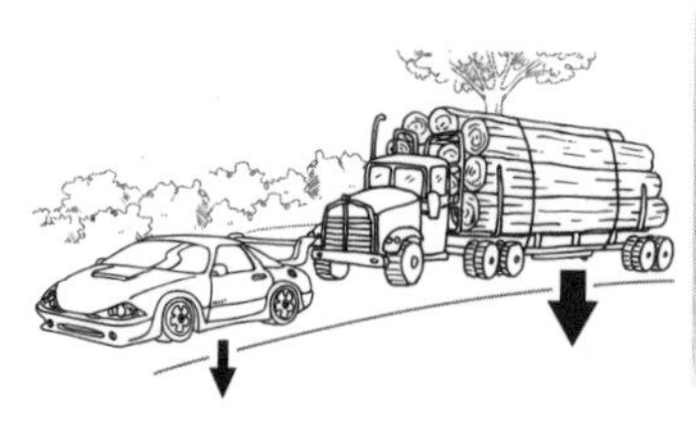

10 Materials and Design

A. 1. A
2. C
3. B
4. C
5. C
6. A

B. 1. portability
2. water resistance

C. (Individual answers)

11 The Particle Theory of Matter

A. 1. tiny ; moving ; spaces ; Heat
2. true
3. false
4. false
5. true
6. false

B.

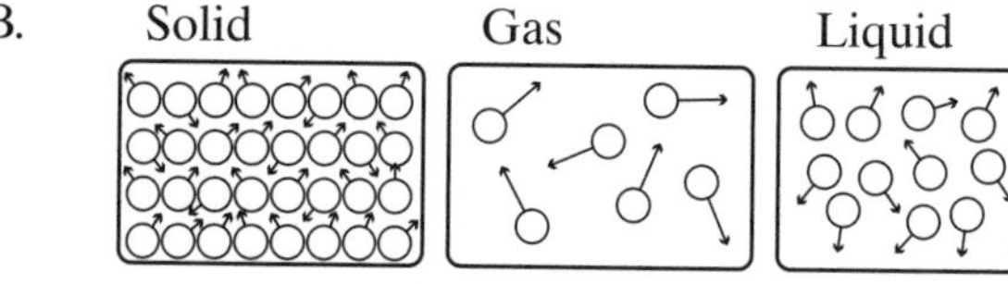

C.

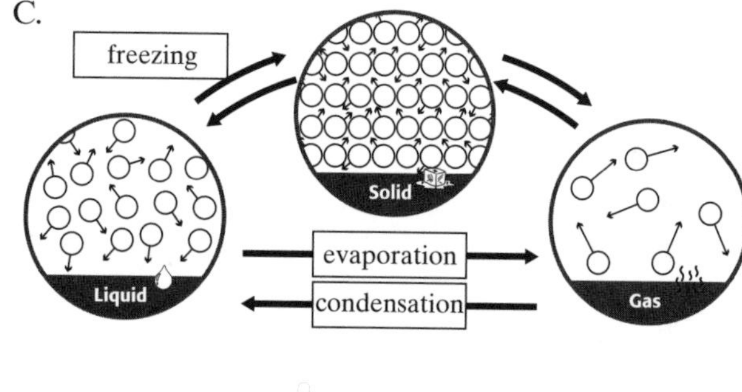

12 Pure Substances and Mixtures

A. 1. identical
2. two

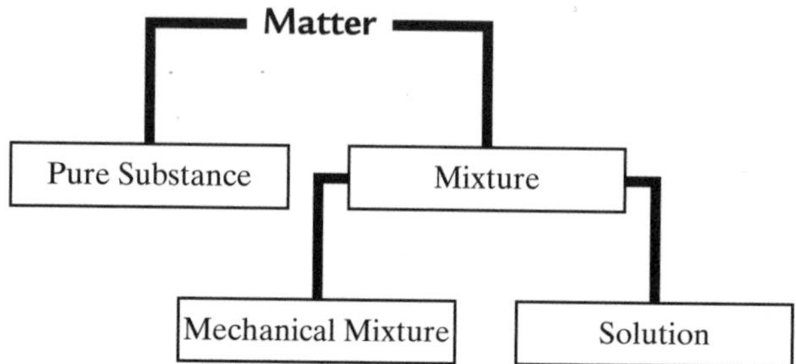

B. 1. m
2. ps
3. ps
4. m
5. m
6. ps
7. m

C.

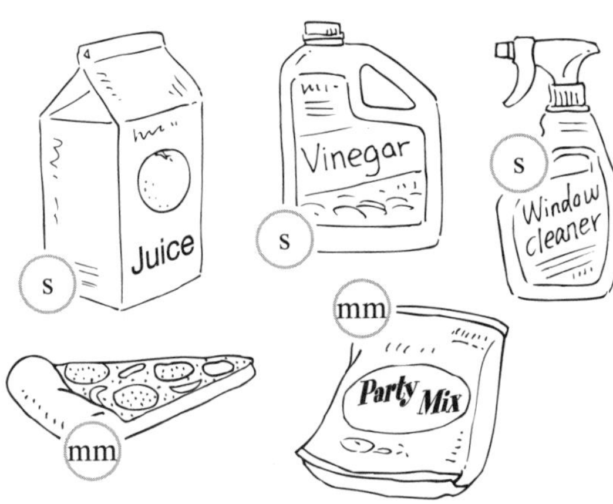

13 All about Solutions

A. 1. solute ; solution
2.

Solution	Solute	Solvent	Solution Type
pop	carbon dioxide (gas)	water (liquid)	gas – liquid
salt water	salt (solid)	water (liquid)	solid – liquid
vinegar	acetic acid (liquid)	water (liquid)	liquid – liquid
brass	zinc (solid)	copper (solid)	solid – solid
air	nitrogen (gas)	oxygen (gas)	gas – gas
maple tree sap	sugar (solid)	water (liquid)	solid – liquid

B. 1. saturated
2. unsaturated
3. saturated
4. unsaturated
5. unsaturated
6. saturated

C.
concentration
dilute
solvent
solute
solubility
insoluble
saturated
unsaturated

14 Separating Mixtures

A. 1. filtration ; D
2. evaporation ; B
3. density ; C
4. magnetism ; E
5. distillation ; A

B. 1. size
2. density
3. dissolvability
4. evaporability

C. 1. filtration
2. density
3. evaporation
4. magnetism

15 Solutions, Mixtures, the Environment, and You

A. 1.

2.

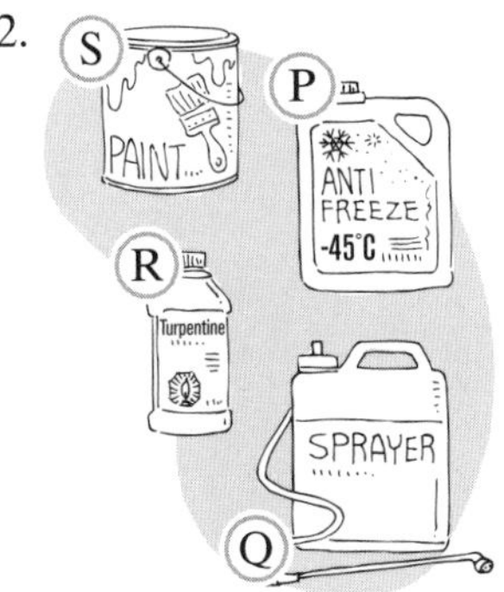

B. 1. acid rain
2-3. industry / automobiles
4. acid solution
5. plant life
6. drinking water
7. (Individual answer)
8. Reducing the use of fossil fuels can help reduce acid rain-causing emissions.

16 Heat and the Particle Theory of Matter

A. 1. tiny ; moving ; faster

2a. (Suggested temperature)

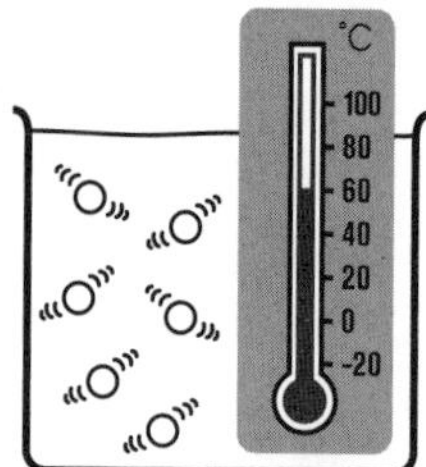

b.

B. 2 ; 1 ; 4 ; 5 ; 3

C. 1. A
2. B
3. A
4. B

17 Heat and Volume

A. 1. less
2. more
3. more
4. more
5. less

B. 1. expand
2. contract

C. water ; ice

D. When heated, the particles of the lid move faster and take up more space. As a result, the lid has a greater volume and makes contact with the jar less tightly.

18 The Transmission of Heat

A. 1. conduction ; A
2. convection ; B
3. radiation ; A

B. 1. conduction
2. convection
3. conduction
4. conduction
5. convection

C. 1. TI
2. TC
3. TI
4. TC

19 Heat and How It Is Produced

A. 1. Mechanical Force
2. Electrical Energy
3. Geothermal Energy
4. Nuclear Energy
5. Chemical Energy
6. Solar Energy

B. 1. electrical
2. solar
3. nuclear
4. mechanical
5. chemical

C. 1. T
2. F
3. F
4. T
5. F
6. T
7. T

20 The Greenhouse Effect

A. 1. atmosphere
2. Earth
3. sun's rays
4. radiation
5. Greenhouse
6. trapped

B. Common Greenhouse Gases:
carbon dioxide ;
methane ;
ozone ;
nitrous oxide ;
water vapour
Sources of Greenhouse Gases:
B ; C ; D ; G ; H

C. 1. rise
2. Methane
3. respiration

Review

A. 1. Ecosystem:
a natural area where living and non-living things interact with each other
Biotic elements:
the living elements of an ecosystem, such as plants, animals, and microorganisms
Abiotic elements:
the non-living elements of an ecosystem, such as soil, air, and water

2.

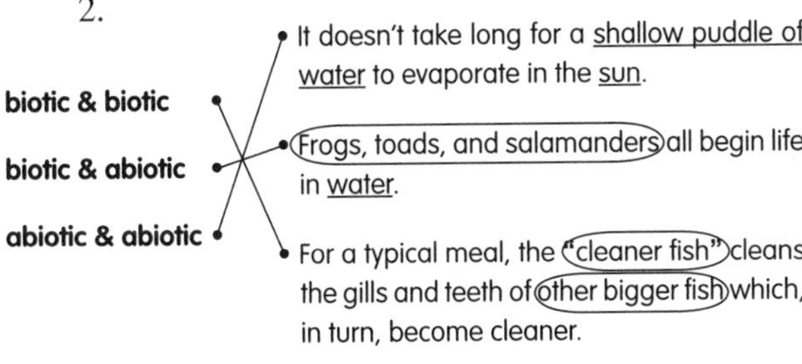

B.

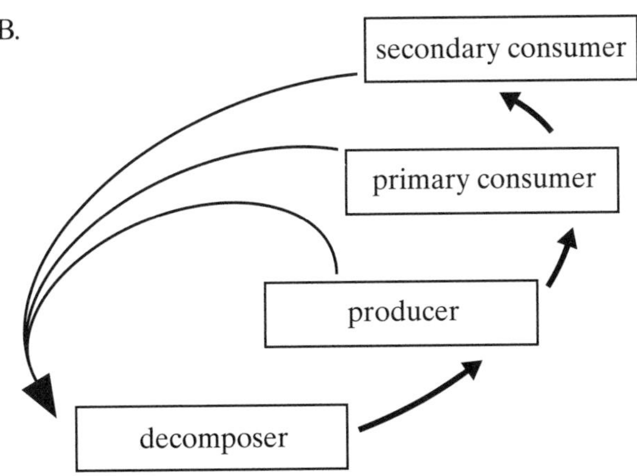

A decomposer converts all organic matter into carbon dioxide and nutrients that become part of the soil and help plants grow.

C. (Individual answer)

D. 1. live
2. dead
3. compressive
4. tensile
5. tension
6. live
7. compression
8. dead

E. 1.

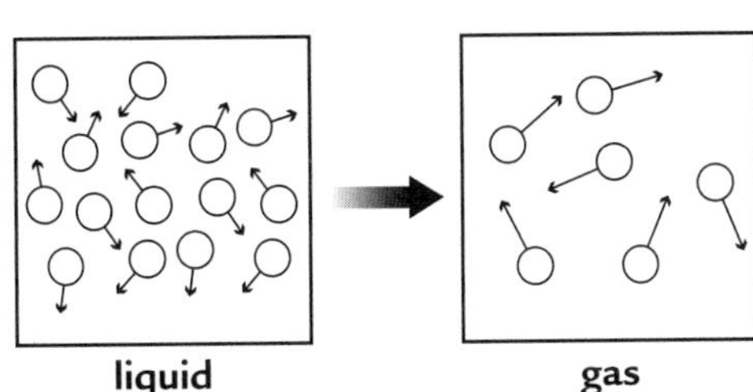

Particles of evaporated water have more energy and take up more space than particles of liquid water.

2.

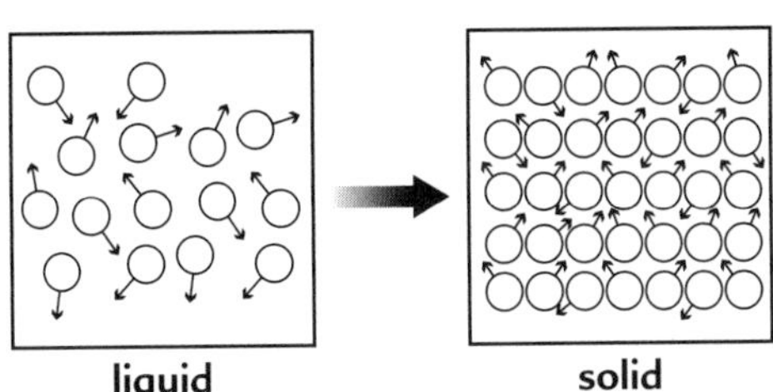

When water changes state to become ice, it expands to take up more space. The particles of ice have less energy.

F.

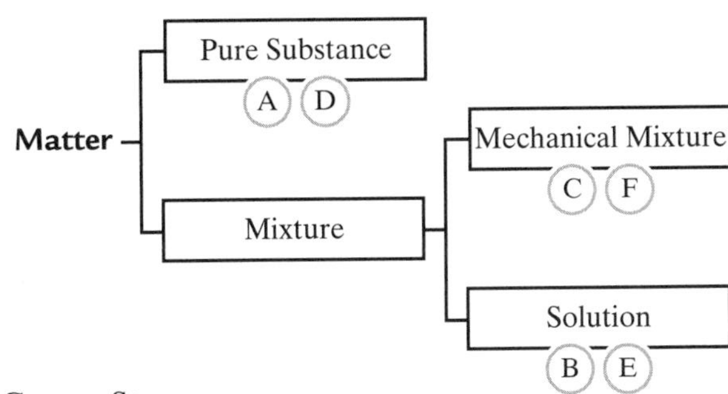

G. Steps:
1st Separate the iron from the mixture by magnetism.
2nd Separate the sand from the remaining mixture by filtration.
3rd Separate the remaining mixture of salt and water by evaporation.

H. 1. Polluting gases from industry and automobiles are released in the air. They combine with the water vapour, and acid rain is created.
2. Acid rain kills aquatic and plant life, damages buildings and cars, and contaminates drinking water. So, all the living things may get sick and die as a result.
3. A ; D

I. 1a. contract
b. greater ; smaller
c. more ; less
d. more ; less
2a. contract
b. greater ; smaller
c. less ; more
d. more ; less

J. (Individual answer for each example)
1. convection
2. conduction
3. radiation
4. Yes, heat in a convection oven moves upward to help food warm evenly and faster.

K. 1. A
2. B
3. C
4. B
5. B
6. A